T0224506

Communications
in Computer and Information Science   1229

Commenced Publication in 2007
Founding and Former Series Editors:
Simone Diniz Junqueira Barbosa, Phoebe Chen, Alfredo Cuzzocrea,
Xiaoyong Du, Orhun Kara, Ting Liu, Krishna M. Sivalingam,
Dominik Ślęzak, Takashi Washio, Xiaokang Yang, and Junsong Yuan

Editorial Board Members

More information about this series at http://www.springer.com/series/7899

Usha Batra · Nihar Ranjan Roy ·
Brajendra Panda (Eds.)

Data Science and Analytics

5th International Conference on Recent Developments
in Science, Engineering and Technology, REDSET 2019
Gurugram, India, November 15–16, 2019
Revised Selected Papers, Part I

 Springer

Editors
Usha Batra (iD)
GD Goenka University
Gurugram, India

Nihar Ranjan Roy (iD)
GD Goenka University
Sohna, Haryana, India

Brajendra Panda (iD)
University of Arkansas
Fayetteville, AR, USA

ISSN 1865-0929 ISSN 1865-0937 (electronic)
Communications in Computer and Information Science
ISBN 978-981-15-5826-9 ISBN 978-981-15-5827-6 (eBook)
https://doi.org/10.1007/978-981-15-5827-6

This Springer imprint is published by the registered company Springer Nature Singapore Pte Ltd.
The registered company address is: 152 Beach Road, #21-01/04 Gateway East, Singapore 189721, Singapore

Preface

Data science employs techniques and theories drawn from many fields within the broad areas of mathematics, statistics, information science, and computer science, in particular from the subdomains of machine learning, classification, cluster analysis, data mining, databases, and visualization. Data analytics seeks to provide operational observations into issues that we either know or do not know. Analysis is a part of any scientific research and it is the first step in building a theory. The second step is synthesis, which actually builds or creates a theory. It is also important to remember that science is not about results, but about a methodology to get them. The focus is on big data applications to tackle the problem of decision-making under uncertainty by using machine learning methods and graph theory to analyze complex structures in big data to build recommender systems and predictive models.

The 5th International Conference on Recent Developments in Science, Engineering and Technology (REDSET 2019), was held at the GD Goenka University, India, during November 15–16, 2019, in association with Springer, is our humble effort in this direction. Promotion of inquiry-based education has been the core competence of the School of Engineering at GD Goenka University since its inception and the present conference was yet another step forward. We aim to promote the interdisciplinary nature of scientific enquiry, which leads to engineering efforts to develop scientific and technologically innovative solutions so as to benefit society as a whole.

We received 353 papers and participation from 12 different countries including India, Canada, Egypt, Lithuania, Malaysia, Nepal, Nigeria, Saudi Arabia, Sweden, UAE, Vietnam, and the USA. After undergoing a rigorous peer-review process following international standards, the acceptance rate was approximately 21%. Selection was based on originality of the idea, innovation, and relevance to the conference theme and relation to the latest trends in the respective domains. We hope that the ideas and subsequent discussions presented at the conference will help the global scientific community to aim toward a nationally and globally responsible society. We also hope that young minds will derive inspiration from their elders and contribute toward developing sustainable solutions for the nation and the world as a whole.

The current proceedings contain the contributions presented during REDSET 2019. We wish to express our sincere appreciation to the members of the Technical Program Committee and the reviewers who helped in the paper selection process. We also thank the authors for their contributions that allowed us to assemble such an exceptional technical set of papers. We thank Springer for being our publication partner for this conference. Our special thanks go to the editorial staff at Springer, especially Ms. Kamiya Khatter and Ms. Alla Serikova, for their outstanding service and support.

April 2020

Usha Batra
Nihar Ranjan Roy
Brajendra Panda

Organization

Patron

Goenka Nipun   Managing Director at GD Goenka Group, India

Co-patron

Bhaskaran Suku   President of GD Goenka Group, India

Conference Program Chair

Panda Brajendra   University of Arkansas, USA

Steering Committee

Chair

Sahu Atma   Coppin State University, USA

Members

Tickoo Sham   Purdue University, USA
Klauss Raul   Technological University of Clausthal, Germany
Rauniyar S. P.   BMRD, Australia
Borana Lalit   Hong Kong Polytechnic University, Hong Kong
Mitra Shayon   Manitoba Public Insurance, Canada
Srivastava Anurag K. Washington State University, USA
Priyadi Ardyono   Institut Teknologi Sepuluh, Indonesia
Goel Lalit   Nanyang Technological University, Singapore

Organizing Committee

Conference Chair

Batra Usha   GD Goenka University, India

Organizing Secretary

Roy Nihar Ranjan   GD Goenka University, India

Members

Agrawal Shilpy   GD Goenka University, India
Arya Vaishali   GD Goenka University, India
Banerjee Alina   GD Goenka University, India

Bashir Jasira	GD Goenka University, India
Chopra Khayati	GD Goenka University, India
Gautam Ashu	GD Goenka University, India
Gupta Niharika	GD Goenka University, India
Jindal Anita Anand	GD Goenka University, India
Kapoor Neha	GD Goenka University, India
Kataria Shipra	GD Goenka University, India
Khurana Shikha	GD Goenka University, India
Kumar Yogesh	GD Goenka University, India
Meenalochani N.	GD Goenka University, India
Mehta Deepa	GD Goenka University, India
Nagpal Arpita	GD Goenka University, India
Pankaj Manchanda	GD Goenka University, India
Priya Rashmi	GD Goenka University, India
Saini Manisha Saini	GD Goenka University, India
Sharma Ganga	GD Goenka University, India
Sharma Manka	GD Goenka University, India
Singh Jaspreet	GD Goenka University, India
Singh Ramandeep	GD Goenka University, India
Sondhi Akanksha	GD Goenka University, India

International Advisory Committee

Srivastava Anurag K.	Washington State University, USA
Priyadi Ardyono	Institut Teknologi Sepuluh, Indonesia
Panda Brajendra	University of Arkansas, USA
Goel Lalit	Nanyang Technological University, Singapore
Yorino Naoto	Hiroshima University, Japan
Kothari D. P.	GP Group of Institutions, India
Al-Rabea Adnan	Al-Balqà Applied University, Jordan
Karki Nava Raj	Tribhuvan University, Nepal
Dharshana Yapa Roshan	University of Peradeniya, Sri Lanka
Eghbal Daniel (Mehdi)	ENERGEX, Australia
Talukdar Kamarul Hasan	Kulna University, Bangladesh
Kapoor Nishal	IBM Corporation, USA
Kuswadi Son	Politeknik Elektronika Negeri, Indonesia
Chari Rama	RRCAT, India
Salazar Alvare German	Stockholm University, Sweden
Girgis Emad	National Research Centre, Egypt
Sharma Paramanand	Tohoku University, Japan
Tickoo Sham	Purdue University, USA
Rauniyar S. P.	BMRD, Australia
Hakim Lukmanul	Lampung University, Indonesia
Klauss Raul	Technological University of Clausthal, Germany
Manis Amigui Gcaro Cocotle Compa	Monterry Institute of Technology, Mexico

Victor Manuel Diez	Interconexion Electrica, Columbia
Mitra Shayon	Manitoba Public Insurance, Canada
Chhabra Amit	Pollard Banknote, Canada
Borana Lalit	Hong Kong Polytechnic University, Hong Kong
Bhalla Subhash	University of Aizu, Japan
Muhammad Akbar Hussain Dil	Aalborg University, Denmark
Abdullah Mohammad FaizLiew	University Tun Hussein Onn Malaysia, Malaysia
Beichelt Frank	University of the Witwatersrand, South Africa
Mueller Eckhard	German Aerospace Centre, Germany

Technical Committee

Yorino Naoto	Hiroshima University, Japan
Huang Miaoqing	University of Arkansas, USA
Kothari D. P.	GP Group of Institutions, India
Al-Rabea Adnan	Al-Balqà Applied University, Jordan
Garg Deepak	Bennate University, India
Raj Karki Nava	Tribhuvan University, Nepal
Dharshana Yapa Roshan	University of Peradeniya, Sri Lanka
Eghbal Daniel (Mehdi)	Energex, Australia
Talukdar Kamarul Hasan	Kulna University, Bangladesh
Kapoor Nishal	IBM Corporation, USA
Kuswadi Son	Politeknik Elektronika Negeri, Indonesia
Chari Rama	RRCAT, India
Alvare German Salazar	Stockholm University, Sweden
Girgis Emad	National Research Centre, Egypt
Vyas Abhilasha	GSFC University, India
Kumar Abhinav	Amity University, India
Kumar Singh Abhishek	BIT, India
Swaroop Abhishek	BPIT, India
Priyam Abhishek	NIT, India
Singh Abhishek Kumar	BIT, India
Elngar Ahmed	Beni-Suef University, Egypt
Kumar Ajeet	AmesGoldsmith, USA
Dureja Aman	PDM College of Engineering, India
Landage Amarsinh	Government College of Engineering, India
Singh Amit	Guru Gobind Singh Indraprastha University, India
Choudhary Amit	Maharaja Surajmal Institute, India
Upadhyay Amrita	NIT, India
Nayyar Anand	Duy Tan University, Vietnam
Garg Anjali	The NorthCap University, India
Kumar Ankit	Uppsala University, Sweden
Choudhary Ankur	Amity University, India
Vij Ankush	Amity University, India

Gupta Anuj Kumar	IKG Punjab Technical University, India
Nagpal Arpita	GD Goenka University, India
Seth Ashish	Inha University, Uzbekistan
Khanna Ashish	MAIT, India
Garg Atul	Chitkara University, India
Bhati Bhoopesh Sinigh	Ambedkar Institute of Advanced Communication Technologies and Research, India
Garg Bindu	Bharati Vidyapeeth College of Engineering, India
Panda Brajendra	University of Arkansas, USA
Shekhar Chander	Amity University, India
Banerjee Chitreshh	Amity University, India
Babu D. Veerabhadra	iNURTURE Education Solutions Pvt. Ltd., India
Mehta Deepa	GD Goenka University, India
Gupta Deepak	GGSIPU, India
Kamthania Deepali	IIT, India
Garg Deepika	GD Goenka University, India
Kumar Devendra	ABES Engineering College, India
Singh Dimple	Amity University, India
Nandan Durgesh	Accendere Knowledge Management Services Pvt. Ltd., CL Educate Ltd., India
Sharma Ganga	Guru Gobind Singh Indraprastha University, India
Rani Geeta	NSIT, India
Yadav Harikesh	NIT, India
Kumar Harish	GL Baja Institute of Engineering and Technology, India
Purohit Hemant	JIET, India
Singh Jaspreet	GGSIPU, India
Jadon Jitendra	Amity University, India
Patel Jyotirmay	Shri Ram Murti Smarak College of Engineering, Technology and Research, India
Sagayam K. Martin	Karunya University, India
Rai Kajal	Punjab University, India
Punia Kavita	JK Lakshmipat University, India
Sree Kiran	SVECW, India
Seth Kirti	Inha University, Uzbekistan
Prasad Lalit	Galgotias University, India
Kharb Latika	Jagan Institute of Management Studies, India
Sharma Lavanya	Amity University, India
Bhatia Madhulika	Amity University, India
Hooda Madhurima	Amity University, India
Goyal Manik	CDLSIET, India
Gupta Manish Kumar	Symbiosis University of Applied Sciences, India
Saini Manisha	GD Goenka University, India
Gupta Manoj	Rukmini Devi Institute of Advanced Studies, India
Singh Manu	HRIT Group of Institutions, India
Solanki Manu	Manav Rachna International University, India

Iqbal Md	Meerut Institute of Engineering and Technology, India
Nafis Md Tabrez	Jamia Hamdard University, India
Sharma Meghna	The NorthCap University, India
Vasim Baig Mirza Mustaq	Yashwant College Nanded, India
Abdul Ahad Mohd	Jamia Hamdard University, India
Thaseen Mohseena	N.E.S's Science College, India
Dawar Parul	DTU, India
Yadav Mukesh	Gurgaon Institute of Technology and Management, India
Goyal Mukta	JIIT, India
Bhatele Mukta	OIST, India
Ojha Muneendra	IIITR, India
Sharma Naresh	GD Goenka University, India
Thakur Narina	BVCOE, India
Jain Neelesh	JUET, India
Kumar Neeraj	Thapar University, India
Goel Neetu	VIPS, India
Sharma Neha	GD Goenka University, India
Gupta Neha	Manav Rachna International Institute of Research and Studies, India
Goel Neha	VIPS, India
Arora Nidhi	GD Goenka University, India
Roy Nihar	GD Goenka University, India
Patidar Nitesh	IIT, India
Malik Nitin	The NorthCap University, India
Alshorman Omar	Najran University, India
Gahlot Pallavi	IIT, India
Nand Parma	IIT, India
Nayak Pinki	Amity University, India
Thakar Pooja	Vivekananda Institute of Professional Studies, India
Sapra Pooja	WCTM, India
Ahlawat Prachi	The NorthCap University, India
Prakash Prashant	BIT, India
Johri Prashant	Galgotias University, India
Pandya Prateek	Amity University, India
Negi Prateek	IITD, India
Kumar Praveen	Amity University, India
Pappula Praveen	SR Engineering College, India
Pandey Purnendu	BML Munjal University, India
Dutta Pushan	Amity University, India
P. Raghu Vamsi	JIIT, India
Singh Rajinder	Guru Kashi University, India
Rajak Ranjit	JNU, India
Mahajan Rashima	Manav Rachna International Institute of Research and Studies, India
Priya Rashmi	GD Goenka University, India

Mishra Renu	GCET, India
Babbar Richa	Thapar University, India
Kumar Rishi	Thapar University, India
Chhikara Rita	The NorthCap University, India
Vaid Rohit	Maharishi Markandeshwar University, India
Madaan Rosy	GD Goenka University, India
Ojha Rudra Pratap	Galgotias College of Engineering and Technology, India
Goyal S. B.	City University, Malaysia
Sinha S. K.	Amity University Noida, India
Abbas Sadiqa	Manav Rachna International University, India
K. Pachalla Sameer	Mahindra Ecole Centrale, India
Mathur Sandeep	Amity University, India
Singh Sandeep	JIIT, India
Saxena Sandeep	NIT, India
Tarar Sandhya	Gautam Buddha University, India
Makkar Sandhya	LBSIM, India
Mondal Sandip	NIT, India
Gupta Sanjay	Manav Rachna International University, India
Pippal Sanjeev	MNNIT, India
Sahu Sanjib	Indira Gandhi Delhi Technical University for Women, India
Das Sanjoy	Indira Gandhi National Tribal University, India
Chauhan Sansar Singh	MNNIT, India
Vishwakarma Santosh	Manipal University, India
Juneja Sapna	BMIET, India
Varshney Sapna	University of Delhi, India
Jain Sapna	University of Petroleum and Energy Studies, India
K. Saravanan	Anna University, India
Tanwar Sarvesh	Chitkara University, India
Sharma Satendra	Yobe State University Damaturu, Nigeria
Srivastava Satyajee	Galgotias University, India
Mishra Saurabh	Chandigarh University, India
Ahlawat Savita	Maharaja Surajmal Institute of Technology, India
Jain Shaily	Chitkara University, India
Vashisth Sharda	The NorthCap University, India
Arora Shaveta	The NorthCap University, India
Suhail Sheikh	J&K Forensic Science Laboratory, India
Sachdeva Shelly	NIT, India
Agrawal Shilpy	GD Goenka University, India
Saluja Shivani	GD Goenka University, India
Sharma Shivnjali	Rajiv Gandhi Institute of Petroleum Technology, India
Mongia Shweta	Jamia Millia Islamia, India
Singh Shyamli	Indian Institute of Public Administration, India
Biswas Siddhartha	Jamia Millia Islamia, India
Menon Sindhu	KLEIT, India

Sood Smita	GD Goenka University, India
Patnaik Soma	Manav Rachna International University, India
Tanwar Sudeep	Nirma University, India
Sengupta Sudhriti	Amity University, India
Mishra Sudipta	GD Goenka University, India
Radha Suja	VIT University, India
Kumar Sumit	NIT, India
Gupta Sumit Kumar	KIET, India
Raheja Supriya	NCU, India
A. Suresh	Nehru Institute of Engineering and Technology, India
Kumar Sushil	KIET, India
Narayanan Swaminathan	QIS College of Engineering and Technology, India
Jha Swati	BML, India
Choudhury Tanupriya	UPES, India
Kumar Tapas	Lingayas University, India
Choudhary Teja Ram	JNU, India
Khatoon Thayyaba	Malla Reddy College of Engineering and Technology, India
Tewari Tribhuwan	JIIT, India
Tiwari Twinkle	JIIT, India
Batra Usha	GD Goenka University, India
Juyal Vandana	BCIIT, India
Saini Varinder	IIT, India
Arora Vasudha	GD Goenka University, India
Tayal Vijay	Amity University, India
Yadav Vijay	Bundelkhand University, India
Tayal Vijay Kumar	Amity University, India
Singh Vijendra	The NorthCap University, India
Shanmuganathan Vimal	National Engineering College, India
Jain Vishal	Bharati Vidyapeeth's Institute of Computer Applications and Management, India
Kumar Yogesh	UTU, India
Gigras Yogita	NCU, India
Kumar Yugal	Hindu College of Engineering, India

Contents – Part I

Next Generation Computing

Contents – Part II

Data Centric Programming

An Efficient Approach for Selection of Initial Cluster Centroids for k-means

Manoj Kr. Gupta$^{(\boxtimes)}$ (iD) and Pravin Chandra (iD)

USIC&T, Guru Gobind Singh Indraprastha University, Dwarka, India
manojkgupta5@gmail.com, chandra.pravin@gmail.com

Abstract. Choice of initial centroids has a major impact on the performance and accuracy of k-means algorithm to group the data objects into various clusters. In basic k-means, pure arbitrary choice of initial centroids lead to construction of different clusters in every run and consequently affects the performance and accuracy of it. To date, several attempts have been made by the researchers to increase the performance and accuracy of it. However, scope of improvement still exists in this area. Therefore, a new approach to initialize centroids for k-means is proposed in this paper on the basis of the concept to choose the well separated data-objects as initial cluster centroids instead of pure arbitrary selection. As a consequence, it leads to higher probability of closeness of the chosen centroids to the final cluster centroids. The proposed algorithm is empirically assessed on 6 different well-known datasets. The results confirms that the proposed approach is considerably better than the pure arbitrary selection of centroids.

Keywords: Data mining · k-means algorithm · Cluster initialization · Clustering · Cluster validation

1 Introduction

Data mining is widely used in numerous applications [1, 2]. It includes a number of functionalities/tasks which are used in diverse applications for multiple purposes. Clustering is also considered as an important task of data mining based on unsupervised learning approach. On the basis of (dis)similarity or distance, objects are grouped into a number of clusters. Like/closer objects are allocated to the same cluster and alike/distant objects are allocated to another clusters. The distance or (dis)similarity is computed as the function of distance or similarity among the behavior or characteristics of the objects by the various clustering methods [2–9].

In the literature, several clustering algorithms are offered. However, basic k-means is the easiest and frequently used clustering algorithm. Algorithm 1 describes the basic k-means [2, 3, 7, 8, 49]:

© Springer Nature Singapore Pte Ltd. 2020
U. Batra et al. (Eds.): REDSET 2019, CCIS 1229, pp. 3–13, 2020.
https://doi.org/10.1007/978-981-15-5827-6_1

Algorithm 1: Basic k-means

Input: *k - # of Clusters, D - Dataset*
Output: *Cluster Assignment of each Data-object (x_i)*

1. *Arbitrarily initialize cluster centroids $C = \{c_1, c_2, \dots, c_k\}$*
2. *Repeat*
   a. *For each x_i in D*
      i. *Find distance of x_i with all centroids*
      ii. *Allocate x_i to the closest cluster*
   b. *Refine the centroid of each cluster*
3. *Until no change occurred in the cluster assignment for all x_i.*

The centroids chosen, as per Step 1 of Algorithm 1, leads to construction of different clusters in every run [8, 49].

The performance and accuracy of basic k-means is mainly rest upon the initialization of cluster centroids. So, the cautious choice of initial centroids, which are closer to the tangible centroids, improves the performance and accuracy of the algorithm. Therefore, several efforts have been made by the investigators to improve the performance and accuracy of the basic k-means. Numerous methods for choice of initial centroids are offered in the literature [6, 12–14].

The initial attempt for cluster initialization was made by Forgy [15] based on the random selection. The Forgy's method was slightly modified by several researchers [16–19]. New methods based on data distribution, estimation of density, deterministic divisive method, maximin initialization and hierarchical method was proposed in [20–24] respectively. Arthur and Vassilvitskii [25] proposed k-means algorithm based on improved cluster initialization method called as k-means++. Numerous other attempts have also been made by a number of other researchers [26–47].

In Sect. 2, an efficient approach for selection of initial centroids for k-means algorithm is proposed and explained. In Sect. 3, experiment design is described. In Sect. 4, the empirical results are presented. These results are compared based on some popular cluster evaluation techniques such as Performance, Cluster Compactness [10], Cluster Separation [10], Precision [11], Recall [11] and F-Measure [11]. To end with, the concluding remarks are drawn in Sect. 5. The empirical results and comparisons confirm that the suggested approach is considerably better than basic k-means.

2 Proposed Method

For the improvement of the performance and accuracy of k-means, an efficient approach for selection of initial cluster centroids for k-means algorithm is proposed on the basis of the concept to choose the well separated objects as initial centroids instead of pure arbitrarily selected initial centroids. In the proposed approach, first centroid is chosen arbitrarily and rest data points are chosen as centroids such that the chosen data objects are well separated or far off from the other data objects. The Step 1 of Algorithm 1 is modified in the k-means based on proposed approach and is presented as Algorithm 2.

Algorithm 2: k-means algorithm based on proposed on approach

Input: k - # of Clusters, D - Dataset, f – Factor, e - Exponent; where f is the normalization factor $(1 \leq f \leq \infty)$ and e is the exponent of the cluster count $(1 \leq f \leq \infty)$

Output: Cluster Assignments of each Data-object (x_i)

1. Initialize cluster centroids $C = \{c_1, c_2, \ldots, c_k\}$ as
   a. Choose any data-object arbitrarily, P_1
   b. Find distance from P_1 to all other data-objects
   c. Choose Farthest data-object, P_2
   d. Consider distance between P_1 and P_2 as $d = dis(P_1, P_2)$
   e. Compute $\alpha = \dfrac{d}{.k^e}$
   f. Eliminate all data-objects near P_1 and P_2 at distance $d \leq \alpha$
   g. Compute $P_1' = $ centroid of P_1 at distance α
   h. Compute $P_2' = $ centroid of P_2 at distance α
   i. Calculate distances of all data-objects to be considered from P_1' and P_2' and call them d_1 and d_2 respectively
   j. Compute $\beta = \dfrac{d_1 + d_2}{2}$ d_1, d_2
   k. Identify data-objects such that $d_1 > \beta$ and $d_2 > \beta$
   l. From the identified objects , find the inter-distances
   m. The data-objects which are most distant, d_3 from each other
      i. If $k < 4$ then choose any one data-object
      ii. If $k = 4$ then choose both data-objects
      iii. If $k > 4$ then choose both data-object; choose $d = min(d, d_3)$ and repeat step 2 (e) through step 2(m).
2. Repeat
   a. For each x_i in D
      i. Find distance of x_i with all centroids
      ii. Allocate x_i to the closest cluster
   b. Refine the centroid of each cluster
3. Until no change occurred in the cluster assignment for all x_i.

---

3 Experiment Design

In MATLAB, the proposed approach based k-Means and basic k-means are implemented. Both the algorithms are performed on 6 well-known datasets. The presented results are the mean of 200 runs of each aforesaid methods with each below mentioned datasets. No special optimization is applied in the implementation.

3.1 Datasets Used

Both k-means using proposed approach and basic k-means are assessed on 6 well-known datasets: Wine, Spambase, Pen Digit, IRIS, Image Segmentation and Animal Milk. First 5 datasets are downloaded from the website of "UCI Machine Learning Repository" whereas last dataset Animal Milk is downloaded from the website of "Hartigan". These datasets are listed in Table 1.

Table 1. Datasets used

Dataset	No. of attributes	No. of instances	No. of clusters
Wine	13	178	3
Spambase	57	4601	2
Pen Digit	16	7494	10
IRIS	4	150	3
Image Segmentation	19	2100	7
Animal Milk	4	16	5

3.2 Metric

Both k-Means algorithms have been executed on the above mentioned datasets. The results, presented in the Sect. 4, are the mean of 200 runs of each aforesaid methods with datasets.

3.3 Clustering Evaluation Measures

Clustering evaluation measures evaluate the validity of goodness of the clustering [10, 11, 47, 48]. They can be broadly categorized into external and internal measures [47, 48].

Internal Measures
These are generally founded upon two principles: cluster compactness [10] and cluster separation [10]. These criteria are employed on the basis of the intrinsic features of the dataset itself and the cluster assignment. Numerous internal measures are offered in the literature [10, 11, 47, 48]. In this paper, Cluster Compactness [10] and Cluster Separation [10] internal measures are used to compare the results.

External Measures
These are founded on the concept of supervised learning and compare the clustering result against the ground truth or prior knowledge about the cluster assignments. Numerous external measures are offered in the literature [10, 11, 47, 48]. However, Precision [11], Recall [11] and F-measure [11] external measures are used to compare the results in the paper.

4 Results and Discussions

The empirical results of basic k-means and the k-means based on proposed approach are listed in the Tables 2, 3, 4, 5, 6, 7 and 8. The results of both the algorithms are assessed and compared on the basis of (i) Performance, (ii) Accuracy, (iii) Cluster Compactness, (iv) Cluster Separation, (v) Precision, (vi) Recall and (vii) F-Measure of the clustering.

Table 2. Performance

Dataset	Basic k-means	Variant_1	Variant_2	Variant_3	Variant_4
Wine	11.87	11.14	11.34	11.13	11.18
Spambase	7.13	7.56	7.07	7.80	7.36
Pen Digit	28.65	32.42	29.77	29.72	29.26
IRIS	9.22	10.23	10.25	9.85	9.84
Image Segmentation	13.89	13.33	14.56	14.97	14.24
Animal Milk	38.42	45.59	42.55	45.07	45.97

Table 3. Accuracy

Dataset	Basic k-means	Variant_1	Variant_2	Variant_3	Variant_4
Wine	71.70%	70.98%	71.26%	71.19%	71.11%
Spambase	98.92%	99.01%	99.22%	98.77%	98.89%
Pen Digit	75.89%	75.85%	75.71%	75.77%	75.79%
IRIS	88.81%	88.75%	88.83%	88.70%	88.82%
Image Segmentation	97.09%	98.01%	97.63%	97.42%	96.78%
Animal Milk	96.96%	97.40%	97.57%	97.32%	97.99%

The proposed approach based k-means algorithm is executed using four different combinations of its two input parameters factor (f) and exponent (e). In this paper, these four different combinations are referred to as Variant_1 to Variant_4 and described below:

- **Variant_1 ($f = 1$ and $e = 2$)** – To set the value of $\alpha = (k^2)^{th}$ part of the total distance (d) via dividing the total distance (d) by k^2.
- **Variant_2 ($f = dim$ i.e. number of dimensions and $e = 2$)** – To set the value of $\alpha = (dim.k^2)^{th}$ part of the total distance (d) via dividing the total distance (d) by the product of dim and k^2.

Table 4. Cluster compactness

Dataset	Original-Values					Normalized-Values				
	Basic k-means	Variant–1	Variant–2	Variant–3	Variant–4	Basic k-means	Variant–1	Variant–2	Variant–3	Variant–4
Wine	841436.80	824383.10	831385.92	831665.70	828800.24	10.00	0.00	4.11	4.27	2.59
Spambase	6202113350.51	622831435.07	628944965.71	615844542.92	619337988.99	3.33	5.33	10.00	0.00	2.67
Pen Digit	3510918.33	3561756.53	3529796.43	3536274.86	3532873.68	0.00	10.00	3.71	4.99	4.32
IRIS	27.14	27.67	27.35	28.21	27.46	0.00	4.94	1.99	10.00	2.99
Image Segmentation	4274503.45	4582433.32	4332766.67	4388329.29	4348107.09	0.00	10.00	1.89	3.70	2.39
Animal Milk	7.67	7.51	7.04	7.19	6.82	10.00	8.14	2.57	4.35	0.00

Table 5. Cluster separation

Dataset	Original-Values					Normalized-Values				
	Basic k-means	Variant–1	Variant–2	Variant–3	Variant–4	Basic k-means	Variant–1	Variant–2	Variant–3	Variant–4
Wine	296495.06	290130.54	292529.93	292273.49	291418.17	10.00	0.00	3.77	3.37	2.02
Spambase	7088425076.79	7206433053.63	7481784999.58	6891745115.39	7049089084.51	3.33	5.33	10.00	0.00	2.67
Pen Digit	109851.99	112867.01	113393.07	112928.90	113059.69	0.00	8.51	10.00	8.69	9.06
IRIS	13.05	12.99	13.04	12.93	13.02	10.00	4.48	8.59	0.00	7.60
Image Segmentation	2273924.87	2228667.99	2232671.57	2222797.13	2202387.98	10.00	3.67	4.23	2.85	0.00
Animal Milk	682.73	686.74	697.27	689.60	701.48	0.00	2.14	7.75	3.66	10.00

Table 6. Precision

Dataset	Basic k-means	Variant_1	Variant_2	Variant_3	Variant_4
Wine	0.7406	0.7346	0.7367	0.7361	0.7355
Spambase	0.6671	0.6664	0.6649	0.6682	0.6673
Pen Digit	0.7718	0.7920	0.7901	0.7880	0.7919
IRIS	0.8972	0.8943	0.8968	0.8923	0.8963
Image Segmentation	0.8042	0.8046	0.8019	0.8028	0.8025
Animal Milk	0.9582	0.9598	0.9635	0.9605	0.9680

Table 7. Recall

Dataset	Basic k-means	Variant_1	Variant_2	Variant_3	Variant_4
Wine	0.6561	0.6693	0.6637	0.6630	0.6656
Spambase	0.5073	0.5067	0.5052	0.5084	0.5076
Pen Digit	0.7167	0.6913	0.6944	0.6952	0.6955
IRIS	0.8807	0.8753	0.8790	0.8703	0.8780
Image Segmentation	0.2162	0.1956	0.2124	0.2085	0.2116
Animal Milk	0.9160	0.9190	0.9270	0.9210	0.9360

- **Variant_3 ($f = 1$ and $e = 1$)** – To set the value of $\alpha = k^{th}$ part of the total distance (d) via dividing the total distance (d) by k.
- **Variant_4 ($f = dim$ i.e. number of dimensions and $e = 1$)** – To set the value of $\alpha = (dim.k)^{th}$ part of the total distance (d) via dividing the total distance (d) by the product of dim and k.

Tables 2 and 3 lists the comparative performance (i.e. average number of iterations taken to converge) and accuracy of both the approaches respectively. Tables 4 and 5 present the Cluster Compactness and Cluster Separation respectively. In Tables 6, 7 and 8, the Precision, Recall and F-Measure, of both the approaches, are presented respectively.

For Image Segmentation and Wine datasets, as shown in Table 2, the performance of proposed method is superior to basic k-means. The accuracy is superior in all datasets except Pen Digit and Wine as shown in Table 3. Tables 4 and 5, show that cluster compactness and cluster separation of the proposed approach are superior to basic k-means in most of the datasets. The Precision, Recall and F-Measure of the proposed approach are also superior than basic k-means for most of the datasets as shown in Tables 6, 7 and 8.

Table 8. F-measure

Dataset	Basic k-means	Variant_1	Variant_2	Variant_3	Variant_4
Wine	0.6703	0.6812	0.6766	0.6760	0.6782
Spambase	0.3945	0.3930	0.3897	0.3969	0.3950
Pen Digit	0.7079	0.6829	0.6865	0.6869	0.6882
IRIS	0.8789	0.8732	0.8771	0.8680	0.8760
Image Segmentation	0.1151	0.0955	0.1118	0.1078	0.1113
Animal Milk	0.9125	0.9142	0.9229	0.9169	0.9320

5 Summary and Conclusion

Due to ease of use and less complexity in choice of initial centroids, the basic k-Means is generally used. However, the performance and accuracy of k-means algorithm are generally affected due to the arbitrary selection of initial centroids. In proposed approach, k centroids are carefully chosen based on well separated data points so that the chosen initial centroids are closer to the tangible centroids.

The empirical results offered in Tables 2, 3, 4, 5, 6, 7 and 8 show that proposed approach is considerably superior to basic k-means on the basis of Performance, Accuracy, Cluster Compactness, Cluster Separation, Precision, Recall and F-Measure. As shown in the empirical results, based on internal clustering validity measures, Variant_1 and Variant_2 are better whereas based on external clustering validity measures, Variant_3 and Variant_4 are better.

The proposed method seems to be quiet complex for a large number of clusters but the complexity can be improved by applying some optimization techniques in future work.

References

1. Arora, R.K., Gupta, M.K.: e-Governance using data warehousing and data mining. Int. J. Comput. Appl. **169**(8), 28–31 (2017). https://doi.org/10.5120/ijca2017914785
2. Han, J., Kamber, M., Pei, J.: Data Mining Concepts and Techniques, 3rd edn. Elsevier (2012)
3. Jain, A.K., Dubes, R.C.: Algorithms for Clustering Data. Prentice Hall, Englewood Cliffs (1988)
4. Gupta, M.K., Chandra, P.: A comparative study of clustering algorithms. In: Proceedings of the 13th INDIACom-2019; IEEE Conference ID: 461816; 6th International Conference on Computing for Sustainable Global Development (2019)
5. Jain, A.K., Murty, M.N., Flynn, P.J.: Data clustering: a review. ACM Comput. Surv. **31**(3), 60 (1999)
6. Gan, G., Ma, C., Wu, J.: Data Clustering: Theory, Algorithms, and Applications. American Statistical Association and the Society for Industrial and Applied Mathematics. SIAM (2007)
7. Gupta, M.K., Chandra, P.: P-k-means: k-means using partition based cluster initialization method. In: Proceedings of the International Conference on Advancements in Computing & Management (ICACM 2019), pp. 567–573. Elsevier SSRN (2019). https://doi.org/10.2139/ssrn.3462549

8. Gupta, M.K., Chandra, P.: HYBCIM: hypercube based cluster initialization method for k-means. Int. J. Innov. Technol. Explor. Eng. **8**(10), 3584–3587 (2019). https://doi.org/10.35940/ijitee.j9774.0881019

9. Gupta, M.K., Chandra, P.: An empirical evaluation of K-means clustering algorithm using different distance/similarity metrics. In: ICETIT 2019. LNEE, vol. 605, pp. 884–892. Springer, Heidelberg (2019). https://doi.org/10.1007/978-3-030-30577-2_79

10. Halkidi, M., Batistakis, Y., Vazirgiannis, M.: Clustering validity checking methods: part iI. ACM SIGMOD Rec. **31**(3) (2002). https://doi.org/10.1145/601858.601862

11. Rendón, E., Abundez, I., Arizmendi, A., Quiroz, E.M.: Internal versus external cluster validation indexes. Int. J. Comput. Commun. **5**(1), 27–34 (2011)

12. Motwani, M., Arora, N., Gupta, A.: A study on initial centroids selection for partitional clustering algorithms. In: Hoda, M., Chauhan, N., Quadri, S., Srivastava, P. (eds.) Software Engineering. Advances in Intelligent Systems and Computing, vol. 731. Springer, Heidelberg (2019). https://doi.org/10.1007/978-981-10-8848-3_21

13. Jain, A.K.: Data clustering: 50 years beyond K-means. Pattern Recogn. Lett. **31**, 651–666 (2010)

14. Xu, D., Tian, Y.: A comprehensive survey of clustering algorithms. Ann. Data. Sci. (2015). https://doi.org/10.1007/s40745-015-0040-1

15. Forgy, E.: Cluster analysis of multivariate data: efficiency vs. interpretability of classifications. Biometrics **21**(3), 768 (1965)

16. McQueen, J.B.: Some methods for classification and analysis of multi-variate observation. In: Symposium on Mathematical Statistics and Probability, University of California Press (1967)

17. Kaufman, L., Rousseeuw, P.J.: Finding Groups in Data. An Introduction to Cluster Analysis. Wiley, Hoboken (1990)

18. Katsavounidis, I, Kuo, C., Zhang, Z.: A new initialization technique for generalized Lloyd iteration. IEEE **1**(10), 144–146 (1994)

19. Bradley, P.S., Fayyad, U.M.: Refining initial points for K-Means clustering. In: Proceedings of the 15th International Conference on Machine Learning, San Francisco, CA, pp. 91–99 (1998)

20. Pei, J., Fan, J., Xie, W.: A new initialization method of cluster centers. J. Electron. **16**(4), 320–326 (1999). https://doi.org/10.1007/s11767-999-0033-3

21. Khan, S.S., Ahmad, A.: Cluster centre initialization algorithm for K-means clustering. Pattern Recogn. Lett. **25**(11), 1293–1302 (2004)

22. Su, T., Dy, J.: A deterministic method for initializing K-means clustering. Tools with artificial intelligence. In: 16th IEEE International Conference, ICTAI 2004, pp. 784–786 (2004)

23. Hathaway, R.J., Bezdek, J.C., Huband, J.M.: Maximin initialization for cluster analysis. In: Martínez-Trinidad, J.F., Carrasco Ochoa, J.A., Kittler, J. (eds.) CIARP 2006. LNCS, vol. 4225. Springer, Heidelberg (2006). https://doi.org/10.1007/11892755_2

24. Arai, K., Barakbah, A.R.: Hierarchical K-means: an algorithm for centroids initialization for K-means. Rep. Fac. Sci. Eng. Saga Univ. **36** (2007)

25. Arthur, D., Vassilvitskii, S.: k-means ++: The advantages of careful seeding. In: ACM-SIAM Symposium on Discrete Algorithms (SODA 2007) Astor Crowne Plaza, New Orleans, Louisiana, pp. 1–11 (2007)

26. Wu, S., Jiang, Q., Huang, J.Z.: A new initialization method for clustering categorical data. In: Zhou, Z.H., Li, H., Yang, Q. (eds.) PAKDD 2007. LNCS, vol. 4426, pp. 972–980. Springer, Heidelberg (2007). https://doi.org/10.1007/978-3-540-71701-0_109

27. Kang, P., Cho, S.: K-means clustering seeds initialization based on centrality, sparsity, and isotropy. In: Corchado, E., Yin, H. (eds.) IDEAL 2009. LNCS, vol. 5788. Springer, Heidelberg (2009). https://doi.org/10.1007/978-3-642-04394-9_14

28. Maitra, R.: Initializing partition-optimization algorithms. IEEE/ACM Trans. Comput. Biol. Bioinform. **6**, 144–157 (2009)

29. Xu, J., Xu, B., Zhang, W.: Stable initialization scheme for K-means clustering. Wuhan Univ. J. Nat. Sci. **14**(1), 24–28 (2009). https://doi.org/10.1007/s11859-009-0106-z

30. Dang, Y., Xuan, Z., Rong, L., Liu, M.: A novel initialization method for semi-supervised clustering. In: Bi, Y., Williams, M.A. (eds.) KSEM 2010. LNCS, vol. 6291, pp. 317–328. Springer, Heidelberg (2010). https://doi.org/10.1007/978-3-642-15280-1_30

31. Naldi, M.C., Campello, R.J.G.B., Hruschka, E.R., Carvalho, A.C.P.L.F.: Efficiency issues of evolutionary K-means. Appl. Soft Comput. **11**, 1938–1952 (2011)

32. Reddy, D., Mishra, D., Jana, P.K.: MST-based cluster initialization for K-means. In: Meghanathan, N., Kaushik, B.K., Nagamalai, D. (eds.) CCSIT 2011. CCIS, vol. 131, pp. 329–338. Springer, Heidelberg (2011). https://doi.org/10.1007/978-3-642-17857-3_33

33. Bai, L., Liang, J., Dang, C., Cao, F.: A cluster centers initialization method for clustering categorical data. Expert Syst. Appl. **39**(9), 8022–8029 (2012). ISSN 0957-4174. https://doi.org/10.1016/j.eswa.2012.01.131

34. Chen, G.H.: Cluster center initialization using hierarchical two-division of a data set along each dimension. In: Jin, D., Lin, S. (eds.) Advances in Computer Science and Information Engineering. Advances in Intelligent and Soft Computing, vol. 168, pp. 235–241. Springer, Heidelberg (2012). https://doi.org/10.1007/978-3-642-30126-1_38

35. Aldahdooh, R.T., Ashour, W.: DIMK-means distance-based initialization methods for K-means clustering algorithms. Int. J. Intell. Syst. Appl. **2**, 41–51 (2013)

36. Goyal, M., Kumar, S.: Improving the initial centroids of K-means clustering algorithm to generalize its applicability. J. Inst. Eng. (India): Ser. B **95**(4), 345–350 (2014). https://doi.org/10.1007/s40031-014-0106-z

37. Duwairi, R., Abu-Rahmeh, M.: A novel approach for initializing the spherical K-means clustering algorithm. Simul. Model. Practice Theory **54**, 49–63 (2015). ISSN 1569-190X, https://doi.org/10.1016/j.simpat.2015.03.007

38. Poomagal, S., Saranya, P., Karthik, S.: A novel method for selecting initial centroids in K-means clustering algorithm. Int. J. Intell. Syst. Technol. Appl. **15**(3) (2016). https://doi.org/10.1504/IJISTA.2016.078347

39. Dhanabal, S., Chandramathi, S.: Enhancing clustering accuracy by finding initial centroid using k-minimum-average-maximum method. Int. J. Inf. Commun. Technol. **11**(2) (2017). https://doi.org/10.1504/IJICT.2017.086252

40. Golasowski, M., Martinovič, J., Slaninová, K.: Comparison of K-means clustering initialization approaches with brute-force initialization. In: Chaki, R., Saeed, K., Cortesi, A., Chaki, N. (eds.) Advanced Computing and Systems for Security. Advances in Intelligent Systems and Computing, vol. 567, pp. 103–114. Springer, Heidelberg (2017). https://doi.org/10.1007/978-981-10-3409-1_7

41. Kumar, K.M., Reddy, A.R.M.: An efficient k-means clustering filtering algorithm using density based initial cluster centers. Inf. Sci. **418–419**, 286–301 (2017). ISSN 0020-0255, https://doi.org/10.1016/j.ins.2017.07.036

42. Ismkhan, H.: I-k-means −+: an iterative clustering algorithm based on an enhanced version of the K-means. Pattern Recogn. **79**, 402–413 (2018). ISSN 0031-3203, https://doi.org/10.1016/j.patcog.2018.02.015

43. Nguyen, C.D., Duc, T., Duong, T.H.: K-means** – a fast and efficient K-means algorithms. Int. J. Intell. Inf. Database Syst. **11**(1) (2018). https://doi.org/10.1504/ijiids.2018.091595

44. Sandhya, N., Raja Sekar, M.: Analysis of variant approaches for initial centroid selection in K-means clustering algorithm. In: Satapathy, S., Bhateja, V., Das, S. (eds.) Smart Computing and Informatics. Smart Innovation, Systems and Technologies, vol. 78, pp. 109–121. Springer, Heidelberg (2018). https://doi.org/10.1007/978-981-10-5547-8_11

45. Yu, S., Chu, S., Wang, C., Chan, Y., Chang, T.: Two improved K-means algorithms. Appl. Soft Comput. **68**, 747–755 (2018). ISSN 1568-4946, https://doi.org/10.1016/j.asoc.2017.08.032

46. Kurada, R.R., Kanadam, K.P.: A novel evolutionary automatic clustering technique by unifying initial seed selection algorithms into teaching–learning-based optimization. In: Soft Computing and Medical Bioinformatics. Springer Briefs in Applied Sciences and Technology. Springer, Singapore (2019). https://doi.org/10.1007/978-981-13-0059-2_1

47. Halkidi, M., Batistakis, Y., Vazirgiannis, M.: On clustering validation techniques. J. Intell. Inf. Syst. **17**(2/3), 107–145 (2001)

48. Theodoridis, S., Koutroubas, K.: Pattern Recognition, 2nd edn. Academic Press, Cambridge (2003)

49. Gupta, M.K., Chandra, P.: MP-K-Means: modified partition based cluster initialization method for K-means algorithm. Int. J. Recent Technol. Eng. **8**(4), 1140–1148 (2019). https://doi.org/10.35940/ijrte.D6837.118419

Bedsore Ulcer Detection Using Support Vector Machine

Anand Upadhyay, Nida Baig$^{(\boxtimes)}$, and Anishka Pereira

Department of Information Technology, Thakur College of Science and Commerce,
Thakur Village, Kandivali East, Mumbai 400101, India
anandhari6@gmail.com, nida.eve@gmail.com,
pereiraanishka2@gmail.com

Abstract. Bedsore ulcer is a common disease. Fall accidents and occurrence's of bedsore ulcer are common amongst the elderly people which is the typical problem most of the medical institutions are accounting. Absence of effective system to detect bedsore ulcer also contributes to this otherwise preventable situation. Considering this problem of ulcer detection system, there is a requirement for a new and a high accurate processing unit for detection. In this paper we have therefore come up with a low-cost & highly accurate method for the bedsore detection. The support vector machine algorithm. will be used that could ultimately reduce the risk of ulcer damaging the skin up to a greater extend. Use of non-invasive techniques, like image classification techniques, it is possible to get some analysis from ulcers and that can be used to aid in its diagnosis. However, even while bedsore ulcers are becoming a more common problem, paying the cost for its treatment is getting difficult. If they are found or detected at an early stage than there can be a good opportunity of these sores getting healed in few days with very little pain. Effective and early bedsore ulcer detection will greatly reduce suffering and discomfort caused to patient's. The results have indicated that Support vector machine performed better than the other classifiers for bedsore ulcers detection.

Keywords: Bedsore ulcer · Support Vector Machine (SVM) · Detection · Pressure ulcer · Affected area · Non affected area · Confusion Matrix · Kappa coefficient

1 Introduction

Body tissues are soft and sensitive to constant load eventually causing to tissue necrosis in the form of bedsore ulcer. They are also called as pressure ulcers or pressure sores, and initially may just appear like off-color skin. Bedsore ulcer is caused by pressure on the skin for longer time limiting the circulation of blood in neighboring tissues. Bedsore ulcer commonly affects those people who are confined to bed [1] and are unable to change their position. Bedsore ulcers develop quickly, but most of the sores can't be healed completely and over time they can get even more serious growing into deep, open wounds. Bedsores are very painful, takes more time to heal, and, for many people leading to other related health problems [2]. Ulcers can appear on both inside your body

© Springer Nature Singapore Pte Ltd. 2020
U. Batra et al. (Eds.): REDSET 2019, CCIS 1229, pp. 14–23, 2020.
https://doi.org/10.1007/978-981-15-5827-6_2

and outside your body and it may also take many forms. Bedsores ulcer are not just a source of pain for bedridden and chair bounded people but these sores often act as pathway for infection and other serious complications, some of which can also lead to permanent incurable wounds and loss of life.

The main cause of bedsores ulcer is lack of mobility of the person. If the person is not moving or not changing the position than the area that covers bony prominences are under constant pressure which leads to skin breakdown because of the continuous pressure on the same area [1]. This continuous pressure leads to ischemia. Ischemia is inadequate blood supply to an organ or part of the body. There are many reasons and factors related with the development of bedsore ulcers, some primary contributing factor include:

Pressure - Flow of blood to the tissues is reduced due to prolonged pressure on body parts. Flow of blood is very important for providing nutrients and oxygen to the tissues. Lacking of these essential nutrients in the skin and its side by tissues get damaged and die off.

Friction - When the skin rubs against the bedding or clothing the friction occurs.

Shear - when 2 surfaces are moving in the contrary directions the shear occurs.

Factors related for bedsores include age of the patient, mobility and activity levels done by person, some current medical conditions, infections or diseases, malnutrition, skin moisture, incontinent medication usage [3]. Bedsore ulcer can lead to few more problems like joint and infection, cancer in the upper layers of your skin, Sepsis. Some risk factors associated with bedsore ulcer are:

Immobility - Due to poor health of the person or may be due to spinal cord injury and other causes.

Lack of sensory perception - loss of sensation is caused due to injury spinal cord, neurologic disorders and some other conditions.

Poor nutrition and hydration - Healthy and rich diet with high protein, calories, enough fluids, vitamins and minerals for maintaining healthy skin and prevent the breakdown of skin tissues.

Medical conditions affecting blood flow- The risk of tissue getting damaged increases with the health problems that can affect flow of blood, such as diabetes and other vascular diseases.

Treating bedsore ulcers is difficult and costly, therefore detecting it is extremely important [4]. The current approach used to identify Pressure Ulcer are dependent on health care workers, primarily nurses [5]. The primary purpose of this bedsore ulcer using SVM is to provide the caretakers nursing the patients affected with bedsore ulcer to detect the exact area of the ulcer on the patients body with the clear information about affected area. It will be basically detecting the infected wounds once the ulcer has developed on the patient's body. This information can help in treating the bedsore ulcer in an effective way with the a clear appearance of the affected area on the patients body. The system is detecting the bedsores ulcer and damage done to skin and reduce time to detect the ulcer on the patient's body. Detecting the bedsore ulcer can help the patient to reduce the risk of developing a more serious type of ulcer [3]. Due to low cost of bedsore ulcer detection, we have an envision that in near future, ulcer detection system would widely be used as a part of the hospitals, wound caring clinics and nursing homes.

The detection will be done using SVM which has become one of the most popular field in machine learning after the neural networks. A Support Vector Machine is trained by the combination of RGB bands selected pixel to distinguish between the two classes viz. Affected and Non Affected. The end result of the work may be an image with ulcer detected on basis of affected and non affected area.

2 Literature Review

Many people are affected by bedsore ulcer. There are only some prevention methods invented. But these prevention methods use different wireless device, sensor based system, which are very expensive & time consuming methods. Researchers are trying to reduce the cost of the bedsore ulcer detection system and even trying to make it available for use in hospitals [6] and nursing homes. A small wireless device was used for classifying some of the positions of the user's in the bed was presented. To differentiate a set of position of the user's in the bed monitoring the activities of patients not able to make the desirable body movements the RSS measurements were used. The collected data was classified using SVM and K-nearest neighbor techniques to recognize different position of the user's and supporting the bedsore issues [7]. A pressure map of entire body of the patient was created using a commercial pressure mapping system. To keep an informative and unobtrusive record of bed posture of the patient's over time an image processing based algorithm was developed. This algorithm predicted patients bed posture with 97.7% average accuracy [3]. Simulation and system development for the analysis of pressure ulcer is based on the analysis and prevention of pressure ulcer using sensor-based system. The Objective of this research paper was to reduce incidences in bed bounded patients by improving the efficiency of detection in areas vulnerable of developing pressure ulcer or detecting infected wounds once the ulcer has developed [8]. A software platform that facilitates monitoring of patients at risk and gives some preventive measures leading to decrease in the count of pressure ulcer formulation incidents in the hospitals was developed. Since all the above method were prevention based method there is no particular detection based system. So we have selected Bedsore Ulcer Detection using SVM [1]. The patients body area was divided into three horizontal areas and three vertical areas to prevent accident falls and to manage the pressure ulcer. The information of pressure on one of the patients body regions that were divided horizontally was managed by each unit of microcontroller. In this study, The possibilities of bedsores occurrence and falling accidents in older people considering both the intensity of the pressure and also the duration of pressure of specific body parts was presented by a real-time pressure-sensing algorithm. The results demonstrate a smart bed works well for several human models of various heights and weights [9]. Chance of stroke occurrence and other neurological pathologies is prevented by Neurogenic intervention while the accumulation of over pressure on ulcer vulnerable regions is prevented by mechanical intervention. The pressure vulnerable regions are said to be the skin over bony prominences. To prevent the formation of ulcers there were various technology developed. The paper was more focused on what is essential for quick prevention of pressure ulcer and also reviewed existing technology. This system envisages automatically shifting the pressure when excessive pressure is sensed over the high vulnerable regions of ulcer. To identify the accumulating pressure Force sensitive resistors (FSR) were used as sensors. When excessive pressure was sensed over the high vulnerable regions of ulcer the system envisaged automatically shifting the pressure [10]. People in an immovable condition are more liable to pressure ulcers, the skin and underlying tissues are localized to injuries because of prolonged pressure. This paper examined thermal images of one adult old patient at risk of developing pedal pressure ulcers, who had reported pain in right side foot, after many days of a hospital stay. Thermal images of the patient's both the heels left as well as right and malleoli were subjected to undergo Image processing for removal of noise and enhance contrast in the image, selection of region and feature extraction technique was carried out to observe changes in temperature, the difference in temperature between both the heels left as well as was calculated over time. These results suggest that the pressure ulcers formation may be able to detect faster than can be visually observed with thermal imaging, in conjunction with image processing [11].

3 Algorithm

Support Vector Machine
Support vector machine was invented by Vladimir N. Vapnik [12] a popular Russian mathematician and statistician. SVM is a binary classifier. Which is now introduced on the basis of the traditional statistics theory. SVMs are among the best "off-the-shelf" supervised learning algorithm. It attempts to find hyper plane that can separate two class of data by the largest margin. Support vector machine is now one of the most important categories to perform Image recognition. SVM comes under Machine Learning. SVM's are also called as supervised learning algorithm. Support vector machines are the supervised learning models with an associated learning algorithms that analyzes the data used for classification and also regression analysis. Support vector machine is nothing but a binary classification algorithm. It basically comes under the umbrella of machine learning. Image processing is basically the process which combines dealing with manipulation of images. For example, image filtering is a process where we use one input image which is then passed through a laplacian filter which needs to be sharpened. An SVM may be used for performing image classification. Example: for a given input image, the classification task is mainly to decide what actually that image is. For example: if it is a cat or a dog. Any image, which is put into SVM might have possibilities that it might have gone through some or any filtering processing types like feature extraction such as shapes, colors and edges. So basically, if compared both of these are basically different from each other in case of field study (SVM being from Machine Learning and Image Processing a subset if Signal Processing). Image processing is mostly opted before than that of SVM.

The two main elements used for the implementation of SVM algorithm are the kernel functions and the mathematical programming. Variety of the hypothesis spaces are searched with the help of Kernel function. Classification is performed by drawing hyper plane in the SVM algorithm. This hyper plane is at equal distance from both the classes in two class classification. Data instances which are used to define this hyper plane are known as support vectors. A margin is defined in SVM which is the distance between hyper plane and the nearest support vector. For good separation by this hyper plane, the distance of margin should be as large as possible because large distance gives less error. SVM is based on concept of finding a hyper plane that best separates the feature into different domains. Support vector machine, whose main idea is to build a hyper plane as the decision surface, is introduced to solve the problems [13]. SVM is the best algorithm that can be used when classes are separable. The aim of using SVM is to minimize classification error through maximizing the margin between the separating hyper plane and the data sets for which SVM is trained to detect the bedsore ulcer between the two categories i.e. affected and non-affected. The SVM has given more accurate values as compared to other algorithm. This algorithm is widely used classification algorithm for prediction of disease. It is also used to predict diseases like diabetes, breast cancer, lung cancer, heart disease, but in this case it used to detect bedsore ulcer. Using SVM is efficient for Ulcer detection because bedsore ulcer has more dimensional data.

The SVM algorithm is used to categorize data (unlabeled data), and is a very widely used algorithm in applications. In other words SVM uses a hyper plane which is used for separation, regression, classification and detection. Here in this paper SVM is used to categorize and separate the affected and non affected data from image processing technique. The hyper plane creates a gap and separates the data in a wide format.

4 Dataset

Collection of accurate data is very important. We have collected data from https://www. healthline.com/. The data collected consists of various images of bedsore ulcer developed on various parts of body. The selection of right image is very important for training the dataset. Images in the .jpg format were used for creating a training file.

Most of the research is based on gathering of the required and measured data. Earlier datasets were not even published and even if somehow they got published they were never ever considered as a by-product. But there's something interesting observed here that datasets i.e. Combinations of models and parameters are becoming important day by day and are also gaining much popularity as they are very important for any project as they can also be seen as the primary objective of the complete research. Gathering and preserving datasets are therefore so important.

5 Methodology

The methodologies for research paper is the implementation of the proposed algorithm where the algorithm is implemented and tested on the data and the result of the performance, result and accuracy of the algorithm are suggested.

The algorithm is developed in MATLAB, It uses SVM algorithm. MATLAB, is a shortening word for 'Matrix Laboratory', It is one of the best platforms to solve scientific and mathematical problems. Matlab is a programming language which is developed by Mathworks, which allows functions and data plotting, also user interface creations, implementation of algorithms and also interacting with other programs those written in programming languages like C++, C, Java and the list goes on.

The collection of functions which truly extends the capacity of the numeric computing environment is the only actual IPT in MATLAB. A group of reference based standard algorithms and their workflow applications for performing image processing, visualization, analysing and algorithm development is provided. This could be used for performing image enhancement, noise reduction, image segmentation, geometric transformations, image registration and 3D image processing operations. A lot of the IPT functions supports C and C++ code generation for desktop prototyping and embedded vision system deployment.

The flow chart represents the steps involved in Classification (Fig. 1).

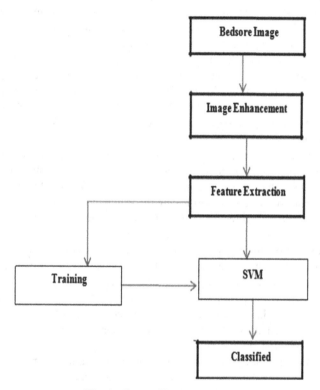

Fig. 1. Stage of implementation

In this phase, the RGB(Red Green Blue) color space feature values of the selected pixels of the bedsore ulcer. These RGB features have been divided into the two major classes of the bedsore ulcer, they are affected area and non-affected area. After the extraction is done of the RGB value of the bedsore ulcer training file is prepared which consist of pixel values of affected area and non-affected area.

Image processing is a technique used for converting any given image into digital format style and are performed desired operations on it. We use image processing techniques for extraction and adoption useful information from it. Changes taking place in the images are usually performed automatically and they do rely on the carefully designed algorithms.

Image processing technique is the best field which has a lot of contributions from many sources of science which includes mathematics, physics, optical and electrical engineering. Not just this but it also has a quality of overlapping with different areas such as artificial intelligence, machine learning, pattern recognition and human research. All the different steps that are involved in image processing includes the importing the image with the help of an optical scanner or with the help of a digital camera, analyzing and manipulating the given image used (image enhancement, image filtering and data compression), and it also generates the desired output image. The only reason to use image processing technique and extract information from images and convert their content has always been the most amazing factor. This technique finds usage in a lot of sectors such as as medicine, industry, and consumer electronics, military and so on is the list. We can take an example of the usage of this technique in medicine, it is used in various diagnostic imaging types such as magnetic resonance imaging (MRI), positron emission tomography (PET), computerized axial tomography (CAT) and functional magnetic resonance imaging (fMRI). Apart from this field, other applications include manufacturing systems such as automated guided vehicle control, quality control and safety systems.

Feature extraction is a very important step in case of the support vector machine's high generation ability of a classifier are realized by feature extraction. For good results of SVM, the features that we give as an input to SVM are required to be reduced. By reducing the feature set it helps in improving the efficiency of the results produced by the algorithm. To reduce features set, only the useful features are selected from the entire set of features.

In feature extraction, the set of features and a method is used for selecting a subset of features that can perform best under the classification system. Classification is a process of dividing the data into separate different and categories, here it gets classifies into two classes i.e.; viz. affected and non-affected. The system will perform the classification of the images into two classes affected and non-affected based on their training model. The results are represented by showing the affected portion in the form of green color and the remaining will be remain the same.

One of the most important part of implementation is training. The Support Vector Machine is trained using the training file which was created before. Once the training has been completed, an image is given in order to detect bedsore ulcer and classify it into affected area and non affected area. And the accuracy of the same is obtained, in order to check the accuracy we have used the Confusion matrix and Kappa Coefficient.

6 Result

Once we are completed with training the sample data, we tested it and the accuracy is required to be checked. To calculate the accuracy we have used Confusion Matrix and the Kappa co-efficient.

6.1 Confusion Matrix

The confusion matrix is used for measuring the effectiveness and performance of our classification model. This matrix also predicts accuracy of the classifier by comparing the actual and predicted values. Confusion matrix helped us to get a better idea of what all our classification model is getting right and to find the errors that were made as it is also known as error matrix.

The Table 1 below shows the confusion matrix of the tested data set by the support vector machine on the basis of the training samples.

Table 1. Confusion matrix

Class	Affected	Non affected	Total	User's accuracy
Affected	2026	31	2057	98.49%
Non affected	33	2028	2061	98.39%
Total	2059	2059	4118	
Producer's accuracy	98.39	98.49		98.44%

$$\text{Accuracy} = (4054/4118) * 100$$
$$= 98.44\%$$

6.2 Kappa Coefficient

Kappa Co-efficient is a measure of how closely the instances are closely classified by the classifier matched with the data named as ground truth image and classified image. The formula was entered in MS Excel and is used to derive the Kappa Coefficient. The Kappa Coefficient is in between the value of 0 to 1. If the Kappa coefficient is 0, then there is less accuracy and if the Kappa coefficient value is closer to 1, then it is more accurate (Figs. 2, 3, 4 and 5).

$$K = \frac{N \sum_{i=1}^{r} xii - \sum_{i=1}^{r}(Xi + *X + i)}{N2 - \sum_{i=1}^{r}(Xi + *X + i)}$$

$$k = 0.9689$$

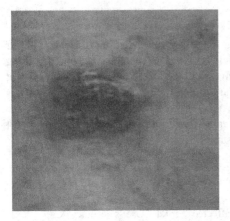

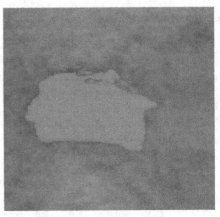

Fig. 2. Image before classification   **Fig. 3.** Image after classification

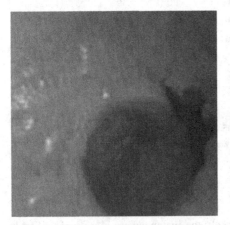

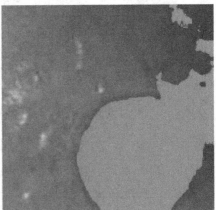

Fig. 4. Image before classification   **Fig. 5.** Image after classification

7 Conclusion

This paper is about, the detection of the bedsores ulcer under two major categories i.e. affected area and non affected area. Support Vector Machine is an elegant and powerful algorithm that can be used to detect bedsore ulcer with more accuracy. From the above Confusion Matrix and the calculated Kappa Value, it is assessed that the accuracy of classifying the image is 98.44% and the Kappa Value is 0.9689. So the results are found to have a very good accuracy. This system can help to reduce time for the detection process of the bedsore ulcer. Advancement in Ulcer detection technique has provided a good opportunities to have bedsore detection in wider portion of body with low costs and high resolution.

8 Future Enhancement

The work carried out is based on the bedsore detection so currently it is only detecting the ulcer. Only detection of the ulcer is not enough to solve the problem what the people are facing and in future with the help of SVM different types of bedsore ulcer can also be detected.

Acknowledgement. We would like to thanks Healthline.com for providing us the required datasets free online.

References

1. Farshbaf, M., Ostadabbas, S., Yousefi, R., Nourani, M., Pompeo, M.: Pressure ulcer monitoring and intervention: a software platform. In: IEEE International Conference on Bioinformatics and Biomedicine Workshops (BIBMW), Atlanta, GA (2011)
2. Sen, D., McNeill, J., Mendelson, Y., Dunn, R., Hickle, K.: A new vision for preventing pressure ulcer: wearable wireless devices could help solve common-and serious-problem. IEEE Pulse (2018)
3. Yousefi, R., et al.: Bed posture classification for pressure ulcer prevention. In: International Conference of the IEEE Engineering in Medicine and Biology Society, 1 August 2011
4. Ostadabbas, S., Yousefi, R., Faezipour, M., Nourani, M., Pompeo, M.: Pressure ulcer prevention: an efficient turning schedule for bed-bound patients. In: Proceedings of the 2011 IEEE/NIH Life Science System and Applications Workshop, LiSSA, 8 May 2011
5. Yousefi, R.: A smart bed platform for monitoring & ulcer prevention. In: International Conference on Biomedical Engineering and Informatics (BMEI), Shanghai, IEEE (2011)
6. Yip, M., Da He, D., Winokur, E., Balderrama, A.G., Sheridan, R., Ma, H.: A flexible pressure monitoring system for pressure ulcer prevention. In: EMBC, pp. 1212–1215, September 2009
7. Barsocchi, P.: Position recognition to support bedsores prevention. IEEE Trans. Inf. Technol. Biomed.: Publ. IEEE Eng. Med. Biol. Soc. (2012)
8. Díaz, C., Garcia-Zapirain, B., Castillo, C., Sierra-Sosa, D., Elmaghraby, A., Kim, P.J.: Simulation and development of a system for the analysis of pressure ulcer. In: IEEE International Symposium on Signal Processing and Information Technology (ISSPIT), Bilbao (2017)
9. Hong, Y.-S.: Smart care beds for elderly patients with impaired mobility. Wirel. Commun. Mob. Comput. **2018** (2018). Article ID 1780904
10. Nageswaran, S., Ramanathan, P.: Analysis of pressure relieving mechanisms for the prevention of decubitus ulcers. Biomed. Res. **27**(4) (2016)
11. Bennett, S.L., Goubran, R., Knoefel, F.: Long term monitoring of a pressure ulcer risk patient using thermal images. In: 39th Annual International Conference of the IEEE Engineering in Medicine and Biology Society (EMBC). IEEE, 14 September 2017
12. Vapnik, V.N.: Statistics for Engineering and Science. The Nature of Statistical Learning Theory. Springer, Heidelberg (1995)
13. Sun, X., Liu, L., Wang, H., Song, W., Lu, J.: Image classification via support vector machine. In: International Conference on Computer Science and Network Technology (ICCSNT), Harbin. IEEE (2015)

Model Performance Evaluation: Sales Prediction

Abhishek Singh$^{(\boxtimes)}$ and Satyajee Srivastava

Galgotias University, Greater Noida, India
`singh.ab2709@gmail.com, drsatyajee@gmail.com`

Abstract. These days, every organization wants to uplift its revenue as well as profit. There are various departments in an organization including the Production department, IT department, Sales & Marketing department and many more. The work is done in hierarchal order but at the end of the day, one of the main objectives of any organization is to increase sales which will lead to increase in profit. For consistent performance in market, the people sitting there at upper level need to take various decisions for the organization's well being. They need to tell the people of production and sales department about the quantity and quality of product that they need to produce within a given time window. Various factors including the location of their stores, population density, direct competitors, etc. play a vital role in prediction of sales in upcoming times. According to a broad study, organizations doing sales predictions correctly are approximately 10% more likely to enhance their revenue growth year-by-year. In this paper, we have used one such data of a very popular store. The major focus is on hypothesis formation, feature engineering and applying various Machine learning Algorithms. At last we have compared the results of all the different algorithms used on the basis of RMSE evaluation metrics and finally predicted the sales as well as the major factors that play significant role in their sales upliftment.

Keywords: Machine learning · RMSE · Hypothesis · Feature engineering · Revenue

1 Introduction

Sales Prediction is the method of making an estimate of future sales. The more accurate the prediction of sales, the more aware/informed decisions a business can take and subsequently perform better in the short-term as well as long term. Nowadays, even many companies try to base their predictions primarily on data of past sales, economic trends, and industry-wide comparisons. Comparatively it becomes easier for well-established companies to forecast future sales on the basis of many years of past data of running business [3]. But on the contrary, newly established/founded companies need to base their predictions on comparatively less-verified data such as thorough market research and their competitors' strategies and actions to predict their future sales. Sales prediction provides insight into how an organization should try to manage its workforce, resources, and cash flow. Sales prediction allows organizations to:

© Springer Nature Singapore Pte Ltd. 2020
U. Batra et al. (Eds.): REDSET 2019, CCIS 1229, pp. 24–37, 2020.
https://doi.org/10.1007/978-981-15-5827-6_3

- Predict which products will be demanded more by consumers in the near future.
- Predict sales revenue
- Efficient allocation of resources
- Future growth plans

In this paper, we will be focusing on the better approach in prediction of sales of every individual product at different Big-Mart stores in different cities. We have used various different regression techniques to predict future sales and measured their performance in terms of RMSE.

RMSE (*Root Mean Square Error*) is one of the best-considered evaluation metrics that is used to measure the performance of regression models used [2]. The only assumption which our evaluation metric makes that too we have taken care of is that errors are unbiased and follow normal distribution.

$$RMSE = \sqrt{\sum_{i=1}^{N} \frac{(Predicted_i - Actual_i)^2}{N}} \qquad (1)$$

The above shown is the mathematical formula to calculate RMSE value where:

N = *Total number of values to be predicted*
$i = i^{th}$ *value*
$Predicted_i$ = *Predicted value*
$Actual_i$ = *Actual Value*

1.1 Why RMSE as Our Evaluation Metric?

- In the formula, you can see that the differences between predicted and actual values are squared first squared and then summed up. This nature helps to produce more robust results as it prevents the cancellation of negative and positive error values.
- It avoids the prominent use of absolute error *(Predicted$_i$ - Actual$_i$)* values.
- In cases where we have more sample data, the reconstruction of error distribution with the use of RMSE becomes more reliable [2].
- As compared to MAE *(Mean Absolute Error)*, our evaluation metric i.e. RMSE gives more weight to large error values and simultaneously punishes them rigorously.

2 Data Collection

Data collection was used to be a very tedious task in previous times but since the world has focused on becoming more and more digital, the reach to data has become easier [1]. Many organizations have started maintaining records of their business in digital form and many among them even share their data on Internet as well as can provide us data on request. We have our data from Analytics Vidya site. Big-Mart Sales data is a part of Hackathon being conducted on their platform.

Our dataset was generated by data scientists at Big-Mart and contains data for 1559 different products across 10 different stores. Each product has certain pre-defined attributes that make it different from other products. Our dataset contains *8523 observations* and *12 unique features*.

2.1 Attributes

See Table 1.

Table 1. Attributes of dataset used

Name	Description
Item_Identifier	Unique Product Id
Item_Weight	Weight of Product
Item_Fat_Content	Low Fat or not
Item_Visibility	Percentage of the total display area in-store allocated to the Product
Item_Type	Category to which Product belongs
Item_MRP	Maximum Retail Price
Outlet_Identifier	Unique Store Id
Outlet_Establishment_Year	Year in which store was established
Outlet_Size	Size of Store
Outlet_Location_Type	Type of City
Outlet_Type	Type of store
Item_Outlet_Sales	Sales of product in a particular store

3 Methodologies

Once we have framed our problem and decided on our performance measure, we started making some assumptions on what could be the possible outcomes that we may expect from our analysis as per available data. This step is known as *Hypothesis Formation* [4]. On the basis of our market knowledge, we thought of possible factors that may affect our sales prediction results.

Factors on which we have formed hypothesis are (Table 2):

Table 2. Hypothesis basis

Store – Level Hypothesis	Product – Level Hypothesis
City Type	Utility
Store Capacity	Display Area
Population Density	Visibility in Store
Ambiance	Advertising
Location	Promotional Offers
Competitors	Brand
Marketing	Packaging
Customer – Level Hypothesis	Macro – Level Hypothesis
Job Profile	Environment
Family Size	Economic Growth
Customer Behavior	
Annual Income	
Purchase History	

3.1 Data Analysis

Our primary was to predict future sales and for that the important thing that needed to be done was to identify the most significant attributes using which we can build different types of regression models and then comparing the results achieved by them and finally

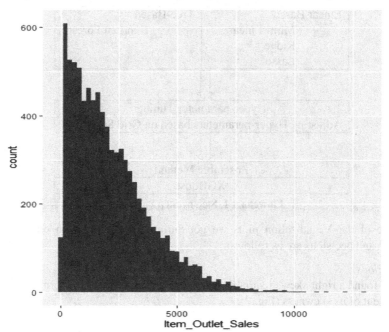

Fig. 1. Target variable

evaluate RMSE score of all of them and see which model along with Good RMSE score also fulfills our hypothesis (Fig. 1).

Hence, our analysis was divided into five critical stages:

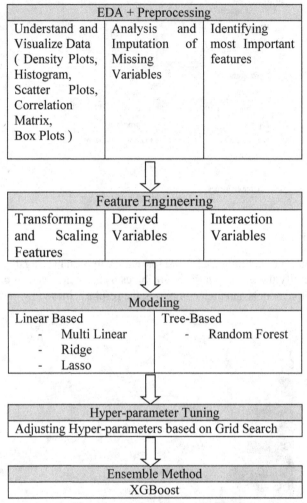

Flowchart 1. Step by Step Process

Some of the Visualization plots we got during EDA along with our analytical approach and decisions are as follows:

Observations
– It was found a right-skewed variable and needed some further transformation for the treatment of its skewness (Fig. 2).

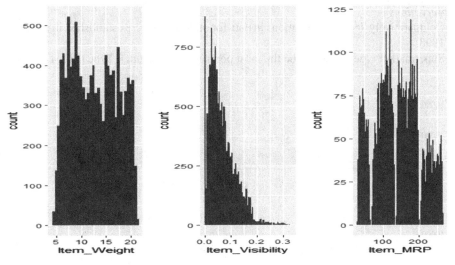

Fig. 2. Univariate analysis I

Observations
- No clear cut pattern was found in Item_Weight
- Item_Visibility was seen right-skewed and needed further transformations to remove its skewness.
- We got an interesting insight by seeing four different distributions in Item_MRP (Fig. 3).

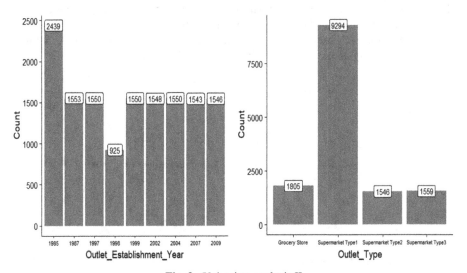

Fig. 3. Univariate analysis II

Observations
- Comparatively, lesser observations in data for outlets that were established in the year 1998.
- Supermarket type I found to be the most popular among Outlet_Type (Fig. 4).

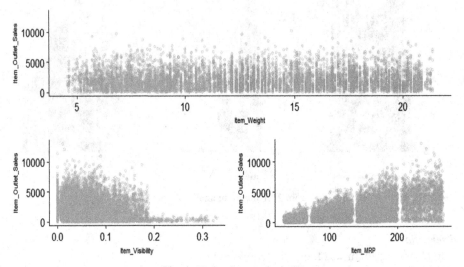

Fig. 4. Univariate analysis III

Observations
- Item_Outlet_Sales was found to be spread well without any of the definite patterns.
- In the second plot, a string at Item_Visibility = 0.0 seemed to be strange as per general knowledge that item visibility can't be completely 0.
- In the third plot, we observed 4 segmentations in the price column that we further used in feature engineering and created a new variable (Fig. 5).

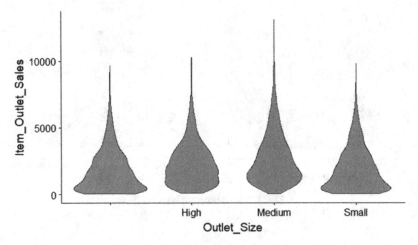

Fig. 5. Univariate analysis IV

Observations
- The distribution of blank Outlet_Size category was found to be identical to a much extent with 'Small' category.

Some points:
- There were many other plots and observations that we got during EDA which are not shown in this paper. Only the most significant ones are presented here.
- Observations that needed actions were considered and worked on by us seriously.
- Missing values treatment, Data transformations using Log Analysis, Feature Engineering, etc. all steps were done before building models for prediction purposes but not shown here as these were not the focus of our research.

3.2 Modeling

After completing all the steps, finally, we arrived the main crux of this paper i.e. building models, applying them on data and measuring their performance like how much error does these models produced in predicting sales of Big-Mart products. As discussed earlier, we have used various kinds of models like Linear-based models, Tree-based models as well as Ensemble modeling for our predictions. Here, we'll start off with very simpler models and subsequently move on to complex models i.e. RandomForest, XGBoost.

1. Linear Regression Model

Linear Regression model is one of the simplest and widely used techniques for predictive kind of modeling. In our case, as there is more than one predictor variable, we call it multi-linear regression model.

$$Y = b_1X_1 + b_2X_2 + b_3X_3 + \ldots + b_nX_n \tag{2}$$

The above equation is the equation of the multi-linear regression model where X_1, X_2, X_3,....., X_n are predictor variables [6]. Y is our target variable and b values are coefficients. The values of b show the weights associated with the corresponding predictor variable [5].

Applying this model on our data and after submission, we got results as written below:

Multiple R-Squared – 0.5636
Adjusted R-Squared – 0.5625
Leaderboard Score (RMSE) – 1202.17

These results were not very satisfying. As we mentioned this research was a part of Hackathon on Analytics Vidya which is currently ongoing. The scores shown there on the public leaderboard were based on 25% of the test data that was public. The results for remaining 75% of test data that were kept private are not shown yet. To solve this problem, and check how robust our model on unseen data is, we've used the Cross-Validation technique.

2. Ridge Regression Model

This is a kind of Regularized regression model. A Regularized regression model has the ability to handle correlated independent variables in a better way and also helps in overcoming the problem of overfitting.

Ridge regression penalizes the coefficients of correlated predictor variables. It shrinks the corresponding coefficients of much-correlated predictor variables towards each other [7]. The magnitude of coefficients of predictor variables decreases, whereas the values shrink towards zero but not to absolute zero magnitudes.

$$\min(||Y - X(\alpha)||_2^2 + \lambda||\alpha||_2^2) \tag{3}$$

The above is the equation of Ridge regression where λ helps in controlling the penalty term. Here α denotes the coefficients of predictor variables. Higher the value, bigger the penalty hence, more reduced the magnitude of coefficient.

Results
Validation Score (RMSE) – 1134.794
Leaderboard Score (RMSE) – 1206.299

3. Lasso Regression Model

It is also a regularized regression model. The difference between Ridge and Lasso is that Lasso tries to pick one of the pairs of correlated predictors while discarding the other one [8]. This is property which is commonly known as feature selection which was lacking in Ridge Regression.

$$\min(||Y - X\alpha||_2^2 + \lambda||\alpha||_1) \tag{4}$$

The above equation is the equation of Lasso Regression. Here α denotes the coefficients of predictor variables.

Results
Validation Score (RMSE) – 1129.781
Leaderboard Score (RMSE) – 1202.344

4. **RandomForest**

It is primarily a tree-based regression model (bootstrapping algorithm). In this kind of modeling, various weak learners i.e. decision trees get combined and make a more powerful and robust prediction model [9]. In our model, we have built it with 450 trees (Fig. 6).

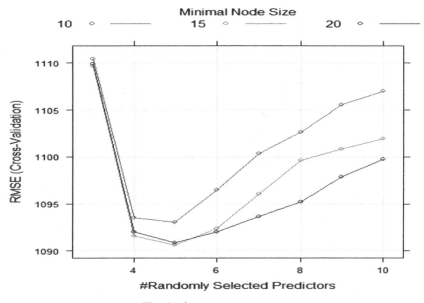

Fig. 6. Best model parameters

Other parameters which we have used in building model are like

$mtry$ = Number of predictors sampled randomly at each split
$min.node.size$ = Minimum size of terminal nodes

Results
Validation Score (RMSE) – 1095.602
Leaderboard Score (RMSE) – 1155.958

With the help of the plot above, we can see that the best score we achieved is at *mtry* = 5 and *min.node.size* = 20 (Fig. 7).

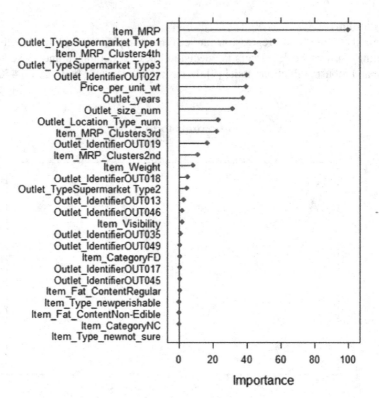

Fig. 7. Variable importance I

As per our expectations, Item_MRP comes out to be the most significant variable in predicting Sales. During featuring engineering step, we created some features like Outlet_Years, price_per_unit_wt, Item_outlet_clusters are also the topmost significant variables. This signifies that we have done feature engineering process correctly.

5. **XGBoost**

XGBoost is primarily an ensemble learning method. Many times, it might not be enough to rely completely on the results of only one model. Ensemble kind of learning as the name suggests provides a well-organized solution to combine the prediction power of more than one learner [10]. The resultant model is only a single model that produces an aggregated output from several combined models. It is fast as well as efficient approach used by many ML practitioners (Fig. 8).

Results

Validation Score (RMSE) – 1089.084
Leaderboard Score (RMSE) – 1154.636

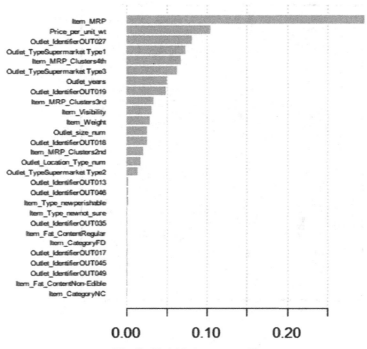

Fig. 8. Variable importance II

Again we can validate that features/variables created by us like Outlet_Years, price_per_unit_wt, Item_outlet_clusters are the topmost significant variables.

4   Result and Conclusion

After several trials and tests of 5 different prediction models on Sales Prediction including the Multi-Linear Regression model, the best score that we achieved on the leaderboard was with the results of XGBoost Ensemble Learning Model. The evaluation scores of each model have been shown above in Fig. 9. The most significant result was that XGBoost has even outperformed the results of RandomForest regression model that was considered the best regression model till now by many beginners and even professionals in industry.

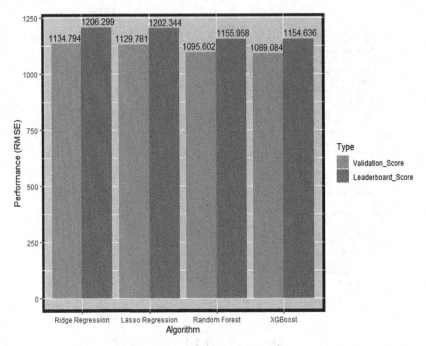

Fig. 9. Different algorithms performance

5   Future Work

There are various things that can be tried still to further improve our models' performance with the help of hyperparameter tuning. We can also look for some other features that can be created with the help of existing features. And after that different models can be used with different subset of features. We can build and train our XGBoost model using the grid search technique to further improve models performance as was done in RandomForest model. More Complex models like Neural network models, LightGBM, etc. can also be tried upon the same dataset to see the performance.

References

1. Ouarezki, S., Nassima SACI: Data Collection methods: Research methodology
2. Chai, T., Draxler, R.R.: Root mean square error (RMSE) or mean absolute error (MAE)? Arguments against avoiding RMSE in the literature
3. Trackmaven – Marketing – Salesforecasting. https://trackmaven.com/marketing-dictionary/sales-forecasting/
4. Bin Tahir, S.: Academia.eu – Hypothesis Formulation
5. Tranmer, M., Elliot, M.: Cathie Marsh Centre for Census and Survey Research – Multiple Linear Regression
6. Schneider, A., Hommel, G., Blettner, M.: Dtsc Arztebi Int - Linear Regression Analysis

7. Marquardt, D.W., Snee, R.: Researchgate - Ridge Regression in Practice
8. Tibshirani, R.: Regression shrinkage and selection via the lasso
9. Ceh, M., Lilibarda, M., Lisee, A., Bajat, B.: Estimating the Performance of Random Forest versus Multiple Regression for Predicting Prices of the Apartments
10. Tianqi, C., Guestrin, C.: XGBoost: A Scalable Tree Boosting System

Predicting Trends of Stock Market Using SVM: A Big Data Analytics Approach

Sneh Kalra[1][✉], Sachin Gupta[1], and Jay Shankar Prasad[2]

[1] Department of CSE, MVN University, Palwal 121102, Haryana, India
snehchhabra@gmail.com, Sachin.gupta@mvn.edu.in
[2] Department of CSE, Krishna Engineering College, Ghaziabad 201007, Uttar Pradesh, India
hello2jsp@gmail.com

Abstract. The huge quantity of data generated by several disparate data sources cannot be processed with traditional database tools and techniques. To analyze and extract events, patterns and useful information from such an enormous quantity of data requires high computational techniques. With embossing technologies like Hadoop and Apache Spark, it becomes feasible to treat this huge amount of data and extract valuable entities from it. In this paper, a stock prediction model is proposed using sentiments of tweets and news data. Classifier Support Vector Machine is implemented for trend prediction of 2 specific companies traded under the National Stock Exchange. A predictive model using Big data analytics has been utilized by considering millions of tweets and news data in Hadoop and Apache Spark framework. The output of the implemented model has been computed for the amalgamation of 3 types of input data. The paper compares the prediction output with existing researches implemented with SVM.

Keywords: Big data · SVM · Apache Spark · Predictive modeling · Apache Hadoop

1 Introduction

Efficient Market Hypothesis theory and Random walk theory was the basis for earlier researches for forecasting stock market trends [1, 2]. These initials methods recommended that stock prices cannot be forecasted since fluctuations in stock prices are dependent on new information instead of current or past prices. Thus, share market prediction accuracy cannot go beyond 50% which follows any random event like tossing a coin [3]. However several studies examined to forecast price movements in share market but financial time series seems to be very composite and noisy to predict There exists many techniques for stock market prediction task and most of them use numerical stock prices and derived technical indicators from them [4]. Most of the prevailing research on technical trading rules and strategies focus on the goal and unambiguous rules supported historical market data while not considering any new information.

Stock movements are often determined by an investor view of particular stock relied on new information collected from divergent data sources. Many studies proved that the public moods or sentiments found in the social media influence the movements in

U. Batra et al. (Eds.): REDSET 2019, CCIS 1229, pp. 38–48, 2020.
https://doi.org/10.1007/978-981-15-5827-6_4

financial markets [3, 6]. The analysis of sentiments fetched through social media data can be able to assess the concerted intelligence of future performance in numerous areas. In the last twenty years, with the development of storing and computational systems the most critical and commercially important data is becoming increasingly available on the internet [5]. There exist miscellaneous types of web financial information sources, such as social media, news articles, financial websites, and blogs. Companies providing financial services are also making their products accessible on the web [6].

This massive quantity of data is out there for assessment hence supervised learning techniques chosen as the key weapon for inventive jobs. Previously, several different supervised learning techniques are applied with varying level of achievement. As this huge amount of data generated by numerous sources is unstructured so along with analysis, this data needs special handling for its storage and processing [7]. For the purpose, researchers move towards big data approach for the stock prediction task. Though, stock forecasting remains strictly limited due to its volatile and unpredictable nature. Big data analysis defines the process to compile and analyse the big quantity of data for decision support system whereas Big data analytics also includes the tools and techniques used to do so.

Big data analytics helps the organization to understand the hidden information that is significant to take strategic decisions [8]. It is performed with specialized tools for text mining, predictive analysis, data optimization, and data mining. Big data analysis is not an easy task. Because the data can be present either in structured or unstructured form collected from different sources using different techniques and it becomes more challenging to work with such data collectively [9]. Leaving these challenges aside, big data analytics can be beneficial to the organization in the following ways:

1. Faster and Better Decision Making
With the availability of big data analytics tools like Hadoop, the process of decision making has become fast. The decisions made are much better than the traditional methods [10]. Analyzing the information has become easier and decisions can be made on what we have learned with more accuracy.

2. Cost Reduction
The usage of Hadoop and cloud computing technologies brings significant cost reduction to save such a massive quantity of data. They also provide a better way of analyzing big data.

3. New Products and Services
With the huge growth of data in data day by day, the analysis also becomes more challenging. These tools with their updated version help to cater to the need of organizations to make the decision-making process more effective.

2   Big Data Analytics with Machine Learning

For data analytics, machine learning helped to manage the big data in a better way. It is employed to train machines by providing them datasets and building algorithms that facilitate machines for decision making and problem-solving [7]. Machine Learning algorithms improve over time as they have the capability to learn from experience. It is the technique that helped to formulate many scrambled processes that formerly required a lot of time and supervision for routine operations [11].

It is an area of research that emphasizes the theory properties, concept, presentation, performance of learning algorithms. Machine learning strategies are generally recognized in several big as well as complex data-intensive areas. These methods afford imaginable remedies to pit the facts hidden within in the data [7]. Machine Learning could also be considered as a scientific tool of data science that generates patterns from data by converting data into knowledge. Many potent machine algorithms are evolved to get insights, make predictions and create a prototype from previous events.

Machine Learning techniques are principally classified into supervised and unsupervised learning types [12]. Supervised learning techniques target correct predictions whereas unsupervised learning has a target to achieve concise descriptions of the Data Clustering, Pattern Mining, Data Classification, Intelligent Decisions, and Predictions are some of its major types [13].

It is necessary to note that experimenting with machine learning algorithms for Big Data solutions is a kind of infinite loop [7]. The algorithms created for specific applications are examined and redesigned over time as the information is entering into the system and going out of the system [11].

2.1 Big Data Role in the Stock Market

Big data has widely opted-in financial industries that help online traders to make good investment decisions. In stock market data, rapid changes keep on occurring. So, big data with mathematical calculations and algorithms has helped investors to gain maximum returns on their investment.

Over the last few years, the computer has been used at a large scale to get more accurate calculations. This inputted data influence online trading decisions. Investor Hangout is a perfect example where a large amount of data is being inputted by investors that act as the main source. Big data with artificial intelligence has the potential to revolutionize stock marketing and surely make data new money. The use of machine learning to compute big data has been increased to speculate the certain stocks that the human mind can't handle. Below points show how big data has influenced online stock marketing:

1. Improving Stock Marketing by Leveling the Playing Field
Algorithmic trading is a buzzword in the stock market. Machine learning has made it easier to make strategic decisions that our normal human mind can't process. Using big data and machine learning together can improve the investment power of stock market industries as well as individuals.

2. Estimating Outcome and Rate of Return on Investment
Financial trading and the stock market are not only about price prediction and behavior anymore. Machine learning over big data helps in predicting the outcomes with more accuracy that helps in calculating the return rate on investment. This helps the individuals not only in putting their price in market meticulously but also mitigates the risks.

3. Delivering Accuracy in Perceptions

As machine learning helps the computer learn and learn to make good strategic decisions based on new and updated information. This can be more effective if the amount of data is large. Big data with machine learning can give more accurate perceptions. This will not only help investors to invest money more wisely but also help in gaining their trust to make decisions more effectively.

Overall, big data can be a great tool to improve investment performance in stock marketing. The more the information we have, the better we will be able to beat the market and execute the trade in a better way. That eventually increases the profit for stock market industries.

3   Proposed Model for Stock Market Prediction

The predictive analysis forecasts future behavior using machine learning techniques based on historical data. The overall process of forecasting direction of trends of the stock market consists of various steps including data collection, text pre-processing, sentiment analysis and predicting the trends with SVM. To carry out the above steps, the Apache Hadoop and Spark framework have been utilized. Figure 1 shows the proposed model for the stock market.

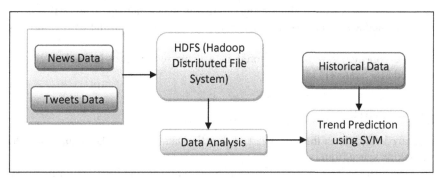

Fig. 1. Proposed model for stock trend prediction

3.1   Data Collection

Data has been collected from Twitter, financial news websites and yahoo finance for the period of July 2018 to December 2018.

3.1.1   Tweets Collection

Among the entire existing social network sites, Twitter is the most significant platforms to share and be in touch with people all around the world. Data from Twitter is quickly obtainable to everyone but only last 7 days of tweets can be easily retrieved. To retrieve the tweets, Rapidminer Process [18] was used and tweets of two companies traded under NSE has been collected and stored.

3.1.2 News Collection

News is accessible to the people when it is publicly shared. In the financial domain, the news about the financial institutions, stocks and government policies about the stock market sectors are reported. The information about the events happening in the companies is also immediately reported through news [6].

To retrieve the company-related news, source of data includes various financial websites named livemint.com, financialexpress.com, ndtv.com, moneycontrol.com, businessstandard.com, economic times, toi.com with different sections like the economy, research, top news, company news, etc. using XML API in MS-Excel. All these websites have a big pool of crucial news catering to the individual stocks.

3.1.3 Historical Data Collection

To train and evaluate the system, historical prices are needed. Historical data for 2 companies from 2 different sectors named Banking and IT sector has collected from yahoo finance [14]. The data extracted is in a CSV format.

3.2 Data Storage

Hadoop is an open-source framework for distributed processing of large data sets across clusters of computers using simple programming models. Hadoop contains two layers named Map-Reduce for data processing and Hadoop Distributed File System for data storage.

All the collected raw data is stored in a dispersed manner in HDFS (Hadoop Distributed File System) [15].

3.3 Data Analysis

Data Analysis is right in the very heart of the Big Data solutions. Data analysis is the act of making sense from raw data.

Apache Spark is one of the most popular analytics engine installed on the top of Hadoop and provides smooth capability with Hadoop [16]. Spark framework was introduced for parallel distributed Systems and is used for data processing and analysis task. The significant feature of Spark is its in-memory cluster computing which is the key

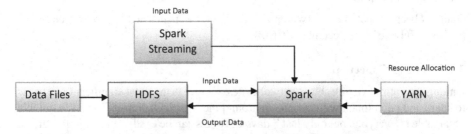

Fig. 2. Hadoop and spark integration

factor for increasing the processing speed. Spark is a potent substitute for the Hadoop MapReduce functions with Yarn for resource scheduling. Spark Streaming is an extension of the core Spark API that allows fault-tolerant, scalable and high-throughput stream processing of live data streams [17]. Figure 2 shows integration of Hadoop and Spark.

The following two steps are adopted for analyzing the raw data:

3.3.1 Data Preprocessing

Fetched tweets contain data that is noisy and irreverent to the stock market. To get the stock relevant tweets for tow specific companies, first of all tweets are filtered using specific company name and a number of stock related terms like dive, rise, plunge, earning, quarter, bear, miss etc. followed by removal of hashtags, removal of URLs, removal of re-tweets, removal of other symbols and conversion to lowercase letters. For news data, pre-processing steps include filtration of specific company news followed by tokenization and stop word removal.

3.3.2 Sentiment Analysis

Sentiment Analysis is an inventive way to extract attitude direction (neutral, negative, positive) from a text segment described for any person, product, organization, or any other object or entity [18]. To find the polarity of a tweet and news data collected from pre-processing step, a lexicon-based approach has been adopted and implemented in Scala language to categorize the news and tweets into 1 and 0 categories [19]. The total number of tweets and news having 1 and 0 polarities are calculated for each day (Fig. 3).

```
1. Load a dictionary of positive and negative keywords.

2. Fetch the pre-processed data from hdfs.

3. Count positive and negative classes for tweets and news.

val neg_count= negWordFiltered.count

val pos_count= posWordFiltered.count

val df_tweets =  Seq((pos_count,neg_count,z)).toDF
("positive_tweets","negative_tweets","date_created")
df_tweets.rdd.map(_.toString().replace("[","").replace("]",
"")).saveAsTextFile("/rs/hive/hdfc_tweets/date_created="+z+h)
h=h+1
```

Fig. 3. Sample of sentiment analysis process for the pre-processed tweets data.

3.4 Trend Prediction Using Support Vector Machine

Support Vector Machine is a widely adopted unsupervised learning technique for classification and regression problems. But, it is mainly used in the classification task. SVM is a capable model for classifying linear as well as nonlinear data. The main objective of the SVM algorithm is to discover a hyperplane in N-dimensional space (N represents the number of characteristics) that categorize the data points differently [11, 13].

In SVM, nonlinear mapping is used to convert the linear dataset into a dataset having higher dimensionality. In the higher dimension, it looks for the linear best separating hyperplane. A hyperplane defines the decision boundary to split two classes. Support vectors are the necessary training tuples from the set of the training dataset. With a sufficiently high dimension and appropriate nonlinear mapping, two classes can be separated with the help of margins defined by the support vectors. Training of SVM is slow, but it generates very accurate results due to its modelling capacity for nonlinear decision boundaries.

The prediction for a new input can be made using the scalar product between the input (x) and every support vector (xi) as shown below [7]:

$$f(x) = B_0 + sum(ai * (x, xi)) \tag{1}$$

The above equation calculates the scalar products of a new input vector (x) with all existing support vectors in the training dataset. The values of coefficients B_0 and ai for each input dataset must be determined from the training dataset using the learning algorithm.

Figure 4 shows SVM algorithm for trend prediction.

Step 1: Import all the required dependencies.

Step 2: Read the CSV files from HDFS with infer schema and then persist it in memory.

Step 3: Split the dataset into a training set and testing set.

Step 4: Create an array of attributes (features).

Step 5: Create a vector assembler for setting input and output columns.

Step 6: Create an array of vector assembler.

Step 7: Create the SVM classifier with a linear kernel for the training dataset.

Step 8: Predict the result of the tested data set.

Fig. 4. SVM algorithm

For making the predictions, data was divided into training and testing set of size 80% and 20%. The classifier has been implemented using Apache Spark-Scala framework and implemented model has predicted the future stock trend as 1 or 0.

4 Experiment and Results

For the experimentation, a total of 3.10 millions of tweets and news data of ICICI Bank and TCS Company have been used [19]. SVM classifier has been implemented and executed against a combination of 4 types of input data: historical price, news sentiments with historical data, tweet sentiments with historical data and finally news and tweet sentiments with historical data. Table 1, Fig. 5 shows the prediction accuracy results for TCS and ICICI bank and its graphical representation.

Table 1. Prediction accuracy for TCS and ICICI bank

Types of input	Prediction accuracy (%)	
	TCS	ICICI bank
Historical Data (HD)	71.21	72.84
News Sentiment with HD	74.43	75.86
Tweets Sentiment with HD	76.78	77.63
News and Tweets sentiment with HD	80.32	83.54

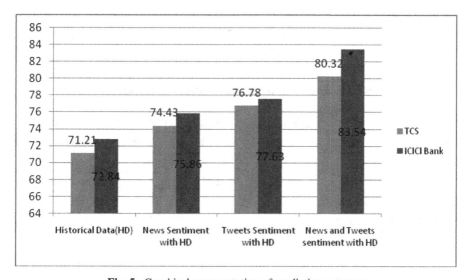

Fig. 5. Graphical representation of prediction accuracy

The minimum prediction accuracy (%) achieved for TCS is 71.21 with historical data and maximum accuracy achieved is 80.32 and the minimum prediction accuracy (%) achieved for ICICI bank is 72.84 with historical data and maximum accuracy achieved is 83.54.

As we can observed in the results, by using only single type of input SVM has achieved less accuracy in comparison to more types of input. When News sentiments are integrated with historical data, accuracy has improved and similarly when tweets sentiments are combined with historical data, it also has generated accuracy more than historic data. Finally at the last step, by integrating news and tweets sentiments with historic data it has improved the accuracy up to a great extent.

4.1 Confusion Matrix

Confusion Matrix summarizes the prediction results for a classification problem. The number of true and false predictions are outlined with count values and countermined by every class. Table 2 and Table 3 shows confusion matrix for ICICI bank and TCS with different types of input data.

Table 2. Confusion matrix for ICICI bank with different input data

Input data	Accuracy (%)	Precision (%)	Recall (%)	F1-measure (%)
Historical data	72.84	81.44	73.23	77.12
News sentiments + HD	75.86	83.14	77.22	80.02
Tweets sentiments + HD	77.63	90.32	74.68	81.76
News sentiments + Tweets sentiments + HD	83.54	94.92	70.89	70.41

Table 3. Confusion matrix for TCS with different input data

Input data	Accuracy (%)	Precision (%)	Recall (%)	F1-measure (%)
Historical data	71.21	83.78	69.65	76.06
News sentiments + HD	74.43	77.23	70.29	73.60
Tweets sentiments + HD	76.78	72.42	70.87	71.64
News sentiments + Tweets sentiments + HD	80.32	81.36	78.69	80.00

Table 4 shows the comparison of implemented work in this paper with the recent studies that utilized SVM classifier for the prediction task.

As it can be observed from Table 4, our implemented model performed best in all the cases except study [24] that has trained the model with 12 years of historical data. This clarifies that the amount of input data provided to classifier has the capacity to increase its prediction results. But, with the qualitative data, we can also improve the performance in the big data environment as we have done.

Table 4. Comparison of prediction results with recent studies

Study and year	Input data	Data set size	Prediction accuracy (%)
[21], 2018	Tweets, News, HD	2 years	62.1
[22], 2018	Tweets, HD	3 years	76.65
[23], 2019	Historical Data (HD)	10 years	78.7
Our Work	**Tweets, News, HD**	**6 months**	**71.21–83.54**
[4], 2018	HD + Technical Indicators	3 years	71.12
[24], 2018	HD + Technical Indicators	12 years	89.52
[25], 2018	HD + News	5 years	56.50
[6], 2019	News	1 year	51.66

5 Conclusion

The input data provided to any prediction model plays a very crucial role. This paper has implemented a stock model that examines the effect of different types of input data with numeric historical data on stock prices. The future trend accuracy is improved by considering tweets and news sentiments and implementing the proposed model with a big data analytics approach. The result of the proposed model is well-matched with previous researches that state that there exists a correlation among public mood or user sentiments with stock prices fluctuations. Future work will focus on considering tweets and news data for more number of months or years for providing this data as input to prediction model which in turn will improve the accuracy. In-addition real-time stock data analysis can be used on Apache Spark.

References

1. Malkiel, B.G.: The efficient market hypothesis and its critics. J. Econ. Perspect. **1**(17), 59–82 (2003)
2. Cox, D.R., Miller, H.D.: The Theory of Stochastic Processes, pp. 1–398. Taylor & Francis Limited, Milton (2017)
3. Bollen, J., Mao, H., Zeng, X.: Twitter mood predicts the stock market. J. Comput. Sci. **2**(1), 1–8 (2011)
4. Himanshu, H., Sopan, A.: Comparative analysis of stock market prediction system using SVM and ANN. Int. J. Comput. Appl. **182**(1), 59–64 (2018)
5. Jagadish, H.V., et al.: Big data and its technical challenges. Commun. ACM **57**(7), 86–94 (2014)
6. Yadav, R., Kumar, A.V., Kumar, A.: News-based supervised sentiment analysis for prediction of futures buying behaviour. IIMB Manag. Rev. **31**(2), 157–166 (2019)
7. Divya, K.S., Bhargavi, P., Singaraju, J.: Machine learning algorithms for big data analytics. Int. J. Comput. Sci. Eng. **6**(1), 63–70 (2018)

8. Silva, B.N., Diyan, M., Han, K.: Big data analytics. In: Silva, B.N., Diyan, M., Han, K. (eds.) Deep Learning: Convergence to Big Data Analytics. SCS, pp. 13–30. Springer, Singapore (2019). https://doi.org/10.1007/978-981-13-3459-7_2

9. Che, D., Safran, M., Peng, Z.: From big data to big data mining: challenges, issues, and opportunities. In: Hong, B., Meng, X., Chen, L., Winiwarter, W., Song, W. (eds.) DASFAA 2013. LNCS, vol. 7827, pp. 1–15. Springer, Heidelberg (2013). https://doi.org/10.1007/978-3-642-40270-8_1

10. Chiang, W.C., Enke, D., Wu, T., Wang, R.: An adaptive stock index trading decision support system. Expert Syst. Appl. **59**, 195–207 (2016)

11. Machine Learning. https://theappsolutions.com/blog/development/machine-learning-and-big-data/. Accessed 18 July 2019

12. Qiu, J., Wu, Q., Ding, G., Xu, Y., Feng, S.: A survey of machine learning for big data processing. EURASIP J. Adv. Signal Process. **2016**, 67 (2016). https://doi.org/10.1186/s13634-016-0355-x

13. Larose, D.T.: Data mining methods and models. In: Proceedings Larose, Data MM, pp. 1–341 (2006)

14. Yahoo finance. https://in.finance.yahoo.com/. Accessed 12 July 2019

15. Yang, T., Hiong Ngu, A.H.: Implementation of decision tree using Hadoop MapReduce. Int. J. Biomed. Data Mining **6**(01), 1–4 (2017)

16. Hadoop. https://www.edureka.co/blog/hadoop-tutorial/. Accessed 18 Aug 2019

17. Spark. https://techvidvan.com/tutorials/hadoop-spark-integration/. Accessed 16 Aug 2019

18. Kalra, S., Gupta, S., Prasad, J.S.: Performance evaluation of machine learning classifiers for stock market prediction in big data environment. J. Mechan. Continua Math. Sci. **14**(5), 295–306 (2019)

19. Kalra, S., Gupta, S., Prasad, J.S.: Sentiments based forecasting for stock exchange using linear regression (unpublished)

20. Sawant, P.A.G., Dhawane, A., Ghate, G., Lohana, P., Kishan, U.: Integrating stock twits and news feed with stock data for better stock market prediction, pp. 142–144 (2019)

21. Zhang, X., Qu, S., Huang, J., Fang, B., Yu, P.: Stock market prediction via multi-source multiple instance learning. IEEE Access **6**, 50720–50728 (2018)

22. Batra, R., Daudpota, S.M.: Integrating StockTwits with sentiment analysis for better prediction of stock price movement. In: Proceedings of the International Conference on Computing, Mathematics and Engineering Technologies: Invent, Innovate and Integrate for Socioeconomic Development, iCoMET 2018, pp. 1–5 (2018)

23. Sadia, K.H., Sharma, A., Paul, A., Padhi, S., Sanyal, S.: Stock market prediction using machine learning algorithms. Int. J. Eng. Adv. Technol. **8**(4), 25–31 (2019)

24. Emami, S.S.: Predicting trend of stock prices by developing data mining techniques with the aim of gaining profit. J. Account. Mark. **7**(4) (2018)

25. Wang, C., Xu, Y., Wang, Q.: Approaches to sentiment analysis for stock prediction, Novel, pp. 1–6 (2018)

Hybrid Entropy Method for Large Data Set Reduction Using MLP-ANN and SVM Classifiers

Rashmi[1(✉)] and Udayan Ghose[2]

[1] ASET, Guru Gobind Singh Indraprastha University, New Delhi, India
rashmibehal@gmail.com
[2] USICT, Guru Gobind Singh Indraprastha University, New Delhi, India
udayan@ipu.ac.in

Abstract. Data reduction has an extreme role in machine learning and pattern recognition with high-dimensional data. It can be achieved with attribute reduction and/or instance selection. The selection of relevant instances and/or attributes from the large amount of data not only affects data reduction (size) but also maintains classification accuracy. Different algorithms have been proposed by many researchers based on instance based learning for attribute reduction to improve classification accuracy. In this paper, based on entropy and fuzzy entropy attribute reduction method is introduced and further tested with different kinds of classifiers. Proposed method helps in reducing storage size and improving classification accuracy. A large number of standard data sets with multiple classes are used to investigate the performance of the proposed method. The performance of this novel approach in terms of reduced data size and mean classification accuracy is measured and compared with existing instance based learning and attribute reduction methods. The experimental result reveals that the performance of the proposed method is positively better than current methods.

Keywords: Data reduction · Attribute selection · Instance selection · Fuzzy entropy · MLP ANN · SVM multiclass data

1 Introduction

In digital era data volume in increasing over many years So there is need to undertake analysis on growing volumes of structured and unstructured data. Data analysis areas like medicine, biology and technology frequently occur in fitting of large data sets to a certain model and in predictive learning.

Attribute reduction can be achieved by two different processes: either by retrieving a low order feature, retaining the properties of original higher dimensional data set or by the meaningful features of original data set. In this work, main focus is on extracting the meaningful features of original data set.

Zhang [30] describes feature selection schemes in to groups named as filters, wrappers and combined scheme. In attribute reduction these schemes find

(c) Springer Nature Singapore Pte Ltd. 2020
U. Batra et al. (Eds.): REDSET 2019, CCIS 1229, pp. 49–63, 2020.
https://doi.org/10.1007/978-981-15-5827-6_5

the selected features. Both schemes varies in subspace generation and subspace selection. In filter scheme, only features selection process happens as it can not generates the subspace and produces relevant attributes. In most of the domains filter scheme is preferred as it is not bounded to any particular learning algorithm. So, a filter scheme is better than wrapper scheme because it has independent subset evaluation criteria. Due to scalability filter scheme is more useful [8]. Supervised approach includes different number of feature selection methods such as explained in [3,18,27,31] which select a subset from the given attribute set.

An attribute reduction algorithm based on conditional entropy of approximation set (ACIEAS) is proposed by [31]. It is based on formulation of the mutual information for relative reduction of knowledge to measure the goodness of feature subset by [9,13]. This algorithm is based on the conditional entropy.

An forward tentative selection with backward propagation of selection decision algorithm (FTSBPSD) given by [3] based on feature selection scheme using RST reducts as the selected features is introduced. The significance of an attribute is measured as the frequency of occurrence in the discernible function. This discernible function is constructed based on the type of reduct definition in RST. The supervised feature selection based on RST with discretization method IOTSU is proposed by [18] which deals with k-mer frequency, where k is chosen as four. RST with discretization method becomes more efficient. This improved OTSU method gives better results with [11] which is based on information entropy. An global discretization approach based on hypercube clustering is introduced [5,30] presented a greedy or nearest neighbor clustering algorithm for discretization. Son [27] has proposed a supervised data reduction technique. Where, each partition is divided continuously based on Shannon entropy. This method accelerates partitioning as compared to existing method [17] and can select relevant attributes. While doing attribute reduction using supervised and unsupervised algorithms significant amount of attribute reduction is observed and other parameters like lesser execution time, training time, number of measurements, model size, and system become more transparent but classification accuracy is not always good. Small input size are more transparent and more comprehensible and faster with no risk of over fitting. Selecting the relevant features or removing the redundant attributes reduces noise and spurious correlations with the output, and removes co linearity problem in inputs. Multi-criteria decision making (MCDM) provides good decision in all domains where the best selection is very complex. In engineering MCDM is combined with fuzzy [20]. Fuzzy entropy weights are considered in computation of fuzzy entropy [15]. Shannon entropy weights are also chosen [16]. Based on different entropy MCDM [32] deal with multi attribute decision making problem even with limited knowledge and ability. In this work hybrid entropy based approach is proposed for attribute reduction. A comparative analysis of this method with four existing feature selection methods ACIEAS method, IOTSU discretization method, FTSBPSD method and on Shannon Entropy [3,18,27,31] proves its effectiveness. Reducts are computed and performance of classification is evaluated on reduced dataset using MLP-ANN and SVM classifiers, validity of the proposed method is also examined with recently developed methods by [3,18,27,31]. In this paper, based on entropy and fuzzy entropy attribute reduction method is introduced and further tested with different kinds of classifiers. Proposed method helps in reducing storage capacity and improved classification accuracy. A large number of standard data sets with multiple classes are used to investigate the performance of the proposed method. The performance of this novel approach in terms of reduced data size and mean classification accuracy is measured and compared with existing instance based learning and attribute reduction methods. The experimental result reveals that the mean classification accuracy rate of the proposed method is significantly better than existing methods.

The rest of the paper is organized as follows: entropy measures, classifiers description multilayer perceptron artificial neural network, and support vector machine classifier are introduced in Sect. 2. The proposed method for attribute reduction is explained in Sect. 3. The experimental, comparison results with discussions are described in Sect. 4. Finally, the Conclusion of the work is presented in this article is drawn in Sect. 5.

2   Related Work

In this section, the entropy is formally defined and some traditional approaches are described. Finally, Hybrid entropy with its foundation are outlined.

2.1   Entropy Measure

Entropy extents the scope of volatality in a data set or how much relevant data is present. Dataset volatality can be extent with different entropy methods. In the existing literature [7,19,25,27] it is found that fuzzy entropy [1] gives better result in terms of data reduction as compared to Shannon entropy [26]. Shannon entropy measures information of each attribute by the formula given as:

$$SE\left(x\right) = -\sum_{m=1}^{n} P_m log P_m \qquad (1)$$

R denotes probability. In Fuzzy entropy, membership function scales the belonging of each attribute while in Shannon's, each attribute either belongs or does not belong to the attribute [22]. The classical set theory's characteristic function in generalized form produces membership function. This generalized function also ranges between [0, 1]. Universal set U comprises of all fuzzy sets F, their cardinality is shown by $\mid F \mid$ in Eq. 2

$$\mid F \mid = \sum_{att \in U} \mu_F\left(att\right) \qquad (2)$$

where $\mu_F\left(U\right)$ denotes the membership value of each element of F. Fuzzy entropy is computed with intersection and union operation. The formulas defined by the two fuzzy sets F and Q are:

$$F \cup Q = max\{\mu_F\,(att)\,,\mu_Q\,(att)\} \tag{3}$$

$$F \cap Q = min\{\mu_F\,(att)\,,\mu_Q\,(att)\} \tag{4}$$

The scope of volatility of a fuzzy set X is defined by the fuzzy entropy as:

$$FE\,(X) = \frac{F \cap Q}{F \cup Q} \tag{5}$$

HE is sum of fuzzy and Shannon entropy which considers the local and global deviation. Where F is the fuzzy set and Q is its complement. Hybrid Entropy (HE) measures degree of randomness in data set with the combined entropy (Shannon and Fuzzy). HE measure is a suitable measure of complete and incomplete information. As the fuzzy sets grasp the partial membership and the entropy considers randomness, the proposed method considers both of these into account.

2.2   Classification Description

MultiLayer Perceptron-Artificial Neural Network (MLP-ANN). It is complete interconnections of all neurons that collectively performs a particular task [10]. The network that learn adaptively; upgrading their weights during training is known as MultiLayer Perceptron (MLP). The layers are connected with weights. In the learning process, a network finds better underlying regularities in the problem domain. It requires proper hardware to process huge data as given by [10]. Here the learning rate η and momentum α of the back-propagation algorithm are constant throughout training. Levenberg-Marquardt algorithm is used to train the data. The MLP-ANN network also has various hidden neurons layers. Here, hidden neurons are taken as 12 which makes the network active for tested problems. According to [21] in visualization of larger data sets, back propagation learning rule has been developed to allow feed forward ANN. This helps in reducing data dimensions using a small number of iterations. The optimized value of control parameters and interval of initial weights produces good results. To extract information, data visualization is must. Sammon's multi layer feed forward neural network analyzed data set without the loss of accuracy [12,24]. It is for clustering data which makes proper subset. Different clustering and classification methods gives different results.

Support Vector Machine. Support Vector Machine (SVM) are becoming more popular as classification tool than ANN. They perform well in practical situations. SVM handles unbalanced data with normal and abnormal cases [23]. They solves problems in a linear way, it does not involve any computations in high dimensional space. Kernels help to perform computaion in input space, so non-linear problems are being converted into linear ones [29]. For multi class problems pattern recognition is performed by determining the separating hyper plane with maximum distance to the closest points of the training set [4,28].

These points are called as support vectors. The SVM classifier make a separating hyper-surface in the input space [29] which maps the input space into a higher dimensional feature space through some nonlinear mapping chosen a priori (kernel); and also make the Maximal Margin Hyperplane (mmh) in this features space; mmh maximizes the distance of the closest vectors belonging to the different classes of the hyperplane. Number of kernels are available to solve linear and non linear problem.classifiers found accurate and collective fault detection with the novel feature selection using non-linear SVM formulation by global optimization theory.

3   Proposed Method

In this section, an efficient attribute reduction method is proposed on the basis of Shannon entropy and Fuzzy entropy for large data sets. It is a supervised learning method. The minimum entropy value of the attribute, makes the certainty of the information in the data set. The method is used to select the efficient attribute in each partition of the data set.

3.1   Attribute Selection Heuristics

The attributes are selected for constructing reducts. The combined entropy values for all attributes in each partition makes them discernible in the data set. Each discernible attribute is fused with existing attribute list to obtain new attribute list. For the attribute selection data pre processing is to be done. The whole process requires qualitative data rather quantitative data because the continuous attribute values takes more computational time and are less efficient. The problem of continuous attributes during entropy calculation is being resolved using pre processing explained in Algorithm 1a. This is achieved using histogram based method to convert data into a specified domain range. The maximal mutual dependence is retrieved with this method. In Algorithm 1b algorithm, attributes hybrid entropy is measured. These attributes evaluates the randomness of information in the data and mean classification accuracy. The fuzzy value is defined if there is zero variance in the data. Algorithm 1c emphasizes on instance retrieval to select non-redundant and relevant instances. The algorithm is simple and considers only distance parameter to control the data as the mechanism of neighborhood algorithm. The reduced data size also saves time and cost. In spite of instance selection from whole data it is employed on partitions retrieved from the data.

Hybrid entropy measures information of each attribute by the formula given as:

$$HE(A) = FE(A) + SE(A) \qquad (6)$$

where HE(A) is hybrid entropy of A computed using Eq. 6 which uses Eq. 1 and Eq. 5 According to decision D for the Table 1 Fuzzy entropy and Shannon entropy values is given in Table 2 Which yields the attribute set as {c}, {c, e}, {c, e, a}, {c, e, a, d}, {c, e, a, d, b} are taken in ascending order as c→e→a→d→b.

Data: An Data Set(DS)
Result: A Discretized DataSet(DDS)
Define domain range;
Normalize the data set using standard deviation σ_{DS} with step 1;
Compute frequency in each domain;
Output DDS;

(a) Pre Processing Algorithm

Data: A Discretized DataSet(DDS)
Result: A relevant attribute Dataset(PDT)
Construct Preprocessed data based on Algorithm 2a;
Create an empty set **Attr_ index** as ϕ;
Create an empty partition dataset **Partition_ Out** as ϕ;
Select the a_{attr_index} with minimum entropy value $HE(a)$;
for *each attribute* $a \in c$ *compute HE;*
  do
  | **if** *(HE(a_1)=HE(a_2)=\cdots= HE(a_n))* **then**
  | | **Return** a_{attr_index}, *partition_out.*;
  | **else**
  | | **Partition** the dataset according to minimum HE(a);
  | **end**
  | **Reduce** the dimensionality of data by using only the selected a_{attr_index}
  | cardinality ($a_{attr_index} <c$) attributes;
  | **Return** a_{attr_index}, *Reduced_dataset*;
end

(b) Attribute Reduction Algorithm

Data: A Partitioned Dataset(PDT)
Result: A Reduced Dataset(RDT)
Initialize the RDT as ϕ;
for *each instance i=1 to n* **do**
  | $par_i \epsilon$ PDT ;
  | compute the *euclidian distance(ED_i)*;
  | Select the instance ins_i satisfies min(ED(ins_i)) condition ;
  | Append RDT for each partition (par_i);
  | RDT$\leftarrow$ RDT $\cup$ ins_i;
  | Separate the instances into partition corresponding to selected attributes;
end
Return RDT as the union of all selected cases in PDT;

(c) Data Reduction Algorithm

Fig. 1. Hybrid entropy based data reduction algorithm

Table 1. Example dataset

SrNo	Conditional attributes					Decision attribute
	a	b	c	d	e	D
1	1	2	1	3	3	4
2	1	2	1	3	3	4
3	1	2	1	3	3	6
4	1	2	1	3	3	6
5	1	2	1	3	3	5
6	1	2	1	3	3	4
7	1	2	1	3	3	4
8	2	2	3	3	1	5
9	2	3	3	2	1	6
10	2	3	3	2	1	6
11	2	3	3	2	1	4
12	2	3	3	2	1	4
13	2	3	3	2	1	4
14	2	3	3	2	1	6
15	2	3	3	2	1	6
16	2	3	3	2	1	4

The attribute c defines the certainty of the system so, it is most likely to be selected first. On this basis, data is partitioned again in the two data sets as shown in partition data set Table 3. The entropy is computed for all the partitions until the information gain value is consistent. Select the attribute with minimum entropy value and update the attribute list. The example data selects c attribute which further divides it into two partition as per the unique values in this attribute. First partition is again divided on the basis on the number of classes exist; as the same data belongs to different classes. From the second partition attribute b is selected and it again creates two partitions of this particular partition. Again HE is computed for all attributes in that particular partition and attribute a is selected. Consequently, attributes are selected until the attribute has unique value, partition data is processed on the basis of classes in that partition.

Table 2. Entropy computation

Entropy method	Conditional attributes				
	a	b	c	d	e
FE	1.8151	2.0663	1.6597	2.0063	1.6597
SE	1.3863	1.2500	1.3863	1.2500	1.3863
HE	3.2014	3.3163	3.0460	3.3163	3.0460

Table 3. Partitioned dataset

SrNo	Conditional attributes					Decision attribute
	a	b	c	d	e	D
1	1	2	1	3	3	4
2	1	2	1	3	3	4
3	1	2	1	3	3	6
4	1	2	1	3	3	6
5	1	2	1	3	3	5
6	1	2	1	3	3	4
7	1	2	1	3	3	4
8	2	2	3	3	1	5
9	2	3	3	2	1	6
10	2	3	3	2	1	6
11	2	3	3	2	1	4
12	2	3	3	2	1	4
13	2	3	3	2	1	4
14	2	3	3	2	1	6
15	2	3	3	2	1	6
16	2	3	3	2	1	4

In this example attributes c, b, and a are selected from the respective partitions. Based on ED 1, 5, 3, 8, 11, 9 instances are selected from the processed data set. The original data $^{16 \times 5}$ converted into reduce data $^{6 \times 3}$. Table 4 shows the six partitions, one row is selected from each partition and final output is shown in Table 5.

3.2 Instance Selection

Initially, partition is the collection of data in each class. ED removes the redundant instances of each partition. In example, the sample data set has 16 instances 6, 2, 8 of three different classes as shown in Table 1. Partition par is a set of instances, par = $\{x_1, x_2, .., x_n\}$ where n is the number of instances. Each instance consists of m attributes, $\{A_1, A_2, ..A_m\}$. Let a $\in \{A_1, A_2, ..A_m\}$. Partition $par_{j..k}$ is a non empty set of instances of the same class such that Each instance is tested to determine whether it is included in the partition or selected as the core of new partition. The first core instances are identified with the minimum ED of each partition $\{c, e, a, d, b\}$. Partition instances starts from an empty set of input vectors and defines the partition adding input vectors iteration. The selected instances in the original partition par are closer to a selective neighbor of the same class them to any instance of a different class in par. Figure 1c emphasizes on instance retrieval to select non-redundant and relevant instances.

Table 4. Processed dataset

SrNo	Conditional attributes					Decision attribute
	a	b	c	d	e	D
1	1	2	1	3	3	4
2	1	2	1	3	3	4
6	1	2	1	3	3	4
7	1	2	1	3	3	4
5	1	2	1	3	3	5
3	1	2	1	3	3	6
4	1	2	1	3	3	6
8	2	2	3	3	1	5
11	2	3	3	2	1	4
12	2	3	3	2	1	4
13	2	3	3	2	1	4
16	2	3	3	2	1	4
9	2	3	3	2	1	6
10	2	3	3	2	1	6
14	2	3	3	2	1	6
15	2	3	3	2	1	6

The method considers ED algorithm to control the redundancy. The mechanism involves neighborhood algorithm which significantly affects run time. In spite of instance selection from whole data it is employed on partitions retrieved from the data as shown in Tables 1, 2, 3, 4 and 5. By the algorithm in Algorithm 1, hybrid entropy of each attribute is measured. These attributes evaluate the randomness of information in the data and mean classification accuracy.

3.3 Combining Attribute and Instance Selection

In this paper, attribute selection process is integrated with instance selection. In the first process, attribute is selected based on minimum hybrid entropy as shown in Eq. 6. Minimum value attribute creates two partition. The partitions are created recursively until the entropy is not stable. Entropy stability gives different partitions according to the attribute value. The number of partitions are created with the attribute entropy. Every partition par has number of instances. The instance from each partition are chosen having minimum ED. This removes the redundant instances. Finally, the attributes used in partitioning are selected. The instance from each partition are selected, and instances are chosen with maintaining the integrity of original data set.

Table 5. Reduced dataset

SrNo	Conditional attributes			Decision attribute
	a	b	c	D
1	1	2	1	4
5	1	2	1	5
3	1	2	1	6
8	2	2	3	5
11	2	3	3	4
9	2	3	3	6

4   Experimental Results, and Comparison Analysis

4.1   The Data Sets

To illustrate the consideration of the proposed method 22 different kinds of publicly available datasets with multiple classes from UCI machine learning data repository [2] is used in our experimental work. These data sets would provide enough insight on the behavior of proposed method. The results of all these data sets in terms of reduced size and mean classification accuracy are listed in Table 6. The description of the results obtained on various data sets is shown in column 4th to 6th of Table 6 is as follows:-

Vehicle Data Set: This data set was gathered by JP Siebert at the Turing Institute (TI), Glasgow, Scotland in 1986-87 and was sourced by Drs. Pete Mowforth and Barry Shepherd (TI). With utilization of an chorus feature clipping to the 2D objects a solution of 3D objects is found. This dataset contains 18 attributes and contains 846 instances. The object is classified into opel, van, bus, and car. The eighteen variables are used in recognition of the object, more detailed can be found on UCI repository.

Ozone Data Set: This data set comes from IBM T.J. Watson Research, University of Lousiana and Houston and was donated by Kun Zhang, Wei Fan, Jing Yuan. The Ozone data set concerns the presence or absence of ozone day. There are seventy two continuous variables which helps in predicting the ozone day.

Glass Data Set: It was created by B. German at Central Research Establishment and was donated by Vina Spiehler. Each variable in the data is particular glass scope, and all data conforms one of 214 glasses in the data where it is stored. The main aim of the data is to classify different types of glasses.

Heart Data Set: This data is composed of a number of tests from healthy person and person with Heart's disease (HD). This data set contains 270 instances and contains 13 variable. In this data variables are of real, ordered, binary, nominal. Data is being normalized using standard deviation and binsize 7. The sum of Shannon and Fuzzy entropy values for each attribute is computed. The performance of proposed method is evaluated on experimental datasets i.e split into two disjoint datasets known as training data as well as testing data. Training and testing data are of equal size. The proposed method is verified with MLP-ANN [14] and SVM [29] classifiers. Original data with reduced data size and accuracy rate is shown in Table 6. The detailed comparisons are listed in Table 7; first column shows the dataset second to sixth column shows the reducts of the methods and seventh to eleventh represents the mean classification accuracy of the comparative method and the highlighted values reveal the improvement by the proposed method.

Table 6. Reduced data sets with classification accuracy

Dataset	Cluster	Original size	Reduced size	MLP mean accuracy	SVM mean accuracy
Zoo	7	101 × 16	41 × 13	98.02	96.19
Iris	3	150 × 4	3 × 3	99.23	99.89
Vehicle	4	846 × 18	160 × 9	82.4	95.48
Vote	2	435 × 16	227 × 16	96.32	99.68
Parkinsons	2	195 × 22	12 × 4	87.2	79.59
Ozone	2	2536 × 72	226 × 30	97.12	99.29
Segmentation	8	210 × 19	44 × 10	95.73	96.92
Heart	2	270 × 13	12 × 4	84.45	92.22
Glass	6	214 × 10	11 × 2	95.33	99.96
Wine	3	178 × 13	10 × 2	88.70	96.73
Sonar	2	208 × 60	58 × 38	86.78	99.11
Dermatology	6	366 × 34	131 × 30	97.81	99.94
Wdbc	2	569 × 31	5 × 2	87.00	92.76
Mushroom	2	8124 × 22	435 × 20	99.45	90.50
Protein	8	336 × 7	26 × 7	88.7	62.5
Ionosphere	2	351 × 34	275 × 33	94.53	99.60
Pima	2	768 × 8	22 × 6	84.45	96.84
Horses colic	2	368 × 23	2 × 1	81.52	80.43
Crx×	2	690 × 15	518 × 15	87.54	99.05
Soybeans	2	307 × 34	150 × 31	98.71	99.90
Land Satellite	6	6435 × 36	5991 × 35	90.03	92.65
LiverBupa	2	345 × 6	48 × 5	78.9	93.53

4.2 Experimental Setup

The mean classification accuracy on the test dataset is used as the performance measure. All chosen datasets are tested on Intel core(TM) i7-4500M CPU 1.80 GHz×4 Ubuntu machine with 8 GB RAM and are verified using MLP-ANN classifier. Binary class datasets are also verified with SVM classifier. The mean classification accuracy rate with SVM and MLP-ANN are listed in Table 6. MAT-LAB 2013 is used for implementation of the proposed method.

4.3   Comparison of Proposed Method Versus the Existing Methods

In this section, the proposed method is compared with the one based on ACIEAS method [31], IOTSU discretization method [18], FTSBPSD method [3], and on Shannon Entropy method [27] in terms of classification rate. The IOTSU method [18] is compared in terms of attribute reduction and classification accuracy. Comparison on data sets Glass$^{214 \times 10}$, Wine$^{178 \times 13}$, Iris$^{150 \times 4}$, Protein$^{336 \times 7}$, Pima$^{768 \times 8}$, Heart$^{270 \times 13}$ is listed in third and eighth column of Table 7. It discretize the data set based on maximum inter class variance. For Glass data set, proposed method gives 2 reduct with mean classification accuracy 95.33% whereas IOTSU method gives 3 reduct with 73.81%. For wine data set reduct cardinality is reduced from 13 to 8 by IOTSU method and the proposed method reduces it to 2 with improvement in mean classification accuracy. For Iris data same reduct cardinality is retrieved with improved accuracy rate. For protein data set reduct cardinality is same while accuracy rate is improved by 5%. On 5 datasets reduct cardinality and mean accuracy rate is improved significantly and one has the same reduct cardinality with improved accuracy rate. The IOTSU method shows result only on few data sets. Table 7 4th and 9th column compare results with [3] FTSBPSD method on 10 different data sets Glass$^{214 \times 10}$, Heart$^{270 \times 13}$, Wine$^{178 \times 13}$, Sonar$^{208 \times 60}$, Wdbc$^{569 \times 31}$, Ionosphere$^{351 \times 34}$, Pima$^{768 \times 8}$, Vehicle$^{846 \times 18}$, Segmentation$^{210 \times 19}$, and Land satellite$^{6435 \times 36}$. Reduct cardinality value for Glass, Vehicle, and Segmentation data, reducts are less then half of the FTSBPSD method [3]. Average classification accuracy for these data set is significant. The mean classification accuracy for Wdbc, Heart, and Wine is not much higher with the proposed method but with the accuracy rate 87.09%, 72.22%, and 88.70% and only 2, 4, 2 features are required respectively. For land Satellite, Ionosphere, and Sonar data set accuracy rate are increased and data sample is being reduced. Pima data set has the same number of reducts with the improved accuracy rate 84.45%.

In Table 7 5th and 10th column shows results using Shannon Entropy method [27] and proposed method can be seen on datasets Zoo$^{101 \times 16}$, Vote$^{435 \times 16}$, Credit approval system$^{690 \times 15}$, Mushroom$^{8124 \times 22}$, Soybean$^{307 \times 34}$. For Zoo and Mushroom datasets the mean classification accuracy is worse by selecting fewer attributes as shown in [27] but proposed method is selecting more features with the better mean classification accuracy. For Vote and Soybean data set accuracy is 96.32% and 98.71% with reduction in sample size and reduct cardinality. For the Credit data the proposed method gives only 10 reducts which are highly significant with the accuracy 97.85%.

Last results with ACIEAS Method given by [31] can be seen in 6th and 11th columns of Table 7 for datasets Credit approval$^{690 \times 22}$, Pima$^{768 \times 8}$, Segmentation$^{210 \times 19}$, Land Satellite$^{6435 \times 36}$, Mushroom$^{8124 \times 22}$, Liver$^{345 \times 6}$. The reduct cardinality is not good with the proposed method but more noticeable is the mean classification accuracy as it is improved for all the data sets except Liver data. The classifiers accuracy depends on the intrinsic dimensionality of the data that means classification data should be properly distributed with the pattern classes to achieve the exact classification rate [6]. The 6th and 11th column of Table 7 shows comparison with ACIEAS Method [31] and it is being analyzed that proposed method has higher accuracy in all the cases except liver data.

Table 7. Comparison results of different algorithms in terms of reducts and classification accuracy

Test data sets	Reducts					Classification accuracy				
	Hybrid entropy	IOTSU	FTSBPSD	Shannon	ACIEAS	Hybrid entropy	IOTSU	FTSBPSD	Shannon	ACIEAS
Zoo	13	NA	NA	9	NA	98.02	NA	NA	92.20	NA
Iris	3	3	NA	NA	NA	**99.23**	99.17	NA	NA	NA
Vehicle	9	NA	17	NA	NA	**82.40**	NA	71.52	NA	NA
Vote	16	NA	NA	NA	NA	96.32	NA	NA	94.00	NA
Segmentation	10	NA	14	NA	3	**95.73**	NA	94.89	NA	79.4
Heart	4	7	9	NA	NA	**81.97**	66.21	81.97	NA	NA
Glass	2	3	7	NA	NA	**95.33**	73.81	76.67	NA	NA
Wine	2	8	5	NA	NA	88.70	88.57	96.63	NA	NA
Sonar	38	NA	13	NA	NA	82.21	NA	86.78	NA	NA
Wdbc	2	NA	13	NA	NA	87.00	NA	96.13	NA	NA
Mushroom	20	NA	NA	6	5	98.99	NA	NA	99.40	77.7
Protein	7	7	NA	NA	NA	**88.7**	82.99	NA	NA	NA
Ionosphere	33	NA	10	NA	NA	92.00	NA	94.53	NA	NA
Pima	6	8	6	NA	4	**84.45**	65.36	78.01	NA	82.60
Crx	10	NA	NA	15	3	**97.85**	NA	NA	97.80	80.90
Soybeans	31	NA	NA	NA	NA	**98.71**	NA	NA	88.35	NA
Land Satellite	35	NA	29	NA	29	**90.03**	NA	84.8	NA	84.80
LiverBupa	5	NA	NA	NA	4	78.90	NA	NA	NA	95.10

5 Conclusion

An entropy and fuzzy entropy based hybrid approach is proposed for boosting the results in terms of data reduction and classification efficiency. The relevance of the attributes are measured with the minimum hybrid entropy value. The duplicate data is also eliminated t o lessen the data size. To eliminate the bias ness, data is normalized using standard deviation and restricts the values in particular domain. The main contribution of the proposed method is that it is an hybrid method, extracting all the relevant features which provides meaningful information. The experimental results are performed on 22 standard datasets and comparison with recently developed schemes like improved OTSU discretization method, FTSBPSD, ACIEAS and Shannon entropy. Finally, the classification accuracy of data sets based on selected attributes are verified by well known machine learning algorithms MLP and SVM. Future directions that need to be scheduled in the field of attribute reduction are as follows: (a) attribute reduction using singular vector decomposition and QR factorization along with rough set theory. (b) attribute reduction using rough entropy and fast machine learning algorithms such as extreme learning machine as a classifier.

References

1. Al-Sharhan, S., Karray, F., Gueaieb, W., Basir, O.: Fuzzy entropy: a brief survey. In: Proceedings of the 10th IEEE International Conference on Fuzzy Systems, pp. 1135–1139 (2001)
2. Asuncion, A., Newman, D.J.: UCI machine learning repository. In: Personal and Ubiquitous Computing, University of California, School of Information and Computer Science, Irvine, vol. 22, no. 5–6, pp. 1083–1091 (2007). http://www.ics.uci. edu/mlearn/MLRepository.html
3. Chebrolu, S., Sanjeevi, S.G.: Forward tentative selection with backward propagation of selection decision algorithm for attribute reduction in rough set theory. Int. J. Reason.-Based Intell. Syst. **7**(4), 221–243 (2015)
4. Cristianini, N., Shawe-Taylor, J.: An Introduction to Support Vector Machines and Other Kernel-Based Learning Methods. Cambridge University Press, Cambridge (2000). Sensors **13**(8), 9604–9623
5. Jiang, F., Sui, Y.: A novel approach for discretization of continuous attributes in rough set theory. Knowl.-Based Syst. **73**, 324–334 (2015)
6. Camastra, F., Staiano, A.: Intrinsic dimension estimation: advances and open problems. Inf. Sci. **328**, 26–41 (2016)
7. Rashmi, Ghose, U., Mehta, R.: Attribute reduction method using the combination of entropy and fuzzy entropy. In: Perez G., Mishra K., Tiwari S., Trivedi M. (eds.) Networking Communication and Data Knowledge Engineering. LNDECT, vol. 3, pp. 169–177. Springer, Singapore (2018). https://doi.org/10.1007/978-981-10-4585-1_14
8. Gheyas, I.A., Smith, L.S.: Feature subset selection in large dimensionality domains. Pattern Recogn. **43**(1), 5–13 (2010)
9. Ge, H., Li, L., Xu, Y., Yang, C.: Quick general reduction algorithms for inconsistent decision tables. Int. J. Approx. Reason. **82**, 56–80 (2017)
10. Haykin, S.: Neural Networks: A Comprehensive Foundation, 2nd edn. Prentice Hall, Upper Saddle River (2004)
11. Hong, X., Haozhong, C., Dongxiao, N.: Rough set continuous attributes discretization algorithm based on information entropy. Chin. J. Comput. **28**(9), 1570–1573 (2005)
12. Ivanikovas, S., Dzemyda, G., Medvedev, V.: Large datasets visualization with neural network using clustered training data. In: Atzeni, P., Caplinskas, A., Jaakkola, H. (eds.) ADBIS 2008. LNCS, vol. 5207, pp. 143–152. Springer, Heidelberg (2008). https://doi.org/10.1007/978-3-540-85713-6_11
13. Zhou, J., Miao, D., Pedrycz, W., Zhang, H.: Analysis of alternative objective functions for attribute reduction in complete decision tables. Soft Comput. **15**(8), 1601–1616 (2011)
14. Hertz, J.A.: Introduction to the Theory of Neural Computation. CRC Press, Boca Raton (2018)
15. Kang, H.-Y., Lee, A.H.I.: Priority mix planning for semiconductor fabrication by fuzzy AHP ranking. Expert Syst. Appl. **32**(2), 560–570 (2007)

16. Kucukvar, M., Gumus, S., Egilmez, G., Tatari, O.: Ranking the sustainability performance of pavements: an intuitionistic fuzzy decision making method. Autom. Constr. **40**, 33–43 (2014)
17. Lam, W., Keung, C.K., Ling, C.X.: Learning good prototypes for classification using filtering and abstraction of instances. Pattern Recogn. **35**(7), 1491–1506 (2002)
18. Liu, Y., Hou, T., Wang, K., Liu, F.: Attribute reduction of gene signal based on improved OTSU discretization method. In: Chinese Automation Congress (CAC), pp. 983–987. IEEE, November 2015
19. Luukka, P.: Feature selection using fuzzy entropy measures with similarity classifier. Expert Syst. Appl. **38**(4), 4600–4607 (2011)
20. Mardani, A., Jusoh, A., Zavadskas, E.K.: Fuzzy multiple criteria decision-making techniques and applications–two decades review from 1994 to 2014. Expert Syst. Appl. **42**(8), 4126–4148 (2015)
21. Medvedev, V., Dzemyda, G., Kurasova, O., Marcinkevičius, V.: Efficient data projection for visual analysis of large data sets using neural networks. Informatica **22**(4), 507–520 (2011)
22. Mehta, R., Rajpal, N., Vishwakarma, V.P.: Robust image watermarking scheme in lifting wavelet domain using GA-LSVR hybridization. Int. J. Mach. Learn. Cybern. **9**(1), 145–161 (2015). https://doi.org/10.1007/s13042-015-0329-6
23. Onel, M., Kieslich, C.A., Guzman, Y.A., Floudas, C.A., Pistikopoulos, E.N.: Big data approach to batch process monitoring: simultaneous fault detection and diagnosis using nonlinear support vector machine-based feature selection. Comput. Chem. Eng. **115**, 46–63 (2018)
24. Pal, S.K., Mitra, S.: Multilayer perceptron, fuzzy sets, and classification. IEEE Trans. Neural Netw. **3**(5), 683–697 (1992)
25. Qian, Y., Liang, J., Pedrycz, W., Dang, C.: An efficient accelerator for attribute reduction from incomplete data in rough set framework. Pattern Recogn. **44**(8), 1658–1670 (2011)
26. Shannon, C.E.: A mathematical theory of communication. ACM SIGMOBILE Mob. Comput. Commun. Rev. **5**(1), 3–55 (2015)
27. Son, S.-H., Kim, J.-Y.: Data reduction for instance-based learning using entropy-based partitioning. In: Gavrilova, M., et al. (eds.) ICCSA 2006. LNCS, vol. 3982, pp. 590–599. Springer, Heidelberg (2006). https://doi.org/10.1007/11751595_63
28. Maulik, U., Chakraborty, D.: Remote sensing image classification: a survey of support-vector-machine-based advanced techniques. IEEE Geosci. Remote Sens. Mag. **5**(1), 33–52 (2017)
29. Vapnik, V.: The Nature of Statistical Learning Theory. Springer, New York (2013)
30. Zhang, X., Mei, C., Chen, D., Li, J.: Feature selection in mixed data: a method using a novel fuzzy rough set-based information entropy. Pattern Recogn. **56**, 1–15 (2016)
31. Zhang, Q., Yang, J., Yao, L.: Attribute reduction based on rough approximation set in algebra and information views. IEEE Access **4**, 5399–5407 (2016)
32. Zhao, N., Xu, Z.: Entropy measures for interval-valued intuitionistic fuzzy information from a comparative perspective and their application to decision making. Informatica **27**(1), 203–229 (2016)

Android Smells Detection Using ML Algorithms with Static Code Metrics

Aakanshi Gupta[1]([✉]), Bharti Suri[2], and Vishal Bhat[1]

[1] ASET, GGS Indraprastha University, New Delhi, India
aakankshi@gmail.com, vishalbhat83@gmail.com
[2] University School of ICT, GGS Indraprastha University, New Delhi, India
bhartisuri@gmail.com

Abstract. Mobile applications development rate is predominantly increasing in comparison with the regular applications. These mobile applications prove to be change frequently according to the user requirements. Moreover, these changes in the code base may introduce some bad design practices that are called as bad smells, which can lead to a higher maintenance cost and degrade quality of the software. A very less attention has been given in the detection of code smells in the mobile applications that are also called as android smells. This research contains the rules in combination of software metrics and their threshold values to detect the bad smells in the android applications. The proposed rules are computed using three different machine learning algorithms. This framework has been applied to 2896 instances of the android applications which are open-sourced on GitHub. The android code smells MIM, LIC, DTWC and SL have been considered for the generation of detection rules and are validated using 10-fold cross validation method. The machine learning algorithm JRip furnished the best result for the android smells up to 90% overall precision, which is quite sufficient to justify the results.

1 Introduction and Motivation

Mobile application market has been explored and extended to a gigantic variety. It has became the most profitable software product markets as compared to other markets and has no end in sight [7]. There are majorly two giants in this market i.e., Android and iOS. According to a research [26], android operating system market worldwide share is 76.23% and iOS operating systems worldwide share is 22.14% and the remaining worldwide share constitutes to some minor operating systems market. The major difference in the android market is due to the lower costs of the smart-phones and the mobile applications which are easily accessible to millions of people around the world [7]. Furthermore, number of available apps in the Google Play Store was most recently recorded to be 2.46 million applications [27], after surpassing 1 million applications in July 2013. Thus, android application market is growing rapidly and is ceaseless. These facts motivate and help in building interests of many researchers in the android application domain.

© Springer Nature Singapore Pte Ltd. 2020
U. Batra et al. (Eds.): REDSET 2019, CCIS 1229, pp. 64–79, 2020.
https://doi.org/10.1007/978-981-15-5827-6_6

Hence, this research work will mainly target the android applications domain. Code smell, according to Martin Fowler, is a surface indication that usually corresponds to a deeper problem [1]. The word code smell was first used by Kent Beck and Martin Fowler. Conventionally, code smells are the marks of the low-level coding practices and bad implementation choices which are adopted by a developer during implementation of a software product [7,22]. Specifically, they are not bugs and do not prevent the code from its actual purpose rather they indicate inefficiencies in the source code and cause low productivity with an increase in the cost of maintainability of the software product [1,7,22]. However, they are considered when the actual design rules are infringed and which may produce long lasting maintainability problems and technical debt [1,2,18,22]. Technical debt was defined by Ward Cunningham, as the dissimilarity between the assumed optimal software product and the produced software product design, which is flawless and successful in any action course [4,10]. This dissimilarity arises when there is more emphasis laid on on-time delivery practice rather than on optimal code delivery practice. Difference in mobile application and desktop application development is carried by different development and programming approaches [21,23]. Mobile application development is confined due to limited resources of mobile phones like Memory, CPU, Battery. Usually, it is governed by strict deadlines and frequent updates as compared to desktop applications [11,14]. More major issues that affect mobile application development are device fragmentation, screen size and building interactive applications as compared to desktop application development. Many researchers and practitioners have also examined code smells as a sinful symptom of maintainability issues which degrades the resources and performance of the android applications [15,21,24]. Previous research work concluded the automatic and manual detection of code smells but both don't go hand in-hand due to very less amount of work was done on automatic detection of android code smells as compared to the manual detection [5]. Reimann et al. proposed a catalogue of 30 types of android specific code smells whose presence affects the performance of android applications [14]. Besides, several techniques were focused for analyzing the code smells in android applications [12,20]. Nevertheless, previous research work analyzed code smells and investigated the impact of code smells on the resource usage (Memory, CPU, Battery) [7], energy consumption [20] in the context of android applications. Researchers have also inspected the software quality along the evolution of android applications [9] and tried to detect android smells using multi-objective programming [12]. They only approached this topic in their explanatory hypotheses and have proposed some tools through which they tried to analyze android code smells but interestingly, this field requires more attention and is yet to be explored further. Precisely, this paper proposes some rules for limiting code smells in android applications. The paper completely tackles and lights up the section of code smells in android applications. It consists of three distinct steps, each of which is supported by different automated tools namely, aDoctor, Understand and Weka. Firstly, collection of data is required for the formulation of uniform dataset with the consideration of 10 android applications. Then aDoctor (version 1.0) tool is used to analyze java-based source code for detection of android specific code smells. Second step consists of a tool called Understand (version 5.0) which is used to generate static metrics. At last step, a tool called Weka (version 3.8) is used to generate rules using different machine learning algorithms in relation to the static metrics. Thus, following sections present the main contributions of the research work done under the paper to uncover the android application domain.

- Applying machine leaning approaches on the Android Smells.
- Determining the accuracy of each considered machine learning algorithms.
- Selecting the best machine learning algorithm for Android Smell detection.
- Selection of most efficient human-readable smell detection rules in the form of metrics.
- Performed validation of the results through 10-Fold cross validation technique.
- Calculated and analyzed the result with performance metrics like: Kappa Statistics, Recall, Precision, TP rate etc.
- Computed the best result upto 90% accuracy with JRip algorithm.

In particular, this research work investigates four different types of android specific code smells as defined by Reimann et al. which are purely dedicated to android applications [14]. The work involves experimentation through the use of three supervised machine learning algorithms for generation of detection rules. The considered four android specific code smells are summarized in Table 1.

Table 1. Summary of considered Android code smells

Android code smells	Description
Data Transmission Without Compression (DTWC)	Arises when a file is transmitted over a network without being compressed
Leaking Inner Class (LIC)	Arises when non-static inner class holding a reference to the outer class
Member Ignoring Method (MIM)	Arises when non-static methods do not access any internal properties of the class
Slow Loop (SL)	Arises when for loop is used instead of for-each loop

The paper is structured in the following sections: Sect. 2 illustrates the background study of the considered topic which describes all the related word. Section 3 represents the proposed methodology carried out in the research work which explains the experimentation process in full detail. Section 4 explains the result analysis using various statistical graphs. Section 5 describes the threats to the validity of the work done. Finally, Sect. 6 provides the conclusions of the work and also predicts the future scope of the work.

2   Background Theory

The quality characteristics that concludes to an optimal software product are correctness, consistent, efficient, performance and maintainability. But developers with lack of knowledge can impediment these characteristics and can introduce code smells in the android applications. The code smells can hinder every possible characteristic and may cause system sensitive bugs and future failures. Furthermore, android code smells take up more resources of the mobile phones and can produce serious crashes which constitute to reduction in efficiency and performance of the software. The future updation process can also be impaired with the bad code smells which definitely increases the maintenance cost of the android application. Thus, the paper applies a methodological view to detect android specific code smells using machine learning with a set of static metrics.

This section is organized as follows: Sect. 2.1 illustrates evolution of code smells in software systems. Section 2.2 deals with the detection of android specific code smells. Section 2.3 describes the elimination of bad android specific code smells.

2.1   Evolution of Android Smells

Code smells, in general, are categorized as software design flaws in object-oriented systems which degrade the quality of the software and may increase the overall cost of maintainability. The effect and occurrence of code smells can vary from one operating system to another operating system. Code smells in android operating system mainly arise when the software design rules vary from the conventional pre-defined optimal design rules. Usually, these rules are violated when a developer is more persistent towards software deadlines rather than on conventional optimal design rules [7,23]. Further, code smells do not directly affect the functioning of an android application rather they affect it indirectly and cause low productivity. This can emerge as a major obstacle in the future maintenance of the application [12]. Previously, Fowler proposed 22 code smells which were not specific to android applications. But, later on, many research works focussed purely on identification of code smells affecting the android applications. Reimann et al. proposed a catalogue of 30 types of android specific code smells which carry a great impact on this domain till now [14]. Roy et al. [23] researched for duplicate code in a software system by conducting a survey on Software Clone Detection. Tufano et al. [16] studied the reasons of bad smells occurred in the software and the survivability of the bad smells over the change history of 200 open source projects from different software ecosystems and investigated when bad smells are introduced by developers, along with conditions and reasons behind their introduction. Zhang et al. [25] reviewed the current knowledge of code bad smells in software systems. Gupta et al. [7] proposed a bad smell prediction model using the concept of Shannon, Renyi and Tsallis entropies. Also, a research emphasis was laid on who to blame for the rise of Android code smells by studying the contributions of developers during evolution of a software [8].

2.2   Detection Techniques and Tools

A tool called aDoctor has been developed to detect 15 android specific code smells with an average precision of 98% and recall of 98% over source code of 18 different android applications [19]. An empirical study investigated the impact of 3 code smells on the smartphones resource usage such as on CPU and memory by applying refactoring techniques [17]. Although, previous research work has analysed various quality metrics that can be used for estimation of the quality of the source code using several existing tools such as InFusion [13] and Paprika [9]. Dustin Lim [14] analysed traditional smell detector tool for detecting code smells in android applications. Hecht et al. [9] introduced a tooled approach to identify 3 object-oriented and 4 Android-specific antipatterns from binaries of mobile apps to track the software quality of android applications along with their evolution. Kessentini et al. [12] generated the rules for the detection of code smells in android applications using a multi-objective genetic programming algorithm.

2.3   Elimination Techniques

Along with, detection, elimination of android specific code smells is aforethought to quench the need of evolving an optimal software. Previous research work delivered detection of android specific code smells using automated and manual techniques. In addition, many research works accounted for increasing the probability of improvement and removal of code smells in the source code of android applications. The improvement in source code is accomplished through refactoring. Refactoring refers to the process of improving the internal properties of a software without affecting its external properties. M. Fowler along with K. Beck proposed a handbook with 70 refracting tips for improving the existing source code through refracting [6]. The consideration of automated and manual refactoring depends on time factor as researchers believe in making best use of available resources while consuming less amount of time. It is known that automated refactoring requires fewer human resources as compared to the manual refactoring. The investigating researchers are ambitious about transforming tools like Leafactor, refractory [12] for automated refactoring of source code of the android applications for the removal of android specific code smells. Luis et al. [3] evaluated in the study whether or not automatic refracting can aid developers in developing energy efficient apps using a tool called Leafactor. The study was done for five code smells in 140 free and open source applications. Palomba et al. [20] examined for the impact of 9 code smells on the energy consumption of mobile applications by applying manual refactoring on 60 android applications.

3   Methodology

With the intention of obtaining human-readable rules for detection of android specific code smells, administration of machine learning algorithms is required on the formularized datasets. Compulsorily, the datasets should be proportionally legitimate for obtaining requisite detection rules. Though, once the rules are detected they will somehow increase the probability of developing a flawless software product and decrease the overhead software maintenance cost. Figure 1 illustrates overview of proposed approach applied in the research work.

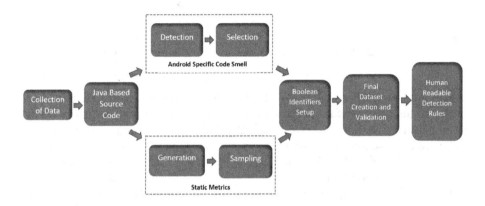

Fig. 1. Research methodology in a schematic way

The initial setup analyses the collection of android applications which can be consider suitable for the extraction of stable datasets. Subsequently, the java source code of these considered android applications is freely available on an open source platform called GitHub. Further, a smell detector tool is used for identification of android specific code smells and a metrics analysis tool is used for evaluation of static metrics. Later in the course of static metrics, sampling is figured out for reducing the complexity of the requisite rules. The final dataset is prepared by assigning Boolean identifiers between the obtained results. More-over, it is further evaluated using machine learning approach with the help of different machine learning algorithms for obtaining optimized human-readable detection rules. The following section is organised as: Sect. 3.1 represents data acquisition and Sect. 3.2 describes the proposed android smell detection approach. Section 3.3 presents static metrics analysis in association with sampling. Section 3.4 examines suitable machine learning approach.

3.1   Data Acquisition

Dataset consistency is accountable for accomplishment and validation of the final results. During entire research work the main concern is to maintain dataset consistency. To achieve the same, different Java-based android application repositories are analysed and 10 are considered suitable for the research work. The source code of the considered android applications is freely downloadable from the open source platform, GitHub. The criteria for selection of these android applications is that their source code should be easily compilable for detection of android specific code smells and figuring out static metrics accurately. Figure 2 illustrates the process of extraction of source code from GitHub.

Inspection   Selection   Download

Fig. 2. Process of extraction of source code from GitHub

The dataset further comprises of two sub datasets which are combined to obtain the final dataset for applying machine learning. In first sub dataset result of the presence/absence of android specific code smell is computed for a particular android source code using aDoctor tool. Also, the second sub dataset contains a large set of static metrics computed over 10 android applications which accounts as individual entity for the machine learning approach. This set of static metrics is computed through Scitools Understand whose metrics bring about property is based on parameters of source code like size, complexity, count and inheritance.

3.2   Detection of Android Specific Code Smells

To explore the presence of android specific code smells proper intimation of design rules should be developed during the software development life cycle. Although keeping the track of this intimation in software developers is very hard to look for. The identification of bad smells in android applications can be effectively achieved through automated detection techniques. Literally, manual detection techniques are extravagant in comparison with automated techniques because it consumes more human resources and there are tremendous chances of errors. So, to curtail these manifestations automated android smell detector tool called aDoctor is considered for examining the android specific code smells [19]. The outlined tool corresponds to android smells with the help of Boolean feature and adequately finds android code smells within instances with comprehensive average precision of 98% and an average recall of 98%. The ideology of the paper comprises detection of four android specific code smells through analysis of 10 android applications. Eventually, the major criteria for the selection of four described android specific code smells is based on their occurrence and diffusion in the analyzed source code of the applications. The paper accounts for most frequently occurring android code smells and identifies their respective detection rules. Apart from that open source availability and high precision of aDoctor conforms its suitability with the demands of the research work.

3.3   Static Metrics Analysis

The main perspective of static metrics analysis is to determine the areas of improvement that affect the evolution of the software development and maintenance. It is used to evaluate statistical properties and characteristics of a software which are analogous to planning, development and maintenance. In order to generate static metrics Scitool Understand is used. It is an IDE (Integrated Development Environment) that is capable of extracting wide range of static metrics and can sensibly generate client-needed reports. The main objective of picking this tool is, its open source accessibility for evaluation of peculiarities in application software. Likewise, the production of static metrics will act as a source of evidence that can predict and anticipate the field of enhancement in the source code of the android application. This enhancement will help to reduce the overhead maintenance cost and will cut down the probability of software failure in the near future. According to the work flow Fig. 1, the source code of different android applications is operated using Understand tool and 40 different types of static metrics are gathered as aftereffect. Remarkably, the rules generated by these 40 static metrics are effectively composite and surely, they would not be understood by a developer. Although, if a developer tries to understand these complex rules than it will be very challenging for the person to deliver the software within the time limits. Alongside, the need to reduce the complexity of the requisite rules, sampling is figured out in the action course of research work. Generally, sampling refers to the situation of selecting a subset from the set of samples to validate the characteristics of the whole set. Also, one more possibility other than reducing complexity of the detection rules is that formation and handling of such big dataset requires a lot of human abilities and efforts. Additionally, sampling is done by keeping two criterion under observation: source code of the analyzed application and the effect of a particular metrics on the analyzed android code smells when estimated using different machine algorithms. The main advantage of sampling is that it helps in reducing the overhead cost and time for formulation of dataset. Table 2 illustrates the 18 sampled static metrics considered for the research work.

In effect, a followed approach is expected to find and allocate the logical values between both the knock down results. The allocation will be responsible for the groundwork of finalised datasets. For finalizing, both the obtained results are validated to form last-minute balanced datasets which are trained further for establishment of detection rules driven by distinct machine learning algorithms. The final datasets are balanced by keeping positive and negative instances in a proper proportion and they account for suitable and appropriate results. At last, four final equitable datasets are obtained with overall 2896 instances in total which correspond to four different android specific code smells as described in the paper.

Table 2. Sampled static metrics

Static metrics	Description
ACM	AvgCyclomaticModified
AL	AvgLine
ALC	AvgLineCode
CDC	CountDeclClass
CDCV	CountDeclClassVariable
CDF	CountDeclFunction
CDIM	CountDeclInstanceMethod
CDIV	CountDeclInstanceVariable
CDMP	CountDeclMethodPrivate
CL	CountLine
CLC	CountLineCode
CLCD	CountLineCodeDecl
CLC	CountLineComment
CS	CountSemicolon
MCM	MaxCyclomaticModified
MCS	MaxCyclomaticStrict
MN	MaxNesting
SC	SumCyclomatic

3.4   Machine Learning Approach

The formalization of final uniform data-set involves machine learning approach which is accordingly applied through different supervised machine learning algorithms. The basic prospect is to evaluate each machine learning algorithm performance for different data-set obtained and to raise the most appropriate algorithm among them for determining best suitable detection rules for investigated android specific code smells. Initially, it yields by erecting proportionate data-set in equivalence with each android specific code smell taken into account. Then implementing these data-set over explicit machine learning algorithms for the sake of unmasking detection rules. For achieving the motive, three distinct machine algorithms are recorded in Table 3.

Further, implementation of the section is carried through an open source data mining software called Weka (pronounced Weh-Kuh). The tool integrity can handle a wide range of data preparation and analytics and meta-learners with attribute selection and visualization features using different techniques. The research work demands for one data specification throughout, which is achieved by Weka. The results of the discussed machine learning algorithms in Table 3 generate human-readable detection rules which are validated through 10-fold cross validation technique. Besides, each dataset comprises of different columns in which first column represents the instances which correspond to android specific

Table 3. Machine learning algorithms and their brief description

Classifiers	Description
JRip	A propositional rule learner, Repeated Incremental Pruning to Produce Error Reduction.
J48	Class for generating a pruned or unpruned C4.5 decision tree.
Naive Bayes	A probabilistic classifier which uses estimator classes and works on Bayes theorem

code smells and other columns displays the object-oriented static metrics which are specified over several discussed parameters. The effectiveness of each classifier is approximated through 12 performance measures in the research process. The performance measures are estimated by Weka and some of these includes Precision, Recall, F-Measure, Percentage Accuracy, Kappa Statistic etc. In the paper, Weka classifies whether the instance is affected or unaffected by android code smell using True or False values respectively.

4   Implementation and Result Analysis

The implementation is based on the process of analysing final created dataset for generation of detection rules for android specific code smells. The final dataset is associated with 10 android mobile applications with overall 2896 instances for investigation of considered android code smells (Table 1). The generation of final dataset demands for boolean administration in association with sampled static metrics which is extremely important for applying different machine learning algorithms (Table 3). Further, the validation of results is established through 10-fold cross validation technique. Cross Validation technique helps in dividing the original sample into a number of folds which is further used to evaluate the predictive models. The final results are also justified on the basis of 12 performance measures which are discussed below:

True Positives Rate (TP Rate): It is defined as the total number of instances predicted positive that are actually positive. It is also referred as sensitivity. False Positives Rate (FP Rate): It is defined as the total number of instances predicted positive that are actually negative. Positive Predictive Value (Precision): It is defined as the fraction of instances predicted positives that are actually positive. It is also referred as PPV.

$$Precision = TP/TP + FP \qquad (1)$$

where FP is the false-positive rate.

Recall: Recall determines what fraction of those instances that are actually positive were predicted positive.

$$Recall = TP/TP + FN \tag{2}$$

where FN is the false-negative rate.

F-measure: It is a measure of a test's accuracy and is defined as the weighted harmonic mean of the precision and recall of the test.

$$F\text{-}measure = 2 * Precision * Recall/Precision + Recall \tag{3}$$

Matthews Correlation Coefficient (MCC): It is used to measure the quality of binary classifications.

Receiver operating Characteristic (ROC Area): It is a plot of true positive rate versus false positive rate at distinct threshold points.

Precision Recall Curves (PRC Area): It is a plot of precision versus recall at different scores.

Kappa statistic: It identifies the random chance by measuring the relation between the Observed Accuracy with Expected Accuracy. Pr(a) is Observed Agreement among the raters and Pr(e) is hypothetical probability of the raters.

$$K = Pr(a) - Pr(e)/1 - Pr(e) \tag{4}$$

Accuracy: It is defined as the percentage of correctly classified instances by used considered classifier.

Mean Absolute Error (MAE): It is used to measure the accuracy and average magnitude of errors for continuous variables. It is a linear score which measures all the difference averages are equally weighted.

Relative Absolute Error (RAE): It is defined as the relativity to what it would have been if a simple predictor had been used.

The evaluation criteria of each classifier by Weka tool accordingly validates the obtained results. The computed data are properly stored and are displayed for 8 performance measures in form of tables. Table 4 represents performance measures evaluated by each considered machine learning algorithm for statistical analysis of DTWC android smell. Table 5 depicts the statistical data for LIC android smell. Table 6 presents the performance efficiency of each algorithm for MIM android smell. Finally, Table 7 shows the results of computation for SL android code smell.

The considered java-based projects are estimated for android specific code smells and static metrics using aDoctor and Understand tools respectively. The obtained results are stored in comma delimited file. Further, machine learning approach is accountable for extracting results using Weka tool. This process involves good amount of human efforts for handling the dataset throughout the experimentation. Further, generated dataset is also trained for finding

Table 4. Statistical analysis for DTWC android smell

Algorithm	TP rate	FP rate	Precision	Recall	F-measure	MCC	ROC area	PRC area
JRip	0.927	0.396	0.922	0.927	0.92	0.635	0.766	0.883
J48	0.923	0.451	0.918	0.923	0.913	0.605	0.783	0.893
Naïve Bayes	0.851	0.554	0.845	0.851	0.848	0.309	0.844	0.898

Table 5. Statistical analysis for LIC android smell

Algorithm	TP rate	FP rate	Precision	Recall	F-measure	MCC	ROC area	PRC Area
JRip	0.894	0.225	0.898	0.894	0.895	0.647	0.841	0.88
J48	0.833	0.33	0.846	0.833	0.839	0.47	0.885	0.881
Naïve Bayes	0.818	0.573	0.795	0.818	0.803	0.289	0.84	0.87

Table 6. Statistical analysis for MIM android smell

Algorithm	TP rate	FP rate	Precision	Recall	F-measure	MCC	ROC area	PRC area
JRip	0.885	0.114	0.886	0.885	0.885	0.771	0.897	0.863
J48	0.856	0.143	0.859	0.856	0.856	0.715	0.867	0.823
Naïve Bayes	0.682	0.323	0.737	0.682	0.661	0.414	0.866	0.856

Table 7. Statistical analysis for SL android smell

Algorithm	TP rate	FP rate	Precision	Recall	F-measure	MCC	ROC area	PRC area
JRip	0.91	0.438	0.902	0.91	0.904	0.539	0.74	0.875
J48	0.902	0.68	0.903	0.902	0.875	0.424	0.617	0.83
Naïve Bayes	0.856	0.551	0.852	0.856	0.854	0.314	0.838	0.903

out the accuracy in accomplishment of the project. The evaluation of classifiers between classifiers is also established through Cohen's Kappa Statistic. The Mean Absolute Error and Relative Absolute Error represents percentage of errors in each classifier while measuring considered android code smells. Figure 3 shows the remaining 4 performance measures which are Percentage Accuracy, Cohen's Kappa Statistic, Percentage Mean Absolute Error, and Percentage Relative Absolute Error of each considered machine learning algorithms.

It has been observed from the above obtained results that JRip algorithm proved to be the best algorithm in terms of accuracy among all the considered three machine learning algorithms for detection of android specific code smells. JRip can detect DTWC, LIC, MIM and SL android smells with almost 92.68%, 89.36%, 88.54% and 91.02% accuracy respectively. These are the highest in comparison with other machine learning algorithms (Table 3). Further, J48 and Naïve Bayes proved to be the second best and third best machine learning algorithms respectively. Furthermore, JRip detects android code smells with high precision

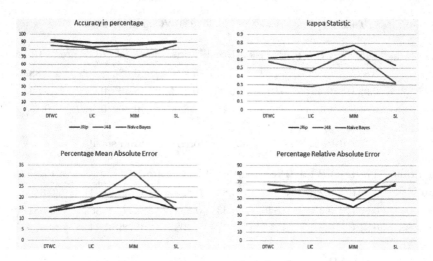

Fig. 3. Performance measures of different ML algorithms

Table 8. Extracted rules from JRip ML algorithm

Android smell	Rules by JRip
DTWC	CountLineComment >= 40 and CountLineCodeDecl >= 89 and CountDeclFunction <= 30
LIC	CountDeclClass >= 4 and CountDeclMethodPrivate <= 1
MIM	CountDeclInstanceMethod >= 5 and SumCyclomatic >= 17
SL	MaxNesting >= 3 and SumCyclomatic >= 102

and less errors as compared to other algorithms. For identification of android specific code smells, JRip proposed simple and efficient human-readable detection rules. JRip detects DTWC smell when CountLineComment is greater than or equal to 40 and CountLineCodeDecl is greater than or equal to 89 and CountDeclFunction is less than or equal to 30. Likewise, LIC smell is detected when CountDeclClass is greater than or equal to 4 and CountDeclMethodPrivate is less than or equal to 1. The detection of MIM smell is carried out when CountDeclInstanceMethod is greater than or equal to 5 and SumCyclomatic is greater than or equal to 17. Finally, SL smell is detected by JRip when MaxNesting is greater than or equal to 3 and SumCyclomatic is greater than or equal to 102. These detection rules are also summarized in Table 8.

5   Validity Threats

While researching several factors could raise questions on validity of the experimentation performed. These factors upraise many limitations which need to be considered in the course of the research work. The first source of limitation could be the experimentation not being performed by experts which may possibly induce errors in the collection and formularisation of the dataset. Secondly, aDoctor tool detects the presence/absence of android code smells using boolean values by analysing instances but does not specifically guarantee that by how much amount the android code smell affects the source code. The output of a Doctor corresponds to upper layer (class-wise) detection of android code smells. Thirdly, sampling of the results of Understand tool could affect the formularised dataset because it is done completely on a random basis where the need of the hour was to obtain a minimal set of static metrics that might predict results working with different machine learning algorithms. Fourthly, the experiment features only 4 android code smells as there exists many more code smells purely dedicated to android applications. Though the instances possessed by dataset are purely significant but the size of dataset could act as fifth barrier because machine learning algorithms can produce better results while working on huge datasets. Moreover, the experiment involves manual addition of boolean identifiers in the formation of final dataset which could act as a source of discontinuity in the results. Rather having self-made models, the experimentation is based on the Weka tool application which applies pre-defined models on the dataset. These pre-defined models could have less impact on the results.

6   Conclusion and Future Work

The research work accounts for generation of human-readable rules for detection of four android specific code smells DTWC, LIC, MIM and SL (Table 1) using machine learning algorithms with the use of static metrics. The considered machine learning algorithms are JRip, J48, NB (Table 3). Firstly, source code of 10 collected android applications are analysed for android specific code smells through aDoctor tool. The results are stored in a CSV file format where values are locally stored in form of boolean values. Next, the same source code is accounted for the evaluation of static metrics through the Understand tool. The result obtained consisted of different static metrics and then sampling was done to establish a minimal set of static metrics. The minimal set contains 18 static metrics and they were accordingly assigned boolean identifiers for the creation of final dataset. This was done similarly for each considered android code smell and dataset obtained correspondingly. Further, each obtained dataset is computed over different machine learning algorithms using Weka tool in order to obtain human-readable detection rules. The impact of each classifier is approximated with the help of 12 performance measures. Finally, 10-fold cross validation technique is used for verification of the results. After comparison, JRip classifier emerged as the best machine learning algorithm for generation of human-readable detection rules. Although, SMO has better scores than JRip but it is considered over-fitted for obtaining results as discussed previously. The final conclusion administers the fact that supervised machine learning algorithm could be used for identification of detection rules for android code smells.

The domain of android applications requires more attention for study of design defects which affect the characteristics of the software systems. The accurate size of the dataset for obtaining more efficient results is still an unanswered question. The detection of android code smells beforehand can help the developer to maintain the overall cost of the software systems. The paper uses pre-defined models, whereas self-made compatible models with huge dataset might provide more accurate results. Further, detection rules for unconsidered android code smells can be generated with an increased dataset and can be validated through k-fold cross validation technique. This research work is language specific as it only targets software written in Java. Thus, targeting software written in languages other than in Java can help developers to increase the scope of detection of android code smells.

References

1. Belle, A.B.: Estimation and prediction of technical debt: a proposal. arXiv preprint arXiv:1904.01001 (2019)
2. Brown, W.H., Malveau, R.C., McCormick, H.W., Mowbray, T.J.: AntiPatterns: Refactoring Software, Architectures, and Projects in Crisis. Wiley, New York (1998)
3. Cruz, L., Abreu, R.: Using automatic refactoring to improve energy efficiency of android apps. arXiv preprint arXiv:1803.05889 (2018)
4. Cunningham, W.: The WyCash portfolio management system. ACM SIGPLAN OOPS Messenger 4(2), 29–30 (1993)
5. Fontana, F.A., Braione, P., Zanoni, M.: Automatic detection of bad smells in code: an experimental assessment. J. Object Technol. 11(2), 5:1–38 (2012)
6. Fowler, M.: Refactoring: Improving the Design of Existing Code. Addison-Wesley Professional, Boston (2018)
7. Gupta, A., Suri, B., Kumar, V., Misra, S., Blažauskas, T., Damaševičius, R.: Software code smell prediction model using Shannon, Rényi and Tsallis entropies. Entropy 20(5), 372 (2018)
8. Habchi, S., Moha, N., Rouvoy, R.: The rise of android code smells: who is to blame? In: Proceedings of the 16th International Conference on Mining Software Repositories, pp. 445–456. IEEE Press (2019)
9. Hecht, G., Benomar, O., Rouvoy, R., Moha, N., Duchien, L.: Tracking the software quality of android applications along their evolution (T). In: 2015 30th IEEE/ACM International Conference on Automated Software Engineering (ASE), pp. 236–247. IEEE (2015)
10. Hecht, G., Rouvoy, R., Moha, N., Duchien, L.: Detecting antipatterns in android apps. In: Proceedings of the Second ACM International Conference on Mobile Software Engineering and Systems, pp. 148–149. IEEE Press (2015)
11. Husien, H.K., Harun, M.F., Lichter, H.: Towards a severity and activity based assessment of code smells. Procedia Comput. Sci. 116, 460–467 (2017)
12. Kessentini, M., Ouni, A.: Detecting android smells using multi-objective genetic programming. In: Proceedings of the 4th International Conference on Mobile Software Engineering and Systems, pp. 122–132. IEEE Press (2017)
13. Kumar, N.A., Krishna, K.H., Manjula, R.: Challenges and best practices in mobile application development. Imp. J. Interdisc. Res. 2, 12 (2016)

14. Lim, D.: Detecting code smells in android applications (2018)
15. Mannan, U.A., Ahmed, I., Almurshed, R.A.M., Dig, D., Jensen, C.: Understanding code smells in android applications. In: 2016 IEEE/ACM International Conference on Mobile Software Engineering and Systems (MOBILESoft), pp. 225–236. IEEE (2016)
16. Tufano, M., et al.: When and why your code starts to smell bad. In: 37th IEEE/ACM International Conference on Software Engineering, ICSE 2015, pp. 403–414. IEEE Computer Society Press (2015)
17. Oliveira, J., Viggiato, M., Santos, M.F., Figueiredo, E., Marques-Neto, H.: An empirical study on the impact of android code smells on resource usage. In: SEKE, pp. 314–313 (2018)
18. Ozkaya, I., Kruchten, P., Nord, R.L., Brown, N.: Managing technical debt in software development: report on the 2nd international workshop on managing technical debt, held at ICSE 2011. ACM SIGSOFT Softw. Eng. Notes **36**(5), 33–35 (2011)
19. Palomba, F., Di Nucci, D., Panichella, A., Zaidman, A., De Lucia, A.: Lightweight detection of android-specific code smells: the adoctor project. In: 2017 IEEE 24th International Conference on Software Analysis, Evolution and Reengineering (SANER), pp. 487–491. IEEE (2017)
20. Palomba, F., Di Nucci, D., Panichella, A., Zaidman, A., De Lucia, A.: On the impact of code smells on the energy consumption of mobile applications. Inf. Softw. Technol. **105**, 43–55 (2019)
21. Parikh, G.: The Guide to Software Maintenance. Winthrop, Cambridge (1982)
22. Reimann, J., Brylski, M., Aßmann, U.: A tool-supported quality smell catalogue for android developers. In: Proceedings of the Conference Modellierung 2014 in the Workshop Modellbasierte und modellgetriebene Softwaremodernisierung-MMSM, vol. 2014 (2014)
23. Roy, C.K., Cordy, J.R.: A survey on software clone detection research. Queen's Sch. Comput. TR **541**(115), 64–68 (2007)
24. Saifan, A.A., Al-Rabadi, A.: Evaluating maintainability of android applications. In: 2017 8th International Conference on Information Technology (ICIT), pp. 518–523. IEEE (2017)
25. Zhang, M., Hall, T., Baddoo, N.: Code bad smells: a review of current knowledge. J. Softw. Maint. Evol.: Res. Pract. **23**(3), 179–202 (2011)
26. Zhu, D., Xi, T.: Permission-based feature scaling method for lightweight android malware detection. In: Douligeris, C., Karagiannis, D., Apostolou, D. (eds.) KSEM 2019. LNCS (LNAI), vol. 11775, pp. 714–725. Springer, Cham (2019). https://doi.org/10.1007/978-3-030-29551-6_63
27. Flaten, H.K., St Claire, C., Schlager, E., Dunnick, C.A., Dellavalle, R.P.: Growth of mobile applications in dermatology-2017 update. Dermatol. Online J. **24**, 2 (2018)

Parallel Solution to LIS Using
Divide-and-Conquer Approach

Seema Rani[1,2(✉)] and Dharamveer Singh Rajpoot[3]

[1] Jaypee Institute of Information Technology, Noida, India
seema20thmay@yahoo.co.in
[2] Dronacharya Government College, Gurugram, India
[3] Computer Science and Engineering Department, Jaypee Institute of Information Technology,
Noida, India
drdharmveer16382@gmail.com

Abstract. This paper presents parallel solution to the LIS problem. The presented approach works by dividing the problem into smaller sub problems and then combining their solutions. The individual sub problems are handled in parallel by multiple processors. The solution produces optimal result in O(n log n) time using n/2 processors. The time taken by a single processor to implement this approach is $O(n/2 \ (\log 2 \ n)^2)$.

Keywords: Longest Increasing Sub sequence (LIS) · Divide-and-Conquer (D&C) · Longest Common Subsequence (LCS)

1 Introduction

For a finite integer sequence, XY is an increasing sub sequence when its elements are in ascending order and if an element appears before another element in Y, then that element should appear before the later element in X also. The increasing subsequence having largest number of elements is termed as Longest Increasing Sub sequence [16].

The LIS problem is a kind of LCS problem. When we try to solve the LCS problem for a pair of sequences using the solution of the LIS, we require to consider the order of characters of the sequence which has larger domain (among the two input sequences). We can use the LIS solution to solve the LCS problem only if there is one sequence which does not contain redundant elements. Pattern recognition, file comparison and data compression can be done using the concept of LCS [1].

LCS-based diff techniques have been designed for extracting long common sequences and Patience Diff extracts the common text [20] of two sequences which does not occur frequently. The nutshell technique aligns sequences by working on the common content which is appearing once in both the sequences [19]. The nutshell technique uses the LIS solution. Thus, the parts of the text appearing once in both the text sequences are identified. An integer value is allotted to each identified part of the text. Integer values are allotted to the common text subsequences of one of the given sequences as: the first text subsequence is allotted one; the second text subsequence is allotted two

U. Batra et al. (Eds.): REDSET 2019, CCIS 1229, pp. 80–90, 2020.
https://doi.org/10.1007/978-981-15-5827-6_7

and so on. Using the allotted integer values, the other sequence is also changed into integer sequence and then the LIS procedure is applied on this changed sequence. Thus the input sequences are mapped by using the solution of the LIS.

More efforts are being put by experts and scientists to align genomes by comparing it with other similar sequenced genome. The LIS solution is used during the alignment of whole-genome [2]. The MUM is highlighted using LIS solution. A MUM is a Maximum Unique Match which is common in both sub sequences but is not repeated in any of the given sequences. Thus, LIS finds the varying portions of the genome sequences. The problem of LIS is also linked with the concept of Young Tableau [3].

We present a D&C approach [18] to solve the LIS problem using which can be executed sequentially and in parallel. Earlier LIS problem has been solved using D&C approach by Alam and Rahman [6] and by Dharmveer and Seema [16]. The approach presented by Alam and Rahman provides optimal solution in many cases, but it fails to output correct solution in few cases. The authors Dharmveer and Seema [16] present the enhancement to the solution proposed by Alam and Rahman [6]. We are presenting a D&C approach which does not need sorted sequence and it uses simple method for dividing the sequence into two sub sequences.

2 Related Work

Many scientists have solved LIS problems using various techniques.

Schensted [4] proposed different types of sequences like increasing and non-increasing sequences in 1961. Suppose a sequence has n elements, a and b are the lengths of the LIS and LDS for this sequence respectively, the paper claimed that the number of different subsequences is sum of squares of numbers of Young Tableaux with distinct shapes with b rows and a columns. Schensted also introduced the LIS problem. The problem of LIS has been solved by using the concept of Young Tableau. For any given sequence A, a sub sequence B is generated such that the position of any element a_i, $a_i \varepsilon A$ in B indicates the |LIS| which ends with a_i. This sub sequence B is the Main Row of Young Tableau (MRYT). An efficient approach to maintain the MRYT was proposed by Fredman [5]: place the first element of A at first index in B. Then consider all the other elements one by one and do: for next element a_i, an element is found (using binary search) in B such that it is smallest element which is greater than a_i. Replace this found element with a_i. Repeat this process for all elements of A. To find an appropriate element for replacement, instead of performing binary search every time, first compare the current element a_i of A with the last element of B, if this current element is greater, then place a_i at the end of B, otherwise do binary search. Thus according to Fredman, the upper bound to find the LIS is $((n - L) \log L + n)$. The LIS problem using D&C technique was first of all addressed by Alam and Rahman [6]. The input sequence is recursively divided to form two sub problems having same size. The smaller elements form the first sub problem and larger form the second sub problem. These sub problems are handled independently to provide optimal LISs for both sub problems. Then these solutions are merged using Fredman's approach to find the optimal LIS for the input sequence. The proposed solution executes in $O(n \log n)$ time. Further this approach [6] has been improved by Rani and Rajpoot [16]. Bespamyatnikh and Segal [7] combined the Fredman's technique with van EmdeBoas's [8] data structure to solve the LIS problem. van Emde Boas data structure is implemented as: A record for the given sequence is maintained such that for each element of the sequence a block is allocated sequentially. Whenever an element is inserted, the corresponding block contains 1 and the deletion of an element is marked by replacing 1 with 0. The insertion, deletion and search operation executes in (log log n) time. Thus their solution took O(n log log n) time using this Boas data structure. Crochemore and Porat [9] solved the LIS problem by dividing the sequence into m blocks each of size s such that s is greater than the |LIS|. All the elements in each block are arranged in ascending order. The elements belonging to p^{th} block appear immediately before the elements of $(p + 1)^{th}$ block in ascending order. An output sequence is generated from the first block such that the element present at k^{th} location in output sequence is the last element of LIS of length k. And this is the smallest element where the LIS of length k ends. The generated output list is then combined with the second block. For this merged sequence, another output sequence is generated. This process is continued till all the blocks are processed. When this process is done for all the blocks, an optimal LIS is obtained. The time required to implement this technique is O(n log log p). The problems with this approach are: the approximated length of the LIS is required, the sequence need to be sorted, some elements need to be processed multiple times and this solution is applicable only when the length of the LIS is very very small.

Lavanya and Murugan [15] worked on the database of lists. They presented approaches to find the ascending sub lists, increasing sub lists in sliding windows, decreasing sub lists and increasing sub lists in windows having variable lengths. The authors worked on multiple sequences and windows of varying lengths. Suppose $[k_1, k_2, \ldots k_m]$ is a sub sequence K of one of the sequences P_i of the database, then (i, $[k_1, k_2, \ldots k_m]$) pair represents P_i's instance. The concepts of overlapping and proper subsets are considered to improve the efficiency of the work. The time required to execute the approach is O(n!). A variation of LCS-repetition-free LCS has been considered in paper [17]. The reason of consideration is to take into account at most one representative for each group having similar genes. The number of times a appears in x is represented by $n(x, a)$. The duplicate sequences were eliminated in multiple ways. In the first procedure, where there are multiple copies of same pattern, all the copies were deleted except the one. The decision about which pattern would be kept is random. In the second procedure, if a pattern is repeatedly occurring p times, then the period [0, 1] is partitioned into p parts and a particular part h is chosen. Then all the entries except the hth entries are deleted. The authors proposed a mathematical model.

When we have large data set to work with, we may prefer efficiency over optimality. Saks and Seshadhri [10] put their efforts to improve an existing approximate solution of LIS problem. The proposed solution works with error δn ($\delta < 0$) and it takes (log n)^c(1/δ)$^{o(1/\delta)}$ time. The procedure works as follows: A 2-d plane contains all the elements such that x-axis represents the its value and y-axis represents its position in the input sequence. An element from this plane is found such that it has high probability of being part of LIS. This element is called a *'splitter'*. The 2-d plane is divided into four parts by drawing one line parallel to x-axis and other line parallel to y-axis. Both theses lines intersect the splitter. From these four parts, upper left and lower right parts are ignored and recursive procedure is applied on lower left and upper right parts and so on. Since in each next iteration, the size of the problem reduces, approximation to LIS also improves. The authors improved the existing 2 times approximation solution to (1 + approximation) solution.

Many experts and researchers have worked on different variants of LIS. There may be situations where we do not need exact LIS but we may be looking for an LIS which is almost increasing. That is an output sequence where the next element is either greater than the previous element or if it is not greater, then the difference between these two elements is not greater than d (d is a small value). This sequence is named a Longest almost Increasing Sub sequence (LaIS) by iElmisasry [11]. Consider two elements a and b from the output sequence such that $b > a$ and b is the closest successor of a. Consider each element x appearing between a and b in the input sequence. This element x will also appear between a and b in output sequence if $(a-x) <= d$. This LaIS is achieved recursively. The authors found an LaIS with q as largest element as follows: they find an LaIS' such that it has largest element $p(p < q)$. Then q is appended to LaIS' to get LaIS. To find this LaIS, authors found the largest element (for each length) where the LIS ends. This entire approach can be executed in O(n log k) time, k is number of elements in LaIS. Solution to find LISs of windows having fixed size was proposed by Albert et al. [12]. The work was done to find the LISs of all the suffixes of active window. A data structure was maintained to keep record of all theses windows and their respective LISs. The proposed procedure is: the next element x of input sequence is inserted using the Young Tableau approach. Suppose x is inserted in place of Y in principal row. Then y is inserted in the next row by using the same technique. This way the element x is inserted in each row and a new row is created with x alone. The information obtained from the first window is analyzed and it is updated to reflect the information for the next window. This way, reducing the work to create the data structure for each window separately. This procedure can be executed in O(n log log n + OUTPUT) time. The sum of all |LIS| is termed as OUTPUT. Chen et al. [13] discussed another variant which has windows with variable lengths. These variable length windows are considered simply by ignoring few elements from front and appending few next elements to the previous window. For any element x, the length of the LIS which ends with x is termed as height of x. In this approach, the authors connected all the elements having same height. Also for each element, its predecessor and successor in LIS are recorded. For the next window this information is obtained by updating the information about the previous window. If it takes D_i time for deletion of ith data, the this entire approach can be implemented in $O(n + OUTPUT + \sum D_i)$ time.

Albert et al. [21] put their efforts on LICS (finding the LIS for a circular sequence for different pairs of first and last elements, keeping the relative order of the elements same. The notation t_p^d indicates the pth element of the LIS having p elements when the first d elements are processed. The authors found different LISs having same length but ending with distinct elements. Then the different LISs in various parts are compared to find the LICS. This approach takes $O(n^{3/2}\log n)$ time. Deorowicz S. [22] has also considered the same variant of LIS–LICS. He has worked with a belief that the LICS can be obtained by considering only few circular sequences and there is no need to work for all possible sequences (circular). He found the covers for sequences by merging the already computed covers. This procedure executes in $O(\min(nl, n \log n, l^3 \log n))$ time. Tseng et al. [1] have proposed an efficient solution to the LIS having minimum height. Here height refers to the sum of differences between all adjacent integers. According to the authors, such LIS can be obtained in two steps: 1) The length of the LIS which ends with each ith element is computed, (suppose this length is t). 2) Then they maintained a data structure for keeping a record of all those elements which has the same length of the LIS which ends with these elements. Then an element k is chosen such that the |LIS| which ends with k is t − 1 and the difference between t and k is minimum. It takes $O(n \log n)$ time to obtain the desired LIS. The authors also computed the LIS such that a particular given sequence is a part of the LIS.

3 Problem Definition

Consider a given finite sequence X of integers, a sub sequence Z is its increasing sub sequence iff all elements in Z are in ascending order and for every pair of elements (c, d) in Z with d > c, d appears after c in X also. A sub sequence Z which has maximum elements is termed Longest Increasing subsequence. Or ex. X = [8, 9, 2, 0, 3, 5,13, 11,12] then its LIS, Z = [0, 3, 5, 11, 12].

4 Proposed Work

We address the solution to LIS problem by dividing the problem into two equal size sub problems. Both sub problems are solved independently and then the second sub problem is solved again. We have used the Fredman's approach [5] to solve sub problems.

Consider a sequence of n elements. Form two sub problems by putting first n/2 elements in first sub problems and rest in second sub problems. While solving the sub problems, an output sequence is generated using Fredman's approach [5] and best predecessor is found for each element. While combining two sub problems, we need to work for only elements which belong to the second sub problem. The output sequence for the first sub problem is used to find optimal predecessors for the elements of the second sub problems.

Divide Phase: The LIS problem for n elements is divided into two sub problems such that elements from 1 to n/2 are placed in the first sub problem and the elements from n/2 + 1 to n are placed in the second sub problem. When there is single element, that element itself form the output sequence with single element and its predecessor is set to 0. After solving individual sub problems their solutions are combined. The algorithm for the divide phase is given below as Divide_LIS.

Combine Phase: The second sub problem and the solution of the first problem are the inputs to the combine phase. The elements of the second sub problem are addressed one by one. The solution of the first sub problem, say O^1 is used and extended to find predecessors for the elements of the second sub problem. For each element x of the second sub problem, a smallest element such that it is greater than x is found in O^1. Update the O^1 by replacing the found element with x. If such an element is not found then extend O^1 by putting x at the end of O^1. In both situations the element which appears before x in O^1 becomes the predecessor of x. The procedure for the combine phase is given as Combine_Sequential.

```
Divide_LIS(X, i, j)
    {
if(i==j)
                pred[i] = 0;
                max_len_I = i;
                return o^i = {A[i]};
    if(j>i)
                n = j-i +1;
                mid = ⌊((j-i+1)/2)⌋;
divide_LIS( X, i, i+mid-1);
divide_LIS ( X , mid+i, j);
                combine(X, i,j, mid, o^i);
}


Combine_Sequential (X, i, j, mid, o^i)
{
max_len = length(o^i);
c= i+mid-1;
n = j-i+1;
for p = c to n do
search smallest element in o^i such that it
is greater than X[c] using binary search;
// Suppose the found element is m in o^i at
// index b and (b-1)th element of o^i is at
// index d in X. if m is at 1st index in o^i
// then d is 0
If (found)
                Replace m with X[c] in o^i;
Else
                Place the element at end of o^i;
Pred[c] = d;
Len[c] = b;
If(b >= max_len)
                    max_len = b;
                    max_len_I = c;
Return o^i ;
}
```

Consider an example sequence $X = [8, 3, 9, 5, 2, 6, 1, 7]$. Now $X' = [8, 3, 9, 5]$ and $X'' = [2, 6, 1, 7]$. The O^1 generated while solving X' is $[3, 5]$ and predecessors for X' are $[0, 0, 2, 2]$. Here 8 and 3 do not have predecessors, and predecessors of 9 and 5 are 8 and 3 respectively. That is predecessors of 3rd and 4th elements is 2nd elements. Similarly while solving X'', we get the O^2 as $[1, 6, 7]$ and predecessors are $[0, 5, 0, 6]$. Now when we combine the solutions to solve entire X, the inputs we need are X and O^1. We start from the 5th element, that is we search an element in O^1 which is smallest but greater than 2, this element comes out to be 3 so we replace 3 with 2 and O^1 now becomes [2, 5] and since there is no element which appears before 2, so the predecessor of 2 is 0.

Next consider 6, and we do not find any element greater than 6, so it is placed at the end of O^1. Now O^1 becomes [2, 5, 6] and predecessor of 6 is set to 5. And so on. At the end O^1 becomes [1, 5, 6, 7] and predecessors of X becomes [0, 0, 2, 2, 0, 4, 0, 6]. The O^1 is now the output sequence for entire X. And LIS of X is found from the predecessors vector from the right end. The last element of LIS is 7, second last is 6 (6th element), 3rd last is 5 (4th element) and 1st element is 3 (2nd element). We need to maintain the index which achieves maximum length. The state space diagram for this sequence is shown in Fig. 1.

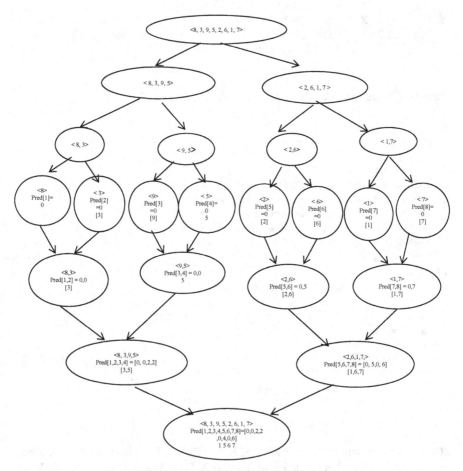

Fig. 1. State space diagram for <8, 3, 9, 5, 2, 6, 1, 7>

Here last index achieves maximum length. So while outputting the LIS, we started from the last element and moved towards left as shown in Fig. 2.

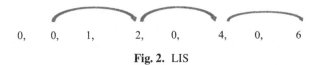

0,   0,   1,   2,   0,   4,   0,   6

Fig. 2. LIS

5 Multiprocessing

We have addressed the solution to LIS by partitioning it into two sub problems which can be solved independently. These sub problems can be executed using multiple processors simultaneously. But the solutions of two sub problems can be combined only after solving the sub problems. Thus here parallel and sequential processing is done in coordination (algorithm given as Parallel_LIS) with each other using the keywords *spawn* and *sync* [14]. To execute two methods in parallel, make each procedure call using *spawn* keyword. Since the *combine* procedure should start only after solving both sub problems, a keyword *sync* is required. If this keyword is not used then any statement after a spawned procedure does not wait for the spawned methods for completing their execution [6].

```
Parallel_LIS(X, i, j)
{
// Before the process starts set Pred[i,…,j] =
   // [0,…,0].
// for each k from i to j set O^i = {X[k]}.
// max_len_I   =k
If (j>i)
            n = j-i +1;
            mid = floor((j-i+1)/2);
            spawn Execute divide_LIS( X, i, i+mid-1)
            using processors P₁;
            spawn Execute divide_LIS ( X , mid+i, j)
            using processors P_{n/2};
            Sync Execute combine(X, i,j, mid, Oi) using
            processor P₁;
}
```

6 Analysis and Comparison

The time taken to divide a problem of size n into two sub problems is constant and is independent of the number of elements. The time needed to combine the solutions of solved sub problems is n/2(log n). Since the only elements (n/2) appearing in the second sub problem needs to be processed, so we included the factor n/2. We need to find the best predecessor for each element using binary search from the output of the first sub problem. The output sequence of the first sub problem can have maximum n/2 elements. During the combine phase this output sequence is modified and/or extended. So during the combine phase output sequence may extend maximum up to n elements. So for each element a binary search from a sequence of size n (maximum) is required. The size of the output sequence indicates the length of LIS. It is n when the input sequence is non-decreasing. So we have included the factor (log n). If we assume L as the |LIS| of the input sequence, then the factor (log L) can replace (log n). Hence the complexity equation becomes:

$$T(n) = 2T(n/2) + n/2 \text{ (log n)}$$

So the total time,

$$
\begin{aligned}
T(n) &= n/2 \log n + n/2 \log n/2 + n/2 \log n/4 \ldots\ldots \\
&= n/2(\log n + \log n/2 + \log n/4 \ldots) \\
&= n/2 \left(\log 2k + \log 2k - 1 + \ldots + \log 2\right) \left(\text{assuming } n = 2^k \text{ hence } \log n = k\right) \\
&= n/2 \left(k + (k-1) + (k-2) + (k-3) + \ldots 1\right) \\
&= n/2 \left(k(k+1)/2\right) \\
&= O(n/2 \text{ (k)2)} \\
&= O(n/2 \text{ (log n)2)} \qquad \text{since } k = \log n
\end{aligned}
$$

Now consider the time required to find the LIS for a given sequence of size n using n/2 processors T(n, n/2).

$$
\begin{aligned}
T(n, n/2) &= n/2 \log n + n/4 \log n/2 + n/8 \log n/4 + \ldots \\
&< n/2 \log n + n/4 \log n + n/8 \log n + \ldots \\
&= \log n(n/2 + n/4 + n/8 + \ldots) \\
&= \log n \left(2k - 1 + 2k - 2 + 2k - 3 + \ldots\right) \quad \text{(assuming } n = 2k) \\
&= \log n \left(2k - 1\right) \\
&= \log n \left(n - 1\right) \\
\Rightarrow T(n, n/2) &= O(\text{ n log n})
\end{aligned}
$$

Using single processor the presented approach executes in O(n/2 (log n)2) time and outputs optimal solution. Using n/2 processors, by solving independent sub problems in parallel, the proposed approach can be executed in O(n log n).time. The best solution using single processor has the time complexity of O(n log n). The proposed solution using multiple processors do not achieve the linear speed up. The total work carried out by using n/2 processors T(n, n/2) is (n/2 (n log n)). The efficiency achieved using multiple processors is T(n)/(n/2 * T(n, n/2)) = O(n log n)/(n/2 (n log n)) = 2/n. Hence the algorithm is not work optimal. The advantage with the proposed solution using single processor is that problem is solved by reducing it in size and for very large values of n it can be beneficial. Also, parallel processing can be done to handle large sized input sequence since the proposed approach is divide-and-conquer. The recurrence tree is shown in Fig. 3.

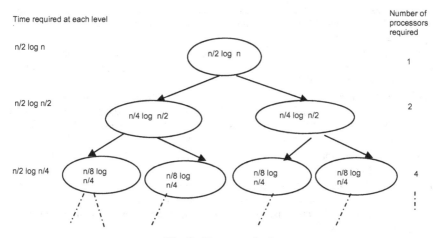

Fig. 3. Time complexity

7 Conclusion

The proposed sequential solution has time complexity $O(n/2 (\log n)^2)$. The D&C sequential solution presented in [6, 16] has the worst case run time of $O(n \log^2 n)$. The proposed solution using $n/2$ processors can be executed in $O(n \log n)$ time. The advantage with the proposed solution using single processor is that problem is solved by reducing it in size and for very large values of n it can be beneficial. A large input sequence can be processed in parallel by multiple processors that reduces time and computation overhead.

References

1. Tsai, Y.T.: The constrained longest common subsequence problem. Inf. Process. Lett. **88**(4), 173–176 (2003)
2. Delcher, A.L., Kasif, S., Fleischmann, R.D., Peterson, J., White, O., Salzberg, S.L.: Alignment of whole genomes. Nucleic Acids Res. **27**(11), 2369–2376 (1999)
3. Lascoux, A., Leclerc, B., Thibon, J.-Y.: The plactic monoid. In: Algebraic Combinatoric on Words, p. 10 (2002)
4. Schensted, C.: Longest increasing and decreasing subsequences. Can. J. Math. **13**(2), 179–191 (1961)
5. Fredman, M.L.: On computing the length of longest increasing subsequences. Discrete Math. **11**(1), 29–35 (1975)
6. Alam, M.R., Rahman, M.S.: A divide and conquer approach and a work-optimal parallel algorithm for the LIS problem. Inf. Process. Lett. **113**(13), 470–476 (2013)
7. Bespamyatnikh, S., Segal, M.: Enumerating longest increasing subsequences and patience sorting. Inf. Process. Lett. **76**(1–2), 7–11 (2000)
8. van Emde Boas, P.: Preserving order in a forest in less than logarithmic time and linear space. Inf. Process. Lett. **6**(3), 80–82 (1977)
9. Crochemore, M., Porat, E.: Fast computation of a longest increasing subsequence and application. Inf. Comput. **208**(9), 1054–1059 (2010)

10. Saks, M., Seshadhri, C.: Estimating the longest increasing sequence in polylogarithmic time. In: 2010 51st Annual IEEE Symposium on Foundations of Computer Science (FOCS), pp. 458–467. IEEE, October 2010

11. Elmasry, A.: The longest almost-increasing subsequence. In: Thai, M.T., Sahni, S. (eds.) COCOON 2010. LNCS, vol. 6196, pp. 338–347. Springer, Heidelberg (2010). https://doi.org/10.1007/978-3-642-14031-0_37

12. Albert, M.H., Golynski, A., Hamel, A.M., López-Ortiz, A., Rao, S.S., Safari, M.A.: Longest increasing subsequences in sliding windows. Theoret. Comput. Sci. **321**(2–3), 405–414 (2004)

13. Chen, E., Yang, L., Yuan, H.: Longest increasing subsequences in windows based on canonical antichain partition. Theoret. Comput. Sci. **378**(3), 223–236 (2007)

14. Cormen, T.H., Leiserson, C.E., Rivest, R.L., Stein, C.: Introduction to Algorithms. MIT Press, Cambridge (2009)

15. Lavanya, B., Murugan, A.: Discovery of longest increasing subsequences and its variants using DNA operations. Int. J. Eng. Technol. **5**(2), 1169–1177 (2013)

16. Rani, S., Rajpoot, D.S.: Improvised divide and conquer approach for the LIS problem. J. Discrete Algorithms **48**, 17–26 (2018)

17. Adi, S.S., et al.: Repetition-free longest common subsequence. Electron. Notes Discrete Math. **30**, 243–248 (2008)

18. Horowitz, E., Sahni, S.: Fundamentals of Computer Algorithms. Galgotia Publication Pvt. Ltd., New Delhi (2004)

19. Mouratov, M. https://stackoverflow.com/questions/12458641/applications-of-longest-increasing-subsquence. Accessed 10 Oct 2018

20. Journal of a Programmer. http://bryanpendleton.blogspot.in/2010/05/patience-diff.html. Accessed 20 Sept 2018

21. Albert, M.H., Atkinson, M.D., Nussbaum, D., Sack, J.R., Santoro, N.: On the longest increasing subsequence of a circular list. Inf. Process. Lett. **101**(2), 55–59 (2007)

22. Deorowicz, S.: An algorithm for solving the longest increasing circular subsequence problem. Inf. Process. Lett. **109**(12), 630–634 (2009)

US Air Quality Index Forecasting: A Comparative Study

Rishipal Singh[✉], Vanisha Singh, and Nonita Sharma

Department of Computer Science and Engineering,
Dr. B R Ambedkar National Institute of Technology, Jalandhar, Punjab, India
95rishipal@gmail.com, vanishasingh58@gmail.com,
nsnonita@gmail.com

Abstract. Air pollution refers to the release of pollutants that are harmful to human health and the entire planet, into the air. To publicize the extent of pollutants in the air at any point in time, government agencies use an air quality index. As the air quality index rises, public health risks increase. Many time series forecasting methods have been proposed to predict the air pollution so that effective measures can be taken to control it. Different methods work with different aspects and types of time series data. In light of these methods, this study aims to provide a comparative study of some of these models based on their forecasting accuracy. The data chosen for this study has been collected four times a day on a daily basis from the year 2000 to 2016, from different monitoring stations in California, USA.

Keywords: Air Quality Index (AQI) · ARIMA · SVR · ETS · Time series data

1 Introduction

Air pollution occurs due to the release of harmful gases, particulate matter, or liquid aerosol into deep air. When the concentration of these pollutants exceeds then naturally it is absorbed by the air. It is the property of air that these chemicals are absorbed into the air, it has harmful health and aesthetic effects. The main gaseous pollutants include sulfur dioxide, nitrogen dioxide, carbon monoxide and ozone. Other than these, minute solid or liquid particles known as particulates are also major air pollutants [1].

Time series data refers to the data which is time-dependent, i.e., each observation is recorded at a particular point in time. Such a series usually has three components – trend, seasonality, and residual. The trend shows the direction in which the series is moving, such as an upward trend or downward trend. Time series forecasting is widely being employed today in order to analyze univariate and multivariate time series data, and predict future values. Analyzing and forecasting the data helps in devising important measures that will be helpful in the future. Numerous forecasting models have been developed for this purpose [13, 18].

© Springer Nature Singapore Pte Ltd. 2020
U. Batra et al. (Eds.): REDSET 2019, CCIS 1229, pp. 91–102, 2020.
https://doi.org/10.1007/978-981-15-5827-6_8

As urbanization and industrialization are increasing, the air quality is decreasing day-by-day. Some of the major cities in the developed and the developing countries are already facing serious health issues due to the increasing air pollution. Therefore, it is necessary to analyze the AQI and predict the forthcoming quality so that actions can be taken to control it. Forecasting methodologies help in this area by providing various models and techniques to estimate future AQI values based on past observations. In this study, these models are used for forecasting the AQI of various cities in California, USA.

2 Problem

The aim of this study is to analyze and forecast the Air Quality Index values of different cities in the state of California (USA) based on the data available for the years 2000–2016.

In order to convey the extent of air pollution to the public, the government agencies use a metric known as the Air Quality Index (AQI). Quality of air is reported daily by the government. This AQI report includes how clean or polluted the air is and the content of various gases present in the air. Each country has its own formula for calculating AQI. The higher is the value of AQI, the greater is the level of air pollution. So health risks increase as the AQI rises.

The air quality index is divided into six groups to categorize the level of health concern based on its value. The Table 1 presented here shows each of the six groups and the associated level of health concern. For example – an AQI of 50 reflects good air quality and no serious effect on public health. On the other hand, an AQI of 300 shows very poor air quality and severe impact on human health [2].

Table 1. AQI and corresponding level of health concern

Air quality index	Level of health concern
0 to 50	Good health
51 to 100	Moderate health
101 to 150	Unhealthy for sensitive groups
151 to 200	Unhealthy
201 to 300	Very unhealthy
301 to 500	Hazardous to health

Each of the six categories can be described as follows –

- 0 to 50: "Good" air quality index and the level of air pollution has little or no health effect.
- 51 to 100: "Moderate" air quality. Air quality is acceptable but it might have a moderate health concern for sensitive people
- 101 to 150: "Unhealthy for Sensitive Groups". The air pollution level may not affect the general public but people with lung or heart disease will be at greater risk.

- 151 to 200: "Unhealthy" air quality. The general public will have some adverse health effects.
- 201 to 300: "Very unhealthy" air quality. Extremely serious health concerns will be in line for everybody.
- 301 to 500: "Hazardous" air quality. Emergency conditions of severe health impacts for the entire population.

The following Table 1 gives a summary of the different AQI ranges and their corresponding level of health concern.

The dataset chosen for this study is the U.S. Air Quality Index (January 2000–May 2016). The observations were recorded four times a day every day at various monitoring stations situated in different states of USA. Since the dataset is quite large, a portion of it is used in this study. Data of 34 cities in the state of California are selected. It consists of AQI values depending on major pollutants such as nitrogen dioxide, sulfur dioxide, ozone and carbon monoxide.

A time series can be stationary or non-stationary depending on the nature of its components. If the mean, variance and co-variance of the series do not vary with time, then the series is stationary. So, a series with seasonality or trend in the data is not stationary. The AQI data used here showed stationarity in most of the cities. According to the model used, different components of the data are taken into consideration.

3   Existing Forecasting Models

A number of models exist for time series analysis and forecasting. Some of the most widely used models are described below.

3.1   ARIMA Model

ARIMA stands for Autoregressive Integrated Moving Average. It is a forecasting method for univariate time series data. This group of models aims to describe the autocorrelations in the data [3]. It is generalized from the Autoregressive Moving Average (ARMA) model. There are three components in this model –

- AR: Autoregression. This means that the variable is regressed against itself. We use linear combination of past values for forecasting the current values.
- I: Integrated. This component shows the use of differencing of the observations in the time series [4]. In differencing, an observation is replaced by the difference between its value and the previous value.
- MA: Moving Average. A linear combination of the error terms makes up the regression error [5]. It uses past errors in a regression-like model.

Each of these components is provided as a parameter to the ARIMA model. The standard notation used is ARIMA (p, d, q). The parameters are non-negative integers and are described as follows –

- p - This is the order of the autoregressive model. It is the number of lag observations in the model.
- d - This is the order of differencing, i.e., the number of times the observations are differenced.
- q – This is the order of the moving average model.

Based on the non-zero parameter, the model can be referred in different ways. For example, ARIMA(1, 0, 0) is AR(1).

ARIMA models are applied where the time-series data is stationary, i.e., the properties of the time series do not depend on the time when the series is observed. In case the data has non-stationarity it can be differenced (more than once) to make it stationary.

An autoregressive model of order p, AR(p), can be written as

$$z_t = c + \phi_1 z_{t-1} + \phi_2 z_{t-2} + \cdots + \phi_p z_{t-p} + e_t, \tag{1}$$

A moving average model of order q, MA(q), can be written as

$$z_t = c + e_t + \theta_1 e_{t-1} + \theta_2 e_{t-2} + \cdots + \theta_q e_{t-q} \tag{2}$$

An ARIMA model can be given as

$$z'_t = c + \phi_1 z'_{t-1} + \cdots + \phi_p z'_{t-p} + \theta_1 e_{t-1} + \cdots + \theta_q e_{t-q} + e_t \tag{3}$$

Where z'_t is the differenced series and e_t, is white noise. The predictors on the right-hand side include both lagged values of z_t and lagged errors [3].

3.2 Seasonal ARIMA Model

ARIMA models can be also be used to model seasonal data. SARIMA is a variation of the ARIMA model suitable for analyzing seasonal univariate time series data. The seasonal components are included as the parameters of the models. The SARIMA model is given as SARIMA(p, d, q) (P, D, Q) m, where the lowercase parameters depict the non-seasonal part and the uppercase parameters depict for the seasonal part [6]. The four new elements in this model are –

- P – seasonal autoregressive order
- D – seasonal differencing order
- Q – seasonal moving average order
- m – the period of time series

The remaining non-seasonal parameters are same as that in the case of ARIMA model.

Here, the m parameter influences the other seasonal parameters. For example, in SARIMA(2, 1, 0) (1, 1, 0) 12, the value m = 12 means that the data is monthly and suggests a yearly seasonal cycle. Also, a P = 1 means that the first seasonally offset observation will be used in the model; D = 1 will calculate a first order seasonal difference and a Q = 1 will use the first order errors in the model.

To eliminate the additive seasonal effects, this model performs differencing at a lag equal to the number of seasons. Using the ACF and PACF plots, the correlation at seasonal lags give the values to be used for seasonal elements.

3.3 Support Vector Regression

Support Vector Regression (SVR) is based on the same principles as Support Vector Machine (SVM) classification. The difference is that in the former case the dependent variable is numerical instead of categorical. SVR uses the concept of kernel tricking. Kernel tricking means converting data from lower dimensions to higher dimensions such that classes can be easily classified. Those planes which divide the classes into higher dimensions are called hyperplane. Higher degree linearly separating hyperplanes is basically formed by SVMs. The vectors divide the higher dimensional space. We represent data point as $(\vec{x}, y)$, where, $\vec{x} = (x_1,..., x_p)$ is vector of attributes or features and y is tuple in classification class. Mathematicians use attributes while data scientists use features. In case of SVM mostly we use two classes, one for positive and another for negative [7].

Consider p dimensional attribute and features where x is feature vector of size p dimensional, i.e. $\vec{x} = (x_1,...,x_p) \in R_p$, then we can mathematically define an affine hyperplane by the following equation:

$$b_0 + b_1 X_1 + ... + b_p X_p = 0 \tag{4}$$

$b_0 \neq 0$ gives us an affine plane (i.e. it does not pass through the origin). We can also write as:

$$b_j + \sum_{j=1}^{p} b_j x_j = 0 \tag{5}$$

Equation 5 is dot product of multidimensional (an inner dot product). We can write as:

$$\vec{b} \cdot \vec{x} + b_0 = 0 \tag{6}$$

If an element $\vec{x} \in R_p$ then it lies on hyperplane the p − 1-dimensional. Elements $\vec{x}$ above the plane satisfy:

$$\vec{b} \cdot \vec{x} + b_0 > 0 \tag{7}$$

While those below it satisfy

$$\vec{b} \cdot \vec{x} + b_0 < 0 \tag{8}$$

We can calculate the sign and determine which side of the hyperplane the point lies on. The element is classified in two classes either positive or negative (+ or −) by calculating the sign of the expression $\vec{b} \cdot \vec{x} + b0$. This concept will form the basis of a supervised classification technique [7]. We have basically four kernels that are used to manipulate data points in the given data. For non-linear distribution, we can use kernel functions. The commonly used kernel functions are − (i) Linear, (ii) Polynomial, (iii) Radial Basis and (iv) Sigmoid. Linear kernel function is used for linearly separable distribution as we saw in SVM [9]. For polynomial separable distribution, we use the polynomial kernel and for radial, i.e., if the data points are circularly separable then we can use radial basis. Sigmoid is a rare case of kernel function that is used for special distribution which is in shape of a sigmoidal function [9].

3.4 Error, Trend and Seasonality

Exponential smoothing is mostly used by ETS which stands for error, trend and seasonality. ETS works well with seasonality and is often used for time series analysis. Exponential smoothing is used as a window for calculating weighted average exponentially. In many other streams of engineering ETS is used for signal processing, in particular, dynamic signal processing for removing noise [11].

To predict the future values of time series $z_{T+1}, \ldots, z_{T+\tau}$, where τ is a time horizon, we mostly use exponential forecasting. Exponential smoothing is widely used for forecasting time series. Exponential forecasting uses exponential decrease in past observations so it can predict with high accuracy. Here $\alpha > 0$ is a smoothing parameter [12]. Older observation has lesser value than recent observations. So in exponential method, older values get less weight than the newer values [8].

When there is no trend or seasonal pattern, then exponential smoothing works very well. Exponential consider past values where recent values don't depend tend wise or seasonal wise. Then the past and recent values are independent. Exponential method is an expert in this property.

Initial series estimate at time period t = 0 is

$$l_0 = \vec{y} = \frac{\sum_{t=1}^{n} y_t}{n} \tag{9}$$

Updated estimate by using the smoothing equation

$$l_T = \alpha y_T + (1 - \alpha) l_{T-1} \tag{10}$$

Where $\alpha \in (0, 1)$
Note that

$$l_T = a y_T + (1 - \alpha) l_{T-1}$$
$$= \alpha y_T + (1 - \alpha) \left[\alpha y_{T-1} + (1 - \alpha) l_{T-2} \right]$$
$$= \alpha y_T + (1 - \alpha) \alpha y_{T-1} + (1 - \alpha)^2 l_{T-2} \tag{11}$$

$$l_T = \alpha y_T + (1 - \alpha) \alpha y_{T-1} + (1 - \alpha)^2 \alpha y_{T-2} + \cdots + (1 - \alpha)^{T-1} \alpha y_1 + (1 - \alpha)^T l_0 \tag{12}$$

4 Results

Out of a number of time series forecasting methods available, three methods – ARIMA, ETS, and SVR, have been used in this study. The measure of accuracy chosen tells which model performed the best on our data. In this case, root mean square error (RMSE) and mean square error (MSE) have been chosen as the deciding criteria for measuring the performance of the models.

$$RMSE = \sqrt{\frac{\sum_{i=1}^{n}(y_t - \hat{y}_t)^2}{n}}. \tag{13}$$

Where

y_t is the actual value at time t
$\hat{y}_t$ is the fitted value at time t
n is the number of observations

The lower the RMSE value, the lesser is the error in modelling. So, the model which gives the smallest value of RMSE is chosen as the one with the best predictions.

The dataset used consists of the air quality index of 34 cities in California, USA, recorded four times a day every day from January 2000 to May 2016. For forecasting purpose, recent data from January 2014 to May 2016 has been used, averaged per day. This portion consists of 22 cities, 14 of which show a daily frequency and the remaining cities have a monthly frequency. Each model is applied separately to every city in the dataset and the results are analyzed to find out which model can make the most accurate predictions [9].

ARIMA works on univariate time series data with the non-stationarity (if exists) and seasonality component removed. Since all of the cities, except one, showed stationarity, there was no need to perform differencing on those observations. A differencing of order 1 was performed on the non-stationary data [14]. Many variations of the model (different values for p and q) were applied, including auto ARIMA. The autocorrelation function (ACF) and partial autocorrelation function (PACF) plots are used for determining the order of the AR and MA components. These plots determine the relationship between the lagged values of a time series. In auto ARIMA, the values of the parameters are automatically chosen by the algorithm, i.e., the user doesn't need to provide these values explicitly. Using the automated ARIMA algorithm, the RMSE values observed for some of the cities are given in Table 2. Since the data originally had seasonality and trend components, ARIMA didn't provide satisfactory results.

ETS considers the error, trend and seasonality components of the time series. The main advantage of ETS is that it also considers the previous error in an exponential manner. It defines some parameters like additive, multiplicative or auto. For example, if we want to consider error additively, then we need to use "AZZ". We can make different combinations of ETS. In our case, the data has trend and seasons so we only use additive; multiplicative does not work well [8].

Table 2. RMSE values for ARIMA

City	RMSE
Concord	3.708047
Long Beach	10.75845
Arden-Arcade	4.999121
Burbank	8.09347
Calexico	9.250098
Capitan	1.142004
Los Angeles	8.357455

Dimensionality does not depend on computation complexity which is the main advantage of SVR. As we know, SVR is next version of SVM, so versatility is also included. We can not only predict in linearly fashion, but we also need some kind of polynomial form of regression since our data includes many ups and downs. As we know our data has seasons and trends, SVR fits very accurately where we have a uniform pattern and in our data, seasonal pattern ups and downs are uniformly distributed [10]. The above description leads us to use SVR. The second reason why we are using SVR in this study is that it is robust to outliers, i.e., outliers will not affect the forecast. SVR can predict by measuring confidence especially when confidence is low. Confidence is used in classification while classification is based in posterior distribution. Due to the posterior distribution, we can easily forecast in SVR. In the formula of SVR, we can use the linear kernel for a simple classification like SVM; for more complex classification we can use polynomial, radial basis kernels. The polynomial kernel is the most commonly used kernel for regression and for circular regression, we use radial kernel. In our case, we can only use polynomial because the time series is never in a circular shape. We can also define how many degrees we want in polynomial with degree parameter. In our case, we are working in 2d shape and we will not move in any direction except in the front as in the case of sin or cos function so we will define 2 for the degree. For making SVR soft or hard we can define Cost(C); if we increase C we are making SVR softer and if C is near to 0, SVR is getting harder and harder [16].

In this comparative study, three different time series analysis and forecast models have been used on the data to find the one which fits and performs the best. The entire process has been depicted in Fig. 1. With ARIMA, it was found that forecast results are not very accurate and the error is higher than the other two models. A straight line is seen as the prediction in the graph which shows that due to non-seasonal data input, no variations are considered in the forecasting.

Since the type of time series applicable to each of the model varies, the predictions are also different. The automated ARIMA algorithm performs poorly on the time series since the data is quite varying for some cities with seasonality and trend included. SVR, on the other hand, performs quite well with the existing seasonality in the data.

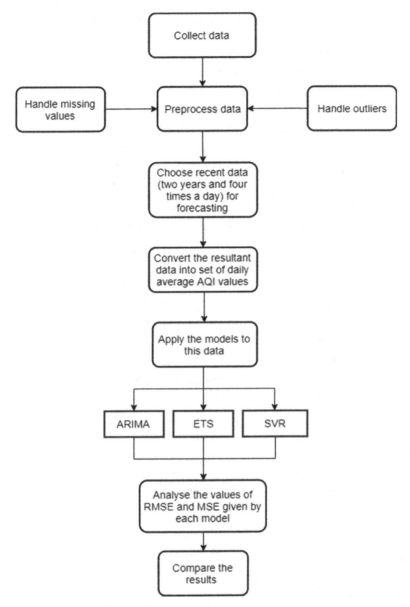

Fig. 1. Flowchart of the methodology used

The RMSE values for each of the models applied in all the cities are shown below in Table 3.

Mean squared Error (MSE) calculates the average squared difference between estimated value and original value. Lower value of MSE indicates lower error.

Table 3. RMSE values for ARIMA, ETS and SVR

City	ARIMA	ETS	SVR
Concord	3.708047	5.464905	0.011123
Bethel Island	2.925316	4.315601	0.008877
Long Beach	10.75845	11.67406	0.53461
Arden-Arcade	4.999121	7.422555	0.035755
Burbank	8.09347	8.866629	0.518429
Calexico	9.250098	12.14948	0.204191
Capitan	1.142004	1.574987	0.001263
Los Angeles	8.357455	9.143726	0.00341
Lompoc	3.48618	4.912189	0.001487
Costa Mesa	7.519503	8.218879	0.052072
Oakland	5.065092	7.4637	0.016167
San Pablo	4.656862	6.454437	0.009891
Rubidoux	8.374225	8.982876	0.046649
Vallejo	5.134612	7.515312	0.012834
V. Air Force Base	1.47653	2.201293	0.009974
Victorville	7.234753	11.42314	0.026
Eureka	2.777908	3.949711	0.029509
Fontana	9.493484	10.56789	0.069085
Fresno	5.451755	8.300154	0.107313
San Jose	7.121869	7.66132	0.004482

Mathematically, MSE can be computed as follows:

$$\text{MSE} = \frac{\sum_{i=1}^{n}(y_t - \hat{y}_t)^2}{n} \tag{14}$$

Where

y_t is the actual value at time t
$\hat{y}_t$ is the fitted value at time t
n is the number of observations

The model with the lowest MSE values shows the best performance since its predicted values are closest to the actual ones. Among the three models employed in this study, the Support Vector Regression model gives the lowest mean squared error values for all the cities. This suggests that it fits well over the data and can give much better forecasting results.

The MSE values for each of the models applied to all the cities are shown below in Table 4.

Table 4. MSE values for ARIMA, ETS and SVR

City	ARIMA	ETS	SVR
Concord	13.7496	29.8652	0.0001
Bethel Island	8.5575	18.6244	0.0001
Long Beach	115.7442	136.2837	0.2858
Arden-Arcade	24.9912	55.0943	0.0013
Burbank	65.5043	78.6171	0.2688
Calexico	85.5643	147.6099	0.0417
Capitan	1.3042	2.4806	0.0000
Los Angeles	69.8471	83.6077	0.0000
Lompoc	12.1535	24.1296	0.0000
Costa Mesa	56.5429	67.5500	0.0027
Oakland	25.6552	55.7068	0.0003
San Pablo	21.6864	41.6598	0.0001
Rubidoux	70.1276	80.6921	0.0022
Vallejo	26.3642	56.4799	0.0002
V. Air Force Base	2.1801	4.8457	0.0001
Victorville	52.3417	130.4881	0.0007
Eureka	7.7168	15.6002	0.0009
Fontana	90.1262	111.6803	0.0048
Fresno	29.7216	68.8926	0.0115
San Jose	50.7210	58.6958	0.0000

5 Conclusion and Future Scope

In this comparative study, three different time series analysis and forecast models – ARIMA, ETS, and SVR have been used on the US Air Quality Index data (2000–2016) to find the one which fits and performs the best over this data. ARIMA and ETS do not perform very well in this case. The motto behind applying SVR is that it is desirable to accurately fit the model on the given data. Linear and non-linear regression can be performed using SVR. It performs much better than the other two models because it performs really well with high dimensional and noisy data. It gives the least error compared to the other methods.

The future scope of this study will include taking into consideration the relationship between the air pollutants and also with other geographical factors to better analyze the data. Multivariate relation might improve the existing results. No one method is perfect in all the situations; it will change with the region and pollutants under consideration.

References

1. Nathanson, J.A.: Air pollution, 31 October 2018. https://www.britannica.com/science/air-pollution. Accessed 22 May 2019
2. Air Quality Index (AQI) Basics, AirNow, 31 August 2016. https://airnow.gov/index.cfm?action=aqibasics.aqi. Accessed 22 May 2019
3. Hyndman, R.J., Athanasopoulos, G.: Forecasting: Principles and Practice (2018). https://otexts.com/fpp2. Accessed 22 May 2019
4. Brownlee, J.: How to create an ARIMA model for time series forecasting in Python, 9 January 2017. https://machinelearningmastery.com/arima-for-time-series-forecasting-with-python/
5. Wikipedia, Autoregressive integrated moving average. https://en.wikipedia.org/wiki/Autoregressive_integrated_moving_average. Accessed 20 May 2019
6. Brownlee, J.: A gentle introduction to SARIMA for time series forecasting in Python, 17 August 2018. https://machinelearningmastery.com/sarima-for-time-series-forecasting-in-python/. Accessed 20 May 2019
7. Azoff, E.: Neural Network Time Series Forecasting of Financial Markets, 1st edn. Wiley, New York (1994)
8. Meyer, D.: SVM. https://www.rdocumentation.org/packages/e1071/versions/1.7-1/topics/svm
9. Vapnik, V., Golowich, S.E., Smola, A.J.: Support vector method for function approximation, regression estimation, and signal processing. In: NIPS 1996 (1997)
10. Schiilkop, P.B., Burgest, C., Vapnik, V.: Extracting support data for a given task. In: Proceedings, First International Conference on Knowledge Discovery & Data Mining. AAAI Press, Menlo Park (1995)
11. Chatfield, C.: What is the 'best' method of forecasting? J. Appl. Stat. **15**(1), 19–38 (1988)
12. Hipel, K.W., McLeod, A.I.: Time Series Modelling of Water Resources and Environmental Systems. Elsevier, Amsterdam (1994)
13. Elman, J.: Finding structure in time. Cogn. Sci. **14**(2), 179–211 (1990)
14. Hwang, H.: Insights into neural-network forecasting time series corresponding to ARMA (p, q) structures. Omega **29**(3), 273–289 (2001)
15. Hyndman, R.: Exponential Smoothing State Space Model. https://www.rdocumentation.org/packages/forecast/versions/8.7/topics/ets. Accessed 20 May 2019
16. Astolfi, R., Lorenzoni, L., Oderkirk, J.: Informing policy makers about future health spending: a comparative analysis of forecasting methods in OECD countries. Health Policy **107**(1), 1–10 (2012)
17. Ellis, P.: Error, trend, seasonality - ETS and its forecast model friends, 27 November 2016. http://freerangestats.info/blog/2016/11/27/ets-friends. Accessed 20 May 2019
18. Sharma, N., Juneja, A.: Combining of random forest estimates using LSboost for stock market index prediction. In: 2017 2nd International Conference for Convergence in Technology (I2CT), pp. 1199–1202. IEEE (2017)

Effect Analysis of Contrast Enhancement Techniques on Cancer Classification in Colon Histopathology Images Using Machine Learning

Manju Dabass[✉], Sharda Vashisth, and Rekha Vig

The NorthCap University, Gurugram, India
manjurashi87@gmail.com, {shardavashisth,rekhavig}@ncuindia.edu

Abstract. The glandular morphology analysis done within the colon histopathological images is a crucial step required for grade determination of colon cancer. But the manual segmentation is quite laborious as well as time-consuming. Also, it suffers from the subjectivity present among the pathologists. Thus in order to minimize these limitations, the rising computational pathology has guided the researchers towards the advancement of various unsupervised and automated computerized methods for the gland segmentation task. However, this automated gland segmentation still remains a tricky task owing to numerous aspects like the need for high-level resolution for exact delineation of glandular boundaries, etc. Thus, in order to help researchers to develop automated gland segmentation techniques, various image enhancement techniques based on contrast adjustment are explained in this paper and their enhancement results are analyzed based on both objective qualitative assessment as well as subjective assessment given in the form of scores by the pathologists. And thus based on the qualitative analysis, a new combined technique i.e. Colormap Enhanced Image Sharpening is proposed in order to get an enhanced image in which all the critical elements are easily detectable. These techniques' effectiveness is also checked by applying them to do the image classification into two classes having benign and malignant cancer using the machine learning technique i.e. Bag of Features. The classification accuracy is examined for each enhancement techniques. These techniques' results will thus help pathologists in better colon histopathology image analysis.

Keywords: Bag of features · Colon cancer · Histopathology image analysis · Image enhancement · Image classification

1 Introduction

According to [1], colorectal cancer is among the top five cancers affecting the world population wherein approx 95% of all the colorectal cancers are adenocarcinomas. The colorectal adenocarcinomas typically build up in the colon or rectum linings which formulate the large intestine. It is characterized mainly by the glandular formations. There are four tissue components present in glands i.e. epithelial nuclei, cytoplasm, lumen and stroma (mainly blood vessels, nervous tissues, connective tissues, etc.). The stroma is not considered as a part of the gland while the epithelial cells enclose the cytoplasm

© Springer Nature Singapore Pte Ltd. 2020
U. Batra et al. (Eds.): REDSET 2019, CCIS 1229, pp. 103–119, 2020.
https://doi.org/10.1007/978-981-15-5827-6_9

and lumen and thus, works as gland boundary. The benign i.e. non-cancerous glands as shown in Fig. 1(a) are easily analyzed using the automated segmentation algorithms owing to significant variances in size, texture, staining, shape, and location of glands. But in the malignant i.e. cancerous case, the glandular objects are significantly different as compared to non-cancerous case. Further for well-differentiated cases, more than 95% of the tumor is gland forming. Also, for poorly differentiated cases, the typical glandular appearance is lost as shown in Fig. 1(b). Hence, the glandular formation loss increases with the increase in cancer grading due to which glandular morphology is one of the critical factors in determining the cancer grade. Thus, the Glandular Histologic Examination with Hematoxylin & Eosin stain is the clinical practice applied for differentiation assessment of cancer within the colorectal adenocarcinoma. Also, the degree of glandular formation is used by the pathologists for giving the final decision for the tumor's grade or degree of differentiation.

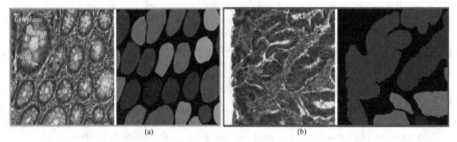

Fig. 1. Examples of gland segmentation challenge dataset (a) benign case with ground truth annotations and (b) malignant case with ground truth annotations. [3]

However, automated gland segmentation is still a tricky task owing to various aspects [2] such as

1. For accurately delineate the glandular boundaries, there is a need for a high-resolution level.
2. There is variation in the size and shapes of glands with the increase in cancer grade.
3. Existence of poignant clustered substances in the tissue samples which makes it complicated for automatic segmentation techniques to divide them into individual entities.
4. The sole gland object output gives very limited information for diagnosis making. To increase the diagnostic making power, extra information is needed like uncertainty prediction, and segmentation of additional histological components such as lumen, dense nuclei area, artifacts, etc.

Thus, to assist pathologists in giving an accurate diagnosis as well as assisting the research community to strengthen the automated segmentation techniques, we have assessed one of the pre-processing techniques i.e. contrast based image enhancement in this paper. The effectiveness of these techniques is also examined by applying the 2-class image classification using the Bag of Features algorithm of machine learning.

2   Literature Review

There are a lot of techniques proposed for medical image enhancement. Some of them are good and some of them lack feasibility in a real-life scenario. The various image enhancement techniques used recently for enhancing various medical imaging modalities are summarized in Table 1.

Table 1. Enhancement techniques applied in various medical imaging modalities

Authors	Imaging modalities	Enhancement technique
Jeevaka et al. [6]	MRI images	Image sharpening
Reddy et al. [7]	Medical imaging	Histogram equalization
Sahu et al. [8]	Color retinal fundus	CLAHE
Cao et al. [9]	Medical imaging	Gamma correction
Duan et al. [10]	Mammograms	Image sharpening using un-sharp masking
Hsu et al. [11]	Medical prostate cancer images	Color histogram equalization
Li et al. [12]	Medical images	CLAHE and un-sharp masking
Ullah et al. [13]	MRI images	Histogram equalization
Mzoughi et al. [14]	MRI brain glioma tumor images	Histogram equalization
Dhal et al. [15]	Color retinal images	Histogram equalization with firefly algorithm
Clark et al. [16]	Radiology images	Image sharpening
Tiwari et al. [17]	Medical images	Adaptive histogram equalization with homomorphic filtering
Bhairannawar et al. [18]	Medical images	Adaptive histogram equalization in HSV space
Dabass et al. [19]	Mammograms	CLAHE

3   Image Enhancement Techniques

The Image Enhancement techniques are those techniques which are applied to enhance the interpretability of the information content present in the images. These techniques are used to smoothen, emphasize, or sharpen specific features like contrast; luminance; brightness, etc. present in an image by in order to improve its visual perception. There are different types of enhancement techniques i.e., contrast adjustment; filtering; morphology; neighborhood and block processing; deblurring; and image arithmetic. From all these techniques we have chosen contrast based image enhancement techniques for the analysis which remaps the image intensity values so that the resultant image has sharp differences between lowest intensity and highest intensity pixels. We applied them to the colon histopathological images and analyze their impact in order to help pathologists in better colon histopathology image analysis. It will also contribute to increasing the analytical as well as the diagnostic accuracy. The various Image Enhancement techniques [3] applied for medical image analyses are elucidated in this section.

3.1 Image Sharpening

Image sharpness is the contrast difference between the different colors present in it. Thus, the image sharpening technique amplifies the contrast along the edges where the different colors convene. Its main aim is to highlight very fine details present in an image and is particularly used for the enhancement of images' high-frequency components. In this paper, the image sharpening is done using the unsharp masking method where first, a smoothened version of the original image is made to subtract from the original image and then it is added to the original image in order to tip the image balance towards the sharper content of the original image. Mathematically, this process is defined as

$$E(m, n) = O(m, n) + \alpha[O(m, n) - \bar{O}(m, n)] \tag{1}$$

Where, $O(m, n)$ is the original image $\bar{O}(m, n)$ is the blurred or smoothened version of the original image, α is the weighting fraction and $E(m, n)$ is the final enhanced sharpened resulted image.

For example, in [5], the image sharpening technique is used for MRI images to enhance the tumor area. Generally, due to the noise, the MRI images become hazy. Thus, by the sharpening technique usage, the tumor was easily and effectively detected as well as segmented from the MRI images.

3.2 Colormap Enhancement

In this technique, scaling by a constant factor is done for all pixels present in an image. Mathematically, this process can be defined as

$$E(m, n) = O(m, n) * K \tag{2}$$

Where, $O(m, n)$ is the original image, K is the scaling constant and $E(m, n)$ is the final enhanced image.

It is applied for altering the contrast of the image in order to change the range of luminance values present in it.

3.3 Proposed Colormap Enhanced Image Sharpening

In this technique, the above two techniques are merged where first the image contrast is changed by applying the contrast adjustment technique and then the image sharpening technique is applied to the resultant image where the smoothened version is subtracted from the resultant image and scaled by a weighting fraction and then added to the resultant image. Thus, change in the range of luminance values and the alignment of the image balance towards the sharper content present in the original image both are done in order to get a better-enhanced image. Mathematically, this process is defined as

$$E(m, n) = \left[O(m, n) + \alpha \left\{ O(m, n) - \bar{O}(m, n) \right\} \right] * K \tag{3}$$

Where, $O(m, n)$ is the original image, $\bar{O}(m, n)$ is the blurred or smoothened version of the original image, α is the weighting fraction, K is the scaling constant and $E(m, n)$ is the final enhanced image.

3.4   Histogram Equalization

The histogram is a very prominent way to show the intensities summary present in an image. The technique of histogram equalization is applied for spreading out the gray levels present in an image in order to make them uniformly distributed across their range. It reassigns the pixels' brightness values based on the image histogram in order to make the histogram of the resultant image as flat as possible. This technique is applied for making the minor variations present within various regions to be seen adequately which earlier were appearing nearly uniform in the original image. This process can be defined as

$$S = T(R) \quad 0 \leq R \leq L - 1 \tag{4}$$

Where R is denoting the intensities present in the original image, L is denoting the gray levels present in the original image, T is denoting the transformations (intensity mapping) applied and S is denoting the output intensity levels produced for every pixel in the original image having the intensity R.

3.5   Contrast Limited Adaptive Histogram Equalization (CLAHE)

This technique is used for the improvement of low contrast issue found in images by limiting the contrast enhancement. The contrast enhancement can be defined as the slope of the function linking the original image intensity with the preferred resultant image intensities and is directly correlated to the histogram height at the intensity value. Thus, contrast limitation can be performed by restraining the slope of this linking function and stipulating the clip limit for the histogram height according to the contrast need.

While histogram equalization works upon the complete input image, CLAHE works on small portions in the image, called tiles. It augments the contrast of each tile in order to match the histogram of the output region approximately to a specified histogram. After applying the equalization, CLAHE unites neighboring tiles by the use of bilinear interpolation so that artificially induced boundaries get eliminated. Here unlike the histogram equalization, the noise does not get enhanced with the contrast enhancement.

3.6   Gamma Correction

This technique can be defined by the non- linear power-law transformation i.e.

$$E(m, n) = [O(m, n)]^\gamma \tag{5}$$

Where γ is the gamma constant and can take either integer or fraction value.

This non-linearity must be compensated by using different values of γ so that the correct reproduction of intensity is achieved. For color images, this is performed by either decomposing the color image into RGB components or HSV components. Each plane is transformed separately by choosing different values of γ and then after the transformations, all individual planes are merged back into one enhanced image.

4 SVM Classifier Using Bag of Features

This technique is adapted from natural language processing. This technique basically does the classification by using the vocabulary constructed by extracting SURF features from each image category. The following algorithm is used for this:

1. Feature point locations are selected using the Grid method. Then,
2. SURF features are extracted from the selected feature point locations and balancing of the number of features across all image categories is performed by keeping a certain percentage of the strongest features from every category.
3. K-Means clustering is used to create a visual vocabulary of SURF features known as 'bag of Features' which will provide an encoding method for measuring the visual word occurrences in an image. Here, a histogram for every image is produced which has a new and reduced representation of that image. This histogram forms a basis for training a classifier and for the actual image classification. Basically, it utilizes an encoding method using the input bag object in order to formulate feature vectors representing each image category from the Training Set.
4. The SVM classifier is trained using visual vocabulary features i.e. 'bag Of Features' object in which Encoded training images from each category are fed into this classifier.
5. Test the images for cancer classification and evaluate classification accuracy.

5 Performance Analyzing Qualitative Matrices

For evaluating the quality of the resulted enhanced medical images, two criteria in the form of objective criteria and subjective criteria are used.

5.1 Objective Criteria

For evaluating the objective assessment, the following quantitative matrices [23] are used:

- **Entropy:** It is a statistical quantitative measure of randomness which can be used to illustrate the image texture. It gives the degree of information content present in images. For good enhancement techniques, the entropy value of the enhanced image should remain near to the entropy value of the original image. It can be calculated as

$$E(Image) = -\sum_{k=o}^{l-1} p(k) \log_2 p(k) \tag{6}$$

Where $p(k)$ is the occurrence probability for the value of k in the image $Image$ and $l = 2^q$ indicates the number of grey levels present in the image. Closer the entropy value to q indicates the high information content. For example, if the value of q is 8 then entropy value closer to this indicates high information content.

- **Mean Square Error or MSE:** It represents the cumulative squared error between two images. If O is the original image and E is the enhanced image with both having physical size of M × N, then MSE can be calculated as

$$MSE = \frac{\sum_{x=0}^{N-1} \sum_{y=0}^{M-1} O^2(x, y)}{\sum_{x=0}^{N-1} \sum_{y=0}^{M-1} \{O(x, y) - E(x, y)\}^2} \tag{7}$$

For having a high quality enhanced image, the MSE should be minimum.

- **Peak Signal to Noise Ratio (PSNR):** It is defined as a measure of peak error and can be calculated as:

$$PSNR = 10 \, Log_{10}\left(\frac{Max^2}{MSE}\right) \tag{8}$$

The high value of PSNR signifies that the enhanced image is of high quality. The PSNR and MSE matrices estimate absolute errors.

- **Structure Similarity Index Measure (SSIM):** It is an image quality assessing metric that is used for assessing the illustrative impact of the three distinctiveness of an image i.e. luminance, contrast and structure and is calculated as

$$SSIM(x, y) = \frac{(2Mean_x.Mean_y + C_1)(2CV_{xy} + C_2)}{\left(Mean_x^2 + Mean_y^2 + C_1\right)\left(SD_x^2 + SD_y^2 + C_2\right)} \tag{9}$$

Where $Mean_x$ & $Mean_y$ are the Local means, $SD_X \& SD_y$ are the Standard Deviations, and CV_{xy} is the Cross-Variance for images X & Y.

5.2 Subjective Criteria

In this, a team of pathologists gave scores for the enhanced images in the scale of 0–9 where 9 represents the best score i.e. excellent fidelity and 0 represents worst score i.e. worst fidelity for the information content present in them which can be useful for accurately predicting cancer grade. It is shown as pathologists' score in the qualitative assessment metric given in Table 3.

6   Dataset

The implemented techniques are assessed on the database made available by the Gland Segmentation (GlaS) Challenge held in MICCAI 2015 [4] given at [5]. This dataset consists of 165 Colon Histopathology images mostly having a size of $775 \times 552 \times 3$. We have taken 151 images from it which was of the same size i.e. $775 \times 552 \times 3$.

7   Experiments

All the contrast enhancement techniques are implemented in MATLAB 2019a. The techniques are implemented as below:

7.1   Image Sharpening

Image sharpening is performed using the un-sharp masking. Here, the input color image is first converted into LAB color space and then un-sharp masking is applied to L channel only. And, in the end for producing output enhanced image, the LAB color space image is again converted into RGB color space.

7.2   Color Map Enhancement

It is performed by mapping the intensity values of the input image to new values in output image such that values between [bottom_in] and [top_in] map to values between [bottom_out] and [top_out]. In our experiment we have taken [bottom_in] value as [0.1, 0.1, 0.8] and [top_in] as [0.9, 0.95, 0.95] for R, G, and B plane respectively. Also, the [bottom_out] value is taken as zero and [top_out] value is taken as one. This technique enhances the contrast values in the output image.

7.3   Proposed Color Map Enhanced Image Sharpening

In this technique, first the contrast is enhanced by mapping the intensity value of the input image to new values by taking lower values as [0, 0.3, 0] and top values as [1, 0.3, 1] i.e. saturating the intensity values in green plane only while keeping the original intensity values of red and blue plane. After this, the RGB image is converted into LAB space and image sharpening is performed on L channel using the un-sharp masking. In the end, the LAB color space image is again converted to an RGB color image in order to produce an output image.

7.4   Histogram Equalization

In this technique, the colormap associated with the input image is transformed such that the histogram of the resultant image approximately matches the histogram $hisgram$, calculated by

$$hisgram = one(1, n) * prod(size(input\, image\, A))/n \qquad (10)$$

then, the transformation T is chosen to minimize

$$|C_1(T(k)) - C_0(k)| \tag{11}$$

Where C_0 is the cumulative histogram of the input image i.e. A, C_1 is the cumulative sum of the above calculated *hisgram* values for all intensities k. Then the histogram equalization uses the transformation $b = T(a)$ to map the gray levels present in input image colormap to the new values.

Here, we tried to match the output image histogram with a flat histogram with 64 bins.

7.5 Contrast Limited Adaptive Histogram Equalization (CLAHE)

In this technique first, the RGB image is converted into LAB space. Then, the CLAHE is performed on the L channel by taking the tile size of $[4 \times 4]$ matrix and contrast enhancement limit factor as 0.7. This contrast enhancement limit is used in order to prevent image over-saturation specifically in homogeneous areas which are characterized by a high peak in the histogram shown in a particular image tile as a result of its maximum pixels falling inside the same gray level range. After this, the Rayleigh distribution is applied for creating a bell-shaped contrast transform function. In succession of this, Exponential distribution is applied for creating a contrast transform function having a curved histogram. In the end, the LAB space image is converted to an RGB output image.

7.6 Gamma Correction in RGB Plane

In this technique, intensity values of an input RGB image are mapped into a new colormap image by saturating the top 10% and bottom 10% intensity values of each plane along with keeping gamma value as 0.8 in order to weights the mapping towards the higher i.e. brighter output values. The gamma value is used to specify the curve shape which defines the relationship between the intensity values in input and output image.

7.7 Gamma Correction in HSV Plane

In this technique, the input image is first converted into HSV space and then its intensity values are mapped into a new colormap image by saturating the top 10% and bottom 10% intensity values of each plane along with keeping gamma value as 0.8. In the end, the HSV image is converted to an RGB output image.

7.8 SVM Cancer Classifier Using Bag of Features

The algorithm used for this is given below:

Step 1. Create Bag-Of-Features for image categories Benign and Malignant using the following:

1.1   Feature point locations are selected using the Grid method by taking the GridStep of [8 8] and the BlockWidth of [32 64 96 128].

1.2 SURF features are extracted from the selected feature point locations. In this 2090756 features were extracted.
1.3 Number of features are balanced across all image categories by keeping 80 percent of the strongest features i.e. 732099 from each category for improving clustering.
1.4 K-Means clustering is used to create a 500-word visual vocabulary by taking 1464198 features and 500 clusters

Step 2. The SVM classifier is trained using visual vocabulary features i.e. 'bag Of Features' object. This 'bag Of Features' object supply an encoding method for counting all the visual word occurrences in each and every image. It resulted in creating a histogram representing a new-fangled and compact depiction for every image. These histograms are thus outlining as a source for training the classifier and for performing the real image classification. In core, it encodes every image into feature vectors. Encoded training images in form of feature vectors derived from bag of features from each category are then fed into the multiclass linear SVM classifier from the Statistics and Machine Learning Toolbox.

Step 3. Testing the images for cancer classification and then evaluating the classification accuracy using the classifier of step 2.

8   Results and Discussion

In order to scrutinize the effectiveness of different image enhancement techniques first, they were assessed for objective qualitative parameters like Entropy, SSIM, PSNR, and MSE. And after that the resulted images were sent to the pathologists in Dharamshila Narayana Hospital, New Delhi for getting their score in the range of 0 to 9 where 9 was given to the excellent image and the decrease in score indicates the less image fidelity. The resulted images along with their resulting histogram plots are shown in Table 2 while the objective and subjective parameters are given in Table 3. The plots of the objective qualitative parameters Vs database images are shown in Fig. 2, 3, 4, and 5.

By the analysis of these techniques, we see that all the techniques like Contrast adjustment, Histogram equalization, and CLAHE are making the epithelial nuclei area darker and due to which the presence of cytoplasm was not coming clear along with the shape of the gland. On the other hand, the Gamma Correction in the HSV plane is blurring the image along with the dye color. Thus, these techniques are not suited for histopathological image analysis. The gamma correction in RGB plane is better than these techniques but it also produces small circles like blocking artifacts at some places. Also, it is found out that techniques like Image sharpening, Colormap enhancement, and Colormap-enhanced image sharpening are giving better results in terms of increase in visibility of lumen, cytoplasm, and epithelial nuclei. Thus these techniques can be used for image enhancement in histopathological image analysis. From the histogram plots of each image, it can be easily interpreted that image sharpening, Colormap enhancement, and Colormap-enhanced image sharpening are giving more uniform histogram plots along with coverage of all the available dynamic histogram range as compared to other

Table 2. Implementation results of various image enhancement techniques.

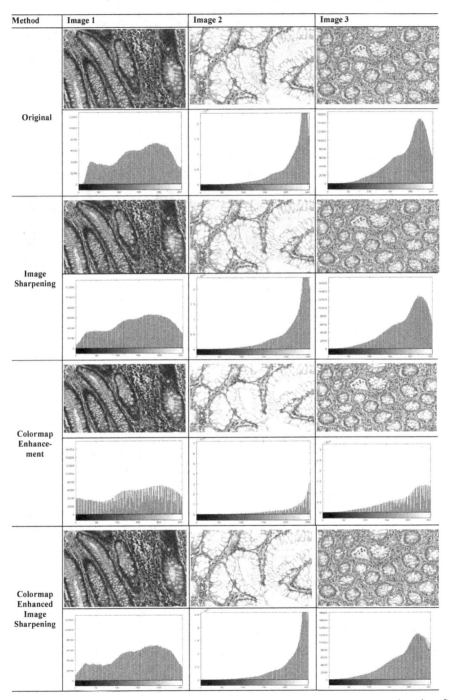

(*continued*)

Table 2. (*continued*)

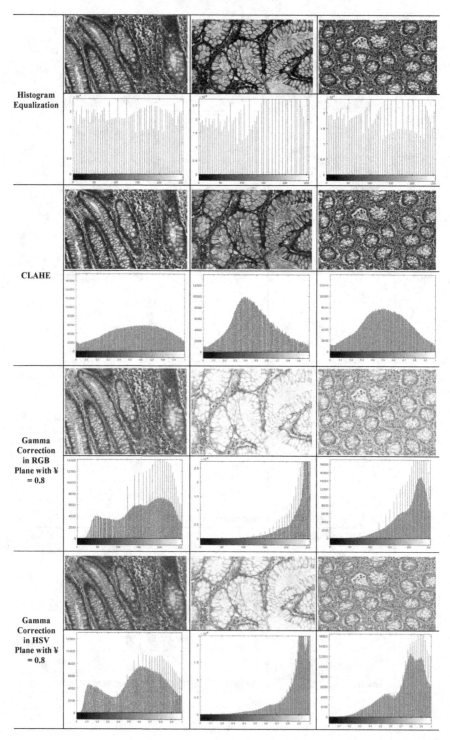

Table 3. Qualitative evaluation of different image enhancement techniques

S. No.	Enhancement method	Entropy	MSE	PSNR	SSIM	Pathologist score*
1.	Image sharpening	7.2861	47.9766	32.9155	.9864	8.8013
2.	Colormap enhancement	6.9183	149.9092	26.4179	.9785	7.8675
3.	**Colormap enhanced image sharpening**	**7.6469**	**34.7820**	**36.4650**	**.9886**	**8.8675**
4.	Histogram equalization	5.9362	3674.4	13.8063	.7916	5.7947
5.	CLAHE	6.7319	34643	4.8086	.0077	4.2052
6.	Gamma correction in RGB plane with ¥ = 0.8	7.4316	171.4274	25.9569	.9629	7.7947
7.	Gamma correction in HSV plane with ¥ = 0.8	7.1892	34554	3.8190	.0011	5.2052

*Pathologist Score is the mean score given by the team of pathologists of Dharamshila Narayana Superspeciality Hospital according to the critical information preservation and thus, become the deciding factor for choosing the appropriate enhancement technique.

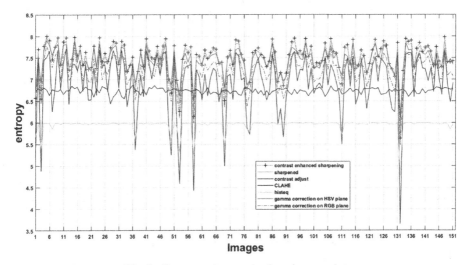

Fig. 2. Entropy values vs database images plot

techniques. In all other techniques, there is a sharp difference between low and high contrast value which is resulting in loss of information.

From the Qualitative analysis shown in Table 3, the above-mentioned results can be justified. From this table, it is easily interpreted that techniques like Image Sharpening and Colormap Enhancement are giving better results for colon histopathology images than techniques like Histogram Equalization, CLAHE, and Gamma Correction. Thus,

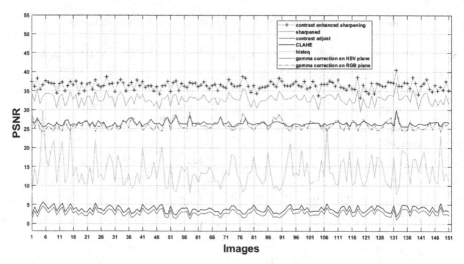

Fig. 3. PSNR values vs database images plot

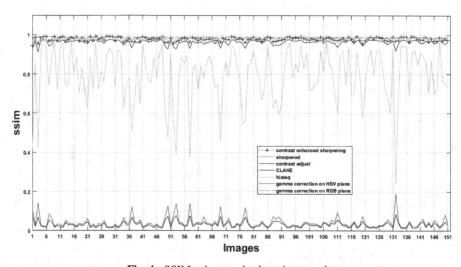

Fig. 4. SSIM values vs database images plot

taking these results into account, we have proposed Colormap Enhanced Image Sharpening technique which is not only giving better visual results but also the Qualitative Evaluation results which are shown in bold letters in Table 3. All the Qualitative parameters are evaluated for each of the 151 images and their individual values are represented in Fig. 2, 3, 4 and 5. In Table 3, the Qualitative parameter values are given by taking mean of all the values coming for each of the 151 images.

From Fig. 6, the classification accuracies are evaluated and analyzed for each enhancement technique and it is found out that two of the enhancement techniques i.e. the

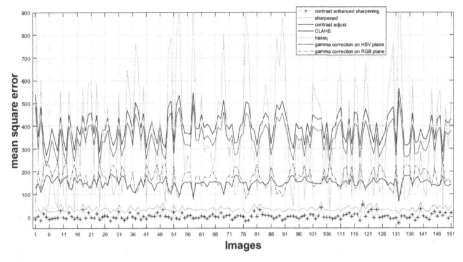

Fig. 5. Mean square error values vs database images plot

colormap enhancement and the proposed colormap enhanced image sharpening are not only enhancing the image quality but also enhancing the classification accuracies. The proposed colormap enhanced image sharpening is increasing the cancer classification accuracy by three percent.

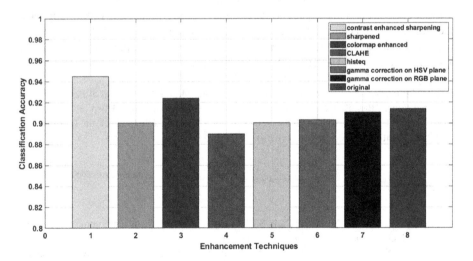

Fig. 6. Classification-accuracy plot for enhancement techniques

9 Conclusion

The main rationale of the Image Enhancement techniques is to perk up the interpretability of the information content present in the images. These techniques emphasize specific features present in an image in order to improve its visual perception. These techniques are particularly application-specific. Thus, here we are taking only some of the image enhancement techniques which are already used for various medical images such as Magnetic Resonance Imaging (MRI), X-Ray, CT scans, etc. As discussed earlier, for detecting and predicting cancer grades, there are some important parts in the colon histopathological tissue samples like gland morphology, lumen, nuclei, etc. Thus, these techniques are applied and tested for their ability to highlight those areas.

In this paper, a total of seven image enhancement methods were applied to colon histopathology images. From these methods, six techniques were the classical techniques and when we applied them on our database, the objective results, as well as the subjective result in terms of pathologists' score, were coming best for image sharpening and colormap enhancement so we proposed a new technique by combining both these techniques in such a way so that the results will improve further. As only pathologists have to work on these techniques, so their score is the most important deciding factor in determining the efficacy of the applied enhancement techniques and thus, based on their score along with other objective qualitative measures we can conclude that the proposed technique can be best suited for the histopathological image analysis. Also, these techniques are further used for cancer classification and it has found out that the proposed colormap enhanced image sharpening is not only enhancing the image quality but also increasing the 2-class cancer classification accuracy by three percentage than the original dataset without any enhancement. These results will also help in finding better cancer classification accuracies without using complex models. A less complicated model can also give better classification results. This technique can be further used to increase the analytical as well as diagnostic accuracy of various applications like Cancer Classification ([20, 21]) and Tumor Segmentation ([22]).

Acknowledgments. The authors are grateful to Dr. Hema Malini Aiyer, Head of Pathology and Dr. Garima Rawat, Pathologists at Dharamshila Narayana Superspeciality Hospital, New Delhi for their support to our research, without their help we will not be able to check the feasibility of the applied algorithm in the real-life scenario.

References

1. Fleming, M., Ravula, S., Tatishchev, S.F., Wang, H.L.: Colorectal carcinoma: pathologic aspects. J. Gastrointest. Oncol. **3**(3), 153 (2012)
2. Gurcan, M.N., Boucheron, L., Can, A., Madabhushi, A., Rajpoot, N., Yener, B.: Histopathological image analysis: a review. IEEE Rev. Biomed. Eng. **2**, 147 (2009)
3. Gonzalez, R.C., Woods, R.E.: Image processing. In: Digital Image Processing, Intensity Transformations, and Spatial Filtering, Chap. 3 (2018)
4. Sirinukunwattana, K., et al.: Gland segmentation in colon histology images: the glas challenge contest. Med. Image Anal. **35**, 489–502 (2017)

5. Warwick-QU image dataset description. https://warwick.ac.uk/fac/sci/dcs/research/tia/glascontest/about/
6. Jeevakala, S.: Sharpening enhancement technique for MR images to enhance the segmentation. Biomed. Signal Process. Control **41**, 21–30 (2018)
7. Reddy, E., Reddy, R.: Dynamic clipped histogram equalization technique for enhancing low contrast images. Proc. Nat. Acad. Sci. India Sect. A: Phys. Sci. **89**, 1–26 (2018)
8. Sahu, S., Singh, A.K., Ghrera, S.P., Elhoseny, M.: An approach for de-noising and contrast enhancement of retinal fundus image using CLAHE. Opt. Laser Technol. **110**, 87–98 (2019)
9. Cao, G., Huang, L., Tian, H., Huang, X., Wang, Y., Zhi, R.: Contrast enhancement of brightness-distorted images by improved adaptive gamma correction. Comput. Electr. Eng. **66**, 569–582 (2018)
10. Duan, X., et al.: A multiscale contrast enhancement for mammogram using dynamic unsharp masking in Laplacian pyramid. IEEE Trans. Radiat. Plasma Med. Sci. **3**(5), 557–64 (2018)
11. Hsu, W.Y., Chou, C.Y.: Medical image enhancement using modified color histogram equalization. J. Med. Biol. Eng. **35**(5), 580–584 (2015)
12. Li, L., Si, Y., Jia, Z.: Medical image enhancement based on CLAHE and unsharp masking in NSCT domain. J. Med. Imaging Health Inform. **8**(3), 431–438 (2018)
13. Ullah, Z., Lee, S.H.: Magnetic resonance brain image contrast enhancement using histogram equalization techniques. 한국컴퓨터정보학회학술발표논문집**27**(1), 83–86 (2019)
14. Mzoughi, H., Njeh, I., Slima, M.B., Hamida, A.B.: Histogram equalization-based techniques for contrast enhancement of MRI brain Glioma tumor images: comparative study. In: 2018 4th International Conference on Advanced Technologies for Signal and Image Processing (ATSIP), pp. 1–6. IEEE, March 2018
15. Dhal, K.G., Das, S.: Colour retinal images enhancement using modified histogram equalisation methods and firefly algorithm. Int. J. Biomed. Eng. Technol. **28**(2), 160–184 (2018)
16. Clark, J.L., Wadhwani, C.P., Abramovitch, K., Rice, D.D., Kattadiyil, M.T.: Effect of image sharpening on radiographic image quality. J. Prosthet. Dent. **120**(6), 927–933 (2018)
17. Tiwari, M., Gupta, B.: Brightness preserving contrast enhancement of medical images using adaptive gamma correction and homomorphic filtering. In: 2016 IEEE Students' Conference on Electrical, Electronics and Computer Science (SCEECS), pp. 1–4. IEEE, March 2016
18. Bhairannawar, S.S.: Efficient medical image enhancement technique using transform HSV space and adaptive histogram equalization. In: Soft Computing Based Medical Image Analysis, Chap. 4, pp. 51–60. Academic Press, January 2018
19. Dabass, J., Arora, S., Vig, R., Hanmandlu, M.: Mammogram image enhancement using entropy and CLAHE based intuitionistic fuzzy method. In: 2019 6th International Conference on Signal Processing and Integrated Networks (SPIN), pp. 24–29. IEEE, March 2019
20. Dabass, M., Vashisth, S., Vig, R.: Review of classification techniques using deep learning for colorectal cancer imaging modalities. In: 2019 6th International Conference on Signal Processing and Integrated Networks (SPIN), pp. 105–110. IEEE March 2019
21. Dabass, M., Vig, R., Vashisth, S.: Five-grade cancer classification of colon histology images via deep learning. In: 2018 2nd International Conference on Communication and Computing System (ICCCS), Taylor and Francis, December 2018
22. Dabass, M., Vig, R., Vashisth, S.: Review of histopathological image segmentation via current deep learning approaches. In: 2019 4th IEEE International Conference on Computing Communication and Automation (ICCCA), pp. 1–6. IEEE December 2018
23. Dabass, M., Vashisth, S., Vig, R.: Effectiveness of region growing based segmentation technique for various medical images - a study. In: Panda, B., Sharma, S., Roy, N.R. (eds.) REDSET 2017. CCIS, vol. 799, pp. 234–259. Springer, Singapore (2018). https://doi.org/10.1007/978-981-10-8527-7_21

A Novel Activation Function in Convolutional Neural Network for Image Classification in Deep Learning

Ochin Sharma[✉]

Manav Rachna International Institute of Research and Studies,
Sector 43, Faridabad 121006, India
ochinsharma2@gmail.com

Abstract. In deep learning, there are various parameters that helps to drive optimal results. One of those parameters is to use the correct activation function. The activation function must have ideal statistical characteristics. In this paper, a novel deep learning activation function has been proposed. Sigmoid activation function generally used in the output layer for bi-classification problem. Recently, swish activation used sigmoid function with hidden layers. Motivated by this, a new activation function is being proposed as (relu (x) + x * sigmoid (x)) to get the significance benefits of relu and sigmoid in a swish like flavour. The proposed function represents the desired statistical characteristics as unboundedness, monotonicity, zero centred and non-vanishing gradient. The experimental outcomes are also quite significant.

Keywords: Relu · Elu · Selu · Monotonic · Swish

1 Introduction

Although, Deep Learning has emerged as a field with great opportunities, but it has also introduced a number of challenges [17]. As deep learning has many areas on which improvements can be done. One of these are improving activation functions to obtain optimize experimental outcomes [18].

Activation functions serve very important role in the neural networks. They help to learn about and create truly complex and non-linear complex functional mappings between input and response variables. They introduce non-linear properties for neural networks. Their main objective is to allow to forward the input signal of a node in the output signal. That output signal is now used as an input to the next layer in the stack. Specifically, in a neural network, the sum of products of the input (X) and their corresponding loads (W) and apply an activation function f (x) to it to obtain the output of that layer and assign it to the next input Feed as Layer.

Without an activation function, the output signal will simply be a simple linear function. The linear function is simply a polynomial of degree one. Now, solving a linear equation is easy, but they are limited in their complexity and have little power to learn complex functional mapping from data. A neural network without an activation function

© Springer Nature Singapore Pte Ltd. 2020
U. Batra et al. (Eds.): REDSET 2019, CCIS 1229, pp. 120–130, 2020.
https://doi.org/10.1007/978-981-15-5827-6_10

would be only a linear regression model, which has limited power and does not perform well, most of the time. In fact, without the activation function, neural network will not be able to learn and model other complex types of data such as images, video, audio, speech, etc., which is why there is a need to use artificial neural network techniques such as deep learning for something complex. It is required to deal with a high-dimensional, non-linear datasets, where the model has many and many hidden layers and a very complex architecture that helps to build knowledge and such complex large datasets [6, 7].

In non-linear functions degree is greater than one and they have curvature though performing non-linear functions. So, there is a requirement of a neural network model to learn and represent almost anything and any arbitrary complex function that maps the inputs to the output. Neural-networks are considered universal function Approximators. This implies that they can calculate and learn any function. Almost any process we can think of can be represented as a functional computation in neural networks.

Another important feature of the activation function is that it must be distinct. We need it in this way to perform a backpropagation optimization strategy propagating backwards in the network to calculate gradients of error (loss) with respect to weight and then gradient descending or any Optimize weight by using other optimization techniques.

In this respect, a new activation function has been explored and proposed; the results attained are better than many activation functions including rectified linear function, Leaky Relu, Tanh and a recently suggested activation function named 'swish' [24]. While doing examination of existing baseline activation function, some interesting things need to be pointed out here:

Sigmoid is a mathematical form of non-linearity

$$\sigma(x) = 1/\left(1 + e^{-x}\right)$$

Sigmoid is not suitable for inner layers of neural network. Rather it is best suited as an output function for bi-classification [25, 26].

Relu is a simple and straightforward activation function. But relu ignores all the negative outputs [23]. It also suffered from vanishing gradient and non-zero centred problem [2]. Sigmoid function generates good results sometimes, but not always due to ignoring some recommended features of activation function. It suffers from zero data centred problem and vanishing gradient problem. The range of functions is 0 to 1. However, signed is still not a useless function and in fact many users love to use this function at the outer layer of the neural network where the problem concerned with bi-classification problem [21, 22].

Leaky Relu has the similar structure as relu does. It tried to overcome the relu function's drawback of non-zero centered data. Statistically,

$$\text{L.Relu(y)} = ax \text{ if } x < 0 \text{ and } x \text{ if } x > 0 \tag{1}$$

The constant value, 'a' should be chosen wisely while training the model. Due to multiplication with a constant scalar, L. Relu has some limitations and show linearity in behaviour, due to this it seems difficult to use L. Relu for complex classification problems as text classification. However, L. Relu fairly outperforms many activation functions including sigmoid & Tanh [3, 12].

Tanh tried to overcome the zero centred problems that is used to exist with sigmoid function. The range of tanh function is between −1 to 1 unlike 0 to 1 of the sigmoid function. However, Tanh also saturate and suffers from vanishing gradient problem after +2 and −2 axis and model's learning becomes negligible [23, 24].

Exponential Linear Unit (Elu) has been projected as an efficient alternative to 'relu' as it doesn't possess zero centred problem, but 'elu' is computationally costly when compared with many of the existing activation functions. Elu is also bounded below and if situation leads it would suffer from gradient saturation [4].

Scaled Exponential Linear Units (Selu) represented statistically as:

$$Selu(x) = \lambda\{x \text{ if } x > 0 \text{ and } \alpha e^x - \alpha \text{ if } x \leq 0\} \tag{2}$$

The value of lambda and alpha are derived using input data. As for mean 0 and standard deviation 1, alpha is 1.6732 and lambda is 1.0507. However, the convergence rate of relu is more than selu. Secondly, Selu is computationally more expensive than relu. Selu is bounded below. Hence it might suffer from the gradient saturation problem [5].

Swish is a recently introduced activation function proposed by Google brain, but it is below bounded function which is not a desirable property of activation function. Secondly, it is a non-monotonic function [11]. So, due to this, there are fair chances of showing unpredictable or inconsistent experimental outcomes depending upon different data sets and experimental environment setup.

2   Analysing Existing Baseline Activation Functions

There are certain essential properties of an activation function. Based on these properties, this section contains the introspection of commonly used activation functions.

2.1   Monotonicity

Back propagation is an important property in a neural network. It influences the next layer weights. A monotonic function leads to a smooth neural network. This emphasis that weight change would be optimised in a predictive and optimized manner. So, it is a very important property while choosing the function as monotonic as well as the derivative of that function should also preserved this property [8]. Refer Table 1 for the functions which possess this property.

Table 1. Essential properties of activation functions

Activation Function	Relu	L. Relu	Sigmoid	Tanh	Softplus	Elu	Selu	Swish	OAF
Desired zero centered property	No	Yes	No	Yes	No	Yes	Yes	Yes	Yes
Vanishing gradient problem	No	No	Yes	Yes	Yes	No	No	No	No
Function monotonicity	Yes	Yes	Yes	Yes	Yes	Yes	Yes	No	Yes
Derivative monotonicity	Yes	Yes	No	No	Yes	Yes	No	No	Yes
Unbounded above	Yes	Yes	No	No	Yes	Yes	Yes	Yes	Yes

2.2 Zero Centred

Zero centred is another desirable property of neural network. This property simply says that the output of the network would be zero centred. So, the output can have positive values as well as negative values. Contrast to this, if data is not zero centred, the output would be either only positive or negative only. Hence, ignoring the potential causes of negatively signed cases. Refer Table 1 for the functions which possess this property.

For a neural network, this seems to be an essential property because without zero centred data, gradient update will always be of similar signs and hence all the weights would be either increased or decreased. For training effective neural network, some weights should be increased and some weights should be decreased to promote the continuous learning of a network [9].

2.3 Unbounded Function

Unboundedness is another desired feature of an activation function. If an activation function is bounded towards either direction (which can be easily seen by a graphical plot of a function) then the output would be restricted to a specific limit and if data is large with high dimensions, output would be saturated to an end, results into bad impact on the overall performance of the network [1, 9] Refer Table 1.

2.4 Vanishing Gradient Problem

It has been observed that the neural networks, which are having vanishing gradient problems suffer from slow learning to no learning as compared to the networks which do not possess this problem. Gradients say about the rate of change of output based on the input. After each epoch (whole dataset) run, the weights of the network are being updated for the next epoch (next time run with the same dataset). When the output of epochs does not show any change in accuracy of classification, whatever input value a network is getting, this is called vanishing gradient problem. An activation function which avoids this situation will lead to the network to its maximum level of optimization and provide the maximum possible accuracy based on the dataset and environment [10]. Refer Table 1 for the functions which is having vanishing gradient problem.

3 Proposed Activation Function (O.A.F)

Optimal Activation Function (O.A.F) statistically, can be represented as:

$$Y = (\text{relu}\,(x) + x * \text{sigmoid}\,(x)) \tag{3}$$

The graph plot for O.A.F is shown in Fig. 1. The derivative of proposed function attains some valuable properties as:

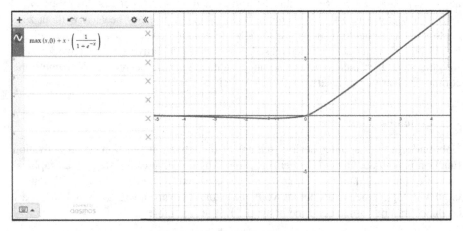

Fig. 1. Graph of OAF function

a) The function is unbounded below and above the x-axis. Hence it avoids the saturated outputs.
b) The function is monotonic.
c) It is a zero centred function and provide valuable outputs for both positive and negative inputs.
d) The function does not suffer from vanishing gradient problem and the model continuously learns.

Due to its unbounded property of above, monotonic functional property, with no zero centred properties, it serves as a potential activation function.

4   Experimental Setup and Result Discussion

MNIST and FASHION MNIST Datasets have been used for experiments. The detail of datasets is described in [15, 16]. For neural network, Mhaskar et al. have discussed that a neural network using a single hidden layer of any nonlinear activation function can approximate any continuous function of any number of real variables on any compact set to any desired degree of accuracy [13]. Cybenko proved that a neural network with two layers of weights and just one layer of a nonlinear activation function formed a model that could approximate any function [14]. So, two hidden layers have been used in image classification.

Window 10 with 64-bit processor has been used. Python 3.5.2 version has been used due to Tensorflow compatibility. Tensorflow and Keras packages have been used to access deep learning functionalities in Python. Additionally, Pycharm is being used as an editor to facilitate the better accessibility. [19, 20].

For image classification, Convolutional 2D Model is being used, one hidden layer with 64 neurons and second hidden layer with 32 neurons, adam is being used as an optimizer, as a loss function sparse_categorical_crossentropy is being used. Output layer is used with 10 neurons and softmax activation functions. Figure 2 and Fig. 3 displays the result of OAF activation function with MNIST and FASHOPN MNIST dataset. Different activation functions are simulated inside the two hidden layers and results of accuracy based on these activation functions are shown in the Table 2.

The experimental results depict that O.A.F activation function is quite competitive for image classification (Figs. 5 and 6).

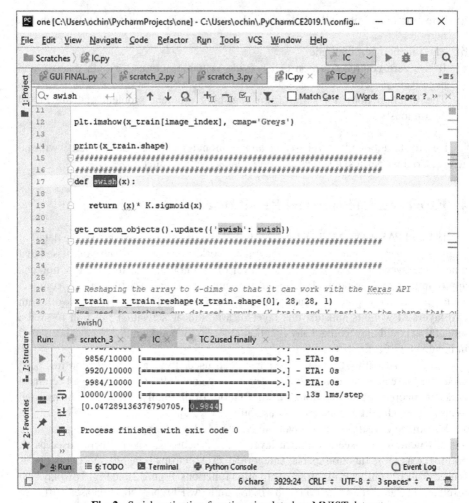

Fig. 2. Swish activation function simulated on MNIST dataset

Fig. 3. Swish activation function simulated on FASHION-MNIST dataset

Table 2. Accuracy comparison by using various activation functions

Dataset	Relu	swish	selu	elu	Proposed OAF	Tanh	L. relu
MNIST	98.4	98.44	98.0	97.99	98.62	87.78	98.39
FASHION MNIST	88.2	88.64	88.21	88.55	90.18	88.20	88.70

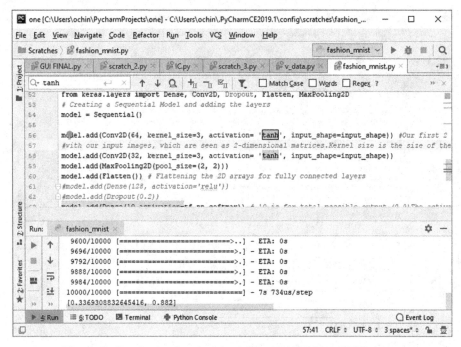

Fig. 4. Tanh activation function simulated on FASHION MNIST dataset

Fig. 5. MNIST Image classification with OAF activation function

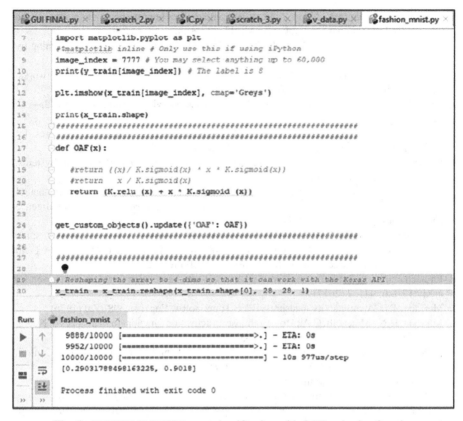

Fig. 6. FASHION MNIST Image classification with OAF activation function

5 Conclusion

The O.A.F is an activation function that has been proposed and discussed statistically and based on the desired properties of an activation functions, namely: monotonicity, unboundedness, complexity, vanishing gradient and zero centred. Various activation functions have been put under observation for this like: Swish, L. Relu, Relu, Tanh, Selu, Elu. Although a new activation function O.A.F has been proposed and experimentally tested and found fairly good, but still there is a need to continue exploring new activation functions for different types of scenarios and data sets to receive the best results.

References

1. Glorot, X., Bengio, Y.: Understanding the difficulty of training deep feedforward neural networks. In: Proceedings of the Thirteenth International Conference on Artificial Intelligence and Statistics, pp. 249–256 (2010)
2. Hahnloser, R.H.R., Sarpeshkar, R., Mahowald, M.A., Douglas, R.J., Seung, H.S.: Digital selection and analogue amplification coexist in a cortex-inspired silicon circuit. Nature **405**(6789), 947 (2000)

3. Maas, A.L., Hannun, A.Y., Ng, A.Y.: Rectifier nonlinearities improve neural network acoustic models. In: International Conference on Machine Learning, vol. 30 (2013)
4. Clevert, D.-A., Unterthiner, T., Hochreiter, S.: Fast and accurate deep network learning by exponential linear units (elus). arXiv preprint arXiv:1511.07289 (2015)
5. Klambauer, G., Unterthiner, T., Mayr, A., Hochreiter, S.: Self-normalizing neural networks. arXiv preprint arXiv:1706.02515 (2017)
6. Schmidhuber, J.: Deep learning in neural networks: an overview. Neural Netw. **61**, 85–117 (2015)
7. Nair, V., Hinton, G.E.: Rectified linear units improve restricted boltzmann machines. In: International Conference on Machine Learning (2010)
8. Sill, J.: Monotonic networks. In: Advances in Neural Information Processing Systems, pp. 661–667, Monotonic (1998)
9. Glorot, X., Bengio, Y.: Understanding the difficulty of training deep feedforward neural networks. In: Proceedings of the Thirteenth International Conference on Artificial Intelligence and Statistics, pp. 249–256 (2010)
10. Hochreiter, S., Bengio, Y., Frasconi, P., Schmidhuber, J.: Gradient flow in recurrent nets: the difficulty of learning long-term dependencies. In: Kremer, S.C., Kolen, J.F. (eds.) A Field Guide to Dynamical Recurrent Neural Networks. IEEE Press (2001)
11. Ramachandran, P., Zoph, B., Le, Q.V.: Swish: a self-gated activation function. arXiv preprint arXiv:1710.05941, 7 (2017)
12. McCabe, T.J.: A complexity measures. IEEE Trans. softw. Eng. (4), 308–320 (1976)
13. Mhaskar, H.N., Micchelli, C.A.: How to choose an activation function. In: Advances in Neural Information Processing Systems, pp. 319–326 (1994)
14. Cybenko, G.: Approximation by superpositions of a sigmoidal function. Math. Control, Signals, and Systems (MCSS) **2**(4) 303–314 (1989)
15. http://yann.lecun.com/exdb/mnist/
16. https://archive.ics.uci.edu/ml/datasets/reuters-21578+text+categorization+collection
17. Sharma, O.: A new activation function for deep neural network. In: 2019 International Conference on Machine Learning, Big Data, Cloud and Parallel Computing (COMITCon). IEEE, February 2019
18. Sharma, O.: Deep challenges associated with deep learning. In: 2019 International Conference on Machine Learning, Big Data, Cloud and Parallel Computing (COMITCon). IEEE, February 2019
19. https://www.tensorflow.org/
20. https://kcras.io/activations/
21. https://ml-cheatsheet.readthedocs.io/en/latest/activation_functions.html
22. https://missinglink.ai/guides/neural-network-concepts/7-types-neural-network-activation-functions-right/
23. https://www.hardikp.com/2017/07/24/SELU-vs-RELU/
24. https://kasperfred.com/posts/computational-complexity-of-neural-networks
25. https://towardsdatascience.com/activation-functions-and-its-types-which-is-better-a9a5310cc8f
26. https://datascience.stackexchange.com/questions/14349/difference-of-activation-functions-in-neural-networks-in-general

Evaluation of Nephrology Dataset Through Deep Learning Technique

Neha Dohare[1] and Shelly Sachdeva[2(✉)]

[1] Maharaja Surajmal Institute of Technology, New Delhi, India
nehadohare@gmail.com
[2] National Institute of Technology, Delhi, New Delhi, India
shellysachdeva@nitdelhi.ac.in

Abstract. Multiple parameters need to be analyzed for making diagnosis in patients with renal disorders. An automatic system that would analyze these parameters and provide diagnosis without the help of a specialist would decrease the burden on already overburdened clinicians. Deep learning has already made a huge impact on medical fields like cancer diagnosis, precision medicine, and can be applied to build this automated system which can diagnose renal disorders. This study has been carried out using the data of nephrology related diseases extracted from a standard based healthcare dataset based on openEHR standard. A feed forward neural network has been used for the creation of the model that would predict the kidney disease present in the patient based on several parameters (such as abdominal ultrasonography, enrolled for transplantation, vascular access, HbsAg, venous fistula amount, urea reduction rate, HIC antibodies and HIV). An accuracy of 98.7% has been achieved through the experiments.

Keywords: Deep learning · Kidney disease · Feed forward neural network · ORDBA dataset · Nephrology

1 Introduction

In past few years, Deep Learning has become more and more popular and has been applied to a large number of areas, health and medicine being one of them. In the treatment of several diseases like stroke and cancer, deep learning has been used for survival and risk prediction. It is estimated that 5 to 10 million people die annually from kidney diseases [1]. Thus, current study makes an effort to apply one of the deep learning techniques for diagnosis of kidney related diseases based on several parameters like abdominal ultrasonography, enrolled for transplantation, vascular access, HbsAg, venous fistula amount, urea reduction rate, HIC antibodies and HIV.

1.1 Deep Learning

Deep learning is widely applied in several applications like image classification, video recommendation, text mining, etc. [2]. It has emerged from conventional neural networks

U. Batra et al. (Eds.): REDSET 2019, CCIS 1229, pp. 131–139, 2020.
https://doi.org/10.1007/978-981-15-5827-6_11

and it significantly outperforms all its predecessors. Deep Learning networks are multi layered networks with transformations among neutrons in each layer. One of the main plus points of deep learning techniques is that they perform feature extraction in an automated way. This enables researchers to extract all the important features even with minimal domain knowledge and effort [3]. The layered architecture of deep learning networks allows for the high level features to be extracted from the upper layers and low level features from the lower layers. These architectures mimic how the human brain works and this is one major advantage of deep learning.

Feed Forward Neural Networks. In current study, a feed forward neural network has been used for classification of kidney disease. Feed forward neural networks are the most typical examples of deep learning models. They contain at least three types of layers- input layer, hidden layer and output layer. The first layer is known as the input layer, the last layer is known as the output layer and all the layers in between are called the hidden layers. In these deep learning networks, the information flows in a single direction only, that is from the input layer to the output layer (via the hidden layers). All the values and functions are computed along the forward pass path. Three steps are involved in training the neural network. First is the acquisition of training and testing datasets, followed by the training of model using the training dataset and the final step is testing the model using the testing dataset [4].

1.2 Healthcare Dataset

Electronic Health Record (EHR) is a lifelong health record of an individual. EHRs can store data for huge electronic exchange so that the patient's data can be electronically shared with any doctor, hospital, clinic, pharmacy and laboratory. OpenEHR [5] is a standard that defines specifications of EHRs, highly generic architecture, and facilitate sharing of EHR. The dataset used in this research is known as ORBDA (OpenEHRBench-mark Dataset) [6]. It is a standardized dataset based on openEHR (standard for semantic interoperability of electronic health records). It was developed using data supplied by the Brazilian Public Health System (SUS) through the Department of Informatics of SUS (DATASUS) database. The dataset consists of high-complexity procedure (APACs) and hospitalization (AIHs) made publically available by DATASUS without the patient identification information.

2 Related Work

Deep learning is a new and fast growing field of research. It has been applied to several areas including, but not limited to sentiment analysis [7], machine translation [8], multi-media systems and computer vision [9], biomedicine and so on. Current study employs a feed forward neural network for prediction of kidney related disease. Several other types of neural networks exist which include- Recurrent Neural Network (RNN), Radial Basis Function Neural Network, Kohonen Self Organizing Neural Network and Modular Neural Network [4]. Table 1 gives an overview of all these types of neural networks. Feed forward neural network has been selected for purpose of this study because of its simple and easy to implement architecture.

Table 1. Overview of different types of neural networks

Neural Network	Summary	Advantages
Feed Forward Neural Network	Information flows in only one direction, from the input layer to the output layer	It is Simple and easy to implement
Recurrent Neural Network	The processing units form a loop. It contains feedback loops	The network has memory about the previous states It is useful for applications that require processing sequence of time phased data like speech or video
Radial Basis Neural Network	It consists of an input, output and hidden layer with the hidden layer including a radial basis function and each node represents a cluster center	It can be trained faster than a multi-layer perceptron
Kohonen Self Organizing Neural Network	It self organizes the network model into the input data. It consists of two fully connected layers- the input layer and the output layer	It is useful for unsupervised learning
Modular Neural Network	It breaks down a large neural network into several small neural networks, with each performing specific tasks which are later combined	It breaks down a big task into smaller tasks which makes it easy to implement it

Deep learning has also been employed in several healthcare related fields. Ciresan et al. [10] has used deep neural networks for mitosis detection in breast cancer histology images. Litjens et al. [11] deployed a Convolutional Neural Network (CNN) based autoencoder for the sectioning of basal cell carcinoma in breast cancer. Advances in deep learning have now enabled machines to learn and detect things which were previously beyond current human knowledge [2]. Poplin et al. [12] exploit deep leaning for prediction of cardiovascular risk factors from retinal fundus photographs. The prediction of cardiovascular risk factors was previously thought to be undetectable by human beings.

In current study data has been acquired from the ORDBA dataset which is a standardized dataset based on openEHR which is the standard for semantic interoperability of electronic health records [5]. Several studies have used EHRs data for a variety of tasks including learning of lower dimensional representations for medical concepts [13] and future diagnosis prediction [14]. Ma et al. [14] proposed a bidirectional Recurrent Neural Networks for modeling EHRs data and interpreting the prediction results.

Some work has also been done in the field of nephrology that uses deep learning. Sharma et al. [15] used deep learning for automatic segmentation of kidneys for total kidney volume quantification in autosomal dominant polycystic kidney disease, which is the most common inherited disorder of the kidneys. They used convolutional neural networks for the same.

In addition to the input parameters chosen, other parameters that may help in the diagnosis of various kidney diseases are glomerular haematuria, protein urea, albumin urea, antinuclear antibodies, anti-double-stranded DNA, HbA1c, etc. [16] These parameters were not present in the dataset chosen for the study.

To the best of the authors' knowledge, the application of deep learning and neural networks on the nephrology dataset extracted from the standard based (ORDBA) dataset is a first attempt as detailed in the current study.

3   Problem Statement

Nephrologists have to take into consideration many parameters in order to make the diagnosis of the renal disease that a patient is suffering from. Thus an automated system can help them make the diagnosis of the condition just by feeding the parameters. This reduces the chances of error as it doesn't depend on human memory and enables nephrologists to make a quicker diagnosis.

4   Evaluation of Nephrology Dataset Through Deep Learning Technique

After rigorous analysis, the current study considers the evaluation of nephrology dataset through feed forward neural network. The authors use a three layer neural network as shown in Fig. 1. The first layer or the input layer consists of 8 nodes corresponding to the eight input features. There are two hidden layers with 16 and 12 nodes respectively. The output layer consists of 9 nodes corresponding to each output class (kidney diseases).

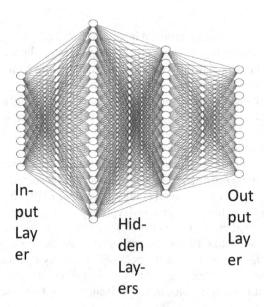

Fig. 1. Architecture of the neural network (with hidden layers consisting of 16 and 12 nodes)

4.1 Analysis of Dataset

The dataset of ORDBA consists of hospitalization data and patient medical information data. It contains two types of records- AIH (5.73 million records) and APAC (9.56 million records). The APAC records contain 7.76 million patient information records out of which 5.07% belong to the chosen problem domain (nephrology). Consider Fig. 2, it gives an overview of the dataset with the filtered problem domain, i.e. nephrology (shown as highlighted).

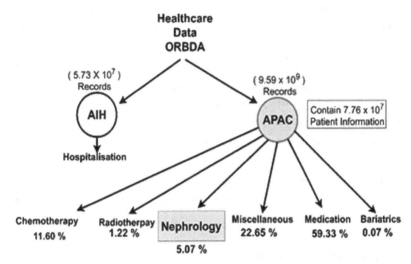

Fig. 2. ORDBA overview with filtered problem domain (Nephrology)

The dataset chosen for this study contains 2205203 entries which were reduced to 1098574 entries after the removal of noisy data and extracting entries for required output classes. For this study eight input features out of eighteen have been considered. Table 2

Table 2. Input features chosen

	Input features
x1	abdominal_ultrasonography
x2	enrolled_for_transplantation
x3	vascular_access
x4	HbsAg
x5	venous_fistula_amount
x6	urea_reduction_rate
x7	HIC_antibodies
x8	HIV

shows the eight input features named as x1, x2, x3....x8. The authors exclude other features (like name, date of admission, etc.) because their values wouldn't affect the diagnosis.

The output or the prediction that has been made is main_diagnosis (y). There are nine output classes which are shown in Table 3. The diagnosis codes follow ICD10 codes.

Table 3. Output Classes

Class	ICD 10 codes	Disease	No. of entries
0	E14_2	Unspecified diabetes mellitus with renal complications	530
1	I10	Essential primary hypertension	1542
2	I12_0	Hypertensive chronic kidney disease	3472
3	N03_9	Chronic nephritic syndrome with unspecified morphologic changes	1217
4	N08_3	Glomerular disorders in disease classified elsewhere	1112
5	N08_8	Glomerular disorders in disease classified elsewhere	690
6	N18_0	Chronic Kidney Disease (CKD)	1084781
7	N18_8	End stage renal disease	937
8	N18_9	Chronic Kidney Disease, unspecified	4293

4.2   Deep Learning on the Dataset

A feed forward neural network with one input layer, one output layer and two hidden layers was used during the evaluation of nephrology dataset. For the classification, eight input features have been chosen, abdominal_ultrasonography (x1), enrolled_for_transplantation (x2), vascular_access (x3), HbsAg (x4), venous_fistula_amount (x5), urea_reduction_rate (x6), HIC_antibodies (x7), HIV (x8). The output feature whose value has been predicted, is main_diagnos.

The dataset was split into testing and training sets with the train set containing 878859 entries and the test set containing 219715 entries. The model was then trained using the training dataset and was tested using the testing dataset.

The first layer or the input layer consists of 8 nodes, followed by a hidden layer with 16 nodes, followed by another hidden layer with 12 nodes and finally an output layer with 9 nodes corresponding to nine output classes.

5   Results

This section presents the results of applying feed forward neural network on standardized nephrology dataset.

5.1 Hardware and Software Details

Experiments have been performed on MacBook Pro 2017 (macOS Mojave OS), 3.1 GHz Intel Core i5 with 8 GB RAM ad Intel Iris Plus Graphics 650 1536 MB.

For developing the model TensorFlow [17] and Keras [18] have been used. Tensorflow, which is implemented by Google, provides a series of functions that provide easy implementation of deep neural networks based on the static computational graph. Keras which supports TensorFlow allows users to design deep learning architectures with ease and without worrying about the internal design. Google Colaboratory, or Colab, which provides free of charge cloud GPU for education and research purposes [19], had been used for the implementation of this study.

The model achieved a training accuracy of 98.74% and test accuracy of 98.75% as shown in Fig. 3. Figure 4 shows the training loss and the test loss (around 8%). The results indicate that feed forward neural networks predict disease with a high accuracy and less loss.

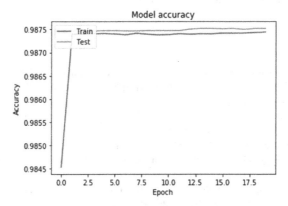

Fig. 3. Model accuracy

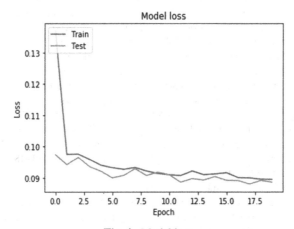

Fig. 4. Model loss

6 Conclusion

Taking the importance of human life into consideration, timely and accurate diagnosis of diseases is extremely important for better treatment and management. With this in mind, in the current study a deep learning based model using feed forward neural networks has been created that is able to predict the kidney disease based on several important parameters. The model is trained on nephrology dataset and achieves a high accuracy of 98.75%. The presence of such an automated system for the prediction of kidney diseases can help reduce the burden of clinicians. They can simply put in the input parameters and obtain the diagnosis as output.

In future, other deep learning algorithms/techniques can be tested for the nephrology dataset. The current architecture may be enhanced through a feedback box which can be evaluated by a medical practitioner/doctor (nephrologist). Some more input parameters like glomerular haematuria, protein urea, albumin urea, antinuclear antibodies, anti-double-stranded DNA and HbA1c may be added to the input parameters. Correspondingly the model training may be enhanced.

References

1. Luyckx, V.A., Tonelli, M., Staniferc, J.W.: The global burden of kidney disease and the sustainable development goals. Bull. World Health Organ. **96**, 414–422 (2018). https://doi.org/10.2471/BLT.17.206441
2. Pouyanfar, S., et al.: A survey on deep learning: algorithms, techniques, and applications. ACM Comput. Surv. **51**(5), Article 92 (2018). https://doi.org/10.1145/3234150
3. Najafabadi, M.M., Villanustre, F., Khoshgoftaar, T.M., Seliya, N., Wald, R., Muharemagic, E.: Deep learning applications and challenges in big data analytics. J. Big Data **2**(1), 1–21 (2015). https://doi.org/10.1186/s40537-014-0007-7
4. Shrestha, A., Mahmood, A.: Review of deep learning algorithms and architectures. IEEE Access **7**, 53040–53065 (2019). https://doi.org/10.1109/ACCESS.2019.2912200
5. openEHR. http://www.openehr.org. Accessed 11 Oct 2019
6. Teodoro D., Sundvall E., João Junior M., Ruch P., Freire, S.M.: ORBDA: an openEHR benchmark dataset for performance assessment of electronic health record servers. PLoS ONE **13**(1), e0190028. https://doi.org/10.1371/journal.pone.0190028
7. Wehrmann, J., Becker, W., Cagnini, H.E.L., Barros, R.C.: A character-based convolutional neural network for language- agnostic Twitter sentiment analysis. In: International Joint Conference on Neural Networks, pp. 2384–2391. IEEE (2017)
8. Cho, K., et al.: Learning phase representations using RNN encoder-decoder for statistical machine translation. In: The Conference on Empirical Methods in Natural Language Processing, pp. 1724–1734 (2014). https://doi.org/10.3115/v1/d14-1179
9. Ha, H.-Y., Yang, Y., Pouyanfar, S., Tian, H., Chen, S.-C.: Correlation-based deep learning for multimedia semantic concept detection. In: Wang, J., Cellary, W., Wang, D., Wang, H., Chen, S.-C., Li, T., Zhang, Y. (eds.) WISE 2015. LNCS, vol. 9419, pp. 473–487. Springer, Cham (2015). https://doi.org/10.1007/978-3-319-26187-4_43
10. Cireşan, D.C., Giusti, A., Gambardella, L.M., Schmidhuber, J.: Mitosis detection in breast cancer histology images with deep neural networks. In: Mori, K., Sakuma, I., Sato, Y., Barillot, C., Navab, N. (eds.) MICCAI 2013. LNCS, vol. 8150, pp. 411–418. Springer, Heidelberg (2013). https://doi.org/10.1007/978-3-642-40763-5_51

11. Litjens, G., et al.: Deep learning as a tool for increased accuracy and efficiency of histopathological diagnosis. Sci. Rep. **6**, article number 26286 (2016). https://doi.org/10.1038/srep26286

12. Poplin, R., et al.: Prediction of cardiovascular risk factors from retinal fundus photographs via deep learning. Nat. Biomed. Eng. **2**, 158–164 (2018)

13. Choi, E., et al.: Multi-layer representation learning for medical concepts. In: ACM SIGKDD International Conference on Knowledge Discovery and Data Mining, vol. 22, pp. 1495–1504 (2016). https://doi.org/10.1145/2939672.2939823

14. Ma, F., Chitta, R., Zhou, J., You, Q., Sun, T., Gao, J.: Dipole: diagnosis prediction in healthcare via attention based bidirectional recurrent neural networks. In: ACM SIGKDD International Conference on Knowledge Discovery and Data Mining, vol. 23, pp. 1903–1911 (2017). https://doi.org/10.1145/3097983.3098088

15. Sharma, K., et al.: Automatic segmentation of kidneys using deep learning for total kidney volume quantification in autosomal dominant polycystic kidney disease. Sci. Rep. **7**, article number 2049 (2017). https://doi.org/10.1038/s41598-017-01779-0

16. Glomerular disease: Evaluation and differential diagnosis in adults. www.uptodate.com/contents/glomerular-disease-evaluation-and-differential-diagnosis-in-adults. Accessed 19 Oct 2019

17. TensorFlow. http://www.tensorflow.org. Accessed 11 Sept 2019

18. Keras Documentation. http://www.keras.io. Accessed 11 Sept 2019

19. Colaboratory. http://colab.research.google.com. Accessed 11 Sept 2019

Prediction of Ticket Prices for Public Transport Using Linear Regression and Random Forest Regression Methods: A Practical Approach Using Machine Learning

Aditi[1] , Akash Dutta[1] , Aman Dureja[2(✉)] , Salil Abrol[2] , and Ajay Dureja[2]

[1] Department of Computer Science and Engineering, PDM University, Bahadurgarh, India
aditi958205@gmail.com, akashdutta57@gmail.com
[2] Department of Computer Science and Engineering, Faculty of Engineering and Technology,
PDM University, Bahadurgarh, India
amandureja@gmail.com, salilabrol@hotmail.com,
ajaydureja@gmail.com

Abstract. Spanish High-Speed Train Service (Renfe AVE) is a ticket pricing monitoring system. It scrapes tickets pricing data periodically and stores it in a database. Ticket pricing changes based on demand and time, and there can be significant difference in price. This dataset has been designed the team of Data Scientists named Pedro Muñoz and David Cañones. The data is well collected for using it with machine learning models to predict fare (price) of a ticket depending upon the date, arrival and destination location, train class and train type. The dataset contains few null values which has to be taken care of to execute this research effectively. Two machine learning models were used (linear regression and random forest regression) and it was found out that random forest regressor gave a better accuracy score with both training and testing dataset of 79.06% and 80.10% respectively. Random forest model wins with more accuracy and can help a user check for train journey with automatically computed ticket fare by machine learning model.

Keywords: Machine learning · Fare prediction · Linear regression · Random forest regression

1 Introduction

Machine learning is a subfield of artificial intelligence (AI) that gives systems to learn the network and to improve based on learning acquired by the system without intervention of explicitly programmed by any human. While the machine learning gives the faster and more accurate results and observation for identify the profitable opportunities or various risk. This is also required the more time and resources to train the network in accurate manner [1]. The learning of system is started with observations of data, such as direct experience, examples, instruction, for finding the important data and useful data in form of useful patterns and make better decisions in the future based on examples

© Springer Nature Singapore Pte Ltd. 2020
U. Batra et al. (Eds.): REDSET 2019, CCIS 1229, pp. 140–150, 2020.
https://doi.org/10.1007/978-981-15-5827-6_12

provided. The various approaches have been found to that can be used to determine the price of the house, the one of them is prediction analysis. A quantitative approach utilizes time-series data, that is based on quantitative prediction [5]. The ML model is a mathematical representation of a process or a scenario that exists in real world and has to be analyzed. We provide the training data to the ML algorithm to build up our own ML model [3]. Using Machine Learning Algorithms, computer programs allow us to learn from the input data to get desired output within the specific range by using statistical analysis. The data is fed to machine learning algorithm rather than writing codes and build logic based on that data [6]. There exists a set of functions that can have similar characteristics and from those set of functions there is a need to choose the function that fits the training data most appropriately. These functions have the characteristics similar to the properties of a linear regressor, and combining the functions together, we term them as linear regression algorithm. While training, the data is fed to algorithm. The learning algorithm will then find pattern in the data. The output of this process will be a machine learning model which is finally used to predict the output on a given set of test input. The above explained process is called as "learning". Predictions on the dataset are made by splitting the data into test and train. We train the model using Train Set and we test the accuracy of the model with the test set [1].

1.1 Supervised Learning

Supervised Learning is the learning where the teacher signal is present i.e. this learning is worked in the presence of teacher. The presence of teacher means that the target output is known, and we apply the input data to train the network to get the expected output with the targeted output. This is done by some error optimization techniques to reduce the error. When the error is minimized then that trained network can be used to making prediction or decision when the new related input or query is applied to that network.

1.2 Unsupervised Learning

The unsupervised learning is based on no teacher approach, i.e. the leaning is done through no teacher signal in which through observation prediction are made. Basically, in this learning algorithms the systems make observation based on useful and very similar patterns near to each other and make them label or categories also called calibration. This process of making group of most similar pattern based on observation by applying shorted distance method is called clustering. The unsupervised leaning can be more unpredictable than the alternate model because the network is trained by itself without the target output known. The advantage of unsupervised learning is that it can perform more complex tasks than supervised systems.

1.3 Linear Regression

Linear regression is the technique to find the straight line which is best-fitted through the number of points. This line is called regression line. The below figure shows the line (black) is the best-fitted line and shows the predicted score on Y axis for each possible value of X (Fig. 1).

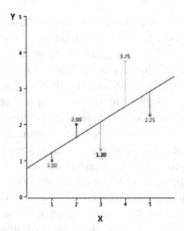

Fig. 1. Line of linear regression fit

The vertical lines (in different colors) shows the error of prediction which is far from the regression line. The Linear regression approaches uses the least squares methods for fitting in the point to find the best-fitted line. The other approaches are also available like least absolute deviation regression method that minimize the "lack of fit" form. Or also this can be done using ridge regression that minimize the penalized version of least squares cost function.

The Linear Regression Equation

Linear regression could be a way to model the connection between 2 variables. We may conjointly acknowledge the equation as slope formula. The equation has the shape Y = a + bX, where Y is dependent variable (that's the variable that goes on the Y axis), X is variable quantity (i.e. it's planned on the X axis), b is slope of the road and a is y-intercept during this equation.

$$a = \frac{(\Sigma y)(\Sigma x^2) - (\Sigma x)(\Sigma xy)}{n(\Sigma x^2) - (\Sigma x)^2}$$
$$b = \frac{n(\Sigma xy) - (\Sigma x)(\Sigma y)}{n(\Sigma x^2) - (\Sigma x)^2}$$

The first step is to find a linear regression equation is to work out if there's a relationship between the 2 variables. this is {often|this can be} often a judgment involve the research worker. You'll additionally want a listing of your information in x-y format (i.e. 2 columns of information—freelance and dependent variables). Linear Models (GLM): It uses linear models to hold out regression, single stratum analysis of variance and analysis of variance [5].

Advantages of Linear Regressor
- Linear regression is an especially easy technique. it's very straightforward and intuitive to use and perceive.
- This approach works in almost all the cases. Even the dataset could not fit in this approach specifically, it may be accustomed find the character of the connection between the 2 variables.

Disadvantages of Linear Regressor

- Linear regression solely models' relationships between dependent and freelance variables. The linear regression actually sees the straight-line relationship between them as it works on Linear Line that is inaccurate typically.
- Linear models fails for the number of variables as it assumes as the noise between the variables instead of finding the connection between them if the number of variables are large.

1.4   Random Forest Regressor

A Random Forest technique has the advantages of using the associate ensemble technique that can be used for regression as well as classification tasks by using the multiple decision tress structure and this method is popularly known as Bootstrap Aggregation also called Bagging. In Random Forest technique, the Bagging involves the coaching of every decision tree onto the unique formation sample. The multiple decision trees are chosen for finding the ultimate output instead of single decision tree as it is useful for finding the best solution path to a problem. The features (Z) and the dependent(y) variable values of the information from the datasets is passed to this random forest method for creating the decision tree. The grid search cross validation technique is employed from the sklearn library to work out the best values to be used for the hyper parameters of the model from a such that vary of values. once making a random forest regressor object, it's passed to function called the cross_val_score() which performs K-Fold cross validation on the input data and produces as an output, an error value (in form of metric), which can be used to determine the performance of the model [2, 4, 5] (Fig. 2).

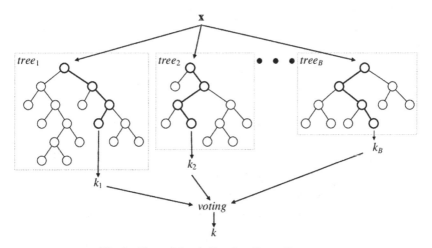

Fig. 2. Flow of data in Random Forest Regressor

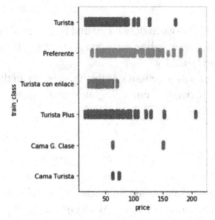 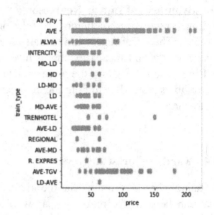

Fig. 3. Categorical Graph b/w train_class & Price

Fig. 4. Categorical Graph b/w & Price train_type and Price

Advantages of Random Forest Regressor

- The advantage of Random Forest Regressor is that it uses the precise learning algorithms and various functions to solve the complex problem and to find the more accurate results for different datasets.
- The approach used in Random Forest Regressor is the forest building, which helps to find and unbiased estimate the generalization error.
- This model still maintains the accuracy even if model is dealing with the very less amount of data as it has the capability to estimate the missing data (Figs. 3, 4 and 5).

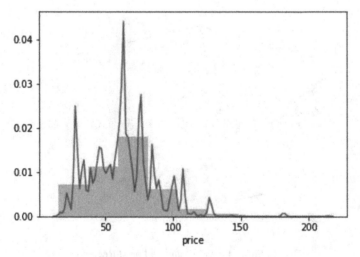

Fig. 5. Distribution graph of price

Disadvantages of Random Forest Regressor
- The problem with the Random forest regressor is that it is overfitted for some datasets and also add the noisy classification/ regression tasks.
- Another problem with Random Forest Regressor method occurs for data having various categorial variables which is of different number of levels. Random forests are biased in these cases.

Rest of the paper is written in the manner where Sect. 2 contains the literature survey, Sect. 3 of this research paper contains methodology explaining the approach in detail, Sect. 4 of this paper contains the results of the tested model, Sect. 5 carries the algorithm framed and followed, Sect. 6 contains conclusion with discussion on future work, At the end there are references to all the papers and books which were referred to do this work (Tables 1 and 2).

Table 1. Description of the features

Feature	Information
insert_date	Date and time when price were collected (UTC)
Origin	Origin City
Destination	Destination city
start_date	Train departure time (European Central Time)
end_date	Train arrival time (European Central Time)
Train_type	Train service name
Price	Price of ticket (Euros)
train_class	Ticket class, tourist, business etc.
Fare	Ticket fare, round trip etc.

Table 2. Sample data set

Target (Price)	insert_date	Origin	Destination	Start date	End date	train_type	train_class	Fare
68.95	2019-04-11 21:49:46	MADRID	BARCELONA	2019-04-18 05:50:00	2019-04-18 08:55:00	AVE	Preferent	Promo
115.65	2019-04-11 21:49:46	MADRID	BARCELONA	2019-04-18 19:00:00	2019-04-18 21:30:00	AVE	Preferent	Promo
	2019-04-11 21:49:46	MADRID	BARCELONA	2019-04-18 21:25:00	2019-04-18 23:55:00	AVE		
107.7	2019-04-11 21:49:46	MADRID	BARCELONA	2019-04-18 13:25:00	2019-04-18 16:24:00	AVE-TGV	Turista	Flexible
43.25	2019-04-11 21:50:04	MADRID	BARCELONA	2019-05-22 07:15:00	2019-05-22 16:37:00	R. EXPRES	Turista	Adultoida

2 Literature Survey

In year 2019, research paper titled "Inflation and Economy Growth: Random Forest Methodology" by Sidika Basci and Houcine Senoussi highlighted use of Random forest methodology to track inflation growth and concluded by using random forest methodology is used in order to capture the relationship between inflation and growth [7].

In year 2019, research paper titled "Linear Regressions of Predicting Rainfall over Ka-ley Region" highlighted accurate predicting using supervised learning and concluded by using linear regression model for accurately predicting rainfall [8].

In year 2018, research paper titled "Forecasting wheat prices in India" by Ashwini Darekar and A Amarender Reddy highlighted use of ARIMA model for predicting and concluded by predicting the future prices of wheat in India with 95% accuracy level [9].

In year 2005, research paper titled "Exploring the Goodness of Fit in Linear Models" by Scott A. Sinex highlighted insights on how to analyse how well the linear regression model fits the data and concluded by Measurement of how good the linear mathematical model fit the data [10].

In year 2019, research paper titled "Bitcoin financial forecasting" by Amit Chauhan highlighted on predicting bitcoin prices and concluded with predicting bitcoin prices [11].

In year 2002, research paper titled "Lazy Learning: A local method for supervised learning" by Gianluca Bonetempi and MauroBirattari was published, highlighted Deep analysis and data on supervised learning and concluded by introducing local modelling, and its is a Lazy Learning version, which is a great alternative to existing techniques [12].

In year 1998, research paper titled "Adaptive Memory Based Regression Model" by Gianluca Bontempi, Hugues Bersini and Mauro Birattari highlighted memory based methods obtain accurate predictions from empirical data and concluded by showing that this method reduces the problem of learning an input output mapping to a collection of simpler local estimation problems [13].

In year 2014, research paper titled "Predictive Model for ECX Coffee Contracts" by Addis Ababa highlighted price prediction model used to predict the daily selling price of all coffee contracts and concluded by proposing prediction model that assists the market to undertake efficient coffee trading system [14].

In year 2017, research paper titled "Forecasting oilseeds prices in India: Case of groundnut" by Ashwini Darekar and A Amarenderv Reddy highlighted use of ARIMA model for predicting market prices of oilseeds and concluded by predicting prices of oilseeds which will definitely be helpful not only to producers and consumers but also to wholesalers, retailers, government agencies [15].

3 Methodology

The methodology used in this paper is given in the flowchart below. The data set is collected from authenticated dataset repository. The data set contains over 7 million rows.

The second step is to check for null values and there are 3106821, 9664 and 9664 null values found in price, train_class and fare respectively. Mean of price column was taken out and was filled in null values. The feature train_class had "Turista" value occurring the most so it was used to fill null values of the same feature. Also, the unnecessary columns are deleted from the data set. In the fourth step, we started with visualizing the data.

In fifth step, some of the columns were passed in label encoder to convert them into int64 type and help the model to find a pattern. This data set formed is then divided into train and test in which test data set gets 10% share. They are further divided into x_train, x_test, y_train and y_test to fit in different Machine Learning models.

In the sixth step, the models are trained to get the training accuracy. Depending on the winner of training phase, the winning model is selected to apply test data for finding the testing accuracy and the results are formulated.

4 Results

Linear Regression and Random Forest Regression models were used in the project and in the sixth step, data is fitted one by one to get a training accuracy. Training accuracy of 62.18% was achieved with Linear Regressor and accuracy of 79.95% with Random Forest Regressor. In the eighth step, Random Forest Regressor was chosen as it has better accuracy and tested it with the test data. In the end, an accuracy of 80.10% was achieved using this model.

Finally in the end for the result analysis, it was found that the dataset had a lot of null entries which had to be filled by us which off course reduced the accuracy but still accuracy of 80.10% was achieved which is quite good and this model can be used to predict the price of the ticket (Table 3).

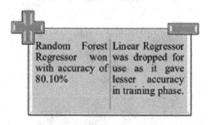

| Random Forest Regressor won with accuracy of 80.10% | Linear Regressor was dropped for use as it gave lesser accuracy in training phase. |

Table 3. Training and testing accuracy

Model	Training accuracy in %	Testing accuracy in %
Linear Regressor	62.18	Dropped
Random Forest Regressor	79.95	80.10

5   Algorithm

Step 1: Importing all necessary library required.

Step 2: Importing the dataset using pandas library.

Step 3: Check for null values and remove them, thus cleaning the dataset.

Step 4: Visualize the dataset using seaborn library.

Step 5: Remove all unnecessary columns hence doing feature selection.

Step 6: Label Encode / One hot encode the required columns.

Step 7: Split the data into train and test using train_test_split.

Step 8: Further split train and test dataset into X_train, Y_train, X_test and Y_test.

Step 9: Try different models with training dataset and choose the one with highest accuracy.

Step 10: Apply the model with highest accuracy on test dataset.

6   Conclusion and Future Work

The values of price (ticket price) are calculated using the data collected by Spanish High-Speed Train Service (Renfe AVE). Mean of price column was calculated which was found out to be 63.38 and this value was used to fill null values present in price column. The feature train_class had "Turista" value occurring the most so it was used to fill null values of the same feature. Origin, destination, train_type, train_class, and fare values are used as independent variables in linear regression and random forest regression to predict values of price column. Random forest regression gave a better accuracy of 79.80% with training data and thus the model was chosen to work with testing data. Upon using the model with testing data, an accuracy of 80.20% was recorded.

The dataset provided although had more than 1 million (1048574) entries, still duration of all entries were from 19/04/2019 to 30/04/2019. Due to this model may not be very accurate in predicting train ticket price during winters or later months. Having data with entries from different months can help improve accuracy of this model as a whole. Doing this is kept for future work.

References

1. Donges, N.: 6 concepts of Andrew NG's book: "Machine Learning Yearning", 18 February 2019. https://machinelearning-blog.com/2019/02/18/6-concepts-of-andrew-ngs-book-ma-chine-learning-yearning/

2. Random Forest Algorithm for Regression: A Beginner's Guide, 6 November 2018. https://acadgild.com/blog/random-forest-algorithm-regression

3. Machine Learning: what it is and why it matters (n.d.). https://www.sas.com/en_in/insights/analytics/machine-learning.html

4. Figure 2f from, Irimia, R., Gottschling, M.: Taxonomic revision of Rochefortia Sw. (Ehretiaceae, Boraginales). Biodivers. Data J. 4, e7720 (2016). https://doi.org/10.3897/BDJ.4.e7720. Random Forest Regression, pp. 1–12 (n.d.). https://doi.org/10.3897/bdj.4.e7720.figure2f

5. Ghodsi, R.: Estimation of housing prices by fuzzy regression and artificial neural network. In: Fourth Asia International Conference on Mathematical/Analytical Modelling and Commuter Simulation, no. 1 (2010)

6. Sharma, S., Sodhi, A., Nagpal, N., Dureja, A., Dureja, A.: Practical approaches: machine learning techniques for image processing and text processing. Int. J. Inf. Syst. Manag. Sci. 2(2), 389–396 (2019)

7. Basci, S., Senoussi, H.: Inflation and economy growth: random forest methodology (2019)

8. Myint, O.: Linear regressions of predicting rainfall over Kalay Region. Int. J. Trend Sci. Res. Dev. (IJTSRD) 3, 1681–1685 (2019)

9. Darekar, A., Reddy, A.A.: Forecasting wheat prices in India, Wheat and Barley Research (2018)

10. Sinex, S.: Exploring the goodness of fit in linear models. J. Online Math.Appl. 5 (2005)

11. Chauhan, A.K., et al.: Bitcoin financial forecasting. Int. J. Adv. Res. Ideas Innov. Technol. 5, 1923–1925 (2019)

12. Bontempi, G., Birattari, M., Bersini, H.: Lazy learning: a logical method for supervised learning. In: Jain, L.C., Kacprzyk, J. (eds.) New Learning Paradigms in Soft Computing. Studies in Fuzziness and Soft Computing, vol. 84, pp. 97–136. Springer, Heidelberg (2002). https://doi.org/10.1007/978-3-7908-1803-1_4

13. Bontempi, G.: Adaptive memory-based regression methods. In: Proceedings of IEEE (1998)

14. Ababa, A.: Predictive model for ECX coffee contracts (2014)

15. Darekar, A., Reddy, A.A.: Forcasting oilseeds prices in India: case of groundnut. J. Oilseeds Res. 34(4), 235–240 (2017)

Identification of Novel Drug Targets in Pathogenic *Aspergillus Fumigatus*: An *in Silico* Approach

Reena Gupta and Chandra Shekhar Rai[✉]

University School of Information, Communication and Technology,
Guru Gobind Singh Indraprastha University, New Delhi, India
{reena,csrai}@ipu.ac.in

Abstract. Invasive aspergillosis due to fungus *Aspergillus fumigatus* is considered a major human disease infecting immunosuppressed patients. Screening of novel drug targets for this opportunistic pathogen is a need of the hour due to the constraints of antifungal remedies, reactions, drug resistance & toxicities, expense and drug-drug interactions. In order to overcome these limitations, novel antifungal drug targets are needed. Thus, to find putative drug targets, we explored combination of subtractive and comparative genomics approach in the current work Whole proteome of *A. fumigatus* is screened for homology analysis via target identification tool 'TiDv2'. TiDv2 classifies proposed drug targets as new and virulent in less time and at low cost. Genes from homology analysis are compared with humans and gut flora to achieve non homology with them to attain broad spectrum drug target. Thereafter, druggability and virulence factor analysis is performed. The resultant dataset is prioritized for metabolic pathway analysis. In addition, functional annotation and subcellular localization is accomplished. The results reveal that 5 genes namely His6, FasA, PabaA, FtmA and erg6 might work as promising wide-spectrum drug targets for *A. fumigatus*. Hence, these genes may improve current curative failures in the medication of invasive aspergillosis. However, these possible drug targets should be verified to confirm before target based lead discovery.

Keywords: Drug targets · *Aspergillus fumigatus* · Subtractive genomic analysis · Target identification · TiD · Comparative genomics

1 Introduction

Invasive aspergillosis is a fatal infection caused by pervasive fungus *A. fumigatus* in immunosuppressed hosts [1]. Qualitative or quantitative deficiencies are manipulated by *Aspergillus fumigatus* in the host resistant defence to induce intrusive infection. It is extremely difficult to treat this infection in immunocompromised hosts. The fatality from intrusive aspergillosis surpasses 50% even post chemotherapy. In 1996, in U.S., the estimate of curing diagnosed patients of intrusive aspergillosis was $633 M, where the amount of each case was roughly $64,500 [1]. In acute immunosuppressed patients,

© Springer Nature Singapore Pte Ltd. 2020
U. Batra et al. (Eds.): REDSET 2019, CCIS 1229, pp. 151–160, 2020.
https://doi.org/10.1007/978-981-15-5827-6_13

presently accessible antifungals have moderate efficiency [2]. According to a 2009 article in the journal Emerging Infectious Diseases, exponential increasing issue in curing Aspergillus infection is drug resistance [1, 3, 4]. Moreover, therapeutic medication is usually unsuccessful and is obstructed by harsh side effects of available antifungals. Hence, new drug targets are required which would be successful in curing aspergillosis and have less side effects on host [5].

Traditional approach has been used to screen drug targets and vaccines against aspergillosis for last two decades [5]. The screening of novel potent drug targets is limited due to lack of data, methodology and information. All these major problems have necessitated to screen possible drugs against this hazardous pathogen. Search of new curative drug targets resulted in screening of novel drug candidates. Due to the online availability of newer genes, genomes and protein databases, comparative genomic analysis is considered one of the most reliable strategy for potential drug designing [6, 7]. In the present work, we have attempted to develop a procedure to resolve the restraints of studies done so far. Our computational procedure incorporates whole genome analysis, subtractive/comparative analysis, metabolic pathway analysis and sub cellular localization analysis.

In the present work, we have used subtractive/comparative genome analysis where deduction of identical protein set is accomplished followed by comparison of pathogen and human host genome. Essential gene set is the smallest set of genes necessary for the growth and sustenance of the pathogen. In the proposed work we have adopted in silico approach through subtractive/comparative genomics on the whole proteome of *A. fumigatus* to identify unique gene set in the metabolic pathways using KEGG and gene set related with the membrane using CELLO [8]. This computational approach is successfully adopted to identify drug targets in many other fungi and bacteria such as *Helicobacter pylori* [9], *Staphylococcus aureus* [10], I [11], Bacillus anthracis [12], *Neisseria meningitides* [13] etc. Hence, we have adopted in silico approach to detect the potential novel drug targets which are virulent and have unique metabolic pathways. However, these putative drug targets should be verified before drug designing.

2   Materials and Methods

Pathogenic proteins of *A. fumigatus* were screened to a wide-spectrum anti-aspergillus drug target detection procedure that incorporates comparative and subtractive genomics technique. The complete description of protocol of the target detection procedure is shown in Fig. 1.

2.1   Program and Data Acquisition of Pathogen Protein

Complete proteome of *A. fumigatus* was fetched from NCBI protein database (http://www.ncbi.nlm.nih.gov/) and subjected to TiDv2, a target identification software. Fasta file format was chosen among various file formats for drug target identification. TiDv2 is a standalone software developed by us. It is an extension of TiD developed by our team [14]. It includes functions for paralog analysis, essentiality analysis and non-homolog analysis that excludes paralogous proteins, includes essential genes from DEG, CEG or

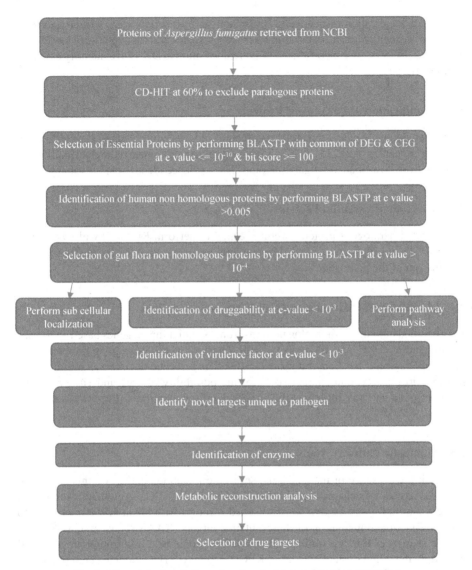

Fig. 1. Complete description of protocol of target detection procedure

common of both DEG and CEG and excludes host and gut flora homologous proteins from the essential gene dataset [12, 15].

Target prioritization analysis tab characterized the resultant essential gene dataset on druggability and virulence. Virulent proteins are vital for the progression, pathogenicity and sustenance of the pathogen [1].

Target prioritization was done on gutflora non homologous proteins with the help of online target prioritization tools such as Kyoto Encyclopedia of Genes and Genomes (KEGG), INTERPROSCAN and Cello for pathway analysis, functional annotation and subcellular localization respectively. BioPython v2.7.10 scripts were written and integrated with executables and datasets in Microsoft Visual Studio 2015 platform for designing TiDv2. In TiDv2, we incorporated fungal radio button in DEG tab to identify essential genes of fungus.

2.2 Identification of Paralogous Proteins

Target detection and characterization parameters and procedures were followed as mentioned in our earlier work [14]. CD-HIT suite was used to eliminate redundant paralogous proteins from downloaded fungal proteome. The sequence identity cut off value is 60%.

2.3 Selection of Essential Proteins

The selected paralogous proteins were screened to perform BLASTP with DEG at e-value 10^{-10} and bit score $>=100$. The resultant genes are vital for the sustenance and progression of the pathogen.

2.4 Identification of Human and Gut Flora Non-homologs

We identified human non-homolog proteins from essential fungal genes based on threshold e-value at 0.005 and bit score $>=100$. Gutflora non homologous proteins were obtained at e-value 10^{-4} and bit score $>=100$. The screened dataset was postulated as possible drug targets and characterized for the possibility of drug and virulence. The resultant gene set was further outlined with UniProt identifiers (http://www.uniprot.org/).

2.5 Metabolic Pathway Analysis

To check the presence of mapped gene set in the metabolic pathways, this dataset of potential targets was characterized at the KAAS server (KEGG Automatic Annotation Server). Further, these targets were screened through BLAST in KEGG database to achieve functional annotation of these putative targets. KAAS server assigns K numbers to sequences that are similar and has bi-directional best hit through programmed procedure that allows establishment of KEGG pathways. The outcome gene set has KO (KEGG Orthology) assignments of sequences that determine metabolic proteins [16].

2.6 Subcellular Localization

We have analysed the metabolic set of proteins in CELLO v2.5 for subcellular localization and biological significance. Subcellular localization detects the potential proteins as cytoplasmic, periplasmic, outer membrane, extra cellular and inner membrane protein [16].

2.7 Identification of Druggability and Virulence Factors

The genes obtained after non homologous analysis with gut flora were further subjected to druggability analysis and virulence analysis. Virulence factor provides new insight in the development of potential anti-fungal drugs [17].

2.8 Selection of Anti Fungal Drug Targets

Finally, proteins obtained after subtractive analysis are putative anti-fungal drug targets. These targets would be experimentally validated before lead discovery. These targets would be potential for the screening of novel anti-fungal drug targets.

3 Results and Discussion

Due to active progression of bacterial proteins, resistance to the present antibiotics is expanding which leads to global health hazard. This entails the exercise to design antibacterial candidates targeted at novel drug targets. The correlation of genomes and gene products have been promoted by the desegregated databases, computerized sequencing of genes, algorithms and tools, which further recommend genome-based drug target designing. Moreover, a computerized, quick and effective methodology to identify drug targets for a specific pathogen from whole proteome of bacteria or fungi develop an effective way to deal with bacterial or fungal proteins expanding with drug resistance in present scenario [14].

The present work is based on advanced comparative and subtractive genomic approach. The unique and vital proteins are critical for *A. fumigatus* progression, pathogenicity and survival [6]. A compelling approach to tackle the demanding aspergillosis infection is to find target proteins and their essential metabolic pathways. The results of the systematic procedures for mining putative drug targets are presented in Fig. 2.

3.1 Identification of Paralogous Proteins

Whole genome sequence (*.faa) of *A. fumigatus* which is responsible for causing infectious disease was successfully retrieved from NCBI and screened through TiDv2 tool. In the prevailing examination, 56757 proteins were retrieved from NCBI. These proteins were screened in CD-HIT suite at 60% identity value as threshold which produce 10815 non paralogous genes.

3.2 Identification of Essential Protiens

Non-paralogous proteins were run in Essentiality Analysis Tab of TiD. These 10815 proteins were run on BLASTP with common of DEG and CEG at e-value $<= 10^{-10}$ and bit score $>= 100$. 1860 proteins were observed to be essential for the growth of *A. fumigatus*.

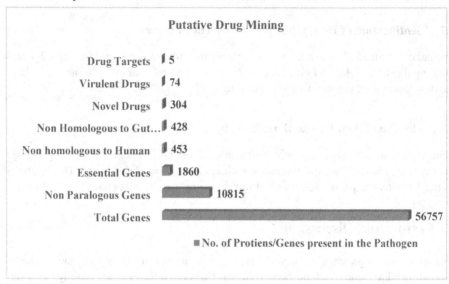

Fig. 2. Results of putative drug mining

3.3 Selection of Human and Gut Flora Non-homologs

1860 essential proteins were screened in Non-Homology Analysis Tab of TiD. Human non homologous proteins were detected by screening through BLASTP at e-value > 0.005. By performing BLASTP, we detected ample analogies between pathogen and human host at e-value < 0.005. Proteins identified as homologous are excluded so that target candidates are safe for human host and has less side effects. We found 453 pathogenic proteins non homologous to human host. Further, out of 453 human non homologous proteins, we identified 428 proteins as non homologous to gutflora at e-value > 10^{-4}.

3.4 Metabolic Pathway Analysis

We found 395 uniprot identifiers when 428 gut flora non homologous proteins were mapped with uniprot identifiers of *A. fumigatus*. To study the relationship of these genes in metabolic pathways, the mapped geneset of potential drug targets was characterized at the KAAS server (KEGG Automatic Annotation Server). Further, these targets were screened through BLAST in KEGG database to achieve metabolic pathway of these potential targets. The outcome gene set contains KO (KEGG Orthology) assignments of sequences that determine metabolic pathway. There were 13817 total KO assignments in the whole proteome.

3.5 Subcellular Localization

Subcellular localization of probable drug targets in the present examination revealed that 137 drug targets were cytoplasmic, 132 were inner membrane, 81 were periplasmic, 51 were outer membrane and 26 were extra cellular proteins (as shown in Table 1). Position of these putative drug targets is vital in future at the time of designing drug or vaccine. A vital condition in rational drug design is the balance between the subcellular localization report of a drug target with the pharmaceutical features of lead molecules focused to it.

Table 1. Subcellular localization of putative drug targets

S.No.	Accession no.	Name of protein	KO number	Pathways	Enzyme
1.	EAL84512.1	sterol 24-c-methyltransferase	K00559	Steroid biosynthesis	Yes
2.	EAL85149.1	nonribosomal brevianamide peptide synthase FtmA	K18281	Staurosporine biosynthesis	Yes
3.	EAL85558.1	para-aminobenzoate synthase PabaA	K13950	Folate biosynthesis	Yes
4.	EAL86700.1	fatty acid synthase alpha subunit FasA	K00667	Fatty acid biosynthesis	Yes
5.	KMK59268.1	5-proFAR isomerase His6	K01814	Histidine metabolism	Yes

3.6 Identification of Druggability and Virulence Factors

We identified 304 proteins as novel drug targets, when 428 gut flora non homologous proteins were screened for druggability analysis. Out of 428 proteins, 74 proteins were found to be virulent. Virulence factor analysis is essential to identify drug targets of the pathogen [17]. The drug targets with virulence factor are vital for inception of infection and perseverance in host. Hence, experimental lead molecules which are developed on the basis of these potential drug targets are integral for formulating a novel curative procedure against pathogens.

3.7 Selection of Anti Fungal Drug Targets

Using subtractive genomic analysis, we detected 5 proteins as novel drug targets having virulence factor and unique metabolic pathway. Out of 5 novel drug targets, 1 was outer membrane protein and 4 were cytoplasmic proteins. The detailed information of proteins with uniport identifier and gene name is shown in Table 2.

This subtractive/comparative genome analysis has been efficiently practiced in various bacterial and fungi genes such as *Mycoplasma pneumoniae* M129 [18], *Staphylococcus aureus* N315 [8], *Mycobacterium tuberculosis* F11 [19], *Neisseria meningitides* serogroup B for screening of drug targets [13]. The proteins screened in the present study will fairly lead to a positive way in developing potential therapeutic drugs for future researchers.

Table 2. Detailed information of putative drug targets

S.No.	Description	Gene name	Uniprot identifier	Subcellular localization
1.	EAL84512.1 sterol 24-c-methyltransferase, putative [Aspergillus fumigatus Af293]	erg6	Q4W9V1	cytoplasmic
2.	EAL85149.1 nonribosomal brevianamide peptide synthase FtmA [Aspergillus fumigatus Af293]	FtmA	Q4WAW3	cytoplasmic
3.	EAL85558.1 para-aminobenzoate synthase PabaA [Aspergillus fumigatus Af293]	PabaA	Q4WDI0	Outer membrane
4.	EAL86700.1 fatty acid synthase alpha subunit FasA [Aspergillus fumigatus Af293]	FasA	Q4WEX7	cytoplasmic
5.	KMK59268.1 5-proFAR isomerase His6 [Aspergillus fumigatus Z5]	His6	A0J5PRW7	cytoplasmic

4 Conclusion

In this era of bioinformatics, previous traditional methods of drug discovery and designing are becoming obsolete. Mammoth of biological database restructures the process of drug discovery and designing procedures. In order to reduce the hazards of dangerous aspergillosis, we have to design novel probable drug targets. In this study, we have executed subtractive genomics and comparative genomics analysis on pathogenic proteins of A. *fumigatus* and identified 5 novel potential drug targets (His6, FasA, PabaA, FtmA and erg6) for designing of drug and development of vaccine. Moreover, these putative drug targets execute an important role in the vital metabolic pathways. However, outcomes of the present work can be authenticated by further clinical research to confirm their execution in restraining the production and disturbing the virulence factor of A. *fumigatus* pathogen. Promisingly, this study would help to design new anti-A. *fumigatus* drugs against aspergillosis. Hence, this study would be undoubtedly favourable because of recent findings which state the growing risk of resistance of A. *fumigatus* pathogen.

References

1. Hohl, T.M., Feldmesser, M.: Aspergillus fumigatus: principles of pathogenesis and host defense. Eukaryot. Cell **6**, 1953–1963 (2007). https://doi.org/10.1128/EC.00274-07
2. Fair, R.J., Tor, Y.: Antibiotics and bacterial resistance in the 21st century. Perspect. Med. Chem. **6**, 25–64 (2014). https://doi.org/10.4137/PMC.S14459
3. Cramer, R.A., et al.: Calcineurin target CrzA regulates conidial germination, hyphal growth, and pathogenesis of Aspergillus fumigatus. Eukaryot. Cell **7**, 1085–1097 (2008). https://doi.org/10.1128/EC.00086-08
4. Davison, J.: Essential gene identification and drug target prioritization in Aspergillus fumigatus. PLOS Pathog
5. Ebel, F., Schwienbacher, M., Beyer, J., Heesemann, J., Brakhage, A.A., Brock, M.: Analysis of the regulation, expression, and localisation of the isocitrate lyase from Aspergillus fumigatus, a potential target for antifungal drug development. Fungal Genet. Biol. **43**, 476–489 (2006). https://doi.org/10.1016/j.fgb.2006.01.015
6. Abadio, A.K.R., Kioshima, E.S., Teixeira, M.M., Martins, N.F., Maigret, B., Felipe, M.S.S.: Comparative genomics allowed the identification of drug targets against human fungal pathogens. BMC Genom. **12**, 75 (2011). https://doi.org/10.1186/1471-2164-12-75
7. Ou-Yang, S.-S., Lu, J.-Y., Kong, X.-Q., Liang, Z.-J., Luo, C., Jiang, H.: Computational drug discovery. Acta Pharmacol. Sin. **33**, 1131–1140 (2012). https://doi.org/10.1038/aps.2012.109
8. Hossain, M., et al.: Identification of potential targets in Staphylococcus aureus N315 using computer aided protein data analysis. Bioinformation **9**, 187–192 (2013). https://doi.org/10.6026/97320630009187
9. Dutta, A., Singh, S.K., Ghosh, P., Mukherjee, R., Mitter, S., Bandyopadhyay, D.: In silico identification of potential therapeutic targets in the human pathogen Helicobacter pylori. Silico Biol. **6**, 43–47 (2006)
10. Uddin, R., Saeed, K., Khan, W., Azam, S.S., Wadood, A.: Metabolic pathway analysis approach: identification of novel therapeutic target against methicillin resistant Staphylococcus aureus. Gene **556**, 213–226 (2015). https://doi.org/10.1016/j.gene.2014.11.056
11. Shanmugham, B., Pan, A.: Identification and characterization of potential therapeutic candidates in emerging human pathogen mycobacterium abscessus: a novel hierarchical in silico approach. PLoS ONE **8**, e59126 (2013). https://doi.org/10.1371/journal.pone.0059126
12. Rahman, A., et al.: Identification of potential drug targets by subtractive genome analysis of Bacillus anthracis A0248: an in silico approach. Comput. Biol. Chem. **52**, 66–72 (2014). https://doi.org/10.1016/j.compbiolchem.2014.09.005
13. Narayan Sarangi, A.: Subtractive genomics approach for in silico identification and characterization of novel drug targets in Neisseria Meningitides Serogroup B. J. Comput. Sci. Syst. Biol. **02** (2009). https://doi.org/10.4172/jcsb.1000038
14. Gupta, R., Pradhan, D., Jain, A.K., Rai, C.S.: TiD: standalone software for mining putative drug targets from bacterial proteome. Genomics **109**, 51–57 (2017). https://doi.org/10.1016/j.ygeno.2016.11.005
15. Yeh, I., Hanekamp, T., Tsoka, S., Karp, P.D., Altman, R.B.: Computational analysis of Plasmodium falciparum metabolism: organizing genomic information to facilitate drug discovery. Genome Res. **14**, 917–924 (2004). https://doi.org/10.1101/gr.2050304
16. Gupta, R., Verma, R., Pradhan, D., Jain, A.K., Umamaheswari, A., Rai, C.S.: An in silico approach towards identification of novel drug targets in pathogenic species of Leptospira. PLoS ONE **14**, e0221446 (2019). https://doi.org/10.1371/journal.pone.0221446
17. Gauwerky, K., Borelli, C., Korting, H.C.: Targeting virulence: a new paradigm for antifungals. Drug Discov. Today **14**, 214–222 (2009). https://doi.org/10.1016/j.drudis.2008.11.013

18. Kumar, G.S.V., Sarita, S., Kumar, G.M., Kk, P., Pk, S.: Definition of potential targets in mycoplasma pneumoniae through subtractive genome analysis (2010). https://doi.org/10.4172/jaa.1000020
19. Hosen, M.I., et al.: Application of a subtractive genomics approach for in silico identification and characterization of novel drug targets in Mycobacterium tuberculosis F11. Interdiscip. Sci. Comput. Life Sci. **6**, 48–56 (2014). https://doi.org/10.1007/s12539-014-0188-y

Comparing Classifiers for Universal Steganalysis

Ankita Gupta$^{(\boxtimes)}$, Rita Chhikara, and Prabha Sharma

The NorthCap University, Sec23A, Gurugram 122017, India
{ankita17csd005,ritachhikara,prabhasharma}@ncuindia.edu

Abstract. Universal Steganalysis rely on extracting higher order statistical features that gets disturbed when hiding the message in a clean image. Due to content adaptive steganographies like HUGO, WOW etc. which embed the data more in textured areas of the image rather than smooth areas by minimizing the distortion of the image itself, first order features are not sufficient to differentiate clean and stego images. Thus, rich models come into picture in which a large number of features are extracted based on higher order noise residuals of clean and stego images. Thus, Universal Steganalyser is essentially a supervised classifier built on high dimensional feature set. To work with such high dimensional features on a large dataset of images is a very challenging task due to curse of dimensionality as well as computationally very expensive. This paper aims at comparing performance of three techniques-Ensemble classifier, Logistic regression and K-Nearest Neighbors on Spatial Rich Model features extracted for benchmarked dataset BOSSbase_1.01, for the better discrimination of clean and stego images.

Keywords: Universal Steganalysis · Ensemble classifier · Logistic regression · KNN · HUGO

1 Introduction

Steganalysis and Steganography are the two sides of the same coin. While steganography is a technique to hide information in some digital media especially images [1], steganalysis [2, 3] is a counter attack to steganography. Besides many positive applications of steganography, it is increasingly being used for criminal activities as thousands of digital images are downloaded from the internet on a daily basis. So steganalysis is of utmost importance to detect such altered images which may have some crucial hidden data. These altered images are known as stego images while their unaltered versions are known as clean images.

Starting with the very basic technique of LSB replacement [4], LSB matching [5] etc., steganography has now moved to a completely new era of content adaptive steganographies such as HUGO [6], WOW [7] etc. All the traditional algorithms randomly embed information regardless of the image content whereas in content adaptive steganography message is embedded wisely keeping value of distortion function minimum. These content adaptive steganographies introduce the smallest distortion possible to the cover image making embedding changes more in textured areas and less in smooth areas. Similarly, steganalysis starts with specific steganalysis which aims at breaking the particular steganography technique. e.g. Chi-square attack is particularly used for LSB

© Springer Nature Singapore Pte Ltd. 2020
U. Batra et al. (Eds.): REDSET 2019, CCIS 1229, pp. 161–169, 2020.
https://doi.org/10.1007/978-981-15-5827-6_14

replacement, steganalysis techniques has now completely moved to Universal (Blind) steganalysis [8] which aims at attacking any steganographic technique with reasonable accuracy. It is able to achieve this by the identification of sensitive statistical features which have high discrimination power.

Universal steganalysis starts with the extraction of higher order statistical features followed by a classifier which on the basis of above features able to learn and discriminate clean and stego images well. In order to improve the performance of various classification algorithms, high dimensional feature space from different domains have been constructed over past few years. These features are constructed keeping in mind that message embedding is like adding some independent noise like signal called stego noise in the cover image. During image acquisition and processing various noise components get added to the image along with complex dependences of these noises between neighboring pixels. These dependences get violated by the stego noise and most steganalysis methods try to use these dependences for the detection of stego signal. A lot of research has been done in the area of universal steganalysis [9–11] but finding the best classifier for high-dimensional features is still on its way. In the literature various first order statistical features were used [2, 3] but with increasing complexity of modern content adaptive steganographies, higher order statistical features [11–13] are being computed. Modern content adaptive steganographies typically embed data in such regions of images which do not disturb first order statistical features. Moreover, traditional steganographic techniques embed data without actually considering the content of the image itself whereas content adaptive techniques try to embed data more in textured areas and smooth areas are used at minimum. Thus, extraction of higher order statistical features has become itself a tedious task in modern steganalysis. Moreover, a very large number of such features are required for solving the very purpose of steganalysis. Thus, high dimensional feature set further put a large pressure on the classifier to be trained on it. The purpose of this work is basically to compare the performance of various classifiers on such high dimensional features.

This work is aimed at comparing various classifiers on benchmarked BOSSbase_1.01 [14] dataset for Spatial Rich Model (SRM) features extracted in [12]. Authors of SRM features have assembled a rich model of features which constitute many diverse submodels so as to capture various types of dependencies in the images itself. Section 2 below discusses the various methodologies used in this work for the above dataset and features.

2 General Framework

2.1 Dataset and Features Extraction

The dataset used in this work is benchmarked BOSSbase_1.01 data of 10000 grayscale, 512 * 512 pixels images available at [15]. This dataset has been used by many researchers in the literature [13, 23] for their pioneer work in the field of steganalysis. In this work these 10000 cover images are then converted to their stego counterpart using Highly Undetectable SteGanOgraphy (HUGO) and thus a dataset of 20000 images is formed comprising of 10000 cover and 10000 stego images respectively.

Now SRM features are computed on these 20000 images. These features comprise of 106 diverse submodels as explained by authors in [12]. Each submodel has approximately 300 features created by capturing different types of dependencies among neighboring pixels of images. These dependencies are captured by using various high pass filters on noise residual of images. Each submodel is constructed as a computation of one or many co-occurrence matrices of these residuals and their quantized versions. Various residual symmetries are used to merge these co-occurrence matrices to reduce the overall submodels to 106 including the various quantized versions. These submodels are divided into 6 classes: 1, 2, 3, SQUARE, EDGE 3 * 3, EDGE 5 * 5. Class 1 submodels are quantized with q = 1, 1.5 while all other submodels are quantized with q = 1, 1.5, 2. Thus if we consider only single quantization step for each class there will be a total of 39 submodels only with 11, 6, 11, 1, 5 and 5 respectively in each class.

2.2 Classifiers

The various methodologies used in this paper are simple but robust machine learning classifiers: Logistic Regression (LR), K-Nearest Neighbor (KNN) and Ensemble Classifier. Authors producing SRM features have used ensemble technique with Fisher Linear Discriminant explained in [16] as base classifier. Authors themselves have compared their ensemble technique with Gaussian-SVM (G-SVM) and concluded that due to its strong mathematical foundation G-SVM is best for steganalysis also but with very high computational complexity, on the other hand their ensemble technique is giving comparable results within a few seconds. So, the main motive of this work is to produce results on SRM features by their ensemble technique and comparing with the above methodologies to understand in-depth their working and time complexities.

As G-SVM has already been compared so we are not taking this into consideration. Moreover, authors in [17] have compared G-SVM with LR for the purpose of universal steganalysis and found that LR gives comparable results to that of G-SVM along with the benefits of giving class predictions probabilities. Like SVM, LR can also make use of kernels for nonlinear classification. Thus, authors have concluded that despite a powerful machine learning classifier LR is overlooked in the field of steganalysis. Similarly, KNN has also been used in the literature [18, 19] for steganalysis but mainly in combined form with other classifiers so this paper is trying to study its performance on the above dataset and features so that we can think of its use in combination later. The general model of feature extraction and classification as a part of universal steganalysis used in this approach is shown in Fig. 1 below.

Logistic Regression (LR). In machine learning era LR has also proved to be a simple yet powerful tool for classification problems in the literature [17, 20]. Like linear regression it makes use of linear equation but instead of predicting the variable value, it makes use of a sigmoid function to predict the class probability.

$$z = \theta_0 + \theta_1 x_1 + \theta_2 x_2 + \ldots + \theta_n x_n \tag{1}$$

$$h = g(z) = \frac{1}{1 + e^{-z}} \tag{2}$$

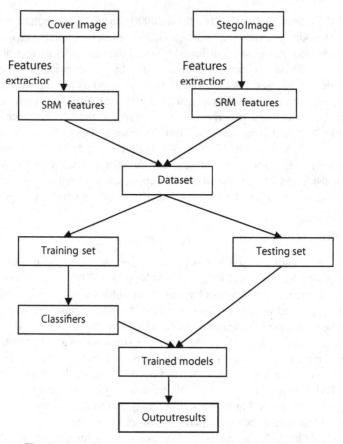

Fig. 1. Flow diagram for features extraction and classification

The sigmoid function g(z) makes all values of z between 0 and 1 and thus these values become the probability that the given data belongs to a particular class.

Also, logarithmic loss function is used to calculate misclassification cost and to predict the values of θ. This misclassification cost is minimized through gradient descent method. Thus, this minimization is time consuming in LR. We are using basic LR in this work but can use various optimizations in LR for our future study.

K-Nearest Neighbors (KNN). KNN algorithm [18] is also another simple and power machine learning classifier, can be easily applied for classification as well as regression problems. In this algorithm to predict the class of test data point, its euclidean distance is calculated with every data point of the training set and then the result is sorted from the lowest distance points to the highest distance points. Then k lowest distance points are considered which are closest to the given test point for the final prediction of that test point class. Out of these k selected training points majority voting is considered for the final output class of the test point. Thus, choosing the optimal value of k is crucial for KNN. We can choose the optimal k by doing cross validation on training set and choose the k having lowest validation error. Euclidean distance measure used in KNN can be expressed as:

$$(\sum (x_i - y_i)^2)^{\frac{1}{2}} \tag{3}$$

where i extends from 1 to no. of features in each training and test point.

Ensemble Classifier. The ensemble classifier used in this work is same as that used by authors in [16]. The benefit of using ensemble techniques is that they can be easily scalable to much larger problem size and even with very simple linear classifier as base classifier they give comparable results with other powerful machine learning classifiers. The base classifier used in this ensemble technique is Fisher Linear Discriminant (FLD), which takes into account that feature which has great inter class separability and less intra class variance is an important feature and should be given more weightage. Thus, in FLD eigen vector is calculated for these features as:

$$v = \frac{mean_{cover} - mean_{stego}}{S_w} \tag{4}$$

where v is the eigen vector, $mean_{cover}$ and $mean_{stego}$ are the mean of cover and stego image features respectively and S_w is within class scatter matrix. Now this eigen vector is multiplied by each datapoint in the test set and result is compared with a threshold to predict the class of that datapoint. This threshold is computed by minimizing the misclassification rate (P_E) on the training set itself as shown below:

$$P_E = \frac{1}{2}(P_{FA} + P_{MD}) \tag{5}$$

where P_{FA} (False Alarms) is the probability of detecting cover as stego image and P_{MD} (Missed Detections) is the probability of detecting stego as cover.

This ensemble classifier is made up of many independent base learners (FLD) which are trained on cover and stego images. The whole dataset is divided into training and testing set. Each FLD makes use of bootstrap aggregation in which training size of each learner is same but training samples are drawn from the training set with replacement Thus each learner has approx. 63% of unique samples with 37% samples are repeated from these 63% samples. The remaining 37% samples are known as out of bag (OOB) samples and are used to calculate misclassification error rate or OOB error rate for each base learner. Thus, for calculating testing error testing set is used in the last when a number of base learners are learnt and minimum OOB error is found. Instead of using all the features each base learner is trained only on a random subset of features so maximum diversity can be achieved among many base learners. Authors of this technique also have given procedure for searching optimal value of subspace dimensionality as well as for searching optimal number of base learners. Ensemble classifier training ends with the minimal OOB error for the above parameters and this trained classifier is then tested on the testing set.

3   Experimental Results

All the experiments in this work are done on the above specified dataset of cover and stego images. HUGO algorithm is used for the purpose of converting cover to stego images with default parameters of $\sigma = 1$ and $\Upsilon = 1$ along with payload of 0.4bpp. Whole dataset is divided into a training set, comprises of 8000 cover and 8000 stego images and a testing set comprises of 2000 cover and 2000 stego images. Same cover stego pairs is necessary for steganalysis problems so division of dataset is done keeping this in mind. All experiments are conducted in MATLAB R2017b.

As ensemble technique is taking lesser time so based on the OOB error best quantized version of each submodel is taken for comparing the results. Authors of SRM features also used the same strategy named as best-q resulting in top 39 submodels out of 106 submodels. All the classifiers taken in this work are run on 39 submodels. Accuracy on the testing set is compared for the 3 classifiers along with the time taken in the most time-consuming operation of each classifier. Table 1 below shows the average accuracy of 3 classifiers:

Table 1.   Comparison of classifiers

Classifiers	Average accuracy (%)	Average training time (secs)
Ensemble	76.38	21.5011
Logistic Regression	76.39	423.839
K-Nearest Neighbor	51.3	600

As observed in above table LR shows comparable performance with respect to ensemble technique on individual models but time taken is 20 times high. Similarly, KNN is showing poorest performance both in terms of average accuracy and time. This is the reason why it has been used in combination with other techniques in the literature in the field of steganalysis. Moreover, accuracy progress of Ensemble and Logistic technique on all 39 models is also plotted in Fig. 2 below so as to gain insight about their competing performance on the used dataset and features.

As the results are compared only for individual models, some containing 325 and some 338 features, exact accuracy can be achieved only by combining these models. Due to time constraint and computational complexity this work combines 39 models resulting in 12,753 features and run ensemble classifier on it, resulting in approx. 87% accuracy. Also, as both the training samples (16000) and features (12753) are of large number linear classifier can also do well so we have also tried LIBLINEAR [21], an online library for linear classification of large data. 80% accuracy is achieved with the help of LIBLINEAR but it takes approx. 1 day to get results so time complexity is high. Similarly, linear SVM is also giving 81% accuracy on such large dataset. Again, due to high time complexities of LR and KNN, they are not checked on these high dimensional features.

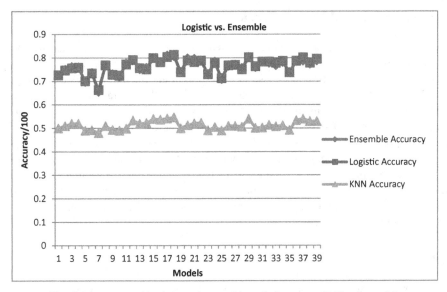

Fig. 2. Accuracy of logistic and ensemble techniques on all 39 sub-models

But with good feature selection techniques on such high dimensional features we can also make use of LR, other linear classifiers, Linear SVM with regularization parameter, G-SVM etc. for getting better results than ensemble technique above. Importance of feature selection techniques has proved in the literature also [22–25]. This paper has also tried a variant of Particle Swarm Optimization (PSO) known as GLBPSO [24] along with ensemble on training dataset of 16000 * 12753 and testing dataset of 16000 * 12753.

GLBPSO is selecting 7250 features with higher accuracy than ensemble but a very high computational complexity. So this further proved that feature selection can improve the results but selection should be done keeping computational complexity in mind. Table 2 below shows the results of classifiers on training set of 16000 * 12753 and testing set of 4000 * 12753:

Table 2. Comparison of classifiers against 12753 features

Classifiers	Accuracy (%)	Execution time
Ensemble	87	153 s
LibLinear	80	1 day
Linear-SVM	80	1 day
GLBPSO with ensemble	87.28	2 days with 7250 features selected

4   Conclusion and Future Work

The main aim of this paper is to develop a clear picture of using various classifiers for rich models both in terms of accuracy and time so that for future it can be decided how to combine feature selection and these or other classifiers for the best results in terms of reduced misclassification and increased accuracy within certain time constraints. Being very high dimensional there are lots of redundant and irrelevant features present, thus there is a need of experimentation with both filter, wrapper and hybrid feature selection approaches. As can be seen above, combining 39 models resulting in a 12753-dimensional feature set, classifiers other than ensemble techniques may take an almost impractical amount of time, it is better to include a better optimization algorithm for classifiers such as logistic regression along with good feature selection strategies. Different metaheuristic techniques can be tried and a novel hybrid approach can be designed for reasonable reduction of features.

References

1. Provos, N., Honeyman, P.: Hide and seek: an introduction to steganography. IEEE Secur. Priv. **99**(3), 32–44 (2003)
2. Zhang, T., Ping, X.: Reliable detection of LSB steganography based on the difference image histogram. In: IEEE International Conference on Acoustics, Speech, and Signal Processing, Proceedings, (ICASSP 2003), vol. 3. IEEE (2003)
3. Westfeld, A., Pfitzmann, A.: Attacks on steganographic systems. In: Pfitzmann, A. (ed.) IH 1999. LNCS, vol. 1768, pp. 61–76. Springer, Heidelberg (2000). https://doi.org/10.1007/10719724_5
4. Chan, C.-K., Cheng, L.-M.: Hiding data in images by simple LSB substitution. Pattern Recogn. **37**(3), 469–474 (2004)
5. Mielikainen, J.: LSB matching revisited. IEEE Signal Process. Lett. **13**(5), 285–287 (2006)
6. Pevný, T., Filler, T., Bas, P.: Using high-dimensional image models to perform highly undetectable steganography. In: Böhme, R., Fong, P.W.L., Safavi-Naini, R. (eds.) IH 2010. LNCS, vol. 6387, pp. 161–177. Springer, Heidelberg (2010). https://doi.org/10.1007/978-3-642-16435-4_13
7. Holub, V., Fridrich, J.J.: Designing steganographic distortion using directional filters. In: WIFS (2012)
8. Lyu, S., Farid, H.: Steganalysis using higher-order image statistics. IEEE Trans. Inf. Forensics Secur. **1**(1), 111–119 (2006)
9. Wang, Y., Moulin, P.: Optimized feature extraction for learning-based image steganalysis. IEEE Trans. Inf. Forensics Secur. **2**(1), 31–45 (2007)
10. Pevny, T., Bas, P., Fridrich, J.: Steganalysis by subtractive pixel adjacency matrix. IEEE Trans. Inf. Forensics Secur. **5**(2), 215–224 (2010)
11. Liu, Q., Sung, A.H., Qiao, M.: Neighboring joint density-based JPEG steganalysis. ACM Trans. Intell. Syst. Technol. (TIST) **2**(2), 16 (2011)
12. Fridrich, J., Kodovsky, J.: Rich models for steganalysis of digital images. IEEE Trans. Inf. Forensics Secur. **7**(3), 868–882 (2012)
13. Holub, V., Fridrich, J.: Random projections of residuals for digital image steganalysis. IEEE Trans. Inf. Forensics Secur. **8**(12), 1996–2006 (2013)
14. Bas, P., Filler, T., Pevný, T.: "Break our steganographic system": the ins and outs of organizing BOSS. In: Filler, T., Pevný, T., Craver, S., Ker, A. (eds.) IH 2011. LNCS, vol. 6958, pp. 59–70. Springer, Heidelberg (2011). https://doi.org/10.1007/978-3-642-24178-9_5

15. http://dde.binghamton.edu/download/. Accessed 10 July 2019
16. Kodovský, J., Fridrich, J.J., Holub, V.: Ensemble classifiers for steganalysis of digital media. IEEE Trans. Inf. Forensics Secur. **7**(2), 432–444 (2012)
17. Lubenko, I., Ker, A.D.: Steganalysis using logistic regression. In: Media Watermarking, Security, and Forensics III, vol. 7880, pp. 78800K. International Society for Optics and Photonics (2011)
18. Mohammadi, F.G., Abadeh, M.S.: A new metaheuristic feature subset selection approach for image steganalysis. J. Intell. Fuzzy Syst. **27**(3), 1445–1455 (2014)
19. Guettari, N., Capelle-Laizé, A.S., Carré, P.: Blind image steganalysis based on evidential k-nearest neighbors. In: 2016 IEEE International Conference on Image Processing (ICIP), pp. 2742–2746. IEEE (2016)
20. Cawley, G.C., Talbot, N.L.: Gene selection in cancer classification using sparse logistic regression with Bayesian regularization. Bioinformatics **22**(19), 2348–2355 (2006)
21. https://www.csie.ntu.edu.tw/~cjlin/liblinear/. Accessed 02 Sept 2019
22. Lu, J., Liu, F., Luo, X.: Selection of image features for steganalysis based on the Fisher criterion. Digit. Invest. **11**(1), 57–66 (2014)
23. Mohammadi, F.G., Abadeh, M.S.: Image steganalysis using a bee colony based feature selection algorithm. Eng. Appl. Artif. Intell. **31**, 35–43 (2014)
24. Chhikara, R.R., Sharma, P., Singh, L.: A hybrid feature selection approach based on improved PSO and filter approaches for image steganalysis. Int. J. Mach. Learn. Cybern. **7**(6), 1195–1206 (2015). https://doi.org/10.1007/s13042-015-0448-0
25. Ma, Y., et al.: Selection of rich model steganalysis features based on decision rough set α-positive region reduction. IEEE Trans. Circuits Syst. Video Technol. **29**, 336–350 (2018)

Airline Prices Analysis and Prediction Using Decision Tree Regressor

Neeraj Joshi[1(✉)], Gaurav Singh[2], Saurav Kumar[2], Rachna Jain[3],
and Preeti Nagrath[3(✉)]

[1] Department of Information Technology, Bharati Vidyapeeth's College of Engineering,
New Delhi, India
neerajjoshi2308@gmail.com
[2] Electronics and Communication, Bharati Vidyapeeth's College of Engineering,
New Delhi, India
singhgaurav2323@gmail.com, sauravkumar1080.0@gmail.com
[3] Computer Science, Bharati Vidyapeeth's College of Engineering, New Delhi, India
{rachna.jain,preeti.nagrath}@bharatividyapeeth.edu

Abstract. The paper analyzes the airline data and predicts the airfare prices. For the purpose of analysis, the features for different airlines is obtained from the dataset, which affect the cost of an airline ticket. The machine learning model Decision Tree Regressor is applied to the features such as Airline, Date of Journey, Source, Destination, Route, Duration, etc., which is used to analyze and predict the air ticket prices. The prediction accuracy is obtained for the model by considering all these features. This paper shows the dependency of each and every feature of flight on determining the cost of airline fare price. For this project, a dataset consisting of 10683 data flights of the different Airlines is collected which is used to train the model via the Decision Tree Regressor algorithm. The result shows that the Decision Tree Regressor model can handle this problem with around 82% accuracy for the existing airline features.

Keywords: Machine learning algorithm · Decision tree regression model · Airline price

1 Introduction

The airline industry utilizes the concept of dynamic pricing strategies [1, 2]. Nowadays, ticket prices vary instantly for the same flights. The price of a flight ticket changes up to 5–6 times in a whole day. Customers try to get as low cost for their airfare ticket, while flight companies seek for increasing their profit by using some tools, to change the airline pricing. However, customers are also becoming more strategic to check and compare prices across various airlines. So, there is a competition among airline companies to choose the optimal price for their customers to generate more avenue. From the last few years, customers research on reducing the airline price for themselves, while airline companies target for an increase in their gain. The researchers obtained a variety of regression techniques [3, 4] to analyze and predict airfare prices. From the view of

© Springer Nature Singapore Pte Ltd. 2020
U. Batra et al. (Eds.): REDSET 2019, CCIS 1229, pp. 170–186, 2020.
https://doi.org/10.1007/978-981-15-5827-6_15

Customers, they target for the minimum cost to buy an airline ticket. It is found that the price of the ticket purchased early have to pay more than of later ones. The ticket price affected due to several factors. Several studies on airline prices show on predicting the cost of airline tickets through a statistical approach [5–7].

Through the ML model, the dataset trained, so as to give the response for unknown data. Some well-known ML models are Multiple Linear Regression model [11, 12], Support Vector Machines [13], Decision Tree [14, 15], Random forest [16, 17], etc. In the machine learning algorithm, the airline fare pricing can be handled in two ways. The prediction of airline fare prices is a *regressor model* [18, 19], it is usually applied for resulting in numerical value, like Price, the mapping function that predicts price model can be approximate through the model used. The other approach is, *classification model* [20, 21], which cannot predict the cost of prices but can take decisions on whether to buy the ticket or not. So, Decision Tree Regressor is implemented on the dataset for predicting the cost of airline price.

The further section continues as follows: Sect. 2, states the related work, Sect. 3 consists of the proposed work, Decision Tree Regressor algorithm is used as the methodology for handling airfare price prediction. Section 4, consist of the experiment performed and the result obtained. Finally, Sect. 5 concludes the overall study of the work.

2 Related Work

Several types of researches on this topic for prediction on the pricing of different airlines. The flight companies considered their starting prediction demand for a given route, which helps them determine the appropriate cost. In simple words, passenger demand affects the generated price. So, airline companies categorized their customers such as businessmen, tourists, normal travelers, etc. The category is classified due to the reason that business customers pay more than normal customers in a search for better facilities.

In the study Malighetti et al., focus on the features to make the profits. The equation of price shows the hyperbola curve with respect to the dates [1]. The factors like the length of the route, frequency of route are the key factors of booking a flight. According to statistics [8], airline companies' approach to calculating the cost price of the ticket through ML algorithms, whereas, dynamic pricing based on factors such as demand enables the prediction of an airline ticket. But dynamic pricing is highly affected by many factors, these consist of features such as Airline, Date of Journey, Route, etc. In simple words, dynamic pricing is like a game between the customers and flight companies, in which each side target for their own profit, this can be shown in diagram Fig. 1. Customers regularly check on the cost of the ticket price, to get the minimum fare ticket. Therefore, airline companies use a dynamically pricing approach. Machine Learning is a keenest topic in the field of computer science [9, 10] and engineering and many disciplines. It provides algorithms, to give machines some kind of intelligence so that it can predict the necessary outcome through that intelligence.

In the study Tziridis et al., the different machine learning algorithms were used such as Multilayer Perceptron (MLP), Random Forest Regression Tree, Generalized Regression Neural Network, Extreme Learning Machine (ELM), Regression Tree, Bagging Regression Tree, Regression SVM (Polynomial and Linear), Linear Regression (LR)

[2]. According to these algorithms, different results were obtained for the study of analyzing and predicting airline fare prices. By using the 10-fold cross-validation procedure to all experiments the models are compared by calculating accuracy and the mean performance of each model. The study results show that ML models can be easily applied to predicting airfare prices. The factors such as data collection and feature selection are important factors in airline ticket price prediction.

In the study Abdella et al., shows the variation of prediction and dedicated fare [8]. It involves varying airline tickets according to the factors. The study includes two models, one for the customer to buy a ticket at a low price and other for the companies to make profits. Therefore, the study suggested a model through machine learning for the purpose of analyses and prediction of the airline ticket prices.

3 Proposed Work

Airline fare prices can be something hard to guess, today's price is entirely different from them tomorrow. It might have been heard from the travelers saying that flight ticket prices are so unpredictable. The price flight tickets for various airlines were provided, and the value of the price has to predict accurately taking considerations of different features.

The objective of this paper is to predict the Price as accurate using Decision Tree Regressor considering all features. But also, to achieve maximum accuracy by using a certain type of features. The paper is comprised as follows: (1) Prediction of cost of the ticket for the dataset, (2) Selection of most impacting features and (3) Analysing of the model for the optimal cost of pricing of a flight ticket. In this study, airline fare pricing can be handled in two ways. The prediction of airline fare prices is a *regressor model* [18, 19], it is usually applied for resulting in numerical value, like Price, the mapping function that predicts price model can be approximate through the model used. The other approach is, *classification model* [20, 21], which cannot predict the cost of prices but can take decisions on whether to buy the ticket or not. So, Decision Tree Regressor is implemented on the dataset for predicting the cost of airline price.

The decision tree regressor algorithm is used building regressor decision trees through covariance [22]. The reduction of the tree through covariance deals with real or numerical target features. The basic formula of covariance is used to select the feature (having low variance) that can be further splitting.

$$\text{Var} = \frac{\sum(X - \bar{X})^2}{N} \tag{1}$$

where, X is actual feature value,
$\bar{X}$ is average feature value,
N is number of terms in the feature.

Figure 1 [8] shows the Dynamic Pricing Concept that how airlines and Customers try to achieve their goal, Airlines to achieve maximizing profits, while Customers to buy the ticket at a lower price.

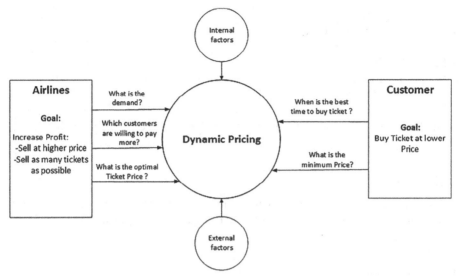

Fig. 1. This diagram showing the Dynamic Pricing.

Steps for Determining the Splitting Through Variance

- The variance of each features calculated,
- Average of the variance of each feature,
- Selection of the node having minimum variance,
- Repeat till leaf node.

Now, considering the methodology comprises four phases as follows:

- The dataset collection for applying model,
- Applying the decision tree regressor model, and
- Evaluation of the decision tree regressor model,
- And the most impacting feature is obtained.

4   Experimental and Result Analysis

4.1   Experimental Analysis

4.1.1   Feature Selection

The features of a flight that determine the cost of air tickets are shown as follows-

- Feature 1 – Airline
- Feature 2 – Date of Journey
- Feature 3 – Source
- Feature 4 – Destination

- Feature 5 – Route
- Feature 6 – Departure Time
- Feature 7 – Arrival Time
- Feature 8 – Duration
- Feature 9 – Total Stops
- Feature 10 – Additional Info

It should be noted out of these features one has the crucial rule in predicting the price.

4.1.2 Dataset

For this purpose, the selection of a single feature is more focused. A set of data for each flight, consist of the ten features (Feature 1 to Feature 10) were collected from the Web, available in [23, 24].

4.1.3 ML Model

The Decision Tree Regressor Model is selected for the flight dataset obtained.

4.1.4 Evaluation of Model

The flight's data collected, were used in a *Decision Tree* to train the aforementioned ML models. The *Linear Discriminant Analysis* [25], *k-best score* [26], *mean squared error* [27] and *absolute error* [28] were calculated for prediction of accuracy that needed to train each model.

Following are the errors and scores-

a) K-Best Score

In Feature selection, some features in our dataset are selected that have more contribution to the target feature Price. Specific modules can be used for this purpose and for improvising accuracy scores.

The benefits of applying this Score:

- Reduction on Overfitting
- Increasing Accuracy
- Minimizing Training Time

b) Mean Squared Error

$$\text{MSE} = \left(\frac{1}{N}\right) \sum_{i=1}^{N} \left(y_i - \hat{y}_i\right)^2 \tag{2}$$

c) **Mean Absolute Error**

$$\mathrm{MAE} \;=\; (1/N) \sum\nolimits_{i=1}^{n} abs(y_i - \lambda(x_i)) \tag{3}$$

d) **Root Mean Square Error**

$$\mathrm{RMSE} \;=\; \sqrt{\left(\frac{1}{N}\right) \sum\nolimits_{i=1}^{N} (y_i - \hat{y}_i)^2} \tag{4}$$

where, N is the number of data points,
y_i is the value obtained by the model,
$\hat{y}_i$ is the actual data point i, and
$\lambda(x_i)$ is the predicted value of x_i.

4.2 Simulation

The project was performed and executed under the Jupyter Notebook [29] environment in an i7-8700 @ 3.2 GHz processor with 8 GB memory. So, the dataset was first cleaned and preprocessed to convert into an appropriate form or machine understanding format [30]. And the dataset was used for analysis purposes consisting of features and the target was separated.

The Decision Tree Regression was built on the dataset for further analysis by making training and testing sets.

The Training and Testing score, as well as root, mean square error was calculated and found to be which is shown in Fig. 2 and Fig. 3.

```
1  print("the training score is ....." ,training_score)
2  print("the testing score is ....." ,test_score)
```

```
the training score is ..... 0.9959071726371508
the testing score is ..... 0.8176251439697398
```

Fig. 2. Training and testing score.

```
print("the Root Mean Square Error is .... ",rmse)
```

```
the Root Mean Square Error is .... 0.43137297674604913
```

Fig. 3. Root mean square error.

4.3 Result

The graph was plotted against *predicted* and *actual price* value of training set as well as testing set, taking whole features (Figs. 4 and 5)-

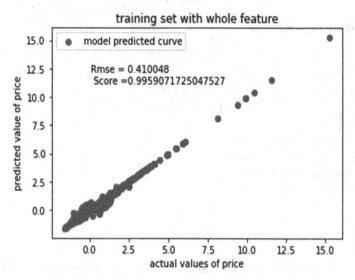

Fig. 4. Actual price vs Predicted price of the training dataset.

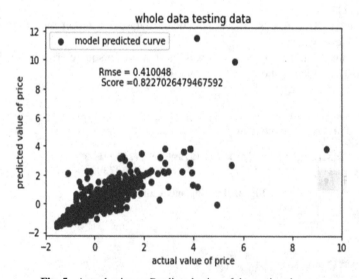

Fig. 5. Actual price vs Predicted price of the testing dataset.

Then, variance-based features are extracted by Analysis of Linear Discriminant and thus a pie graph was plotted as shown in Fig. 6.

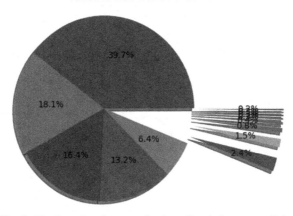

Fig. 6. Pie chart showing contribution of each features on Price.

Then, the best selection was selected out which have a more impact on predicting the target named *price*. And Fig. 7 & Fig. 8, showing the score of each feature on predicting the value of *price* as a table and graph representation.

	Parametre	Score
12	Duration_minute	3344725
3	Route	189036
9	Dep_Min	68390
11	Arrival_Min	50444
4	Total_Stops	23581
6	Day_of_Journey	22599
10	ArrivalHour	18959
0	Airline	14058
8	Dep_Hour	11058
2	Destination	9141
1	Source	7392
7	Month_of_Journey	2438
5	Additional_Info	1024

Fig. 7. Table representation - Parameters vs their score.

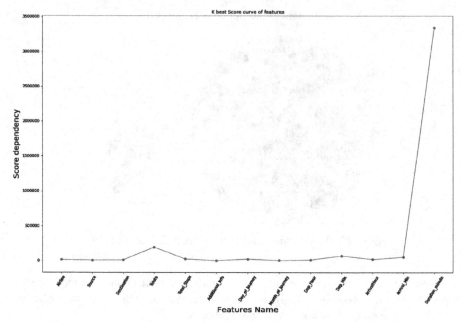

Fig. 8. Graph representation - Features vs their Score.

From the Figures shown above, we found that the Duration_minute (Duration) having more impact, then followed by Route, and then Dep_min (Departure minute), and so on.

Now, the single feature (*Duration_minute*) was selected instead of taking all other features.

Now, the data was further divided into training and testing sets as did before, and the Decision Tree Regression model was applied to the training set and score and root mean square error value was calculated as shown in Fig. 9 and Fig. 10.

```
1  print("the training score is ....." ,training_main_score)
2  print("the testing score is ....." ,test_main_score)
```

```
the training score is ..... 0.4948821093564261
the testing score is ..... 0.5034462408558451
```

Fig. 9. Training and Testing score.

```
1  print("The Root Mean Square Error is: ", rmse_main)
```

```
The Root Mean Square Error is:  0.6536428097105438
```

Fig. 10. Root Mean Square Error.

The graph was plotted between *duration Time* (Duration_minutes) and *price of* Training and Testing set as shown in Fig. 11 and Fig. 12 -

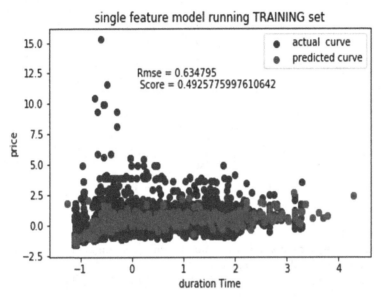

Fig. 11. Duration time vs Price of the training set.

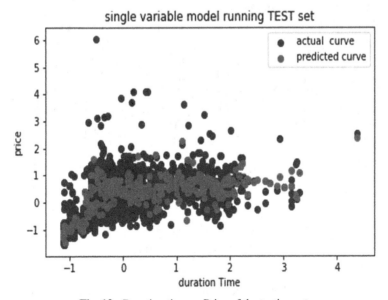

Fig. 12. Duration time vs Price of the testing set.

The accuracy score was found for different value of cv (cross-validation generator) i.e. cv = 50 and cv = 52 as shown in Fig. 13 and Fig. 14.

```
1  accuracies= cross_val_score( estimator=regressor_main,X= test_X1, y=test_y1 ,cv=50)
2  print('Accuracy max....', accuracies.max())
```

Accuracy max.... 0.7178025762260599

Fig. 13. Accuracy score for cv = 50.

```
1  accuracies= cross_val_score( estimator=regressor_main,X= train_X1, y=train_y1 ,cv=52)
2  print('Accuracy max....', accuracies.max())
```

Accuracy max.... 0.6464707358007724

Fig. 14. Accuracy score for cv = 52.

Now dealing with random number value to achieve minimum root mean square as well as absolute error value and maximum scores.

The graph was plotted between *random state* and *rmse* in Fig. 15.

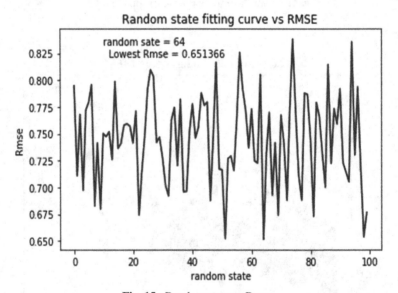

Fig. 15. Random state vs Rmse.

The graph was plotted between *random state* and *mean absolute error* in Fig. 16-

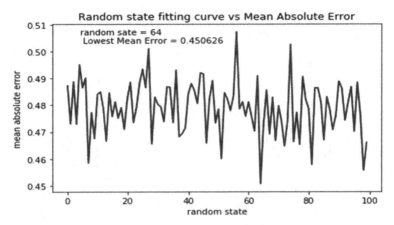

Fig. 16. Random state vs Mean absolute error.

Now, the graph was plotted between *random state* and *training set score* of the training set as shown in Fig. 17 and *random state* and *testing set score* of the testing set as shown in Fig. 18.

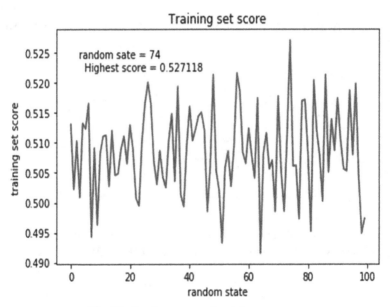

Fig. 17. Random state and training set score.

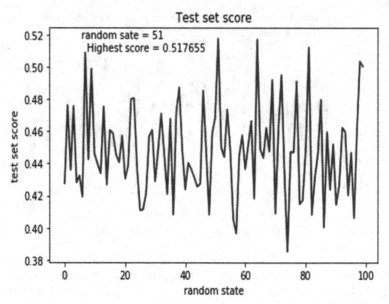

Fig. 18. Random state vs Test set score.

As a result, random state = 64, was taken for better accuracy, as shown below in Fig. 19.

```
1  print('rmse value.... ', rmse_main)
2  print('absolute_error.... ', absolute_error)
3  print('training_main_score.... ', training_main_score)
4  print('test_main_score.... ', test_main_score)
```

```
rmse value....  0.6513664051302884
absolute_error....  0.45062552531954214
training_main_score....  0.49157181062901456
test_main_score....  0.5171099024637804
```

Fig. 19. Errors and scores of training and testing set.

The graph was plotted between *duration time* (Duration_minute) and the *price* of training and testing set as shown in Fig. 20 and Fig. 21 (Fig. 22).

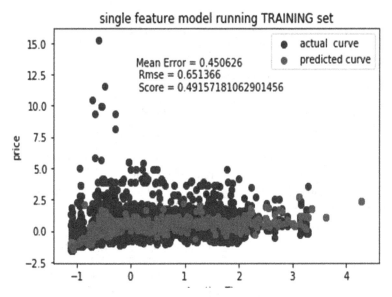

Fig. 20. Duration time vs Price of the training set.

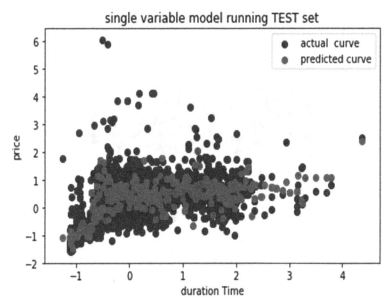

Fig. 21. Duration time vs Price of the testing set.

```
1  print('rmse value.... ', rmse_main)
2  print('absolute_error.... ', absolute_error)
3  print('training_main_score.... ', training_main_score)
4  print('test_main_score.... ', test_main_score)
```

```
rmse value.... 0.6347952165128494
absolute_error.... 0.44415521109255934
training_main_score.... 0.4925775997610642
test_main_score.... 0.5394828942791622
```

Fig. 22. Errors and scores of training and testing set.

Calculating the errors and scores, by reducing testing size-

The graph was plotted between *duration time* (Duration_minute) and the *price* of training and testing set as shown in Fig. 23 and Fig. 24.

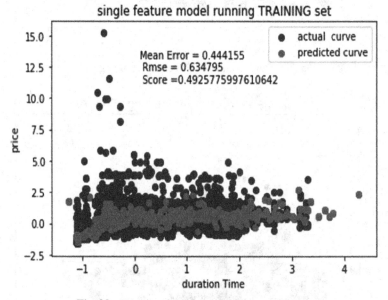

Fig. 23. Duration time vs Price of the training set.

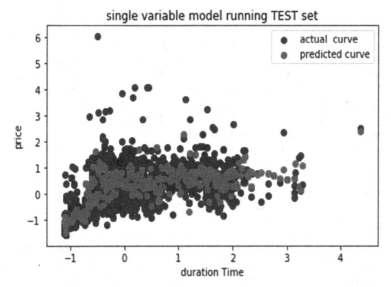

Fig. 24. Duration time vs Price of the testing set.

5 Conclusion

The paper states on the topic "Airfare Prices Analysis & Prediction". The airline fare data was collected and which was feasible for the purposes of analysis as well as prediction of the cost of airline ticket prices. The evaluation of the model experimentally shows that Decision Tree Regressor is satisfactory as well as the beneficiary tool for predicting airline ticket prices. The selection of the dataset and the impacting features is an important part of predicting flight ticket prices. So, the conclusion from the work is that the particular features influence most of the cost of a flight ticket price. Also, the other features having a low impact can be improved for the prediction of better accuracy. However, the perspective of Machine Learning models can guide customers to purchase a cheaply flight ticket. The accuracy obtained was almost 84% considering all features and almost 54% for a particular feature i.e. Duration.

References

1. Malighetti, P., Paleari, S., Redondi, R.: Pricing strategies of low-cost airlines: the Ryanair case study. J. Air Transp. Manag. **15**(4), 195–203 (2009)
2. Tziridis, K., Kalampokas, T., Papakostas, G.A., Diamantaras, K.I.: Airfare prices prediction using machine learning techniques. In: 2017 25th European Signal Processing Conference (EUSIPCO), pp. 1036–1039. IEEE (2017)
3. Groves, W., Gini, M.: A regression model for predicting optimal purchase timing for airline tickets, Technical Report 11-025, University of Minnesota, Minneapolis (2013)
4. Groves, W., Gini, M.: An agent for optimizing airline ticket purchasing. In: 12th International Conference on Autonomous Agents and Multiagent Systems, AAMAS, St. Paul, MN, 06–10 May 2013, pp. 1341–1342 (2013)

5. Dixon, W.J., Massey Jr, F.J.: Introduction to statistical analysis (1951)
6. Makridakis, S., Spiliotis, E., Assimakopoulos, V.: Statistical and machine learning forecasting methods: concerns and ways forward. PLoS One **13**(3), e0194889 (2018)
7. Andrieu, C., De Freitas, N., Doucet, A., Jordan, M.I.: An introduction to MCMC for machine learning. Mach. Learn. **50**(1–2), 5–43 (2003). https://doi.org/10.1023/A:1020281327116
8. Abdella, J.A., Zaki, N., Shuaib, K., et al.: Airline ticket price and demand prediction: a survey. J. King Saud Univ. Comput. Inf. Sci. (2018)
9. Graham, R.L., Knuth, D.E., Patashnik, O., Liu, S.: Concrete mathematics: a foundation for computer science. Comput. Phys. **3**(5), 106–107 (1989)
10. Weiser, M.: Some computer science issues in ubiquitous computing. Commun. ACM **36**(7), 75–84 (1993)
11. King, M.L.: Robust tests for spherical symmetry and their application to least squares regression. Ann. Stat. **8**(6), 1265–1271 (1980)
12. Andrews, D.W., Lee, I., Ploberger, W.: Optimal changepoint tests for normal linear regression. J. Econom. **70**(1), 9–38 (1996)
13. Priya, R., de Souza, B.F., Rossi, A.L.D., de Carvalho, A.C.P.L.F.: Using genetic algorithms to improve prediction of execution times of ML tasks. In: Corchado, E., Snášel, V., Abraham, A., Woźniak, M., Graña, M., Cho, S.-B. (eds.) HAIS 2012. LNCS (LNAI), vol. 7208, pp. 196–207. Springer, Heidelberg (2012). https://doi.org/10.1007/978-3-642-28942-2_18
14. Hara, S., Hayashi, K.: Making tree ensembles interpretable. arXiv preprint arXiv:1606.05390 (2016)
15. https://www.saedsayad.com/decision_tree_reg.htm
16. Liaw, A., Wiener, M.: Classification and regression by randomForest. R News **2**(3), 18–22 (2002)
17. Segal, M.R.: Machine learning benchmarks and random forest regression (2004)
18. King, D.E.: Dlib-ml: a machine learning toolkit. J. Mach. Learn. Res. **10**(July), 1755–1758 (2009)
19. Little, R.J.: Regression with missing X's: a review. J. Am. Stat. Assoc. **87**(420), 1227–1237 (1992)
20. Zhang, M.L., Zhou, Z.H.: A k-nearest neighbor based algorithm for multi-label classification. In: GrC, vol. 5, pp. 718–721 (2005)
21. Schurmann, J.: Pattern Classification. Wiley, Hoboken (1996)
22. https://statweb.stanford.edu/~owen/mc/Ch-var-basic.pdf
23. https://www.kaggle.com/open-flights/flight-route-database
24. https://github.com/Neerajjoshi2308/Airline-Prices-Analysis-and-Prediction/blob/master/Dataset/Data_Train.xlsx
25. Ye, J., Janardan, R., Li, Q.: Two-dimensional linear discriminant analysis. In: Advances in Neural Information Processing Systems, pp. 1569–1576 (2005)
26. http://scikit-learn.org/stable/modules/generated/sklearn.feature_selection.SelectKBest.html
27. https://www.freecodecamp.org/news/machine-learning-mean-squared-error-regression-line-c7dde9a26b93/
28. Sammut, C., Webb, G.I. (eds.): Mean Absolute Error, Encyclopedia of Machine Learning. Springer, Boston (2011). https://doi.org/10.1007/978-0-387-30164-8_525
29. https://jupyter.org/
30. https://achyutjoshi.github.io/btp/dataprep

ANN Based Direct Modelling of T Type Thermocouple for Alleviating Non Linearity

Ashu Gautam[1](✉) and Sherin Zafar[2](✉)

[1] GD Goenka University, Gurugram, India
ashuone@gmail.com
[2] Department of CSE, SEST, Jamia Hamdard, New Delhi 110062, India
zafarsherin@gmail.com

Abstract. Non-linearity related with the sensing elements gives escalation to numerous complications in interfacing chip, for direct digital readout, for various processes of testing, and calibration procedure and control. Furthermore, the static and dynamic performance of a transduction element is pretentious undesirably by ambience variations around them. In fact, the effect of this change in environment on the transducer is quiet non-linear. The delinquent of estimation of transducer static non-linearity and its self-compensation is being gradually tackled by means of software techniques, because of emerging computation techniques and advent in the integrated circuit technology. However, for an indiscriminate non-linear response of transducer characteristic, a software clarification depends upon the choice of proper method using the concept of mathematical modelling of the response curve. To select the best curve fitting procedure for the mentioned set of inputs and outputs data there are no specific rules. The issue is of extraordinary intrigued in measurement and estimation applications. This paper reports on the implementation of a transducer modeling strategy based on an Artificial Neural Network (ANN) to estimate and self-indemnate the static nonlinearity of transducer.

The usage of ANN based on single layer has been proposed in two different researches with fairly good outcomes under the ANN-based transducer modeling system. The first model already exists based on the architecture of Widrow-Hoff's adaptive linear (ADALINE) network. The other is based on the FLANN structure developed with a single layer linear ANN architecture with gradient-descent training with a momentum-based learning algorithm.

Keywords: ANN · FLANN · Modeling of transducer

1 Introduction

In recent decades, industrial world automation has begun to dominate, and automation without sensors and transducers is incomplete. More and more precise, fragile linear measuring sensors are mandated in industrial automation. In all equipment and systems popularly implemented in science and industrial areas, sensors and transducers are essential components. In addition, the computer-based instrumentation is the best option

© Springer Nature Singapore Pte Ltd. 2020
U. Batra et al. (Eds.): REDSET 2019, CCIS 1229, pp. 187–202, 2020.
https://doi.org/10.1007/978-981-15-5827-6_16

for the concurrent surveillance of various parameters. There is a particularly strong need for enhanced sensors for systems comprising fast computer or processing units, where sensor growth is anticipated to be aligned with different needs of applications [1]. The relevant hardware and software modules for processing of the sensor output signal have been created and also developed to enhance their efficiency, both based on analog and digital technologies. But still the low-cost compensation for several parameters of interference is an untouched issue throughout the transducer design. Throughout this case, the classical strategy of a transducer-based twin sensor (i.e. from the same batch) indicates to be inadequate: both sensor responses must be accurately matched to all interfering parameters. In addition, the extensive use of an inverse model may not be satisfactory in digital compensation systems. First, a precise mathematical model with all the sources of mistake is seldom known. More sensors are then required, each of which monitors an interfering parameter. In either event, the analytical concern appears non-linear and multidimensional and demands optimization techniques to be efficient. The environment is extremely dynamic and demanding because there are many issues abandoning this technology, and with increasing sophistication many more is supposed to be added. The following wide-range regions of measuring, instrumentation and control have been illustrated by the soft computational versatile modelling technologies with huge potential and wide applications [2]:

- Intelligent instrumentation system (IIS)
- Virtual instrumentation systems (VIS)
- Soft (or virtual sensor)
- Instrumentation fault detection and isolation (IFDI)
- Web-enabled instrumentation system (WIS)

The ability of the machine to examine and modify its behavior in a limited sense is usually achieved by using various contemporary practices for example knowledge-based structures, artificial neural networks, fuzzy logic, genetic algorithms, and simulated annealing, etc. Key issue behind all these techniques is the knowledge acquisition, knowledge representation and knowledge processing in an intelligent manner. In our pursuit to form intelligent machines we have a logically occurring model available - in form of brain of human. Some how's the brain is capable of using neurons-the brain's basic computing elements which are of the order 5 or 6 orders of scale slower in comparison to the silicon logic gates - to complete certain calculations many times faster than the computer which are exiting. This performance is apparently accomplished one way through using enormous parallel hardware.

Machine-based devices allows any information from anywhere in the globe to be tracked and controlled in real time. It is perhaps one of the most significant inventions in electronic instruments during the last period. In the near future, the device is assumed to be a prevalent device that would even transform a advanced sensor into a plugin [4, 5]. In reality, this situation has forced the scientists to strive very hard for real-time implementations in the developing zone of a unique distributed, cross platform and internet-enabled digital instrumentation technique. Because of such factors, tools relying on the concept of virtual evaluation scheme, the Personal Computer (PC) has already acquired substantial interest and has become one of the most dominant study areas in the recent past. In fact if numerous parameters need to be monitored concurrently PC-based instrumentation is probably the best choice.

Many sets of detectors and transducers work on plants or system monitoring equipment. The accuracy of the detectors and monitoring devices is fully dependent on procedures of calibration carried out in the factory, during planned maintenance or during tiny breakdowns. Essentially, all physically feasible systems, which include sensors and actuators are structured as integrators and usually seem to display remarkably nonlinear response as far as static characteristic of sensor is considered [6]. Moreover, if the measurement is carried out using a PC-based diagnostic scheme, the elements of signal conditioning unit of Data Acquisition System (DAQS) in addition to the intrinsic nonlinearity also invariably add further some nonlinearity. Over period decomposition becomes further liable for adding differences in the characteristics of the device Calibration is most often needed in such situations The issues pertaining to the nonlinearity of the transducer and its self-compensation should therefore be tackled jointly in DAS-connected computer-based estimation systems taking into consideration both nonlinearity connected with the device and that of its signal processing module [4]. In addition, the necessity to introduce intelligence in these schemes has also presented an extra difficulty in dealing with the problems of self-compensation for environmental variations and self-detection and confinement in transducer components. This has been noted that this region is both very vibrant and demanding as the related incidents are also on the rise with the uptick in system complexity.

2 Modeling Based on Artificial Neural Network

Modeling procedures featuring usage of neural networks concentrate on machine learning established on the concept of self-adjustment of the intrinsic system parameters The artificial neural network framework constitutes of five chief parts; learning field, neural networks, learning techniques learning procedure and assessment process [7, 8]. Accordingly, the neural network-based simulation method includes five primary elements: a) knowledge acquisition, analysis and task representation; b) design determination; c) learning scheme decisiveness; d) network training; and e) ANN modeling is categorized into three primary stages: a) design; b) deployment; and c) training and testing the network.

Parameters Selection: ANN based design is made up of distinct (or input) elements and conditional output variables. There are two elements in selecting determinants to be used in model First, the details could be transformed to make the network more useful Second, choice will be centered on restrictiveness and covariance among the transformed factors. Essentially, if the conditional factors are correlated with it, a chosen discrete variable is predictive. In comparison, if two autonomous variables are associated, correlated inputs make the model more susceptible to quantitative oddities in the specific measurements, and the correlated contributions of inputs make the model more prone to the statistical complexities of specific measurements. This in turn enhances the concern of overfitting and prohibits universal usage. For such determinants, the system should only comprise autonomous factors that predict dependent factors but not to variate with each other, regardless of which modeling approach is used.

Parameters representation: Smith (1993) indicated that the way the network's input nodes represent discrete factors has a noticeable effect on network instruction and the derived model's results The network's potential is mainly referred to as its extensive effectiveness Both quantity of computing and the time it takes to learn are severely affected by the type of depiction used. There are two forms of measurements that are autonomous and dependent: 1) linear; and 2) class variables. Any number can be the quantitative or continuous value variable. There's no need to fall within the borders of the sigmoid feature implemented.

Hidden Layer and hidden Node: The invisible layer can, in principle be more than one layer. If it has sufficient contained nodes, the network can predict any complexity of a target function. As a statistical modeling instrument, the concealed parts of nodes create multi-layered perceptron appealing. Hidden node output can reflect new parameter, i.e. input to next subsequent layer or nodes on output layer (or dependent variable). The fresh parameters fired from the nodes onto the cached layer and are known as internal representations along with the net topology, and could make the modeling practice self-explanatory. Thus the neural network approach is a type of machine learning. So few hidden nodes (or too low networks) will allow back-propagation not to converge into some kind of answer for a specific issue. Many concealed nodes, however, trigger a much longer span of teaching. Increasing the amount of concealed nodes at some stage does not significantly enhance the classification capacity of the neural network. At the other hand, excessive units on one layer can over-specify a network, particularly if the number of items in first input processing layer is equivalent to the amount of cases in training set. Too many hidden nodes could fit over, so the network can over fit. Minimum size network containing few hidden units, as possible, is indeed crucial for efficient classification and comprehensive use such that the entire network could model the random arrangement in the sample as well as the underlying target function framework. Thus, it is important for an effective classification and generalization to have a small network with the lowest hidden units.

Weights and biases: The weights are specified as the strength of a tangible amount of input connections. Inputs are provided to the processing nodes via connections. Every connection has its own weight attached. The weight ranges from a value which updates the application nodes, the excitement to get on or even off. The weights are also the comparative strength (mathematical value) of the original input information or the diversified relationships among layers. Each contribution to a processing component is of comparative significance. In practice, before starting the training, weights would be initiated and assigned to the network. The amount of nodes on each link for a specified network, and the amount of preference is the sum of the number of all nodes.

Summation and transformation function: Summing function means that the weighted average for each processing element (or nodes) is determined [9]. It merely multiplies the weight of the input values and sums them up into a weighted amount. The conversion function is a connection between neuronal inner activation level (N) (called activation function) and outputs. The function of conversion is sort of sigmoid function. An f (N) function is a sigmoid function if it has two certain features: firstly it is bounded, and secondly it always rises with N. A number of distinctive features have such features and hence qualify as sigmoid characteristics.

Learning rate and its momentum: When the net volume is big or the amount of training patterns is huge, than back propagation is the most widely used algorithm. However there are certain constraints to back propagation. There seems to be no assurance that perhaps the network will indeed be trained in finite amount of time. It applies gradient descent, i.e. routes descending the error surface slope and adjusts the weights continuously to a minimum. There is therefore the risk that the local minimum will be trapped before the global minimum is achieved. When using back propagation [9–11], it is important to choose the right learning rate and momentum term. Unfortunately, there are very little guidelines apart from perception, based on test-and-error. An elevated rate of learning leads to rapid learning which can push the training to a minimum local level or trigger oscillation. In turn, the time to achieve a global minimum will be significantly improved when implementing tiny learning rates. Each layer of the same network may have distinct learning rates. The solution for learning rate selection issues is to introduce a momentum factor that is amplified by the prior weight change so that the modifications are still speedy while the learning rate is regulated. The function of the momentum metric is to balance out weight adjustments, that also enables prevent network learning from oscillation. A basic rule seems to be that learning rate of last hidden layer should always be two times of output layer.

ANN based networks are used scientifically towards designing of transducer as well as sensor system [22, 24]. The transducer system model must simulate the connection between factors (i.e., temperature, pressures, angular movement) or the relevant corresponding output voltages, i.e. they have the capability to approximate any true non-linear value to any desired precision [12, 17]. Through recurring experiences a neural network learns. Iterative learning obtains expert understanding and facts in neural networks on the grounds of previous examples, but over training should be prevented. Only then can the neural network react to the data for the relevant purposes used to train it. However, first before using well-trained neural networks, the success of the independent data set should be validated. However, when the new data is present, the neural network must also be trained up on-line or off-line both. A lot of intuition and testing are needed to create a adequate neural network artificial model for a specified implementation. The network architecture, topology and neuron properties as well as learning rule it utilizes, are determined by supervised neural networks for given operation. Neural networks include a straightforward and simple strategy to both direct along with inverse transducer modeling. For various types of transducers. The aim is to create an ANN based transducers modelling as a powerful instrument used as a detector so that unknown inputs can be responded in a realistic way. This scheme is similar to the issue of control engineering system identification. The training set for the suggested neural network comprises a known value set of the applied inputs and the respective outputs. In general, a new output is comparable to the right output for input arrays used during training comparable to new input. Nervous system information processing capacity is imitated by artificial neural networks.

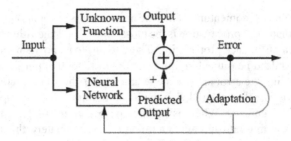

Fig. 1. Universal approximator of neural network

3 Direct Modeling of Transducers Using ANN

Throughout the current work, the non-linear response attributes of a transducer are modeled on an expansion of the power series with a certain range [18, 19, 35]. Adaptive model provide us with an alternative to the current system architecture: rather than developing a feature F mechanism, we generate a framework to understand or adjust to implement F. Adaptive learning methods are appropriate to circumstances in which changes in environmental influences are intrinsically intertwined with input. An adaptive system generally has two distinct components: training (or feedback) and operation. The advantages of such systems are often critical: flexibility and power. The ANN has developed in past few years as a lucrative field of studies since its adaptive nature enables it to conveniently shape a non-linear system. Thus the need of direct model of transducers can be in:

- Approximation of nonlinearity
- Transducers testing
- Standardization of transducers
- Simulation of soft sensors (Virtual sensors)

In channel equalization, system recognition and in-line improvement there are comprehensive applications of adaptive algorithms. The least mean square (LMS) and recursive least squares are two such algorithms which are used for estimating the parameters of different digital systems in above mentioned applications. A function approximation, i.e. curve fitting, is one of the most effective uses for neural networks. A key feature of the solution is that the approximated F function is not provided explicitly but implies through a set of input-output pairs called a training set, readily accessible from measuring system calibration information. As shown in Fig. 1, we have ended up getting some unknown feature we want to estimate. If we apply the same input to both schemes as in Fig. 5, we would adjust the network parameters to generate the same reaction as the unknown feature.

In 1970, Broyden, Fletcher, Goldfarb and Shanno (BFGS) [36–37] inevitably proposed an alternative inverse Hessian update method. The modern Quasi Newton method was produced with their formula. The big distinction between the DFP and BFGS techniques is that with the BFGS technique, instead of the Hesse matrix, the Hessian matrix is updated iteratively (Fig. 2).

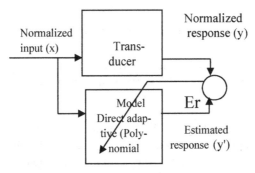

Fig. 2. Polynomial-ANN learning method for direct model equation

Since the inverse of the Hessian matrix is approximated, the BFGS method can be called an indirect update method. Before discussing the BFGS here a Newton Method has been discussed. Newton Method can be extended for the minimization of multivariable functions. Consider the quadratic approach to function f(X) at X = Xi using the expansion of the Taylor series.

$$f(X) = f(X_i) + \nabla f_i^T (X - X_i) + \frac{1}{2}(X - X_i)^T [J_i](X - X_i) \qquad (1)$$

where $[J_i] = [J]_{xi}$ is the matrix of second partial derivatives (Hessian Matrix) of f evaluated at the point X_i. By setting the partial derivatives of equation equal to zero for the minimum of $f(X)$, we obtain

$$\frac{\partial f(X)}{\partial x_j} = 0$$

$$j = 1, 2 \ldots, n \qquad (2)$$

Equations (2) and (1) give

$$\nabla f = \nabla f_i + [J_i](X - X_i) = 0 \qquad (3)$$

If $[J_i]$ is nonsingular, Eq. (3) can be solved to obtain an improved approximation $(X = X_{i+1})$ as

$$X_{i+1} = X_i - [J_i]^{-1} \nabla f_i \qquad (4)$$

Since the higher order terms in Eq. (1) and (4) have been neglected iteratively, it is necessary to find an optimum solution X^*. Newtons method uses the second partial function derivatives (in matrix form) (in the form of the matrix $[J_i]$) and is, therefore, a second order method. Due to the following method characteristics, the technique was not very helpful in practice:

- Matrix $n \times n[J_i]$ need to be saved.
- The components of the matrix $[J_i]$ could not be measured, quite hard and at times impossible matrix.
- At each step the matrix $[J_i]$ needs to be reversed.
- Evaluation of the amount $[J_i]^{-1} \nabla f_i$ is required at every step.

Implementation Direct Modeling of T Type Thermocouple Transducers Using
The T type thermocouple characteristics can be characterized with the sixth order type of characteristic equation. The Real and predictable static response obtained from direct modeling of T-type Thermocouple are as shown in Figs. 3, 7, 11 available from the ANN training with three distinct algorithms. While the learning characteristics of ADALINE based, FLANN based ANN based direct model of are shown in Figs. 7, 11 and the suggested Polynomial ANN based are as shown in Figs. 12, 13, 14 respectively and Table 1 representing effects of direct modeling of T-type temperature transducer with training data using first degree ADALINE based model trained with Widrow-Hoff's algorithm .

3.1   T-Type Thermo-Couple Direct Modeling Results with ADALINE Trained with the Learning Algorithm of Widrow Hoff

See Figs. 4 and 6.

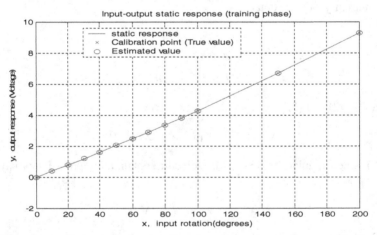

Fig. 3. Real and assessed static response attained from direct modeling of T-type Thermocouple through ADALINE trained with Widrow-Hoff's based Learning

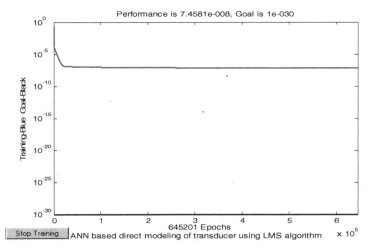

Fig. 4. ADALINE-based direct model T-type Thermocouple Transducer learning traits Trained by Widrow-Hoff

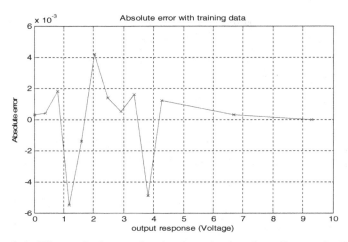

Fig. 5. Absolute difference in the actual and estimated approach to discover details using the Widrow-Hoff based learning algorithm trained ADALINE model

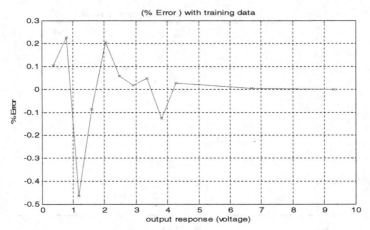

Fig. 6. Error (%FS) between actual and estimated response via ADALINE trained with Widrow-Hoff's based learning

3.2 Results of Direct Modeling of T-Type Thermocouple Transducer Using FLANN Trained with Gradient Descent with Momentum Learning

See Figs. 8, 9 and 10.

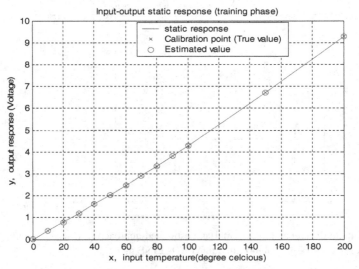

Fig. 7. True and estimated static response obtained from direct modeling of T-type Thermocouple using FLANN trained with Gradient Descent with momentum

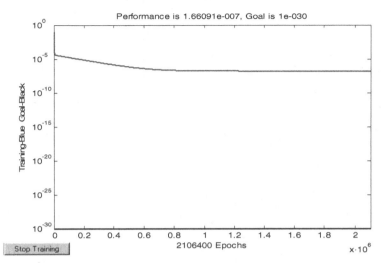

Fig. 8. Learning characteristics of FLANN based direct model of T-type Thermocouple trained with Gradient Descent with momentum

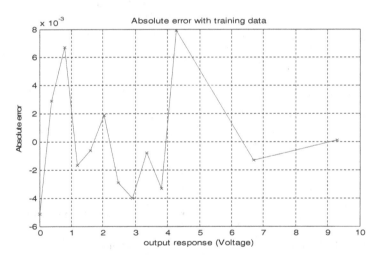

Fig. 9. Absolute error between actual and estimated response with training data using FLANN trained with Gradient Descent with momentum

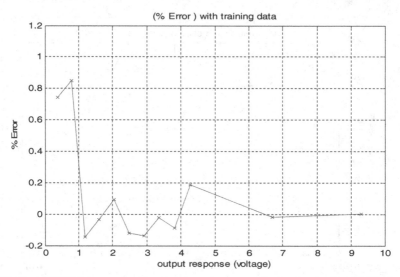

Fig. 10. Error (%FS) between actual and estimated response obtained with using FLANN trained with Gradient Descent with momentum

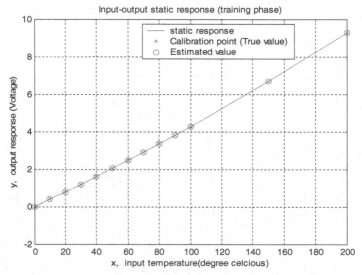

Fig. 11. True and estimated static response obtained from direct modeling of T-type Thermocouple using FLANN trained with Quasi Newton based learning Algorithm

3.3 Results of Direct Modeling of T-Type Thermocouple Transducer Using Polynomial – ANN Trained with BFGS–Quasi Newton

Table compares all the three algorithms ADALINE Trained with Widrow-Hoff's, FLANN Trained with Gradient Descent with momentum and Polynomial-ANN trained with BFGS, for the given number of epochs 645200 for the ANN based direct modeling of T type transducers.

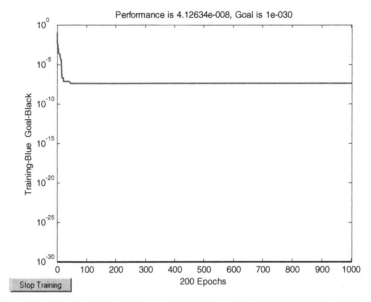

Fig. 12. Learning characteristics of Polynomial ANN based direct Model of T-type Thermocouple trained with Quasi Newton based learning Algorithm

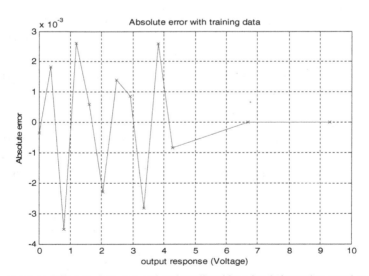

Fig. 13. Absolute difference between real and predicted learning information reaction using the Polynomial ANN model developed using the Quasi Newton BFGS technique.

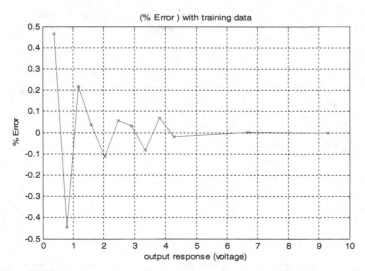

Fig. 14. Error (%FS) between actual and estimated response obtained from the use of Polynomial ANN based model trained with Quasi Newton BFGS method.

Table 1. Evaluation of outcomes of direct modeling of T-type Thermocouple transducer with both existing as well as Polynomial – ANN based proposed model

Algorithm under investigation	Mean square error	Maximum absolute error	Maximum %F.S error	Co-efficients	Estimated value
ADALINE Trained with Widrow-Hoff's	7.4581e−008	0.0049	0.4627	c_0	−0.0000
				c_1	0.8301
				c_2	0.1867
				c_3	0.0049
				c_4	−0.0233
				c_5	−0.0135
				c_6	0.0013
				c_7	0.0137
FLANN Trained with Gradient Descent with momentum	7.4581e−008	0.0049	0.4627	c_0	−0.0000
				c_1	0.8301
				c_2	0.1867
				c_3	0.0049

(continued)

Table 1. (*continued*)

Algorithm under investigation	Mean square error	Maximum absolute error	Maximum %F.S error	Co-efficients	Estimated value
				c_4	−0.0233
				c_5	−0.0135
				c_6	0.0013
				c_7	0.0137
Polynomial-ANN trained with BFGS	4.12634e−008	0.0035	0.4663	c_0	−0.0000
				c_1	0.8559
				c_2	−0.4490
				c_3	5.2102
				c_4	−19.4623
				c_5	36.1844
				c_6	−32.5088
				c_7	11.1696

4 Conclusion

This study work proposes a straightforward methodology built around a single-layer network trained BFGS-Quasi-Newton learning algorithm for direct transducer modeling using Polynomial-ANN. From the present overhaul, the predicted learning algorithm is found to be tremendously quick and very effective in replicating transducer neural models. The estimated transducer features acquired from direct modeling are also in reasonable agreement with the features assessed. This actual fact validates the proposed method's effectiveness. Considering the current discussion, the neural networks are certainly supportive components for transducer data processing.

References

1. Gautam, A.: ANN based direct modeling of permanent magnet DC tachogenerator sensor. Int. J. Hybrid Inf. Technol. **8**, 163–176 (2015)
2. Postolache, O., Girao, P., Pereira, M.: Neural networks in automated measurement systems: state of the art and new research trends. In: Proceedings of IEEE International Joint Conference on Neural Networks-IJCNN 2001, 15–19 July 2001, vol. 3, pp. 2310–2315 (2001)
3. Shukla, K.K.: Neuro-Computers Optimization Based Learning. N.P.H. (2001)
4. Dunbar, M.: Plug-and-play sensors in wireless networks. IEEE Instrum. Meas. Mag. **4**, 19–23 (2001)
5. Potter, D.: Smart plug and play sensors. IEEE Instrum. Meas. Mag. **5**, 28–30 (2002)
6. Patranabis, D.: Sensors and Transducers, pp. 249–254. Wheeler Publishing Co., Delhi (1997)
7. Pereira, J.M.D., Girao, P.M.B.S., Postolache, O.: Fitting transducer characteristics to measured data. IEEE Instrum. Meas. Mag. **4**, 26–39 (2001)

8. Meireles, M.R.G., Almeida, P.E.M., Simoes, M.G.: A comprehensive review for industrial applicability of artificial neural networks. IEEE Trans. Ind. Electron. **50**(3), 585–601 (2003)
9. Bentley, J.P.: Principles of Measurement Systems, 3rd edn. Pearson Education Asia Pte Ltd., Delhi (2000)
10. Grandson, P.E., Neilsen, K.J.H.B., Tingleff, O.: Unconstrained optimization, 3rd edn., March 2004. http://gams.nist.gov
11. Deb, K.: Optimization for Engineering Design, 5th edn. Prentice Hall of India Pvt. Ltd., New Delhi (2002)
12. Arpaia, P., Daponate, P., Grimaldi, D., Michaeli, L.: ANN-based error reduction for experimentally modeled sensor. IEEE Trans. Instrum. Meas. **51**(1), 23–29 (2002)
13. Singh, A.P., Kumar, S., Kamal, T.S.: Versatile virtual transducer response curve tracer based on data acquisition card. IETE J. Educ. **45**(1), 3–8 (2004)
14. Bernieri, A.: A neural network approach for identification and diagnosis on dynamic systems. IEEE Trans. Instrum. Meas. **43**(6), 867–873 (1994)
15. Pratap, R.: Getting Started with MATLAB 5, pp. 114–122. Oxford University Press, Oxford (2001)
16. Hagan, M.T., Menhaj, M.: Training feed-forward networks with the Marquardt algorithm. IEEE Trans. Neural Netw. **5**(6), 989–993 (1994)
17. Singh, A.P., Kumar, S., Kamal, T.S.: Artificial neural network based soft estimator for estimation of transducer static nonlinearity. Int. J. Neural Syst. **14**(4), 237–246 (2004)
18. Singh, A.P., Kumar, S., Kamal, T.S.: ANN based virtual instrumentation system for estimation of non-linear static characteristics of sensors. IETE J. Educ. **44**(2), 63–72 (2003)

Forecasting of Literacy Rate Using Statistical and Data Mining Methods of Chhattisgarh

Aditeya Nanda, Vishwani Sati, and Shweta Bhardwaj[⊠]

Computer Science and Engineering Department, Amity University, Noida, Uttar Pradesh, India
aditeyananda@gmail.com, vishwani.sati@gmail.com,
shwetabhardwaj84@gmail.com

Abstract. Literacy helps in country's overall development and economic growth. Chhattisgarh is one of the states of India and ranks 27th in terms of literacy. This describes about the lack of educational facilities in the state. Predicting literacy rate of Chhattisgarh will help in determining the future status of the state. This will further help to take necessary action in the support of promoting literacy in the state. The main reason for lack of literacy in this area is due to tribal areas in the state and lack of initiatives in educating men and women. Forecasting of literacy rate will help the government to make proper plans to increase literacy rate. Projection for total literacy rate per year is done using geometric mean method. Forecasting is done with the help of time series analysis in R programming language using ARIMA model. As per this method, the forecasted literacy rate of Chhattisgarh in 2021 is 75.502%. This forecasting will help to monitor literacy rate of Chhattisgarh and may help to improve its rank among other states. The main tool used for forecasting is the R language, used for data mining.

Keywords: Forecasting · Literacy rate · Geometric mean · Time series analysis

1 Introduction

The research paper is based on forecasting of literacy rate with the help of data mining method. The data mining methods used in our project is time series analysis. The model used for forecasting and analysis of data is ARIMA model, which is highly accurate and precise. ARIMA also known as Auto-Regressive Integrated Moving Average method serves as a model for obtaining the results.

Time series analysis is an effective method for analysis and processing of data. It accepts data as obtained in a specific time format like daily, monthly, quarterly or yearly data. Based on the format the data is analyzed and processed to perform various tests to check stationarity of data. Data must be regular and stationary to obtain results. The literacy data of Chhattisgarh obtained from census website of India gives the data from 1961 to 2011. The data obtained were processed, analyzed and explored with the help of R language. The software used for the project is R studio.

© Springer Nature Singapore Pte Ltd. 2020
U. Batra et al. (Eds.): REDSET 2019, CCIS 1229, pp. 203–211, 2020.
https://doi.org/10.1007/978-981-15-5827-6_17

2   Theoretical Background

Chhattisgarh ranks 16th in terms of population of states in India but it is ranked 27th in terms of literacy rates in India. This is a very bad and alarming situation for the government as well as the citizens of the state. It becomes necessary to predict the future education scenario of this state so that government policies are created to ensure education for each citizen [1]. Education is considered as a primary objective for a state as well as country's growth and development and promoting it will further enhance the social and economic status of the state and the country as a whole. Poverty has been the main reason behind lack of access to education and proper health facilities in the country. In addition, many children are not able to attend schools and educational programs due to lack of health facilities. Many people due to their low income are not able to afford education in various schools especially private schools where gaining education is getting very expensive. Low income may act as a barrier for gaining proper healthcare facilities in men as well as women. Hence it is very important to allow free access to education and healthcare facilities.

However, literacy rate in Chhattisgarh has increased from 64.66% in 2001 to 71% in 2011. This has been a good improvement. We can further increase this number with the help of more non-government organizations and various government policies that promote free education for all irrespective of their gender, location, social background and economic status [2]. Proper measures should be taken to make people living in tribal areas aware about the benefits of education. Hence it is very important to reach out to the people living in tribal areas and help them in getting free education. Prediction of literacy rate will help government to make educational plans.

3   Methodology

Data collected from the census website of India is explored and analyzed carefully. Since census data done once in every 10 years, it was inefficient for carrying out the forecasting. Thus, with the help of geometric increase method the data was forecasted for every year since 1961 mathematically until 2011.

In the geometric mean method, the data analyzed and forecasted for every year between 1961 to 1971, 1971 to 1981, 1981 to 1991, 1991 to 2001 and 2001 to 2011. The average increase in literacy rate is calculated for each consecutive census data. Based on this value, the data forecasted every year from 1961 to 2011 with the help of the given formula:

$$Rn = Ro(1 + r/100)^i \qquad (1)$$

$$\text{where, } A = r/n, \ i = (Y - y)/10 \qquad (2)$$

A is the average percentage increase in literacy rate
r is total increase in literacy rate
n is the number of observations and i is the number of decades
Ro is the initial literacy rate at year y

Rn is the literacy rate at a given year Y

The average percentage increase in literacy considered constant from decade to decade. After yearly data is calculated using the formula, then graphs are plotted using python language. The data is also loaded in R studio to perform the implementation in coding to obtain the forecasted results [3, 4].

The literacy rate data from 1961 to 2011 based on which the analysis is done is listed below [8] (Table 1).

Table 1. Literacy rate data from 1961 to 2011

Year	Literacy rate (%)
1961	18.14
1962	18.32
1963	18.5
1964	18.68
1965	18.87
1966	19.06
1967	19.25
1968	19.44
1969	19.64
1970	19.83
1971	24.08
1972	24.32
1973	24.56
1974	24.8
1975	25.05
1976	25.3
1977	25.55
1978	25.811
1979	26.068
1980	26.328
1981	32.63
1982	32.95
1983	33.28
1984	33.61
1985	33.95
1986	34.29

(*continued*)

Table 1. (*continued*)

Year	Literacy rate (%)
1987	34.63
1988	34.97
1989	35.32
1990	35.67
1991	42.78
1992	43.2
1993	43.63
1994	44.07
1995	44.51
1996	44.95
1997	45.4
1998	45.85
1999	46.31
2000	46.77
2001	64.66
2002	65.8
2003	65.95
2004	66.61
2005	67.27
2006	67.94
2007	68.62
2008	69.3
2009	69.99
2010	70.69
2011	70.27

The method of forecasting is time series implemented with R language as a tool. Data that collected in regular time intervals is called time series. Example are sales data, weather data, population data forecast, etc. [11]. Time series involves a series of methods. These are creating a time series using ts() function. We have used Geometric increase method to calculate data of previous year's literacy rate of Chhattisgarh, as it is a least error showing method in data analytics.

This gives us very less error calculation between observed data and calculated data [5].

- Understanding the time series- identifying seasonality, trend and error in time series at time t.
- Identifying the time series as stationary or not- In stationary time series, the mean value remains constant over time and the variance do not increase.
- To extract trend, seasonality and error using decompose() function.
- Autocorrelation and partial autocorrelation: It used to determine if the data is stationary or non-stationary. A stationary data will have lines, which drop quickly, but non-stationary data will have lines dropping gradually. For our data, it was checked out to be non-stationary data with the help of graph generated by acf() function.

Basic Time Series Model: As time plays important role in succession of any task it also plays a significant role in success of any business. As it is quite difficult to run with the speed of time. There are few methods with the help of technology by which we can look up for things in ahead of time. Time series model is one of the models out of them we can analyses data for a year, month, day etc. It includes certain steps which are listed here:

Stationary Series: As it is clear in the graph nonstationary graph has its mean value which is increasing continuously, in this graph mean is time dependent variable which violates stationary series condition. According to stationary series mean should not be dependent on time.

According to the condition of stationary series variance should not be dependent on time value which is called homoscedasticity.

ARIMA Time Series Modelling: ARIMA stands for auto regression moving average, it is a time series model method which is used only in case of stationary data not in nonstationary data series. Before applying ARIMA model you should be well aware that your data is in stationary series or not if it is in non-stationary form you should then by applying difference, transformation first make the data series in to stationary form, then we can only apply ARIMA model [6].

Moving Average Time Series Model: As we have studied auto regressive time series model, with few modifications in moving average time series model, one difference in the mathematical formula which is 'beta' factor which is for the long-lasting effect of the previous year. It diminishes earlier previous year data plotting ang focus on the next year criteria.

Difference Between AR and MA Time Series Model: The difference in AR and MA is based on their value of previous year data in MA model the value of $x(t)$ and $x(t-1)$ is zero when $n >$ order of the year that's why it can diminish the effect of previous year plotting, which is a better implementation. As in case of AR the value of two successive year is never null and as n value increases continuously the value of $x(t)$ and $x(t-n)$ decreases or shows declination in the graph.

Hence the difference in AR and MA is completely based on their successive time series objects at two different time intervals [7] (Table 2).

TIME SERIES VISUALISATION -> MAKING THE DATA STATIONARY -> PLOTTING ACF AND PACF GRAPHS AND FINDING PARAMETERS -> BUILD ARIMA MODEL -> FORECASTING

Table 2. Methodology steps

S. no.	Steps
Step 1.	Time Series Visualization
Step 2.	Making the Data Stationary
Step 3.	Plotting ACF and PACF graphs
Step 4.	Finding Parameters
Step 5.	Build ARIMA Model
Step 6.	Forecasting

4 Results

Based on prediction of literacy rate, the following results were obtained. The data was first loaded and plotted to check any pattern, trends, seasonality and stationarity.

The auto-correlation function (ACF) test performed to check our data is stationary or not. If the data is stationary, we can build model based on which prediction done. The below graph shows the data is non-stationary. Hence, the data further differenced and log function used to make it stationary (Fig. 1).

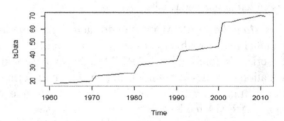

Fig. 1. Data loaded and plotted to check any pattern, trends, seasonality and stationarity

The graph shows gradual decrease in lines, which shows the given data, is non-stationary (Fig. 2).

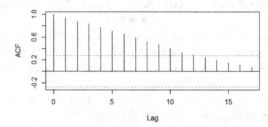

Fig. 2. ACF test

The data further differenced to make it stationary. The result is the below graph. It shows that the lines are random and there is a sudden drop in line after first lag. This shows that the data has become stationary and is suitable for carrying out forecasting. The parameters for ARIMA forecasting obtained from this graph. In the below graph we have sudden drop of line after first lag at 0. Hence, the value for p for ARIMA forecasting is 0. Further the partial auto-correlation function (PACF) is calculated when the data has become stationary to find the value for q that is used as a parameter for ARIMA forecasting. The below graph helps in deciding a model for forecasting.

The partial auto-correlation function (PACF) test performed with the differenced data. The below graph helps in deciding a model for forecasting (Figs. 3 and 4).

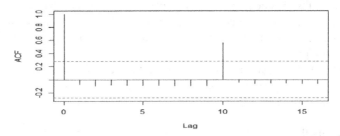

Fig. 3. ACF forecasting

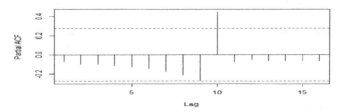

Fig. 4. PACF test

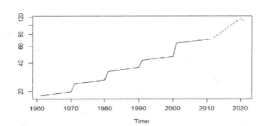

Fig. 5. Final prediction

The final prediction for literacy rate came out to be the graph below which shows the result based on ARIMA model. The prediction is done till the year 2021 (Fig. 5).

```
Time Series:
Start = 2012
End = 2021
Frequency = 1
 [1] 71.04398 71.52602 72.01134 72.49995 72.99187 73.48713 73.98575
 [8] 74.48776 74.99317 75.50201
```

From the above output obtained, we can observe the subsequent forecasting values from 2012 to 2021 every year.

5 Analysis and Discussion

Based on the results obtained, the following analysis can be done. The data processing must be done to check the data is stationary or not. If the data is not stationary, then it must be made stationary with the help of log() and diff() functions or by detrending and differencing methods.

Stationary data has mean value and variance value independent of time. These values don't change with time but remain constant throughout the data. Non-stationary data has varying mean and variance value with time. These values don't remain constant with time.

After making the data stationary, we can check stationarity with the help of 2 tests. The tests are ACF and PACF which generate graphs based on which we determine whether the data is stationary or not by observation. With the help of these graphs, we determine the parameters for building the ARIMA model for forecasting. Hence these graphs must be accurate enough to generate accurate predictions.

The resulting output time series for literacy rate showed the predictions starting from 2012 to 2021 for every year. The resulting forecasted literacy rate for the year 2021 is 75.50%.

6 Conclusion

The prediction for literacy done with the help of ARIMA model for forecasting with the help of time series analysis. The implementation for prediction done with the help of R programming language with R studio software.

The ARIMA model does not work in non-stationary data but works on stationary data. Hence, it is essential to convert data into stationary data before forecasting.

Time series analysis is the method in data mining, which collects data in a specific time period like monthly, quarterly or yearly. The data source must be accurate to do accurate analysis and processing on the data.

As we know literacy rate of any area will depend on various factors like population density of that area, sex ratio, male and female population including child and youth, literate and illiterate population of that area. Calculated literacy rate gives almost accurate results to the actual literacy rate given by per year data. This combinational work prediction for literacy rate would be helpful to the scientists, researchers who work with demographic features and work related to this study.

7 Future Work

Learning about time series analysis using ARIMA model motivates to do further projects based on this concept. This method is an efficient method for forecasting in data mining. The results obtained may be effective for government policy makers to take informed decisions. They can help in improving the literacy status of the state and help to establish measures for promoting education in the state.

By predicting the literacy rate of Chhattisgarh every year, we will get to know the direction of the literacy status of the state. This will help to take following precautionary measures to prevent any illiteracy issues in the country and help to promote literacy in state by developing important government policies. This will help to improve the status of the state as well as the country.

References

1. Ravichandran, R.: A study on population projection using the logistic curve method in time series analysis with reference to India. Indian J. Appl. Res. **3** (2013)
2. Asur, S., Huberman, B.A.: Predicting the future with social media. In: IEEE/WIC/ACM International Conference on Web Intelligence and Intelligent Agent Technology (2010)
3. Jain, S., Mishra, N.: Forecasting of literacy rate using statistical and data mining methods. Int. J. Adv. Comput. Eng. Netw. **3**(8) (2015). ISSN 2320-2106
4. Raftery, A.E., Alkema, L., Gerland, P.: Bayesian population projections for the United Nations. Inst. Math. Stat. Stat. Sci. **29**(1), 58–68 (2014). https://doi.org/10.1214/13-STS419
5. Rajasekhar, N., RajiniKanth, T.V.: Hybrid SVM data mining techniques for weather data analysis of Krishna district of Andhra region. Int. J. Res. Comput. Commun. Technol. **3**(7) (2014)
6. Martínez-Álvarez, F., Troncoso, A., Morales-Esteban, A., Riquelme, J.C.: computational intelligence techniques for predicting earthquakes. In: Corchado, E., Kurzyński, M., Woźniak, M. (eds.) HAIS 2011. LNCS (LNAI), vol. 6679, pp. 287–294. Springer, Heidelberg (2011). https://doi.org/10.1007/978-3-642-21222-2_35
7. Wikipedia for Demographics of India. en.wikipedia.org/wiki/DemographicsofIndia
8. Chhattisgarh Census Data. http://www.census2011.co.in/
9. Achrekar, H., Gandhe, A., Lazarus, R., Yu, S.-H., Liu, B.: Predicting Flu trends using Twitter data. In: IEEE Conference on Computer Communications Workshops (INFOCOM WKSHPS), Shanghai (2011)
10. Rosenberg, D.: Trend Analysis and Interpretation. Maternal and Child Health Information Resource Center, HRSA, PHS, DHHS, December 1997
11. Population Forecasting – NPTEL IIT Kharagpur Web Courses
12. Lutz, W., Scherbov, S.: Global Age-specific Literacy Projections Model (GALP): Rationale, Methodology and Software, Montreal (Quebec), Canada, UNESCO Institute for Statistics (UIS), July 2006
13. Wali, A., Kagoyire, E., Icyingeneye, P.: Mathematical modeling of Uganda population growth. Appl. Math. Sci. **6**(84), 4155–4168 (2012)
14. Liao, S.-H., Chu, P.-H., Hsiao, P.-Y.: Data mining techniques and applications – a decade review from 2000 to 2011. Expert Syst. Appl. **39**, 11303–11311 (2012)
15. Adult and Youth Literacy, National, Regional and Global Trends, 1985–2015, UIS information paper, June 2011

Recommendation System for Prediction of Tumour in Cells Using Machine Learning Approach

Ankit Verma, Amar Shukla, Tanupriya Choudhury$^{(\boxtimes)}$, and Anshul Chauhan

School of Computer Science, University of Petroleum and Energy Studies (UPES) Dehradun, Dehradun, India
avankitverma.2011@gmail.com, amar28071989@gmail.com, tanupriya1986@gmail.com, anshulchauhan9993@gmail.com

Abstract. In today's world cancer is a familiar disease to everyone, people are keen to know the way and approaches for the better diagnosis of the cancer diseases in the early stages, cancer occurs in the different parts of the body which are having the auspicious behaviours of the cancer cell. One of the major cancerous subject where the whole world is affected that is tumour, which is found in the breast region, where more than millions of people are resulting to death by these breast tumours. So the study is made under the face of machine learning algorithms and strengthening the performance of these approaches which tends to classify and prediction based on the data. Therefore, these approaches of the machine learning creates the significance model for the prediction of the cancerous cells and the analysis of those tumour cells in the subject of the breast cancer. This model tends to the development of the recommender system, which helps to bring out the condition whether the breast cancer is benign or malignant. This system use to have of K- nearest neighbour (KNN) algorithm approaches with the univariate and multivariate analysis.

Keywords: Recommender system · K-nearest neighbour (KNN) · Machine learning · Univariate analysis · Multivariate analysis · Principal component analysis

1 Introduction

World is dealing with the most prominent disease that is breast cancer which revenge off and effect the life of the people in the greater aspect where it continues the struggle of the life of the people in the economically and emotionally. Breast cancerous cells are follows with the two region that is benignant and malignant; these are the important aspect to determine the region of the cancer in the subject. Early detection of the tumour can significantly change in the life of the people to survive with better strength and this cancer is the third most dangerous cancerous tissue.

Malignant cells mostly effect the surrounding tissues which were previously unaffected by them through basal membrane. They spread into various body parts through

© Springer Nature Singapore Pte Ltd. 2020
U. Batra et al. (Eds.): REDSET 2019, CCIS 1229, pp. 212–222, 2020.
https://doi.org/10.1007/978-981-15-5827-6_18

bloodstream or via the lymphatic system. Malignant cells are very dangerous because they might reappear after they are removed, often in places, which were free from them. They have modified Deoxyribonucleic Acid (DNA) and chromosomes, which are categorize by abnormally large, variable shape nuclei, which is dark in colour. These can give out chemicals that cause weight loss and weakness during their life cycle.

A person suffering from cancerous cells requires heavy treatment, which includes bone marrow transplant, chemotherapy, Hormone therapy, surgery, radiation, and many other treatments, which are very expensive, and not much advanced and developed.

In the past, not many methods were there to detect cancer; X-ray was the only efficient and effective method. However, in recent years many new and advanced methods have been developed for detection of breast cancer, Methods like artificial intelligence, Genomics, neural networks, immunotherapy, and data mining are taking over, as these are highly reliable and effective methods.

To extract data from an image, we use image processing which provides us information which is required to classify the different types of tumours, and also the data of a patient which is used to predict whether they are affected by the cancerous cells or not.

The working logic of K-nearest neighbour (KNN) algorithm is very easy and straightforward, data is segregated on the basis of class to which the closest neighbours belongs, here K number of neighbours of the data are used.

2 Literature Review

Machine Learning approached the best possible way to predict the cancerous tissues, which helps to rise the tumour, some of the significant approaches for the prediction of the cancerous tumour and to find its intensity of its behaviour in the body. KNN algorithm [1] to diagnose the disorder in the behaviour of the children. Here the user will provide a question, which he can use to refer to for taking advantage from all the consulting services that are described in the behavioural disorder field. In the proposed model, a researcher or master in psychology can group the questions and all the reactions that are needed for the diagnosis and consulting the social issue. The output showed that the accuracy of the KNN model was subjectively effective by the nearest neighbour approach for predicting economic [2] events KNN contributes the different domain specification and the prediction of the diseases and the stress, market study which constitute the better significance and approachable way to demonstrate the study of the subject. There are distinct methods provided [3] to classify closest neighbour with focus on; calculating how close they are i.e. distance, the difficulty faced in computing and recognizing which neighbour is nearest and methods to reduce component of data. The following paper showed the problems where the output of the classifier can be useful in such cases implementing the K nearest neighbour algorithm could be very efficient and effective. Many techniques that help in noise reduction that only work for K nearest neighbour are very useful in noise reduction and improves the accuracy of our classifier. KNN is not much useful for very complex and difficult classification tasks, in such cases techniques like neural networks and support vector machines are superior to KNN. KNN classification contains the having the specific effectiveness and have efficiently applied different machine learning methodologies on the [4] gemstone spectral imaging (GSI) analysis of the cancer caused at the lymph node by the malignant cells that appeared in the gastric cancer. The authors employed the KNN classifier so that they can differentiate between the lymph node metastasis (malignant cells when appear at a location that is different from the primary location of the malignant cells) the only untamed domain was that not enough number of clinical cases were accounted into the research. The significant approach has developed a technique, which uses ultra-wide band antenna microwave [7] for scanning images to detect cancer of the breast. They system used only a single ultra wide band to scan an image. The collected data contains cancerous tissue data, which is used to make a microwave image of the tissue cells, which shows the tumour standing out. The data was then compared with the original data from the doctors to get the accuracy of the system.

ANN artificial neural networks model [8] to detect and predict breast cancer. This algorithm uses precise data taken by instruments of the cancerous cells. This data was fed to Radial basis functional network (RBFN), which produced an output, which was either positive or negative. Since lab results had an accuracy of 60 to 70% only, thus the algorithm worked properly. Almost similar techniques are used to predict or check the plants that might be infected with some diseases. The KNN classifier is used on several features of the plant that gets us a prediction whether that plan is infected or not, [9] this program helped the farmers to stop the spread of diseases into other plants which saves time and money. A digital image of the plant is fed to the program which then takes various features of the plant from the image and then processes it and tells us whether the plant is disease infected or not.

KNN machine learning algorithm [5] to analyse the data that they extracted from the image of a tumour. The data is feed to the KNN algorithm that is used to predict the cancer. Since doctors miss about 15% of the total actual cases of cancer, and develop the significance accrues of the approach above this so that it is actually more useful than the traditional methods. Detecting the cancer in its first stage was the main motive as curing the first stage cancer is easy as compared to higher stage ones. Genetic approach for the k nearest neighbour model [10] to detect the early stage lung cancers using a non-parametric method. This uses CT scan images of a patient and then uses it to produce the results. The total distance between every test and training sample is worked out and the k-neighbour having greatest distance is considered. The accuracy of this method came out to be 90%, which is around 15 to 20% more than the results of traditional methods.

New way of approach [12] have used data mining techniques to provide a method of detecting cancer specifically that of malignant cancer. Support vector machine (SVM), Artificial Neural network (ANN), Principal Component analysis (PCA), have been applied. They worked on the most commonly used cancer data set and applied naïve-Bayes classifier, ad boost, support vector machine, k-fold cross validation, and compared the results from all these methods to find out an optimal one. The advance approach [11] in the data from the repository, have applied KNN and support vector machine techniques on the dataset, have measured the efficiency of both methods, and then have compared the results. The results showed that SVM produced results that were accurate up to 92.7% and is a superior method compared to KNN but KNN was almost equivalent and hence SVM was found to be reliable. This disease starting from the breast tumour, it can spread to other part of the body if early action is not taken. Breast cancer [13] is the prominent disease, which has to be detected in the early stages, if this disease can be cured in the early stages, then it can be cure and prevented easily. Then the [14] Local Binary pattern to extract the features of mammographic images for breast cancer detection. Author try to find the cure of this problem in the different way. Set of images extracted from MiniMammographic Database (MIAS) and Digital Database for Screening Mammography (DDSM) database, which causes the greater effect on curing of the disease in the significant way. The different distances that can be used to apply KNN on the given dataset, which authors took from Wisconsin database (WBCD). Different types of distances like cosine distance, city block distance, correlation distance, Euclidian distance, and Manhattan distance were observed and worked upon. Conclusion made was that for Euclidian distance, the results were most accurate 98.70% and for Manhattan distance, it was 98.45%. To improve the prediction rate [15] of images that were obtained from Raman spectroscopy. They have proposed a EWHK algorithm to identify the spectra, they added weighting of entropy information to improve the accuracy of KNN algorithm. This gave them an accuracy of 92.33%, 93.8% sensitivity and 87.7% specificity.

The proposed a system where they take the Computed Tomography (CT) scan images of the patient's lungs and then store it in MATLAB and apply noise removal, image enhancement, image segmentation to get better and more accurate details from the image. In conclusion, the watershed approach and thresholding approach were compared while watershed produced and accuracy rate of 85.27% the threshold approach showed an accuracy rate of 81.24%. Deep convocational neural network [16] that will work on breast cancer image analysis. Gradient boosted tree classifiers and deep neural networks were used. The overall accuracy of the proposed method came out to be 87.2%, and when they took two class, the accuracy came out to be 93.8%. The specificity was 88% sensitivity was 96.5% and AUC was 97.3%. The overall accuracy surpassed all other known methods that used image classification. KNN algorithm on heart disease database for prediction of heart diseases [17], which cause around 32% of total deaths in Andhra Pradesh and around 35% deaths in USA and Canada. They combined KNN with genetic algorithm and tried to improve the accuracy of the prediction model. The model produced an accuracy rate of 95% when k was 1 and produced 83.3% when k was chosen to be 3. So these literature distinguish the demonstration of the KNN in the various field of medical field, education, share market and many more to have prediction of the scenarios according to the liabilities of the subject is having the high level of acceptance in the different fields, so these study also categorize the different scenarios of the prediction of the cancer, to develop as recommender system for the proper and significance analysis of the cancer in the breast cancer region.

3 Methodology

Firstly, data is collected in the data set and importing it using panda's library in form of data frame. Second step is performing data wrangling operation i.e. removing the null values. Third step is check for the outlier in our dataset and replacing it with particular value so that it cannot alter future prediction. Fourth step is of plotting the data with respect to data sets. Fifth step is Univariate Analysis. Sixth step is Bivariate Analysis.

Seventh step is Multivariate Analysis. Eight step is principal component analysis (PCA). Ninth step is splitting of data in training and testing data set. Finally, we need to Checking for accuracy (Fig. 1).

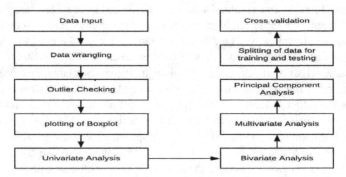

Fig. 1. Flow chart of the different approaches and analysis for the breast tumour and to do the analysis of the cancerous cell whether it is benign or malignant

4   Result and Analysis

Strengthening and analysis of the data sets play a significant role to get the specific approach for the cancerous cell detection and to develop the subsequent recommender system.

Firstly, analysis of the data set that is BCW (Diagnostic) and to establish the multi variable approach for the analysis of the dataset, which is approachable in the table below. The data set contain the 33 columns where 31 prominent features where selected among these columns for the analysis. Then the next step is to subsequently find the column behaviour and the properties has to be categorized so that it brings the appropriate features can come in the role for the detection of the cancerous cell. Then again it required is to check whether the subject is facing the cancer or not, if the subject is facing the cancer then the binary approach is applied for the malignant and the benignant who is effecting from the cancer(M = 1 and B = 0) and then established the correlation between them (Fig. 2).

Then next step is to find out the significant features extraction by the histogram approach, which contains the concave point worst (CPW), perimeter Worst (PW). Fifth step is to develop the final training model for the subsequent features, which results in the heathier mode for the prediction of the disease and then to establish the correlation with respect to the subject and arranged in the ascending order. Then the most prominent approach is to recurred the noise and external outliers, which can subsequently effect the mode of analysis and can reduce the effectiveness of the analysis, each column has to rectify so that the effective results can be concluded, so some of the outliers may be in CPW, PW, RW (radius worst), same procedure will be attained on the each column, again then the overfitting and overfitting issues might arise so again the step is, PCA (principal component analysis) approach is used for the better analysis and the features

id	diagnosis	radius_mean	texture_mean	perimeter_mean	area_mean	smoothness_mean	compactnes s_mean	concavity_mean
842302	M	17.99	10.38	122.8	1001	0.1184	0.2776	0.3001
842517	M	20.57	17.77	132.9	1326	0.08474	0.07864	0.0869
84300903	M	19.69	21.25	130	1203	0.1096	0.1599	0.1974
84348301	M	11.42	20.38	77.58	386.1	0.1425	0.2839	0.2414
84358402	M	20.29	14.34	135.1	1297	0.1003	0.1328	0.198
843786	M	12.45	15.7	82.57	477.1	0.1278	0.17	0.1578
844359	M	18.25	19.98	119.6	1040	0.09463	0.109	0.1127
84458202	M	13.71	20.83	90.2	577.9	0.1189	0.1645	0.09366

Fig. 2. Sample of the Data Set, which consist of the various features [18]

description. In these we describe the two dimensional principal component analysis on the available features and the three dimensional representation analysis from those four principle component (Table 1).

Again we have a significant approach to consider the specific features of the nuclei which is also used in the training that k can be chosen in the method of $k = \sqrt{n}$ where n represents the total number of elements in the row. After this there is, need to determine the different classes these sets belong by determine this value of k and the value of the k by using the [6] Euclidian distance approach

$$\sqrt{\sum_{j=1}^{k} (a - b)^2} \tag{1}$$

Finally, we will check and validate the accuracy of the system with the value of r, which stand for the root mean square for prediction of the cancer whether it is benign or malignant (Fig. 3).

First of all after importing the dataset and converting it into data frame Since we have 32 columns now, we cannot use all the columns for our training our machine learning model so we need to reduce it into 8 columns for that we need to reduce the no of columns for that we need to analyze our given dataset first for that. Then we have converted the columns diagnosis which is categorical variable now we need to convert the data in this column since of the person is suffering from cancer there will be presence of malignant cell and if the person has tumor then it has benign cell. 0-Tumour (Table 2).

For this, we replaced the benign data with 0 and malignant in diagnosis column with 1. Firstly, we made the multivariate analysis that is plotting of heat map. Then we checked how each column are co related with diagnosis columns then we find the 8 columns which are highly correlated with them After that we done the univariate analysis by plotting the histogram and analyzed each 8 columns after that we plotted the bar graph for doing the bivariate analysis and then we proceeded to training. Our recommender system take the dataset of the affected cell that can be either tumor or cancer and do the analysis on it and after performing the data wrangling operation then we can predict whether the person is suffering from cancer or not.

Table 1. Describes the screen shots of the highly correlated columns with respect to the diagnosis of the patient in ascending order

Diagnosis	1
concave points_worst	0.793
perimeter_worst	0.782
concave point s_mean	0.776
radius_worst	0.776
perimeter_mean	0.776
area_worst	0.742
radius_mean	0.733
area_mean	0.708
concavity_mean	0.73
concavity _worst	0.708
compactness_mean	0.696
compactness_worst	0.659
radius_se	0.596
perimeter_se	0.59
area_se	0.567
texture_worst	0.548
smoothness_worst	0.421
symmetry_worst	0.416

Table 2. Describe the Recommender system approached followed in the methodology

0	Tumor
	{
	"Presence of benign cell"
	}
1	Cancer
	{
	"Presence of Malignant cell"
	}

In prediction set when we apply our model for prediction after training the model with a suitable machine learning algorithm then our result firstly check all the parameters and give us the result that are firstly stored in form of array and finally after doing our calculation we stored in form of excel file so that we can check our result in different scenario (Table 3).

Table 3. Prediction process for the recommender system

Predicteer = model. predict(x_test)
Array{(1,0,0,1,0,1,1,1,1,0,0,1,1,1,1,1,0,0,0,0,0,0,0,0,0,0,1,0,0,0,0,0,0,1,0,1,1,1,1,0,0,0, 0,1,0,0,0,0,1,0,1,1,1,0,0,1,0])

In the above table the prediction procedure is taken and the data is stored in the below table, that is way the recommender system proceed to these data sets (Table 4).

Table 4. Data stored in the table after the prediction process takes place by the recommender system.

Diagnosis ID	Diagnosis
87930	1
859575	0
8670	0
907915	1
921385	0
927241	1
9012000	1
853201	1
8611161	1
911673	0

This table tell us the Id of the person along with the diagnosis {whether the person is having the presence of malignancy or not} that is done by our machine learning model. When we input the id of the people with their features our recommender system perform analysis and after performing the data wrangling operation we pass it in our model for predicting the result. Hence, this table describe the significant approach for developing the recommender system for the prediction of the cancerous tissues in the breast cancer and to categorise the category of benign and malignant.

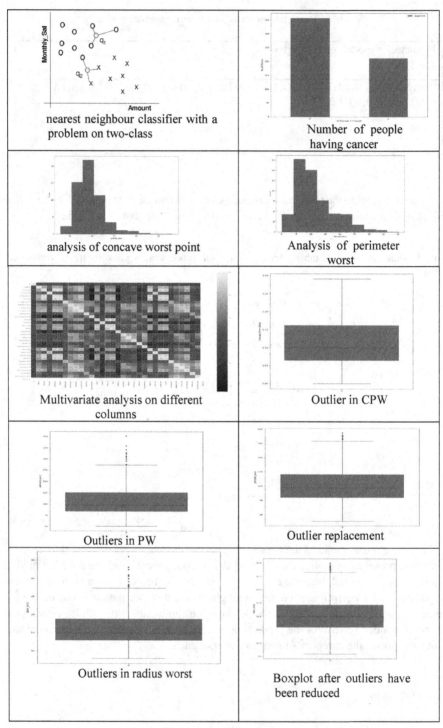

Fig. 3. Describe the overall process involved in the analysis of this study and the flow of the approaches, which has been followed in this research.

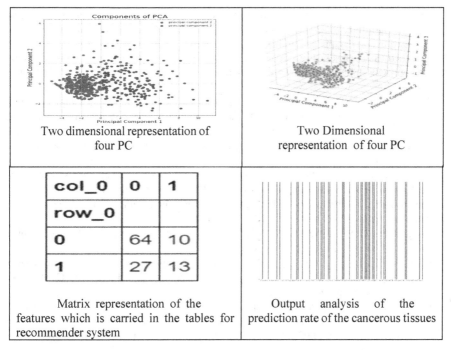

| Two dimensional representation of four PC | Two Dimensional representation of four PC |

| Matrix representation of the features which is carried in the tables for recommender system | Output analysis of the prediction rate of the cancerous tissues |

Fig. 3. (*continued*)

5 Conclusion

There was a significant output based on results that the eight feature that plays a major important role in diagnosis of whether the person has a malignant or benign cells present are CPW, PW, CPM, RW, PM, AW, RM, AM. We found the best accuracy for our prediction made using K Nearest Neighbor that is nearly 80% and when we checked for its accuracy using other classification algorithms like decision tree classifier than it was not up to the requirements.

References

1. Brown, M.L., Houn, F., Sickles, E.A., Kessler, L.G.: Screening mammography in community practice: positive predictive value of abnormal findings and yield of follow-up diagnostic procedures. AJR. Am. J. Roentgenol. **165**(6), 1373–1377 (1995)
2. Al-Hadidi, M.D.R.A., Al-Gawagzeh, M.Y., Alsaaidah, B.A.: Solving mammography problems of breast cancer detection using artificial neural networks and image processing techniques. Indian J. Sci. Technol. **5**(4), 2520–2528 (2012)
3. Übeyli, E.D.: Implementing automated diagnostic systems for breast cancer detection. Expert Syst. Appl. **33**(4), 1054–1062 (2007)
4. Kulkarni, D.A., Bhagyashree, S.M., Udupi, G.R.: Texture analysis of mammographic images. Int. J. Comput. Appl. **5**(6), 12–17 (2010)

5. Alarabeyyat, A., Alhanahnah, M.: Breast cancer detection using k-nearest neighbor machine learning algorithm. In: 2016 9th International Conference on Developments in eSystems Engineering (DeSE), pp. 35–39. IEEE, August 2016
6. Medjahed, S.A., Saadi, T.A., Benyettou, A.: Breast cancer diagnosis by using k-nearest neighbor with different distances and classification rules. Int. J. Comput. Appl. **62**(1), 1–5 (2013)
7. Zhang, H., Arslan, T., Flynn, B.: A single antenna based microwave system for breast cancer detection: experimental results. In: 2013 Loughborough Antennas & Propagation Conference (LAPC), pp. 477–481. IEEE, November 2013
8. Ng, E.Y.K., Kee, E.C.: Advanced integrated technique in breast cancer thermography. J. Med. Eng. Technol. **32**(2), 103–114 (2008)
9. Kaur, N., Kaur, P.: Classification and Segmentation Approach for Plant Disease Detection. Int. J. Comput. Sci. Mob. Comput. **8**(8), 6–16 (2019). ISSN 2320-088X
10. Bhuvaneswari, P., Therese, A.B.: Detection of cancer in lung with k-nn classification using genetic algorithm. Proc. Mater. Sci. **10**, 433–440 (2015)
11. Wang, H., Yoon, S.W.: Breast cancer prediction using data mining method. In: IISE Annual Conference & Expo 2015, pp. 818–828, October 2015
12. Floyd Jr., C.E., Lo, J.Y., Yun, A.J., Sullivan, D.C., Kornguth, P.J.: Prediction of breast cancer malignancy using an artificial neural network. Cancer: Interdisc. Int. J. Am. Cancer Soc. **74**(11), 2944–2948 (1994)
13. Sangeetha, R., Murthy, K.S.: A novel approach for detection of breast cancer at an early stage using digital image processing techniques. In: 2017 International Conference on Inventive Systems and Control (ICISC), Coimbatore, pp. 1–4 (2017). https://doi.org/10.1109/ICISC.2017.8068625
14. Král, P., Lenc, L.: LBP features for breast cancer detection. In: 2016 IEEE International Conference on Image Processing (ICIP), pp. 2643–2647. IEEE, September 2016
15. Li, Q., Li, W., Zhang, J., Xu, Z.: An improved k-nearest neighbour method to diagnose breast cancer. Analyst **143**(12), 2807–2811 (2018)
16. Rakhlin, A., Shvets, A., Iglovikov, V., Kalinin, A.A.: Deep convolutional neural networks for breast cancer histology image analysis. In: Campilho, A., Karray, F., ter Haar Romeny, B. (eds.) ICIAR 2018. LNCS, vol. 10882, pp. 737–744. Springer, Cham (2018). https://doi.org/10.1007/978-3-319-93000-8_83
17. Deekshatulu, B.L., Chandra, P.: Classification of heart disease using k-nearest neighbor and genetic algorithm. Proc. Technol. **10**, 85–94 (2013)
18. Kaggle Link of Data set. https://www.kaggle.com/uciml/breast-cancer-wisconsin-data

A Novel Mobile Based Hybrid Skin Tone Classification Algorithm for Cancer Detection

Paarth Bir[1(✉)] and B. Balamurugan[2]

[1] Department of Electronics and Communication Engineering,
Malaviya National Institute of Technology, Jaipur, India
paarthbir@gmail.com
[2] School of Computer Science and Engineering,
Galgotias University, Greater Noida, India
kadavulai@gmail.com

Abstract. Human skin, epidermis, forms the largest organ of the human body. It plays an integral role as the outermost layer of the body by guarding internal organs from the environment, producing vitamin D which is important for various bodily functions and regulating body temperature. Skin ailments are a growing concern with a significant rise in cases reported in both developed and developing countries. With the rise in exposure to UV radiation, it is very important to detect skin cancer in its nascent stages which significantly increases chances of successful treatment. The proposed method seeks to use a single image captured from a standard smartphone and classify the input image as cancerous or non- cancerous. Multiple algorithms for feature extraction and classification are compared to obtain the maximum accuracy.

Keywords: Deep Convolutional Networks · Image classification · Binary classification · Cancer detection · Transfer learning

1 Introduction

Skin diseases are a major health concern in both developed as well as developing countries, they are the fourth largest cause of non-fatal diseases [1]. Skin diseases may occur due to a host of reasons including but not limited to exposure to UV radiation, alcohol, smoking, increasing air and water pollution, etc. There have been recent studies highlighting mental ailments such as stress, depression, etc as a cause of skin diseases. Skin diseases have serious effects on an individual's quality of life. Studies show that even common ailments like acne and psoriasis can cause depression, anxiety and an increase in suicidal thoughts [2]. Permanent effects may include scarring or disfigurement. Diseases like skin cancer, especially melanoma, may prove to be fatal. It is estimated that 2 to 3 million cases of non-melanoma and 132,000 melanoma skin cancers are reported every year [3].

© Springer Nature Singapore Pte Ltd. 2020
U. Batra et al. (Eds.): REDSET 2019, CCIS 1229, pp. 223–235, 2020.
https://doi.org/10.1007/978-981-15-5827-6_19

It is assumed that the number of cases mentioned are underestimated [4]. Furthermore with the decrease in Ozone layer thickness, the number of cases of skin cancers are only set to increase. An estimated 1.9 billion suffer from skin diseases at any given time, the demand for qualified dermatologists grossly underwhelms the number available. In the United States there are 3.4 trained dermatologists for every 100,000 persons [5]. The lack of trained practitioners along with the high costs of testing greatly increases the need to develop accurate, efficient and cheap methods to detect and identify skin ailments. The aim of this paper is to develop an efficient architecture capable of classifying skin lesions in the form of input images as malignant (cancerous) or benign (non-cancerous) that is capable of running on mobile devices and provides performance equivalent to trained dermatologists.

Kaliyaadan et al. introduced a cost effective method to use smartphones as a dermoscopy device, using a device costing 10 dollars [6].

2   Related Works

A large amount of literature exists on classification of skin lesions into melanomatous or non-melanomatous cancer. Some approaches that have been applied include using Support Vector Machines (SVM) [7], K-Nearest Neighbors (KNN) [7,8], Artificial Neural Networks and Deep Convolutional Networks. Dorj et al. used a ECOC SVM classifier on features extracted automatically by a pretrained deep convolutional neural network (AlexNet) and classified the lesions into four types of cancers. Training and testing was done on 3,573 RGB images. Accuracy of 94.2% was achieved by the proposed algorithm [9].

Hekler et al. used a combination of human and artificial intelligence for skin cancer classification. A total of 11,444 dermatoscopic images were used to train a single CNN. Then 112 expert dermatologists and the aforementioned CNN independently classified 300 verified skin lesions into five categories. The two, human and machine, were combined to create a new classifier with the help of gradient boosting methods. The classifier predicted the category of the lesion and predicted it as either benign or malignant. An accuracy of 82.59% and sensitivity of 89% was achieved by this combination [10]. Brinker et al. compared automatic melanoma classification by CNN trained on 12,378 dermatoscopic images to 145 dermatologists on 100 verified clinical images. Comparison was done on the basis of sensitivity, specificity and receiver operating characteristics. They found a mean sensitivity of 89.4% and specificity of 64.4%, while the CNN exhibited mean specificity of 68.2%. This was the first time, dermatologist-level image classification was achieved on clinical image classification without training on clinical images. The CNN displayed higher robustness compared to human assessment [11].

Esteva et al. devised a new method to classify skin cancers by training a deep CNN using 129,450 clinical images of different skin cancers. They compared the trained network's performance to that of a 21 member board of certified dermatologists. They found their network to be on par with the domain experts. Their use of such an extensive dataset allowed for high accuracy on new skin lesions, as the general trend has been that more data for a deep network equates to better performance. [12] M.H. Jafari et al. proposed a method for accurate extraction of lesion region using deep learning. A high accuracy of 98.5% and sensitivity was achieved, outperforming the existing state of the art models for segmentation of lesion [13]. E. Nasr-Esfahani et al. proposed a Convolutional Neural Network trained to distinguish between melanoma and benign cases. Accuracy of 81% and sensitivity of 81% was obtained making it superior to the existing state of the art methods at the time [14]. A. Mikołajczyk et al. used the concept of data augmentation to improve the existing classification models for medical imaging. They compared and analyzed multiple methods of data augmentation in the task of image classification, including classical image methods like rotation, cropping, zooming, histogram based methods and comparatively newer methods like style transfer and Generative Adversarial Networks (GAN) [15]. Hameed et al. proposed a scheme to classify skin lesion image into five categories healthy, acne, eczema, benign or malignant melanoma. A pretrained CNN, AlexNet was used to automatically extract features for ECOC SVM classifier. An accuracy of 86.21% was obtained [16].

3 Discussed Algorithms

The premise of this paper is to classify input image as either non-cancerous or cancerous. There exists several methodologies, each with their merits and demerits, which can be implemented. We review some of these in the section below.

Local Binary Pattern (LBP) is a non-parametric descriptor that effectively summarizes the local structure of images and is used extensively in feature extraction for face recognition and demographic classification. LBP is especially tolerant regarding monotonic illumination changes. A major advantage of the LBP is that it is a powerful method for feature extraction but is computationally inexpensive. In recent researches it has been modified to be rotationally invariant [17]. The **Histogram of Gradients**, introduced by Dalal and Triggs [18], uses HOG to extract feature vector from the images. This method is based on evaluating well-normalized histograms of image gradients orientations in a dense grid. The HOG method has the basic idea that a shape or an object may be described by the distribution of intensity gradients rather than edges and contours. The HOG has many advantages with the most important being that it is invariant to translations and rotations if they are small enough (Table 1).

K-Nearest Neighbors is a supervised machine learning algorithm, it learns from a set of inputs X and their labels y and learns to map the input vector X to its desired output y. The KNN algorithm 'learns' the entirety of the training data and for predicting on an input X', calculates a distance from X' to each instance in the training set. The 'K' nearest neighbors to the input X' are then put through a voting mechanism and the prediction is obtained. Feature extractors such as HOG or SIFT or one of the many existing extractors can be used to reduce dimensionality of the problem and give improved results. Principal

Table 1. An overview of feature extractors.

Feature extractors		
Name	Advantages	Disadvantages
Histogram of gradients	Invariant to geometric and photometric transformations	Rotationally invariant
Pretrained Deep CNN	High accuracy, no need for domain knowledge	Require large amount of data, computationally very expensive
Linear binary patterns	Computationally inexpensive	Poor performance when faced with flat images

Component Analysis is an extremely popular algorithm for tackling this 'curse of dimensionality'. The KNN is the simplest machine learning algorithm in that it really just finds out the vectors closest to the input vector from the training set and provides an output. It has the advantage of requiring no training but struggles with large datasets and the fact that a majority of its computation is during prediction which ideally is not wanted.

Support Vector Machines are very powerful machine learning models used for classification problems. These are essentially used for binary classification but may be modified for use in multi-class classifications. SVM was introduced by Cortes and Vapnik [19] so as to map inputs to high dimensional feature spaces, where linear or nonlinear boundaries or a hyperplane separates the classes perfectly. These were later known as hard-margin SVM. Soft-Margin SVM were introduced to ensure that no overfitting took place by reducing the complexity of the hyperplane at the cost of the perfect separation of the classes. The SVM may use from the several kernels such as the linear kernel, polynomial kernel and the Gaussian Radial Basis Function (RBF) kernel. **Multi-Layer Perceptron** is a type of feed forward artificial neural network (ANN) [20], that consists of input layer, hidden layers and output layer. Each of these layers contain nodes or neurons in them. These neurons each take a linear combination of their inputs and apply some non-linear activation function to it. There exists many types of these activation functions each with their merits and demerits. Some of the most popular activation functions include sigmoid, ReLu, Leaky ReLu, PReLu, etc. The MLP however requires large amounts of data in order to avoid overfitting. MLP have tended to show greater accuracy compared to the above mentioned classifiers (Table 2).

Deep Convolutional Neural Networks are the most popular classifiers in recent literature owing to their huge success in classification tasks and by often removing the need for domain knowledge. These neural networks generally have convolution and pooling operations on the input which extracts features for the neural network to use. Recent times have seen a huge increase in the depth of the networks with more and more data as well as computational power avail-

Table 2. An overview of classification algorithms.

Classification algorithms		
Name	Advantages	Disadvantages
K nearest neighbors	Simple to implement	Computation during prediction period
Support vector machine	Highly powerful for binary classification	Poor performance for overlapping datasets, not good with large datasets.
Multi layer perceptrons	Highly accurate for binary and multi class classification	Computationally expensive to train

able, these deep networks have matched and sometimes even surpassed human level performance in classification and recognition tasks. The popularity of these networks has increased ever since AlexNet [21] was introduced in 2012 for the ImageNet [22] challenge and significantly reduced the top5 error rate from 25.8% to 16.4%. AlexNet introduced a number of breakthroughs such as using ReLu non-linearity over tanh, dropout, data augmentation, etc that completely transformed how deep networks were viewed. Since then models such as VGGNet [23], GoogleNet [24] and ResNet [25] have further improved performance. These however require large computational power as well as memory for both training as well as for prediction. A dataset of tens of thousands of images and now, typically millions of images are required to train deep networks. Specialised hardware such as GPUs are required for training as well as for inference. However, with the advancement of technology, both in terms of optimized frameworks and hardware for mobile devices, deep learning is taking off for mobile devices. The concept of transfer learning is another aspect that has tremendously improved performance without a large amount of training as by using initial layers of the state-of-the-art models like AlexNet and training the remainder of the network on the new training set, which may have a completely distinct domain to that of ImageNet, a high performance may be obtained.

VGG16 model was runner up in ILSVRC 2014 for the classification challenge was introduced as an investigation into the effect that an increasing depth of convolutional layers had on accuracy in a large scale image recognition problem [23]. VGG16 obtained a top one accuracy of and a top-5 accuracy of on the ImageNet dataset. Due to the huge depth of the network, with convolutional layers of kernel size (3,3) and MaxPooling layers of size (2, 2), stacked one over another, the VGG16 model has a size of around 530 MB having over 138 million parameters.

Inception V3 was runner up in ILSVRC 2015 obtained a top-one accuracy of 77.9% and a top-5 accuracy of 93.7% with less than 25 million parameters. GoogLeNet, winner of 2014 ImageNet challenge, now known as Inception-V1 was improved first with batch normalization (Inception-V2) and then factorizing convolutions (Inception-V3). The model was an effective improvement over the existing state-of-art models having similar performance to VGG but at significantly reduced computation.

MobileNet V1 introduced depthwise separable convolutions to reduce model size and complexity. The model obtained a top-one accuracy of 70.4% and a top-5 accuracy of 89.5% and has a size of around 16 MB, a significant reduction from other deep convolutional networks [26].

4   Dataset

The International Skin Imaging Collaboration (ISIC) has developed the ISIC Archive [27], an international repository of dermatoscopic images, for both the purposes of clinical training, and for supporting technical research toward automated algorithmic analysis by hosting the ISIC Challenges. The HAM10000 [28] ("Human Against Machine with 10000 training images") dataset collected dermatoscopic images from different populations, acquired and stored by different modalities. The final dataset consists of 10015 dermatoscopic images. Cases include a representative collection of: Actinic keratoses and intraepithelial carcinoma/Bowen's disease (akiec), basal cell carcinoma (bcc), benign keratosis-like lesions (solar lentigines/seborrheic keratoses and lichen-planus like keratoses, bkl), dermatofibroma (df), melanoma (mel), melanocytic nevi (nv) and vascular lesions (angiomas, angiokeratomas, pyogenic granulomas and hemorrhage, vasc). They are further divided into 2 classes: malignant and benign. bcc, mel are classified as malignant while nv, bkl and df are considered benign. Due to imbalanced distribution of the two classes, the, majority class(benign) is undersampled to reduce the parity between the two classes (Table 3).

Table 3. Distribution of data.

Distribution			
Name	Training set	Validation set	Testing set
Benign	5000	500	100
Malignant	1663	300	100

5   Method

The dermatoscopic images from the dataset are first pre-processed to resize to fixed size of (256, 256, 3). The images are in RGB format. In order to reduce noise due to hair, the images are passed through morphological black-hat transformation after conversion to grayscale. Black hat transformations are typically used to enhance dark objects of interest in a bright background. A mask is created for inpainting the images and the mask so prepared is used in the original image to restore the noisy part of the image with significant deduction in hair present in the dermatoscopic image. Three networks are used for feature extraction: VGG16, Inception V3 and MobileNetV1 trained on the ImageNet data. With the available dataset being smaller than standard deep network datasets the deep networks are not trained from scratch so as to avoid overfitting, rather the concept of transfer learning is used. Transfer learning is especially useful in cases where the dataset may be limited in nature due to various reasons such as the cost of obtaining data. Transfer learning utilizes the fact that the early layers in a convolutional neural network learn features such as curves, edges and other low level features. The fully connected layers of these networks are replaced with new layers according to the classification problem. Another concept exploited for training deep models is data augmentation, that is increasing the training samples by various affine transformations. The dataset is augmented by introducing zoom, illumination, rotation, linear shifting and horizontal flipping. The features extracted are passed through a neural network.

Classification algorithms under consideration are K-Nearest Neighbors, Support Vector Machines and Multi-Layer Perceptrons. The K-Nearest Neighbor is a lazy algorithm as it has no training phase, but instead all computation is performed during prediction stage where the distance from the input to each training instance is calculated and compared, making the algorithm quite unfeasible for implementation in this problem. Support Vector Machines are extremely versatile classification structures especially for binary classification but show poor performance when the target classes are overlapping. Multi Layer Perceptrons learn through a system called as back-propagation in the dense networks, where the chain rule to calculate gradients is effectively used.

VGG16 + MLP: The VGG16 model is frozen so that it's weights do not update in training of the working dataset. The dense networks of the model are replaced with a MLP structure with the output nodes equal to that of the classes required for classification. Features are extracted from block3 Maxpool layer so that only low level features are learnt. To counter data imbalance in addition to undersampling the majority class, class weights are assigned to the loss function such that the minority class has a greater effect on the loss function. ELu non-linear activation is used for layers to combat the 'dead' neurons caused by the ReLu activation. Adam optimizer is used with a variable learning rate for training [29] in the initial epochs. Stochastic Gradient Descent(SGD) is used as optimizer after to [30]. To further increase the accuracy of the model, the feature extractor is unfrozen and the complete model is trained. After a respectable accuracy was obtained, class weights for the loss function were varied to maximise the F1 score.

InceptionV3 + MLP:A similar methodology is adopted to that used for the VGG16 network. The Inception V3 model is frozen and the dense networks of the model are replaced with a MLP structure suited to the task. Features are extracted from 'mixed4' layer. Feature extraction from deeper layers did not converge but rather overfitted on majority class. Early Stopping was used to prevent overfitting.

MobileNetV1 + MLP:A similar methodology is adopted to that used for the VGG16 network. Features are extracted from "conv_pw_8_relu" layer of the pretrained network. Features from deeper layers of the network led to overfitting on majority class (Fig. 1).

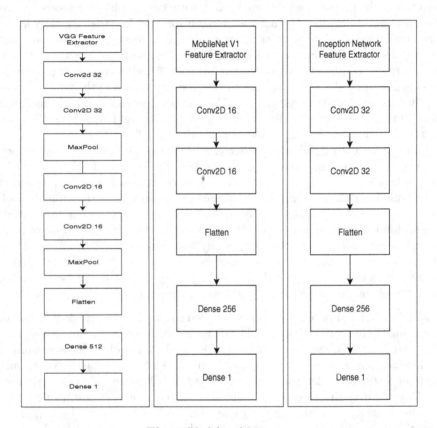

Fig. 1. Model architectures

6 RESULTS

6.1 VGG16 + MLP

See Fig. 2.

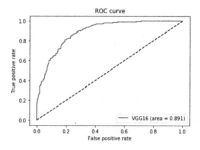

Fig. 2. ROC plot

A validation accuracy of 80.5%, test accuracy of 79.88% and train accuracy of 81.56% was obtained (Tables 4 and 5; Fig. 3).

Table 4. Confusion matrix

407	93
63	237

$$Precision = TruePositives/(TruePositives + FalsePositives) \quad (1)$$

$$Recall = TruePositives/(FalseNegatives + TruePositives) \quad (2)$$

$$F1 = 2 * precision * recall/(precision + recall) \quad (3)$$

Table 5. Results for VGG16 used as feature extractor for MLP.

Scores		
Precision	Recall	F1 score
71.81%	79%	75.23%

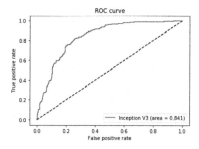

Fig. 3. ROC plot

6.2 Inception V3 + MLP

A validation accuracy of 77.875%, test accuracy of 76.523% and train accuracy of 76.28% was obtained (Tables 6 and 7).

Table 6. Confusion matrix

398	102
75	225

Table 7. Results for Inception V3 used as feature extractor for MLP.

Scores		
Precision	Recall	F1 score
68.80%	75%	71.77%

6.3 MobileNetV1 + MLP

A validation accuracy of 85%, test accuracy of 81.6% and train accuracy of 87.81% was obtained (Fig. 4; Tables 8, 9 and 10).

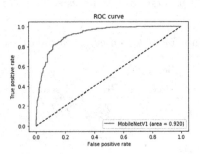

Fig. 4. ROC plot

Table 8. Confusion matrix

441	59
61	239

Table 9. Results for MobileNetV1 used as feature extractor for MLP.

Scores		
Precision	Recall	F1 score
80.20%	79.66%	79.93%

Table 10. Comparison of results

Scores							
Name	Total parameters	Size	Validation accuracy	Precision	Recall	F1 score	Test accuracy
VGG16	2,886,593	15.46 MB	80.5%	71.8%	79%	75.23%	79.88%
Inception V3	10,367,457	79.46 MB	77.875%	68.8%	75%	71.77%	75.52%
MobileNetV1	1,940,449	14.91 MB	85%	80.2%	79.66%	79.93%	81.6%

7 Conclusions and Future Work

As determined in the above results, automated mechanisms may be used to detect malignant and benign tumors with comparable degree of accuracy to dermatologists [10,11]. Feature extraction from very deep layers was avoided to reduce number of parameters which would increase model size as well as cause overfitting. Diagnosing cancer in early stages is very important, however other skin diseases including acne, eczema, psoriasis, etc too are very common and detrimental to the society. A pipeline to automatically diagnose skin disease will be very beneficial to society. For skin cancer, a mechanism for detecting the stage of the diagnosed cancer is another important implementation. Further, the discussed algorithms may be used in a host of other bio-medical fields.

References

1. Hay, R.J., Johns, N.E., Williams, H.C., et al.: The global burden of skin disease in 2010: an analysis of the prevalence and impact of skin conditions. J. Investig. Dermatol. Symp. Proc. **134**, 1527–1534 (2014)
2. Dalgard, F.J., Gieler, U., Tomas-Aragones, L., et al.: The psychological burden of skin diseases: a cross-sectional multicenter study among dermatological outpatients in 13 European countries. J. Invest. Dermatol. **135**(4), 984–991 (2015). https://doi.org/10.1038/jid.2014.530
3. World Health Organization. https://www.who.int/uv/faq/skincancer/en/index1.html
4. Bray, F., et al.: Global cancer statistics 2018: GLOBOCAN estimates of incidence and mortality worldwide for 36 cancers in 185 countries. https://doi.org/10.3322/caac.21492
5. Glazer, A.M., Farberg, A.S., Winkelmann, R.R., Rigel, D.S.: Analysis of trends in geographic distribution and density of US dermatologists. JAMA Dermatol. **153**(4), 322–325 (2017). https://doi.org/10.1001/jamadermatol.2016.5411

6. Kaliyadan, F., Ashique, K.: A simple and cost-effective device for mobile dermoscopy. https://doi.org/10.4103/0378-6323.120740
7. Murugan, A., Nair, S.H., Kumar, K.P.S.: Detection of skin cancer using SVM, Random Forest and kNN classifiers. J. Med. Syst. **43**(8), 1–9 (2019). https://doi.org/10.1007/s10916-019-1400-8
8. Ballerini, L., Fisher, R.B., Aldridge, B., Rees, J.: A color and texture based hierarchical K-NN approach to the classification of non-melanoma skin lesions. In: Celebi, M., Schaefer, G. (eds.) Color Medical Image Analysis, vol. 6, pp. 63–86. Springer, Heidelberg (2013). https://doi.org/10.1007/978-94-007-5389-1_4
9. Dorj, U.-O., Lee, K.-K., Choi, J.-Y., Lee, M.: The skin cancer classification using deep convolutional neural network. Multimedia Tools Appl. **77**(8), 9909–9924 (2018). https://doi.org/10.1007/s11042-018-5714-1
10. Hekler, A., et al.: Superior skin cancer classification by the combination of human and artificial intelligence. https://doi.org/10.1016/j.ejca.2019.07.019
11. Brinker, T.J., et al.: A convolutional neural network trained with dermoscopic images performed on par with 145 dermatologists in a clinical melanoma image classification task. https://doi.org/10.1016/j.ejca.2019.02.005
12. Esteva, A., et al.: Dermatologist-level classification of skin cancer with deep neural networks. Nature **542**(7639), 115–118 (2017). https://doi.org/10.1038/nature21056
13. Jafari, M.H., et al.: Skin lesion segmentation in clinical images using deep learning. In: 2016 23rd International Conference on Pattern Recognition (ICPR), Cancun, pp. 337–342 (2016). https://doi.org/10.1109/ICPR.2016.7899656
14. Nasr-Esfahani, E., et al.: Melanoma detection by analysis of clinical images using convolutional neural network. In: 2016 38th Annual International Conference of the IEEE Engineering in Medicine and Biology Society (EMBC), Orlando, FL, pp. 1373–1376 (2016). https://doi.org/10.1109/EMBC.2016.7590963
15. Mikołajczyk, A., Grochowski, M.: Data augmentation for improving deep learning in image classification problem. In: 2018 International Interdisciplinary PhD Workshop (IIPhDW), Swinoujście, pp. 117-122 (2018). https://doi.org/10.1109/IIPHDW.2018.8388338
16. Hameed, N., Shabut, A.M., Hossain, M.A.: Multi-class skin diseases classification using deep convolutional neural network and support vector machine. In: 2018 12th International Conference on Software, Knowledge, Information Management & Applications (SKIMA), Phnom Penh, Cambodia, pp. 1–7 (2018). https://doi.org/10.1109/SKIMA.2018.8631525
17. Dalal, N., Triggs, B.: Histograms of oriented gradients for human detection. In: 2005 IEEE Computer Society Conference on Computer Vision and Pattern Recognition (CVPR 2005), San Diego, CA, USA, vol. 1, pp. 886–893 (2005). https://doi.org/10.1109/CVPR.2005.177
18. Ahonen, T., Matas, J., He, C., Pietikäinen, M.: Rotation invariant image description with local binary pattern histogram fourier features. In: Salberg, A.B., Hardeberg, J.Y., Jenssen, R. (eds.) SCIA 2009. LNCS, vol. 5575. Springer, Heidelberg (2009). https://doi.org/10.1007/978-3-642-02230-2_7
19. Cortes, C., Vapnik, V.: Mach. Learn. **20**, 273 (1995). https://doi.org/10.1023/A:1022627411411
20. Uhrig, R.E.: Introduction to artificial neural networks. In: Proceedings of IECON 1995 - 21st Annual Conference on IEEE Industrial Electronics, Orlando, FL, USA, vol. 1, pp. 33–37 (1995). https://doi.org/10.1109/IECON.1995.483329

21. Krizhevsky, A., Sutskever, I., Hinton, G.E.: ImageNet classification with deep convolutional neural networks. In: 2012 Advances in Neural Information Processing Systems 25
22. Russakovsky, O., et al.: ImageNet large scale visual recognition challenge. Int. J. Comput. Vis. **115**(3), 211–252 (2015). https://doi.org/10.1007/s11263-015-0816-y
23. Simonyan, K., Zisserman, A.: Very deep convolutional networks for large-scale image recognition. CoRR, abs/1409.1556 (2014)
24. Szegedy, C., et al.: Going deeper with convolutions. In: 2015 IEEE Conference on Computer Vision and Pattern Recognition (CVPR), Boston, MA, pp. 1–9 (2015). https://doi.org/10.1109/CVPR.2015.7298594
25. He, K., Zhang, X., Ren, S., Sun, J.: Deep residual learning for image recognition. In: 2016 IEEE Conference on Computer Vision and Pattern Recognition (CVPR), Las Vegas, NV, pp. 770–778 (2016). https://doi.org/10.1109/CVPR.2016.90
26. Howard, A.G., et al.: MobileNets: Efficient Convolutional Neural Networks for Mobile Vision Applications (2017) arXiv:1704.04861
27. Codella, N.C.F., et al.: Skin Lesion Analysis Toward Melanoma Detection: A Challenge at the 2017 International Symposium on Biomedical Imaging (ISBI), Hosted by the International Skin Imaging Collaboration (ISIC) (2017). arXiv:1710.05006
28. Tschandl, P., Rosendahl, C., Kittler, H.: The HAM10000 dataset, a large collection of multi-source dermatoscopic images of common pigmented skin lesions. Sci. Data **5**, 180161. https://doi.org/10.1038/sdata.2018.161
29. Loshchilov, I., Hutter, F.: Fixing Weight Decay Regularization in Adam. ArXiv, abs/1711.05101 (2018)
30. Keskar, N.S., Socher, R.: Improving Generalization Performance by Switching from Adam to SGD. ArXiv, abs/1712.07628 (2017)

Next Generation Computing

Detection of Lung Cancer Through Image Processing Using SVM

Anand Upadhyay, Ankit Dubey, and Ajaykumar Patel$^{(\boxtimes)}$

Thakur College of Science and Commerce, Kandivali (E), Mumbai 400101, India
anandhari6@gmail.com, dankit913@gmail.com,
ajaypatel.118268@gmail.com

Abstract. Detection of a cancer in a lung through image processing with SVM classification is processed in this research paper. The research could facilitate the detection of a cancer in desired output. The author considered a computer tomography (CT) image of a lung as an input data set which further processed by segmentation of that image. Here water segmentation is proposed on an input image to improve the quality from the image. Once the segmentation of an image is done the author used the SVM classification to train segmented data set to get an accurate reading of lung cancer detection. In every stage of classification image segmentation is done separately. For classification purpose, SVM binary classifier is used to show a higher accuracy in a detection of a lung cancer. The author has makes use of a confusion matrix to determine the predicted groups in group and group hat respectively.

Keywords: Detection of lung cancer · CT scan image processing · Watershed segmentation · SVM classifier

1 Introduction

Nowadays, comparing with other types of cancer, lung cancer has become the major death causing disease. Lung cancer is a disease of an abnormal cells multiplying and growing into a tumor. This growth can spread beyond the lung by the process of metastasis into nearby tissue or other parts of the body. Normally there are Two types of lung cancer i.e. Small-Cell Lung Carcinoma (SCLC) and Non-Small-Cell Lung Carcinoma (NSCLC). NSCLC contribute more than 80% of All lung cancer cases, while SCLC account for about 15% of the cases [5]. Lung carcinoma causes certain mutations in healthy cells. This type of cancer generally extends towards the center of the chest. Metastatis is a condition that occurs when a cancer cell leaves the place where it started and migrate into a lymph node [7]. Each year more people is dying of lung cancer than colon, breast, and prostate cancers combined [8].

The image can be modified to get better information and to isolate the region of interest which help to diagnosis the disease. Each year more people is dying of lung cancer than colon, breast, and prostate cancers combined [8]. The main reason behind high death by lung cancer is just because they are detected very later stages. If the lung cancer is detected at early stage, chances for survival can increase up to 50%–70% [6].

© Springer Nature Singapore Pte Ltd. 2020
U. Batra et al. (Eds.): REDSET 2019, CCIS 1229, pp. 239–245, 2020.
https://doi.org/10.1007/978-981-15-5827-6_20

It is so difficult to recognize the cancer in its initial phase because its symptoms are mostly detectable at final stage or third stage. Because of such reason, the death rate of lung cancer are very high as compared with other types of cancer. As per the statistics and reports recorded by the world health organization that every year 7.6 million people died through lung cancer. Which resultant cost annually 10,000 billion dollars all over across the world. It is also important to notice that there are many techniques to detect lung cancer but it is very expensive to detect the cancer. Our approach is to reduce the cost efficiency so it could be useful for the poor people. This approach could be done by image processing technique which will be very useful for determining whether the lung is cancer defected or not. Imaging technology in medical field is very helpful for the doctor to see the interior portion of the body. However, system cannot give an 100% accuracy but it is still giving highest accurate reading. Here, in this two class of 0 and 1 is feature as affected lung and healthy lung to determine the lungs.

2 Methodology

By referring many research papers, the author came to know that image processing technique widely used by Doctors, Researchers and Scientists to detect lung cancer in early stage. So, the author has implemented image processing technique with SVM classifier to detect cancer affected lung which is good, less costly time saving and gives accurate outputs. Here the classification of a lung cancer and algorithm has been processed using the MATLAB Tool and with its inbuilt functions, in which we use the technique of image processing. The detection of cancer in a lung is done with the help of algorithm. To get the desired output the image segmentation is proposed by the author. With this technique the complete division of the image in separated region are shown which can be easily determined and required low computation time. The author proposed the SVM classification because it gives more accurate value rather than the other neural network.

The following flow chart shows work-flow of proposed system.

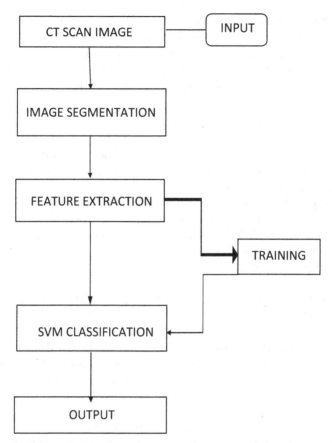

Initial stage: Taking input as CT image of a normal and abnormal lungs from the reference of clinicaladvisor.com and stored it in the folder for the further enhancement and segmentation to get the better and accurate reading of the lung detection whether the lung is affected or not.

Second stage: This stage classifies the further process in which the input image is segmented by watershed segmentation technique which is used to enhance the image to get the best level of quality. Water segmentation return a label matrix that identifies the watershed region of input matrix which can have only dimension. It transforms to find the catchment basins or watershed rigid lines which indicate the different portion or the desired part of the lung detection.

Third stage: The stage is followed by the completion of second stage in which it classifies the features extraction and detection of a lung CT image whether the lung is affected with cancer or it is a healthy lung.

The feature extraction is the process of reclassifying the repeating data or information into an arrangement of element of decreased value. To obtain the general feature and detection of a lung cancer from the enhanced segmented image. Once the feature extraction is done the extracted part of the lungs undergoes for training and makes the data instance. In this research paper the author used the SVM classification to determine the result of lung detection.

Classification: For classification purpose the author has utilize or have been used the SVM classifier to describe the output. SVM is discriminative classifier which formally defined by a separating hyper plane. It is a binary classification in which it deals with only two classes 0 and 1 for the declaration purpose. In this research paper the classifier detects the lungs with the cancer affected and also healthy lungs.

3 Literature Review

As reviewing many papers research, the author has come to know that the researchers have make more utilized of image processing technique and tools for their research to detect the medical related diseases or lung cancer detection. The author also described that the CT image of lung as an input for image processing technique is good because it gives more accurate detection regarding other images.

Paper [1] proposed a CT image of a lung to detect the lung cancer by getting the 97% of accuracy with the classifier.

Paper [2] proposed of a back propagation based gray level feature to detect the nodule in the lungs.

Paper [3] in this paper the author makes use of a PNN with the modified crow – search algorithm for a cancer detection in a lung by obtaining the 82.5% of the classification accuracy.

Paper [4] has proposed an Entropy Degradation Method (EDM) machine learning algorithm with the vectorized histogram features to detect the early malicious cancer present in the lungs. Here author aim is to determine the system to make decision regarding the radiologist to assume the affected cancer or tumor.

The author has proposed a Bayesian classification and mean shift segmentation in order to detect and segment the sputum cells of sputum image as input [10].

Here, the author has proposed the early lung cancer detection by using segmentation and analysis of ct images [9].

As per the above paper reviewing, the author in this research paper has used an SVM classification with image processing technique to identify the cancer present in the lungs. In this work it deals with the binary class such as 0 and 1 for the classification of data set feature. The accuracy for a lung cancer detection can obtained higher accuracy with the support of the conclusive for processing the image technique and tools.

4 Results and Analysis

The result obtain from this research approach is analyzed and discussed, which is represented by the following figures.

In the above Fig. 1 the author has taken CT image as an input which is further segmented by water segmentation technique to make better quality of the image and then on segmented image, SVM classifier is applied which further gives the expected output.

In above Fig. 2, now here also the CT image is taken as input which is later on segmented by water segmentation and SVM classifier is applied to get desired output. During training period, the segmented image clearly shows that the area of dark blue

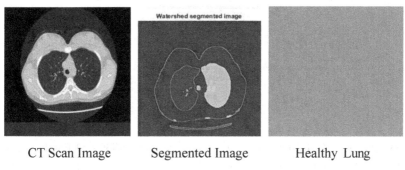

CT Scan Image   Segmented Image   Healthy Lung

Fig. 1. Healthy lung cell

pixel is greater than area of light blue pixel which indicates the normal lung and light blue pixel indicates i.e. smaller one is cancer affected lung.

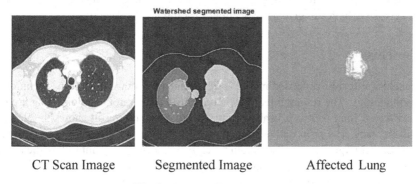

CT Scan Image   Segmented Image   Affected Lung

Fig. 2. Cancer affected lung cell

As per the result of Fig. 1. and Fig. 2. the accuracy of proposed model can be determined by the below Tables 1 and 2.

Table 1. Healthy lung

Image no.	Linear accuracy	Quadric accuracy	Cubic accuracy
1	94.2%	99%	99%
2	94.4%	99%	99.2%

By above tables reading, the accuracy of an affected lung is increasing and giving absolute accurate reading for the detection of lungs. As per the observation of an output more the accuracy is determining less training time is occurred to train the data set. For healthy lungs the linear SVM classify 94.2% accuracy in 1.4152 s for training data

Table 2. Cancerous lung

Image no.	Linear accuracy	Quadric accuracy	Cubic accuracy
1	93.7%	99%	98%
2	94.2%	99%	99.2%

set and in quadric SVM it classifies 99% accuracy with 0.2836 s of training data set. For cancer affected lung linear SVM classifies the 93.7% of accuracy for affected lung which takes 1.3352 s to train the dataset. Quadric gives 99% accuracy for affected lung and it takes 0.3661 s to train the data set. As per the observation and implementation it could be very helpful for the doctors to recognize or detect the cancer present in the lungs easily.

The accuracy for the detection of a cancer in a lung can be improved by the different techniques like p-tile thresholding; binary morphology and can also applied to other neural network which can give more accurate reading for the detection.

5 Conclusion

The conclusion for the proposed model is determined by image processing techniques and methodology. The research facilitates to identify the input image of a lung are the cancer affected lung or it is a healthy lung. In this work the result shows the 93% to 99% of accuracy. The proposed technique gives the higher accuracy result as compare to the other techniques. It can also obtain much better accuracy by improving the image processing enhancement and techniques. The detection process is very promising and gives the expected area for further diagnosis process to recognize the lung cancer.

References

1. Alam, J., Alam, S., Hossan, A.: Multi-stage lung cancer detection and prediction using multi-class SVM classifier. In: 2018 International Conference on Computer, Communication, Chemical, Material and Electronic Engineering (IC4ME2), pp. 1–4. IEEE, February 2018
2. Anifah, L., Harimurti, R., Permatasari, Z., Rusimamto, P.W., Muhamad, A.R.: Cancer lungs detection on CT scan image using artificial neural network backpropagation based gray level coocurrence matrices feature. In: 2017 International Conference on Advanced Computer Science and Information Systems (ICACSIS), pp. 327–332. IEEE, October 2017
3. Rajaguru, H.: Lung cancer detection using probabilistic neural network with modified crow-search algorithm. Asian Pac. J. Cancer Prev. APJCP **20**(7), 2159–2166 (2019)
4. Wu, Q., Zhao, W.: Small-cell lung cancer detection using a supervised machine learning algorithm. In: 2017 International Symposium on Computer Science and Intelligent Controls (ISCSIC), pp. 88–91. IEEE, October 2017
5. Kalaivani, S., Chatterjee, P., Juyal, S., Gupta, R.: Lung cancer detection using digital image processing and artificial neural networks. In: 2017 International conference of Electronics, Communication and Aerospace Technology (ICECA), vol. 2, pp. 100–103. IEEE, April 2017

6. Vas, M., Dessai, A.: Lung cancer detection system using lung CT image processing. In: 2017 International Conference on Computing, Communication, Control and Automation (ICCUBEA), pp. 1–5. IEEE, August 2017

7. Al-Tarawneh, M.S.: Lung cancer detection using image processing techniques. Leonardo Electron. J. Pract. Technol. **11**(21), 147–158 (2012)

8. Hamad, A.M.: Lung cancer diagnosis by using fuzzy logic. IJCSMC **5**(3), 32–41 (2016)

9. Sammouda, R.: Segmentation and analysis of CT chest images for early lung cancer detection. In: 2016 Global Summit on Computer & Information Technology (GSCIT). IEEE (2016)

10. Werghi, N., Donner, C., Taher, F., Alahmad, H.: Segmentation of sputum cell image for early lung cancer detection. In: IET Conference on Image Processing (IPR 2012), pp. 213–213 (2012)

Learning Vector Quantization Based Leaf Disease Detection

Anand Upadhyay, Jyoti Singh[✉], and Rutuja Shinde

Department of Information Technology, Thakur College of Science and Commerce, Thakur Village, Kandivali (E), Mumbai 4000101, India
anandhari6@gmail.com, jyotidsingh23@gmail.com,
rutujashinde876@gmail.com

Abstract. The purpose of this paper is to detect and classify the disease in leaf which may occur and not visible to the human naked-eye. Where the cultivators of this field are beyond the bound of possibilities. The algorithmic solution is based on image-processing for automation of disease detection. Diseases in crops, chiefly on the leaves affect and lead to the reduction of both quality and quantity of agricultural products. As the Indian economy is agriculture based, and farmers cannot afford experts for solution. So this approach is to provide rapid, affordable and precise way to detect. The implementation is done using image processing and LVQ algorithm, then for accuracy confusion matrix is applied.

Keywords: Leaf disease · Neural network · Probabilistic neural network · LVQ · Detection · Image-processing · Classification

1 Introduction

Plant is an important and essential source in terms of energy, oxygen or any other ecosystem. Plant disease has tremendous effect on environment and agriculture and its products, especially on countries which are economically depends on agriculture like Indian economy. If there is a decline in agro products, the entire economy should suffer the effect. Farmers use very expensive fertilizers to prevent it from plant disease or any other harm to agriculture. Disease detection in plant plays very crucial role in today's environment. The whole human civilization will get affected if any agro product or agriculture gets affected. Because the humans are nothing without agriculture. So to protect it from all the harms and disease proper diagnose and care must be taken in less time and more effectively. Image-processing is best, inexpensive and faster way to detect disease in plant. It helps in identifying exactly which area is affected and which is not. Some advanced computer technologies like machine vision; image processing and computer visions provide feasible support to the growers. The naked-eye observation approach is widely fostered, still it requires continuous evaluation from experts which makes it costly when there are large farms. Additionaly in the numerous places, and farmers have to cover large distance to reach people which are expert in identifying and detection plant diseases [5]. Because of this consultation of experts to be exceptionally financially

U. Batra et al. (Eds.): REDSET 2019, CCIS 1229, pp. 246–253, 2020.
https://doi.org/10.1007/978-981-15-5827-6_21

straining, sluggish and a tedious affair. Due to a vast amount of plants are getting affected by such diseases, it majorly affect the quality, quantity and productivity of the vegetation and food production which indirectly affects the economy and also health of mankind. It is very important to detect disease in correct way as well as in timely manner. Most of the diseases are asymptomatic and only appear when it becomes worse. Usually, it is detected by means of advanced measures like use of microscopes. Commonly used method includes remote sensing methods that capture multi and hyper spectral photos. To achieve this, one can use digital image processing instruments. It is beneficial for crop production since it consumes less time and diagnose the disease in effective and automatic manner. [7] One of the main issue amongst all in agriculture is to minimize the expansion of pests on plants and crop yields, an organism which spreads malady is a pest which further cause hazardous effect on yields and plants. Pest cause spasmodic increase of disease which further cause food scarcity and food shortage. There a lot of demand for technologies such as automation in disease detection, disease classification optimizing image processing. The algorithmic solution LVQ (Learning vector quantization) helps achieving it using computational neurons. This machine technique will be much helpful for farmers in order to prevent agriculture and plant from disease in timely manner before the malady is affected in massive region [8].

2 Literature Review

The author Ghaiwat represented the plant leaf disease classification using different techniques of classification and prediction. For example, k-nearest neighbor method looks simpler and easily applicable for prediction. In SVM, it is not easy to determine ideal parameters, when the training set is not linearly separable. This shows one its drawbacks [1].

According to Khirade, identifying and classifying the leaf diseases manually is such a difficult task and also it is not having any assurance of correct results. It may be inaccurate or less accurate. Hiring experts leads to costly process which many farmers can't afford to have it. Applying image processing techniques on detection and classification of plant leaf disease help in faster and improved result. To keep environment and agriculture alive and healthy continuous monitoring and detection is very important [2].

Dhaygude represent the importance of plant leaf disease re occurring on day to day basis and the reason behind that is bacterial viruses, fungi etc. They implemented using four step processing i.e. input as RGB image, then RGB conversion to HSI for color description. Using threshold value, masking and removal of green pixels are done and then segment extraction. At the end plant leaf disease is detected [5].

Author represents automatic detection of plant leaf disease named little leaf using genetic algorithm and image segmentation based on various features found in different leaf images such as texture and color [6].

Author presents detection of diseases and prevention in fauna. Using various textures, colors and features which usually appear in area which are affected and to prevent them different agricultural techniques are acknowledged and classified [3].

Author presented the plant leaf disease detection using image processing technique. SVM is used for classification which consists of two dataset on which further processing is done. At last classifier will classify the disease by extracting other features. LVQ work more efficiently as compared to SVM and gives result more appropriate [7].

According to paper, the author presented different types of techniques which are used for classification and prediction of diseases. These diseases can occur from anywhere in plant such as leaves, stem of tree, roots, etc. The main root cause of continuously occurring these diseases are some human activities produces pollution in large extent and agricultural losses. Comparative study of different techniques helps in electing best among them [4].

According to author, algorithm proposed which is based on support vector machine to classify and detect the disease in plant leaves accordingly because pesticides may harm the plants badly and that too without giving appropriate results, so that automatic diagnosis of plant leaf disease is proposed. Support vector machine may be less appropriate and less effective approach to use for plant leaves disease than learning vector quantization method because, in SVM it is difficult and a bit complicate to understand the weights and also its training time is comparatively long [9].

Author detected the plant leaf disease using image processing which include image pre-processing, feature extraction, segmentation and classification. The methods used are K-mean clustering, GLCM and BPNN which eliminate the background noise in the image acquired and then applying automatic diagnosis to prevent real world plant yields [10].

3 Algorithm

The algorithmic rule for a Learning Vector Quantization will be simply enforced by utilizing a neural network with a competitive layer containing variety of competitive neurons equal with the amount of clusters.

Some of the advantages of LVQ algorithm:

- The network performance of LVQ is good enough.
- The recognition rate of LVQ is comparatively very high.
- LVQ is one of the best model for classification features.
- It is also popular for its easy fault tolerance and potency.

The algorithmic rule of LVQ is repetitive and needs the initialization of the networks weight vectors W_i. In every repetition or epoch a vector, X^n is given as input to the network, the distances from every centroid W_i are calculated and eventually the winner neuron m with the minimum value of Euclidean distance is chosen. The ultimate step is to update the weight vectors by "moving" the winner's neuron centroid W_m "closer" towards input vector X^n. The number of "moving" depends on a η parameter (learning rate).

- Load the input image as datset.
- Apply image pre-processing on acquired image.
- Apply LVQ Cluster algorithm.
- Next step is feature extraction.
- Classification of leaf is done by classifier.

LVQ Cluster algorithm applied:

- Outline the quantity of clusters M.
- Initialize the centroids w_i (0), $i = 1 \ldots M$.
- Initialize learning rate η, epochs counter $k = 0$ and repetitions counter $k = 0$.
- For each epoch k do the subsequent steps:
- Set vector X^n as the Neural Network's input.
- Choose the winner neuron m.
- Update the load vector for the winner neuron.
- $k = k + 1$.
- Check for termination. If not set $k = k = 1$ and return to step four.

4 Dataset

Dataset is created which consists of various leaf images which are required for processing as an input samples. The images clicked in different angles keeping in mind to obtain accurate result and to check overall health of the crop yield. The pixel size of images taken are 256×256 pixels Then the separate dataset is created with featured values by extracting and comparing the simultaneously occurring features of leaves After that train the classifier using train file and use test file to perform further classification process. Then load all the data files (training and testing data files) and make changes to the data accordingly. The training set consist of two classes affected area as 1, non-affected area as 2. Then on testing set LVQ is applied to examine and detect the affected area and non-affected area. The images having texture details help to produce more appropriate results.

5 Methodology

(Fig. 1).

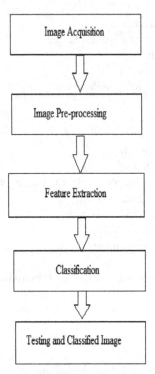

Fig. 1. Flow of classification for leaf disease detection

5.1 Image Acquisition

Image acquisition in image processing is described as the working of recovering an image from fewer sourced, generally for processing the hardware-based source. It is the very foremost pace in the work-flow order because no process is possible without an image. The acquire image is completely unprocessed. In our case, it is the initial step, and with the help of digital camera it is necessity to capture an image. More number of images will give more accurately trained results.

5.2 Image Pre-processing

Image pre-processing is used to enhance the standard of and image and also to detach undesired manipulation from the image. The image of the leaf is clipped and is to achieve the urge in interested image area and then Low-pass and High-pass filters are applied in the order that the image is smoothened. To increase the dissimilarity, image enhancement is additionally done. A Low Pass Filter is a circuit that can be designed to cut all unwanted high frequencies of an associated electrical signal and settle for or pass solely those signals needed by the circuits designer. High Pass Filter is the precise divergent to the low pass filter circuit. There are two components which are interchanged between them with the output signal filters now being taken from across the resistor.

5.3 Feature Extraction

A feature is something that will probably differ among other samples, i.e., and discriminate one sample from another. This call is also to classify the sample to a finite set, cluster the samples supported similarity (clustering) or predict a true value based on those features (regression). Feature extraction is the process of assembling discriminative info from a collection of samples. Feature extraction is that the method within which every given sample is dampened to quantitative (and typically qualitative) attributes. In the observation of computer and image processing, a feature is a segment of a knowledge that has relevance for resolving the calculus task associated with a specific application. This is the same sense as a feature in machine learning, though image process incorporates a very subtle and advanced assortment of the feature. Here we use Learning Vector Quantization algorithm for classification and feature extraction. The result of a feature can be of general zone operation or by the feature detection of a concern image.

5.4 Classification

Classification is a technique comes under supervised learning. Supervised learning means that predicting input values supported the label or the target variable of coaching examples that you previously have antecedently provided. We had classified our RGB image file into affected areas and non-affected areas. This classifies them into two distinct classes. The classifier we have used is the Learning Vector Quantization.

5.5 Testing and Classified Image

We have taken images as input and every pixel of images has Red, Blue and Green component in it and First, LVQ classifier is employed to implement the classification and detection. Then measuring of successful outcome of classification is finished by employing the confusion matrix resulting in providing accuracy.

6 Results and Analysis

For input, samples of plant leaf such as a tomato with septoria disease. The different images are classified into plant diseases. A confusion matrix is a précis of prediction outcomes on a classification problem. The quantity of correct and incorrect predictions are summarized with count values and burst down through each class. This is the significant pointer to the confusion matrix. The confusion matrix gives us insight into the mistakes being made by using a classifier addition to the types of errors that are being made and give accuracy of classification done.

Kappa coefficient is far usually notion for better robust measure than easy percent agreement calculation, as it takes into consideration, opportunity of the settlement taking place through the way of risk. Kappa coefficient measures settlement among two raters, each classify N objects into C at the correlative exceptional categories (Table 1).

Table 1. Confusion matrix.

Class	Affected	Non-affected	Total	Producer's accuracy
Affected	846	28	874	96.79%
Non-affected	42	669	711	94.09%
Total	888	697	1585	
User accuracy	95.27%	95.98%		95.58%

We have calculated the accuracy by implementing the formula mentioned below:

$$Acc = (sum\ (diag(C))\ /\ sum1)\ *\ 100;$$

Accuracy = 95.5835

The Kappa Co-efficient is calculated by the formulation mentioned below:

$$k = \frac{N \sum_{i=1}^{r} xii - \sum_{i=1}^{r} (Xi + *X + i)}{N2 \sum_{i=1}^{r} (Xi + *X + i)}$$

$$k = 0.91056$$

Confusion matrix and kappa coefficient are for the data set which is tested by neural network which is trained with the set which consist of only two feature vector.

Below are the result of classification and detection of disease on tomato leaf with septoria disease by applying algorithm chosen i.e. LVQ(learning vector quantization).

The input and output image are displayed where the input image is a tomato leaf with septoria disease and output image shows the classification of disease using Learning Vector Quantization (Fig. 2).

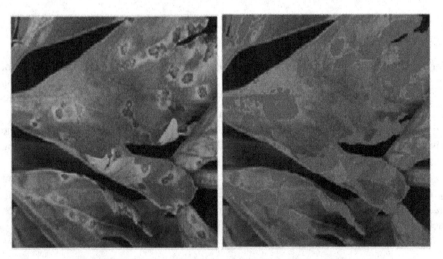

Fig. 2. Original input image and affected area detected image

7 Conclusion

As shown in results, the images taken as input samples are classified and detected on leaf tomato with septoria disease using image processing and LVQ algorithm and we got accuracy of 95.58%,also even the small spot is detected accurately. To increase the rate of detection and more accurate results different types of related disease are also taken into consideration. The potency of LVQ algorithm is shown in the process of classification and detection of disease on infected leaves for septoria leaf spot benefit is of incorporating the above methodology that disease is often known earlier and at initial stage. So, that further precautions can be taken.

8 Future Enhancement

We have taken input data are in the form of images for further processing and predicting the disease on leaf. But in future we can ensure more accuracy and efficiency of detection using video input. Also can predict the exact disease and on which level it is there. So that we can take following measures to overcome the problem, which will have better segmentation, feature extraction and classification to increment the recognition rate in results in order to obtain more accuracy.

References

1. Ghaiwat, S.N., Arora, P.: Detection and classification of plant leaf diseases using image processing techniques: a review. Int. J. Recent Adv. Eng. Technol. 2(3), 1–7 (2014)
2. Khirade, S.D., Patil, A.B.: Plant disease detection using image processing. In: 2015 International Conference on Computing Communication Control and Automation. IEEE (2015)
3. Bashir, S., Sharma, N.: Remote area plant disease detection using image processing. IOSR J. Electron. Commun. Eng. 2(6), 31–34 (2012)
4. Arivazhagan, S., et al.: Detection of unhealthy region of plant leaves and classification of plant leaf diseases using texture features. Agric. Eng. Int. CIGR J. 15(1), 211–217 (2013)
5. Dhaygude, S.B., Kumbhar, N.P.: Agricultural plant leaf disease detection using image processing. Int. J. Adv. Res. Electr. Electron. Instrum. Eng. 2(1), 599–602 (2013)
6. Singh, V., Misra, A.K.: Detection of plant leaf diseases using image segmentation and soft computing techniques. Inf. Process. Agric. 4(1), 41–49 (2017)
7. Namrata, K.P., et al.: Leaf based disease detection using "GLCM and SVM". Int. J. Sci. Eng. Technol (2017). ISSN (O) 2348-4098, ISSN (P) 2395–4752
8. Rastogi, A., Arora, R., Sharma, S.: Leaf disease detection and grading using computer vision technology & fuzzy logic. In: 2015 2nd International Conference on Signal Processing and Integrated Networks (SPIN) (2015)
9. Rashmi, S., Laxmi, K., Priyanka, H.: Plant leaf disease detection based on image processing using MATLAB. Int. J. Innovative Res. Comput. Commun. Eng. 6(5) (2018)
10. Mainkar, P.M., Shreekant, G., Mayur, A.: Plant leaf disease detection and classification using image processing techniques. Int. J. Innovative Emerg. Res. Eng. 2, 139–144 (2015)

Towards Prediction of Energy Consumption of HVAC Plants Using Machine Learning

Monika Goyal$^{(\boxtimes)}$ ⓘ and Mrinal Pandey

Manav Rachna University, Faridabad, India
monikagoyal.er@gmail.com, mrinal@mru.edu.in

Abstract. Today energy optimization has become a great challenge as energy is being consumed at a fast rate in almost every sector including buildings, transport and industries. However, Buildings are the largest consumer of energy followed by Transport and Industry throughout the world. In buildings, most of the energy consumption depends upon the usages of air conditioning plants (Heating, Ventilation and Air Conditioning). Therefore, with the necessity to determine the energy consumption due to HVAC plant in building, this research focuses on Cooling Tower data of HVAC plant of a building as Cooling Tower is an important component of HVAC and carries a major responsibility of maintaining the ambient temperature within a building. In this paper, three popular Machine Learning techniques namely Multiple Linear Regression, Random Forests and Gradient Boosting Machines were experimented for predicting the energy consumption due to HVAC plant within a building. The findings of the experiments reveal that Random Forest outperforms in terms of error measures.

Keywords: Machine Learning · Energy optimization · Heating · Ventilation and Air Conditioning · Random Forests · Multiple Linear Regression · Gradient Boosting Machines

1 Introduction

Technology is spreading in each and every sector in the present world and it has put forward the challenge of quick consumption of energy. The demand of energy is increasing for the smooth functioning of various types of machines in homes, hotels, offices, industries and transport. Although advancements in technology have brought ease and comfort in human lives, but on the other hand, they have put burden on the natural non-renewable resources, because energy is conventionally produced by the burning of fossil fuels like coal, oil and natural gas, which take millions of years to form. If the precious energy continues to be consumed at such high pace, soon the non-renewable energy sources will deplete. Apart from that, burning of fossil fuels releases carbon, more the fossil fuels burnt more carbon is emitted which consequently leads to air and water pollution [1]. To conserve energy on a bigger scale, high energy consuming areas should be identified and targeted. Studies show that globally buildings account for approximately 40% of energy usage throughout the world [2–5] and it is greater than the energy consumed by other two areas, industry and transport which as per reports are 32% and 28% respectively.

© Springer Nature Singapore Pte Ltd. 2020
U. Batra et al. (Eds.): REDSET 2019, CCIS 1229, pp. 254–265, 2020.
https://doi.org/10.1007/978-981-15-5827-6_22

These data motivated to target the biggest energy consumer i.e. buildings. The analysis of energy consumption pattern in a building, revels that the biggest portion of energy is consumed by HVAC (Heating, Ventilation and Air conditioning) system. An HVAC unit consists of different components like Chillers, Cooling towers, Primary Pumps, Secondary Pumps. Each of these components performs their designated task and consumes power to operate. It consumes around 40%–50% of the total energy consumed in a building [6, 7]. This further motivated to analyze and counter the energy consumption profile of HVAC. Therefore, in this research the energy consumption due to HVAC plant, particularly Cooling Tower data was analyzed using regression (Multiple Linear Regression) and two Ensembles based Machine Learning techniques namely Random Forest and Gradient Boosting Technique.

The organization of this paper is as follows: Sect. 1 introduces the problem and gives a brief overview of the Machine Learning techniques. Section 2 describes the Machine Learning techniques. Literature Survey is presented in Sect. 3. Methodology of the work done is described in Sect. 4. Section 5 explains the experiments performed and results obtained. Section 6 gives conclusion of this research.

2 Machine Learning

Machine Learning is the concept in which a machine learns and behaves in a certain manner when a particular type of data is fed as input. Machine Learning can be classified as Unsupervised Learning and Supervised Learning. A common technique in unsupervised learning is clustering in which the given dataset is grouped into a given number of clusters depending upon the similarity index. In Supervised Learning the input data is mapped to the desired output using a labelled set of training data. Two common techniques in Supervised Learning are Classification and Regression. Following section presents the Machine Learning Techniques used in this research.

Regression can be viewed as a statistical methodology generally used for numeric prediction. Regression can be classified as a) Linear Regression which involves finding the best line to fit two variables, such that one variable is independent called Predictor and can be used to predict the other variable which is dependent called Response. b) Non – Linear Regression which involves more complex calculations and finds the best curve instead of best line. A common example is Polynomial Regression. Ensemble based Regression techniques are becoming popular for last few years. In Ensemble techniques, regression is performed by integrating the results of several individual models with the objective of improving the accuracy and robustness of prediction in learning problems having a numerical response variable. Two most popular ensemble methods are bagging and boosting [8, 9].

2.1 Multiple Linear Regression

The concept of Multiple Linear Regression is similar to Linear Regression with a difference that the model consists of one Response variable B which is dependent upon multiple Predictor variables $A_1, A_2, A_3 \ldots.. A_n$. Interpretation of results in MLR is more complex due to the correlation among different predictor variables [10].

2.2 Random Forests

This technique of Machine Learning lies under Ensemble technique category of model development. It is a tree based technique applicable for both Classification and Regression. Various features which enhance the appeal of Random Forests are: Prediction speed, suitability for high dimensional problems, handling of missing values and outliers etc. [11].

2.3 Gradient Boosting Machines

This technique is also a tree based ensemble learning technique, where additive regression models are built by iteratively fitting a simple base to recently updated pseudo residuals by the application of least squares at every consecutive iteration [12].

3 Literature Survey

Machine Learning techniques have been proved highly effective approach to address the issue of energy consumption in buildings [13]. Apart from applying the ML algorithms individually, Ensemble methods can be created by specifically combining different models, which improve the effectiveness of the model in terms of accuracy and performance. Following section presented the application of Machine Learning techniques for energy consumption particularly in buildings.

Authors in [14] proposed two frameworks for anomaly detection in HVAC power consumption. One was a pattern based anomaly classifier called CCAD-SW (Collective contextual anomaly detection using sliding window) which created overlapping sliding windows so that anomalies can be pointed out as soon as possible. This framework made use of bagging for improved accuracy.

Another was prediction based anomaly classifier called EAD (Ensemble Anomaly Detection) which used Support Vector Regression and Random Forests. Experiments were performed on HVAC power consumption data collected from a school in Canada and results show that EAD performed better than CCAD-SW in terms of sensitivity and reducing False Positive rate.

Decision Tree Analysis was performed in [15] to predict the cost estimations of HVAC while designing buildings. The HVAC sub systems are CP (Central Plant) system, WD (Water Side Distribution) system and AC (Air Conditioning) system. Different combinations of these sub systems result in different costs of HVAC plants. The study was carried out in office buildings in Korea. The study showed that AC component of HVAC has maximum impact on the cost followed by CP and then WD has minimum impact.

Authors in [16] applied six Regression techniques: Linear Regression, Lasso Regression, Support Vector Machine, Random Forest, Gradient Boosting and Artificial Neural Network on for estimating Energy Use Intensity in Office buildings and energy usage by HVAC, plug load and lighting based on CBECS 2012, micro data. Out of them, Random Forest and Support Vector Machine were found comparatively robust.

A sensor-based model was proposed by the authors of [2] for forecasting the energy consumed by a multi-family residential building in New York City. The model was built using Support vector regression. Authors analysed the prediction performance through the perspective of time and space and found that most optimal prediction was hourly prediction at by floor levels.

In another paper [3] the authors developed a framework in which they used clustering algorithm and semi-supervised learning techniques to identify electricity losses during transmission i.e. between source and destination. The technique also helps in optimizing the losses. Deep learning is used for semi-supervised machine learning because of its ability to learn both labelled and unlabelled data. The electricity consumption, heating, cooling and outside temperature data was obtained from a research university campus in Arizona.

The work done in [17] used various supervised classifiers- DT (Decision Trees), DA (Discriminant Analysis), SVM (Support Vector Machines) and KNN (K- Nearest Neighbors) to disaggregate the data of power consumption by multiple HVAC units into that consumed by individual HVAC, while the data was retrieved collectively from single meter to reduce cost and complexity. Power consumption information of individual appliances is necessary for accurate energy consumption monitoring. The experiment was performed by collecting data from a commercial building in Alexandria. The results show that K- nearest neighbour was most efficient in power disaggregation.

A component-based Machine Learning Modelling approach was proposed [18] to counter the limitations of Building Energy Model for energy demand prediction in buildings. Random Forest was selected and applied on the climate data collected from Amsterdam, Brussels and Paris. MLMs excel over BEM as they generalize well under diverse design situations.

The work done in [19] witnessed the collection of energy consumption data of a house in Belgium and outside weather data and application of four Machine Learning algorithms namely Multiple Linear Regression, Support Vector Machine with Radial Kernel, Random Forest and Gradient Boosting Machines to predict the energy consumption and to rank the parameters according to their importance in prediction. They proposed that GBM was best at prediction.

The author in [20] proposed an ensemble technique which is a linear combiner of five different predictor models: ARIMA, RBFNN, MLP, SVM and FLANN. The combiner model was applied on stock exchange data for predicting the closing price of stock markets and it proved to be better in terms of accuracy as compared to individual models.

In another paper [21] the authors applied several Supervised Machine Learning techniques including Classification, Regression and Ensemble techniques to estimate the air quality of Faridabad by predicting the Air Quality Index. The algorithms applied include Decision Tree, SVM, Naïve Bayes, Random Forest, Voting Ensemble and Stacking Ensemble. They concluded that Decision Tree, SVR and Stacking Ensemble outperform other methods in their respective categories.

A framework was proposed by the authors of [22] in which they selected 8 different characteristics of a residential building as input parameters and depicted their effect on the 2 output parameters- Heating load and cooling load. Linear Regression and Random Forests were applied and results showed that Random Forests were better at predicting Heating and Cooling load in terms of accuracy.

4 Methodology

The Methodology for this research follows the classical approach and starts with the Data Collection followed by Data Pre-processing which includes Data Cleaning, Integration and Transformation, after pre-processing Model construction and evaluation phases completes the process of traditional Machine Learning approach. Figure 1 shows steps of the methodology adopted.

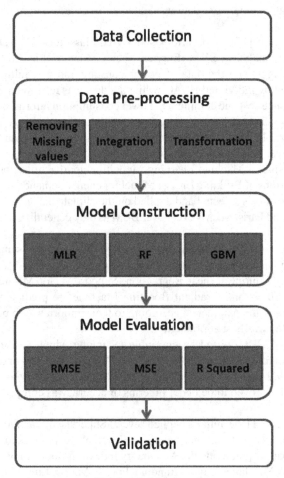

Fig. 1. Methodology

4.1 Data Collection

The dataset of HVAC plants was collected from a hotel building in New Delhi, India for this research. It consists of HVAC data from sensor recordings at every 5-min intervals for one year from Oct 2017 to September 2018. The data were categorized into two categories as Humidity (May–Nov) and Non-Humidity (Dec–April) depending upon two weather conditions. The data contains Inlet temperature, Outlet temperature and energy consumed by Cooling Tower, Dry Bulb Temperature and Relative Humidity. Energy consumed by Cooling Tower depends on Wet Bulb Temperature, so WBT has been calculated using DBT and RH. The experiments were performed on the Cooling Tower data. Table 1 describes the parameters of the data used along with the units in which each parameter is measured.

Table 1. Dataset parameter description

Parameter	Description	Unit
DBT(Dry Bulb Temperature)	Ambient temperature	°Celcius
RH(Relative Humidity)	Amount of water vapour in air relative to its temperature	%age
WBT(Wet Bulb Temperature)	Temperature brought down by water evaporation	°Celcius
CT_INLET	Temperature of water entering into Cooling Tower	°Celcius
CT_OUTLET	Temperature of water exiting from Cooling Tower	°Celcius
CT_POWER	Power consumed by Cooling Tower	Kilo Watts

In this research the data of April and August were considered for analysis & prediction. This is so because April represents non-humid weather and August represents humid weather condition particularly in NCR region of India. It must be mentioned that, HVAC consumes more energy in humid conditions to counter humidity rather than summer or winters.

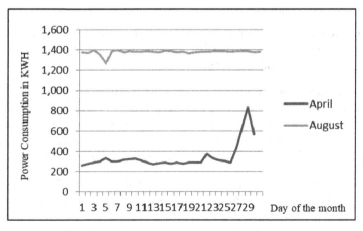

Fig. 2. Energy consumption in April and August

Figure 2 represents the day wise pattern of energy consumed by Cooling Tower in the months of April and August. Here x-axis denotes the days of month and y-axis denotes the power consumed in Kilo Watt Hour.

4.2 Data Pre-processing

Data pre-processing consists of filling the missing values, removing any outliers, transforming it into a form suitable for algorithm application, normalization, feature selection etc. [23]. The dataset used for this research was pre-processed in the following manner:

Although the data has been recorded by sensors at every 5-min intervals but at some instances the readings were mis-recorded at 1 or 2 min intervals. Such records were not complete and most of their fields were blank. In order to avoid any kind of flaws in result calculation, few extra records were removed while few records were filled with the mean of the values of that particular attribute.

As the data was recorded by different sensors installed at different places, there was a problem of integration of files for the values for different parameters into a single file. In order to ensure symmetry of data, extra records were removed from some files so that each record should represent the values of all parameters at same time instance. Data Transformation was done to convert the data into a form suitable for applying Machine Learning algorithms.

The original dataset consists of Dry Bulb Temperature and Relative Humidity as features, but the energy consumption of Cooling Tower also depends on Wet Bulb Temperature, therefore one more feature namely Wet Bulb Temperature is derived from Dry Bulb Temperature and Relative Humidity for the experiments.

4.3 Model Construction

For building the model, three Machine Learning algorithms namely Multiple Linear Regression, Random Forests and Gradient Boosting Machines were applied on the datasets of April and August months.

Data Partitioning. Datasets were partitioned according to 70%–30% rule into Training and Testing data. For partitioning, Random Sampling without Replacement was applied which resulted in 70% Training data and 30% Test data.

Parameter Tuning. In MLR default algorithm was applied on the data. In RF model, there are several parameters like ntree and mtry. Different values of ntree were tried where 500 is the default value. Best results were obtained by keeping ntree at 200. In GBM model also, certain variations were done in the values of some parameters. Best results were obtained by keeping shrinkage at 0.1 and interaction.depth at 6.

Libraries and Functions. All algorithms were implemented using RStudio. MLR was implemented using lm function and another function regr.eval was used to evaluate error metrics- RMSE, MSE, R Squared and MAE. The libraries included for implementing RF were- randomForest, miscTools and caret. GBM implementation used gbm library and function.

4.4 Evaluation

The results of the models were evaluated using three well known performance measures namely RMSE, MSE and R Squared.

Root Mean Square Error can be viewed as the standard deviation of residuals, where residuals indicate the distance of data points from the line of best fit i.e. these are the difference between actual and predicted values. Lower the value of RMSE better is the prediction. Formula for RMSE:

$$RMSE = \sqrt[2]{\sum_{i=1}^{N} \frac{\left(\hat{Y}_i - Y_i\right)^2}{N}}$$

Where

Yi : is the observed value for the ith observation
$\hat{Y}i$: is the predicted value
N   : is sample size

Mean Square Error can be defined as the average of the error squared. It is used as the loss function in least squares regression. MSE is the sum of the square of difference between predicted and actual target variables, spanning over all the data points, divided by the total number of data points. Formula for MSE:

$$MSE = \sum_{i=1}^{N} \frac{\left(\hat{Y}_i - Y_i\right)^2}{N}$$

R Squared is also known as Coefficient of Determination. It is used to statistically measure the closeness of data points to the fitted regression line. R squared can be defined by the following formula:

$$R^2 = 1 - \frac{\sum \left(Y_i - \hat{Y}_i\right)^2}{\sum (Y_i - \bar{y})^2}$$

Where $\hat{Y}i$: is the predicted value of Y
$\bar{Y}$: is the mean value of Y

4.5 Model Validation

In order to validate the generality of the model, the above mentioned Machine Learning algorithms were also applied on another dataset collected from the UCI repository [24]. The dataset was used by researchers [22] to perform regression. The dataset consisted of eight independent variables describing various building parameters and two dependent variables: Heating Load (Y_1) and Cooling Load (Y_2). The comparative result summary is given in Sect. 5.

5   Experiments and Results

The R studio was used for performing various experiments of the research. Three Machine Learning algorithms namely Multiple Linear Regression, Random Forests and Gradient Boosting Machines were experimented on cooling tower data sets both for the month of April and August. The results of the experiments are described in Table 2 and Table 3.

5.1   Results for the Month of April

Table 2 summarizes the results obtained after applying all the three above mentioned algorithms on the dataset of April 2018 in terms of aforementioned performance measures.

Table 2. Results for the month of April 2018

Performance metric	ML algorithm		
	MLR	RF	GBM
RMSE	6.14	5.08	5.32
MSE	37.78	25.88	28.3
R Squared	0.23	0.5	0.65

The values of RMSE are 6.14, 5.08 and 5.32 for MLR, RF and GBM respectively. Corresponding MSE values are 37.78, 25.88 and 28.3 and R Squared values are 0.23, 0.5 and 0.65. It is clear from the Table 2 that RMSE and MSE error measures are minimum for Random Forest for the month of April.

5.2   Results for the Month of August

Table 3 summarizes the results obtained for August 2018. As per the results RMSE is 3.44 for MLR, 3.09 for RF and 3.72 for GBM. MSE values are 11.89, 9.57 and 13.83 for MLR, RF and GBM respectively. R Squared result values are 0.05, 0.43 and 0.57. It can be observed from the Table 3 that in terms of RMSE and MSE Random Forest outperforms among three algorithms.

Table 3. Results for the month of August 2018

Performance metric	ML algorithm		
	MLR	RF	GBM
RMSE	3.44	3.09	3.72
MSE	11.89	9.57	13.83
R Squared	0.05	0.43	0.57

5.3 Comparative Analysis of the Results for Hotel Building Dataset and UCI Dataset Using Random Forest

Random Forests has been proved as the best algorithm for this research in terms of RMSE and MSE. Therefore, same was applied on another dataset obtained from UCI repository. The recorded results are given in Table 4.

Table 4. Comparative Analysis of the results for Hotel Building dataset and UCI Dataset

Performance metric	Dataset			
	Hotel dataset	Hotel dataset	UCI dataset	UCI dataset
	April 2018	August 2018	Predictor Y1	Predictor Y2
RMSE	5.08	3.09	1.19	1.71
MSE	25.88	9.57	1.42	2.95
R Squared	0.5	0.43	0.98	0.96

As per Table 4, when RF was applied on the hotel building dataset, the obtained value of RMSE is 5.08 and 3.09 for the months April and August respectively while UCI dataset RMSE values are 1.19 and 1.71 for Heating Load and Cooling Load respectively. Similarly, the values MSE are 25.88 and 9.57 for April and August for the Hotel dataset while 1.42 and 2.95 for Heating Load and Cooling Load for UCI dataset. The values of R Squared are 0.5 and 0.43 for April and August months for Hotel dataset and 0.98 and 0.96 for Heating Load and Cooling Load for the dataset obtained from the UCI repository.

Figure 3 shows the results comparison of experiments performed on the hotel dataset and dataset collected from UCI repository.

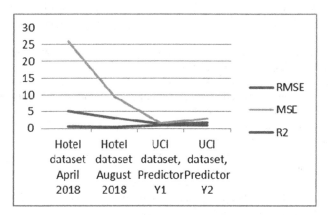

Fig. 3. Comparative analysis of both datasets

6   Conclusion and Future Scope

Energy being a precious resource needs to be utilized in the most efficient manner so that it is conserved while the comfort of consumers is also not compromised. Buildings are the largest consumer of energy globally and within a building HVAC accounts for the maximum energy consumption. This paper targeted cooling tower dataset of HVAC plant for analyzing the energy consumption in buildings. Three well known Regression algorithms namely Multiple Linear Regression, Random Forests and Gradient Boosting Machines were applied to predict the energy consumption due to HVAC plants in buildings. The results were compared on well-known performance measures namely Root Mean Square Error, Mean Square Error and R Square. The analysis of results proved Random Forests as the most suitable algorithm for this study. Further, Random Forest algorithm was also employed on another energy consumption dataset obtained from UCI repository for validation purpose.

The work in this area can further be carried on by experimenting with other powerful algorithms like Support Vector Machines and Extreme Gradient Boosting. Also optimization techniques can be explored and applied in order to work towards energy optimization.

References

1. Goyal, M., Pandey, M.: Energy optimization in buildings using machine learning techniques: a survey. Int. J. Inf. Syst. Manag. Sci. **1**(2) (2018)
2. Jain, R.K., Smith, K.M., Culligan, P.J., Taylor, J.E.: Forecasting energy consumption of multi-family residential buildings using support vector regression: investigating the impact of temporal and spatial monitoring granularity on performance accuracy. Appl. Energy **123**, 168–178 (2014)
3. Naganathan, H., Chong, W.O., Chen, X.: Building energy modeling (BEM) using clustering algorithms and semi-supervised machine learning approaches. Autom. Constr. **72**, 187–194 (2016)
4. Ahmad, M.W., Mourshed, M., Rezgui, Y.: Trees vs neurons: comparison between random forest and ANN for high-resolution prediction of building energy consumption. Energy Build. **147**, 77–89 (2017)
5. Chou, J.S., Bui, D.K.: Modeling heating and cooling loads by artificial intelligence for energy-efficient building design. Energy Build. **82**, 437–446 (2014)
6. Carreira, P., Costa, A.A., Mansu, V., Arsénio, A.: Can HVAC really learn from users? A simulation-based study on the effectiveness of voting for comfort and energy use optimisation. Sustain. Cities Soc. **41**, 275–285 (2018)
7. Drgoňa, J., Picard, D., Kvasnica, M., Helsen, L.: Approximate model predictive building control via machine learning. Appl. Energy **218**, 199–216 (2018)
8. Mendes-Moreira, J., Soares, C., Jorge, A.M., Sousa, J.F.D.: Ensemble approaches for regression: a survey. ACM Comput. Surv. **45**(1), 10 (2012)
9. Prasad, A.M., Iverson, L.R., Liaw, A.: Newer classification and regression tree techniques: bagging and random forests for ecological prediction. Ecosystems **9**(2), 181–199 (2006). https://doi.org/10.1007/s10021-005-0054-1
10. Krzywinski, M., Altman, N.: Multiple linear regression: when multiple variables are associated with a response, the interpretation of a prediction equation is seldom simple. Nat. Methods **12**(12), 1103–1105 (2015)

11. Breiman, L.: Random forests. Mach. Learn. **45**(1), 5–32 (2001). https://doi.org/10.1023/A: 1010933404324
12. Friedman, J.H.: Stochastic gradient boosting. Comput. Stat. Data Anal. **38**(4), 367–378 (2002)
13. Banihashemi, S., Ding, G., Wang, J.: Developing a hybrid model of prediction and classification algorithms for building energy consumption. Energy Procedia **110**, 371–376 (2017)
14. Araya, D.B., Grolinger, K., ElYamany, H.F., Capretz, M.A., Bitsuamlak, G.: An ensemble learning framework for anomaly detection in building energy consumption. Energy Build. **144**, 191–206 (2017)
15. Cho, J., Kim, Y., Koo, J., Park, W.: Energy-cost analysis of HVAC system for office buildings: development of a multiple prediction methodology for HVAC system cost estimation. Energy Build. **173**, 562–576 (2018)
16. Deng, H., Fannon, D., Eckelman, M.J.: Predictive modeling for US commercial building energy use: a comparison of existing statistical and machine learning algorithms using CBECS microdata. Energy Build. **163**, 34–43 (2018)
17. Rahman, I., Kuzlu, M., Rahman, S.: Power disaggregation of combined HVAC loads using supervised machine learning algorithms. Energy Build. **172**, 57–66 (2018)
18. Singaravel, S., Geyer, P., Suykens, J.: Component-based machine learning modelling approach for design stage building energy prediction: weather conditions and size. In Proceedings of the 15th IBPSA conference, pp. 2617–2626 (2017)
19. Candanedo, L.M., Feldheim, V., Deramaix, D.: Data driven prediction models of energy use of appliances in a low-energy house. Energy Build. **140**, 81–97 (2017)
20. Nayak, S.C.: Escalation of forecasting accuracy through linear combiners of predictive models. EAI Scalable Inf. Syst. **6**(22) (2019)
21. Sethi, J.S., Mittal, M.: Ambient air quality estimation using supervised learning techniques. Scalable Inf. Syst. **6**(22) (2019)
22. Tsanas, A., Xifara, A.: Accurate quantitative estimation of energy performance of residential buildings using statistical machine learning tools. Energy Build. **49**, 560–567 (2012)
23. Fan, C., Xiao, F., Wang, S.: Development of prediction models for next-day building energy consumption and peak power demand using data mining techniques. Appl. Energy **127**, 1–10 (2014)
24. https://archive.ics.uci.edu/ml/datasets/Energy+efficiency

Ionic Concentration and Action Potential Differences Between a Healthy and Alzheimer's Disease Person

Shruti Gupta[1]([⊠]), Jyotsna Singh[2]([⊠]), and Kaushal Kumar[1]([⊠])

[1] Computer Science Department, K. R. Mangalam University, Gurugram, India
Shruti.searching@gmail.com, Kaushal.kumar@karmangalam.edu.in
[2] Computer Science Department, IILM College of Engineering and Technology,
Gurugram, India
Singhjyotsna1@gmail.com

Abstract. Depressed Na^+/K^+ ATParse amount and diminished glutamate agreement in Alzheimer's disease brain is coupled through Alzheimer's disease. Cellular ion disparity might be its outcome. As soon as the cell is energized by some inner or exterior spur then action potential in the shape of very small pulses arises. It overreaches the decisive threshold of the membrane. The action potential initiation observed in cortical neurons is not capable to be explained by HH type models. This paper reviews HH model and shows the difference between a HH model with its sodium and potassium ion currents and the ionic concentrations of sodium and potassium of a person with Alzheimer's disease in it. Results are generated in form of graphs. This model is implemented in Matlab software to fairly accurate the differential equations. By using HH model, further parameters are created, Na^+ and K^+. The new parameters need to be carefully considered and analyzed.

Keywords: Ion concentration · Hodgkin–Huxley model · Alzheimer's disease · Hyper polarization · Depolarization · Sodium current · Potassium current

1 Introduction

In widespread network, astrocytes are structured which are balanced to dynamically manipulate neuronal function. The chief antioxidant in the brain is Glutathione (GSH), whose synthesis is restricted by the accessibility of cysteine [1, 2]. Classic procedures namely depolarization, repolarisation plus hyper polarization complete its natural cycle by membrane potential during action potential. A variety of neurological diseases are associated in the direction of the management of ion conduct namely epilepsy, stroke, scattering despair, migraine, hypoxic encephalopathy plus more mind purpose nourishing steadiness [3, 4]. Significant properties of neuron, neuron networks and other biological models are multi stability and coexistence of dynamical regimes. In the pathogenesis of several neurological diseases, such as, Parkinson's disease, essential termers, synchronization plays a key role [5, 6]. Neurological disorders have an effect on millions of people globally which might origin a multiplicity of indications together with paralysis and dementia. Straddling starting the electrophysiological properties of solitary neuron up to system smoothness policy, Spiking neural network (SNN) implements biologically practical neural network models [7, 8]. By reproducing the timing and a form of the spike, the neuron is replaced. All kinds of neurons can be reproduced by HH model with a good precision.

To experiment the supposition that harmed glutamate clearance plus dejected Na^+/K^+ ATParse heights in AD brain be related with Na^+ and K^+ asymmetry. Na^+ and K^+ heights in intellect tissues of standard and AD persons are analysed. A few ionic shortcomings are established in the cortical (Na^+) and cerebella (K^+) sampling of AD intellect [9, 10]. Experiential differences during provisions of ionic concentration between normal and AD intellect tissues might be elucidated through mathematical modelling of the experimental information. The dynamics of ion channels such as Na^+ and K^+ supply to the production of an Action Potential in a neuron is explained by HH model. A pointed voltage spike, action potential, is elicited by motivating a neuron with a current and this current exceeds a definite threshold value [3, 11]. Cells bulge during a large diversity of pathologies, together with shock, ischemia, hypoxia, seizures, and dissemination despair [12]. Cells may modify their quantity through usual action, plus the transform in cell amount through entity AP has been fairly accurate [13].

The result of cell puffiness on sole cell behaviour is partly implicit [14]. With incorporating preservation of particles, arraign as well as accounting for the power necessary to reinstate ionic gradients, the classic HH formalism is expanded. Broad varieties of neuronal actions are reported, from spike to seizure, scattering despair, varied seizure, scattering despair state, and the fatal anoxic sign of loss [15, 16]. The membrane potential is immediately changed as soon as the current is entered into the cell. Ion travels also succeeding action potentials (AP) are now one minute fraction of neurons working. Models smash behind neuron functions and properties via numerical equations. Models that are biologically precise have a propensity to employ additional equations. AP occurs from the synergistic accomplishment of both the channels, which open as well as closes in a current reliant manner. Major characteristic of the representation is that the channels release autonomously of one another; the likelihood with the intention of opening a channel rely simply on record of membrane voltage. The HH model is established during arithmetical simulations a hostile affiliation connecting both variables. We discover to the factors describing beginning speed to beginning distance rely on the quantity of synaptic backdrop movement. Definitely, single series of backdrop movement takes place in which the traditional HH model satisfies among the investigational information.

2 Materials and Methods

A unified method for epileptic seizure (SZ) and Seizure Dynamics (SD) can be exposed, by increasing HH kind structure. This statistical representation frames on earlier work where the membrane potential V of the neurons is modelled through the subsequent deposit of customized HH mathematical statements. By their capacity, the finders were capable to gain thorough equations which describe the variations to the ionic current compactness [17, 18]. They establish this:

$$I = C_M \frac{dV}{dt} + I_i \tag{1}$$

Here I is the total membrane current density calculated in micro amps per centimetre squared, C_M is the membrane capacity calculated in microfarads per centimetre squared which is thought to be stable and equal to 1 μF/cm^2, $\frac{dV}{dt}$ is the transform in the displacement of the membrane potential from its resting value with respect to time and I_i shows the three dissimilar ionic current densities calculated (Na^+, K^+ and leakage).

Equation (1) is written as:

$$C_M \frac{dV}{dt} = I - \sum_{ion} I_{ion} \tag{2}$$

The ionic current density is alienated into the three ionic currents that HH calculated. These ions are sodium (Na^+), potassium (K^+) and leakage current. Leakage includes mainly chloride however might as well contain little portions of another ions. The equation:

$$\sum_{ion} I_{ion} = I_{Na} + I_K + I_{Leak} \tag{3}$$

Is divided into:

$$I_{Na} = g_{Na} h \, m^3 (V - E_{Na}) \tag{4}$$

$$I_K = g_K n^4 (V - E_K) \tag{5}$$

$$I_{Leak} = g_{Leak} (V - E_{Leak}) \tag{6}$$

So,

$$\sum_{ion} I_{ion} = g_{Na} h m^3 (V - E_{Na}) + g_K n^4 (V - E_K) + g_{Leak} (V - E_{Leak}) \tag{7}$$

The parameters contain constants gi which are the utmost membrane conductances per ion calculated in μS/cm^2 and Ei are the assessment at which instance there is denial progress of the equivalent ion among the intra- and extracellular fluid. The standards of gi and Ei were designed by HH to robust their experiential conclusion.

Differential equations used are

$$dm/dt = \alpha m(V)(1 - m) + \beta m(V)m \tag{8}$$

$$dh/dt = \alpha h(V)(1 - h) + \beta h(V)h \tag{9}$$

$$dn/dt = \alpha n(V)(1 - n) + \beta n(V)n \tag{10}$$

$$dp/dt = \alpha p(V)(1 - p) + \beta p(V)p \tag{11}$$

Gating variables are described by the following rate equations

$$\alpha m = 0.1(V + 30)/1 - exp(-0.1(V + 30)) \tag{12}$$

$$\beta m = 4exp(-(V + 55/18)) \tag{13}$$

$$\alpha n = 0.01(V + 34)/1 - exp(-0.1(V + 34)) \tag{14}$$

$$\beta n = 0.125exp(-(V + 44/80)) \tag{15}$$

$$\alpha h = 0.07exp(-(V + 44/20)) \tag{16}$$

$$\beta h = 1/1 + exp(-0.1(V + 14)) \tag{17}$$

$$\alpha p = 0.0001(V + 30)/(1 - exp((-V - 30)/9)) \tag{18}$$

$$\beta p = 0.0001(-V - 30)/(1 - exp((V + 30)/9)) \tag{19}$$

We will compare the ionic concentrations of both sodium and potassium ions in HH and Alzheimer's disease model. The equations for ionic concentration in HH model:

$$INa(i) = gNa(m(i)3)h(i)(V(i) - ENa) \tag{20}$$

$$IK(i) = gK(n(i)4)(V(i) - EK) \tag{21}$$

The equations for ionic concentration in Alzheimer's disease:

$$Nat = Naex + (Nain - Naex)Vin \tag{22}$$

$$Kt = Kex + ((Kex - Kin) * Naex + (Kin - Kex) * Nat) * (Nain - Naex) \tag{23}$$

Here, for the Alzheimer's disease, K_{in} and Na_{in} are the potassium and sodium intracellular volumes. K_{ex} and Na_{ex} are the extra cellular volumes. The values for extracellular sodium and potassium ions remain constant. However, different values are taken for intracellular sodium and potassium ions. We study the graph for intra cellular Na^+ ions i.e. 5, 10, 20 and 40 mM. Also, intracellular K^+ ions are taken as 100, 110, 120 and 130 mM, while relative intracellular volume i.e. Vin remains 1. The regular ion consolidations considering Hodgkin–Huxley model were $[Na^+]out = 145$ mM, $[Na^+]in = 5 - 15$ mM, $[K^+]out = 5$ mM, and $[K^+]in = 140$ mM.

Here, K_{in} and Na_{in} are the potassium and sodium intracellular volumes. K_{ex} and Na_{ex} are the extracellular volumes. The values for extracellular sodium and potassium ions remain constant. However, different values are taken for intracellular sodium and potassium ions. We study the graph for intracellular Na ions i.e. 5, 10, 20 and 40 mM. Also, intracellular K ions are taken as 100, 110, 120 and 130 mM, while relative intracellular volume i.e. Vin remains 1.

3 Results

We have simply computed the graph for HH model, by calculating the inputs which inculcates the currents discussed previously.

The result obtained in Fig. 1, shows the variations of Action potential and ionic conductance. The graph is plotted using HH model without applied current. In Fig. 2, we have included both ionic concentration of Alzheimer's disease. It shows that at intra-cellular $Na^+ = 40$ mH and $K^+ = 100$ mH, hyper polarization takes place and then re polarization takes place in action potential. Here, no channel conductance of either Na^+ or K^+ channel takes place. Also, extracellular $Na^+ = 147$ mH and $K^+ = 2.8$ mH were considered. In Fig. 3, we have included only ionic concentration of Na^+ channel and not K^+ channel. As a result action potential and ionic concentrations of both the chan-nels are generated. Action potential takes a big jump, Na^+ channel conductance remain constant while K^+ channel conductance increases slightly. Intracellular ionic concen-tration of sodium i.e. $Na^+ = 5$ mH is taken into consideration. Figure 4, Intracellular ionic concentration of sodium i.e. $Na^+ = 40$ mH is taken into consideration. Here, the Na^+ channel value disappears. At $Na^+ = 40$ mH, the K^+ channel conductance become constant and action potential takes a small value.

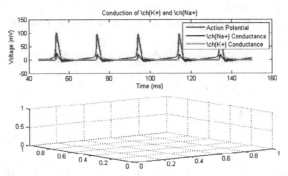

Fig. 1. HH model: It is stimulated with the conductance and action potential generated. Hhrun $(I, tspan, V, m, h, n, Plot)$ purpose replicate the HH replica for the squid massive axon in sup-port of consumer mere principles of the present contribution, time span, early principles of the factors and the explanation process. Since production it shows voltage (membrane potential) time succession plus the plots amid three variables $V vs. m$, n and h.

Figure 5, considering only K^+ ionic concentration values and $Na_t = 5$ mH. Na^+ ionic concentration is not taken here. Also, $K_{in} = 100$ mH, 110 mH, 120 mH, 130 mH and $Na_{in} = 5$ mH, 10 mH, 20 mH, 40 mH. The conductance of both Na^+ and K^+ channels are too small to be displayed in graph. In Fig. 6, we have considered simple HH model with the value of applied current, which displays a big change in all the three parameters. The Fig. 7 shows Hodgkin–Huxley model with applied current included. Figure 8, shows the same model but without I_{app}. We have inculcated the sodium and potassium ionic concentration of Alzheimer's disease person into HH model to learn the differences between a healthy person and a person with the Alzheimer's disease. The same is shown in Fig. 9. In Fig. 10, we have taken one concentration at a time i.e. sodium

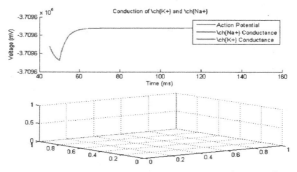

Fig. 2. Hodgkin–Huxley model with ionic consolidations of Na^+ and K^+ in Alzheimer's disease. Graphs were plotted using standard values for extracellular $Na^+ = 147$ mH and $K^+ = 2.8$ mH. At intracellular $Na^+ = 40$ mH and $K^+ = 100$ mH, hyper polarization takes place and then repolarization occurs. This shows that how voltage decreases and then increases with time. Afterwards it remains constant.

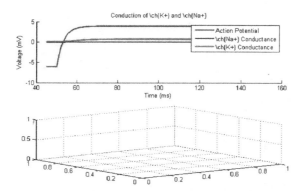

Fig. 3. We have included only Na^+ ion here and not considered K^+ ion This figure shows the ionic conductance's of Na^+, K^+ and action potential. Intracellular ionic concentration of sodium i.e. $Na^+ = 5$ mH is taken into consideration. At this point depolarization of action potential takes place. Within 10 ms of time, the action potential increases rapidly. Voltage of Na^+ channel conductance remains constant with respect to time. Also, slight increase in voltage of K^+ occurs.

ion and plotted the result. The last one i.e. Fig. 11, shows the ionic concentration of only potassium current into HH model. Grades on the basic replica suggest that around could be fundamental customary types for the alliance act we enclose at this time experiment. We complete the HH equations by means of preservation values towards describing in support of the ionic changes plus the energetic necessary towards reinstate ionic angles.

4 Discussions

In this study, we found the differences between Hodgkin–Huxley model and the same model with ionic concentrations of a person with Alzheimer's disease. The graphs are plotted in Matlab R2014a software. They show the action potential, Na^+ and K^+ channel

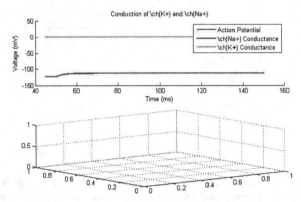

Fig. 4. This figure shows the K^+ conductance and action potential. As the value of Na^+ conductance keeps increasing, the Na^+ channel value fades away. At $Na^+ = 40$ mH, the K^+ channel conductance become constant and action potential takes a small value. The relative intracellular volume $= 1.0$

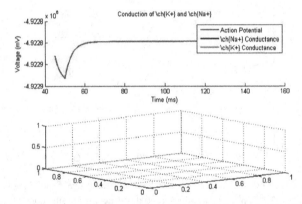

Fig. 5. Considering only K^+ ionic concentration values and $Na_t = 5$ mH. Na^+ ionic concentration is not taken here. Also, $K_{in} = 100$ mH, 110 mH, 120 mH, 130 mH and $Na_{in} = 5$ mH, 10 mH, 20 mH, 40 mH. The conductances of both Na^+ and K^+ channels are too small to be displayed in graph. Only action potential is shown whose voltage is a small value with time.

conductance. Reliance of whole K^+ consolidation happening on entire Na^+ consolidations as the qualified intracellular amount changes among zero to hundred percent [19]. Membrane potential is placed to permit the user to regulate the resting potential, $Vrest$ 0 mV. The time step, dt is set to 0.01 s which is the assessment used in all the graphs in this paper. Only action potential is shown whose voltage is a small value with time. Compotation models beginning with the corporeal aspects of neurons and their artery are built, also the features of ion metabolism, devoid of statistics decent [20]. By means of this essential illustration of the physics of neuronal ways, we blend this illustration through facts – figures incorporation – inside an approach generally useful in meteorology.

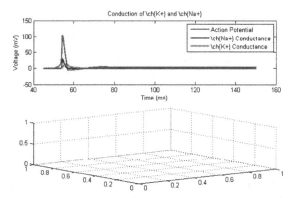

Fig. 6. Hodgkin–Huxley model: It is stimulated with the conductance and action potential generated along with applied current. The graph shows the result of applied current on Action potential, sodium and potassium ions. First graph of HH model was generated without applied current.

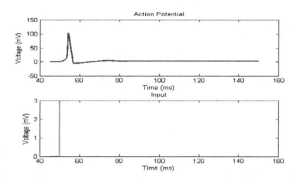

Fig. 7. In addition to sodium, potassium and leak current, applied current is also taken into consideration whose value is 2. This graph shows that the action potential is affected by the applied current. Hyperpolarisation occurs here where action potential is subdued by escalating the stimulus essential to progress the membrane potential to the action potential threshold. Afterwards, action potential remains constant with respect to time.

In support of breakdowns within the integral intellect, plus the integration of cognitive movement, Experiments are in progress exploring the application [21]. The HH working is worn towards modeling neurological syndrome. Beginning with the recording of natural AP, sodium and potassium ion conductance statistics, the ambition is to sculpt the variations among a fit and ailment person. Particularly in the case of HH, big values can significantly influence the ionic current so that the spikes voltage is higher value than the code can handle, or is not logically reasonable, which will end the code from functioning [22]. Configured with an erratic conductance as agreed in the study, each HH cell illustration in the enteric was one solo section [23]. One of the simplest biological models is Hodgkin–Huxley model, which computes membrane potential by means of four differential equations. The time progression of foundation variables depends on the voltage dependent rate constants. During action potential, rate constant shows spiky

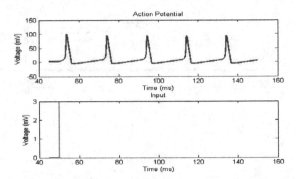

Fig. 8. Applied current is removed from now onwards and the result is shown of the currents: Sodium, potassium and leak. It can be clearly seen that a continuous pattern is formed when no current is applied. Also, input remains same as previous graph.

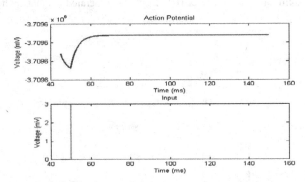

Fig. 9. In this both ionic concentrations of sodium and potassium of a person with neurological disorder is taken into Hodgkin–Huxley model. We have considered the Alzheimer's disease and taken its parameters of sodium ion and potassium ion. Depolarization can be seen clearly after which action potential becomes constant.

transitions as a outcome of speedy changes in membrane voltage [24, 25]. The likelihood of the channels being open, of ions moving from intracellular to extracellular fluid, or vice versa, is represented by the gating variables.

The standards of gating variables are reliant on both time and membrane voltage. These variables i.e. h, m and n can be defined anywhere between 0 and 1. We can amend the original model, in case of learning of neurological diseases, to simply embrace the cell degeneration. The electrical behaviour of an excitable neuron is described quantitatively in the course of the Hodgkin–Huxley equations [25, 26]. The circulation of diverse ionic species through its membrane is the outcome of electrical action of a neuron. Contest among essential neuronal ion currents, sodium-potassium pumps, glia, and dispersal may fabricate sluggish plus huge-amplitude swaying inside ion compressions alike to pragmatic physiologically in breakdowns. All ionic currents are calculated when the summing up is ended. This equality is helpful since it aims on the transform of the membrane potential. The HH, one of the simplest biological models [27, 28], make use of four differential equations to calculate the membrane potential. The four differential

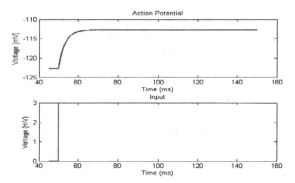

Fig. 10. In this graph we have only considered sodium ion concentration and leak current in the Hodgkin–Huxley model. For a short duration action potential remains constant then it increases over a short period and finally it becomes constant. Potassium ion concentration is not considered in this particular graph study.

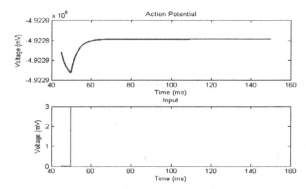

Fig. 11. Potassium ion concentration and leak current is taken while calculating the input value. Sodium current is discarded for this particular graph study. Again like one of the previous graph depolarization of action potential takes place and input remains unaffected.

equations form the ionic stream of the neuron. HH premeditated ionic flow by placing an electrode into the cell and putting a current to compute the course of ions and cell membrane alter formed on this putted current [29, 30].

5   Conclusion

Perturbations of Na^+ and K^+ ion pools, significant for electrophysiological action, membrane transport, and additional cellular processes are basically unstudied in Alzheimer's disease. In the current learning, the effects of ion concentrations on the behavior of HH cell model were investigated in conditions of constancy and management of the generated spikes. The ion concentrations were established to be effectual. Particularly, potassium concentration considerably exaggerated action potential and the steadiness and harmonization of the network conclusion. The graphs obtained at this time showed that the constancy and dependability of brain functions had a sturdy relationship with the cellular ion concentrations, and showed the likelihood of varying the behavior of neurons and therefore the firing rate of spikes in such a cortical network by varying simply the ion concentration balance.

To represent neurological disease and execute a disease neuron by Hodgkin–Huxley parameters is the concluding objective of this study. Afterwards, learn the influence and actions of these neurons incorporated into a neural network. We will employ the compartmental HH model, synapses, and elongated period smoothness to this neural network. The calculations mentioned now elucidate that to appreciate in case the experimental data is steady with the HH graphs. Mixing the hypothetical formalism mentioned in here with dimensions of the variance of synaptic conductances, whereas cautiously domineering for another sources of inconsistency in the dimension, is a brilliant path for prospect study. In total, we learn the impact of dissimilar lengths parameters on HH model and Alzheimer's disease. The HH model is single straightforward models in the unequivocal depiction of neurons grouping. So far, it requires four differential equations as well as eight erstwhile equations and three parameters to model presently the ionic pour of a neuron.

References

1. Vitvitsky, V.M., Garg, S.K., Keep, R.F., Albin, R.L., Banerjee, R.: Na$^+$ and K$^+$ ion imbalances in Alzheimer's disease. Biochim. Biophys. Acta **1822**(11), 1671–1681 (2012)
2. Bagheri, S., Squitti, R., Haertlé, T., Siotto, M., Saboury, A.A.: Role of copper in the onset of Alzheimer's disease compared to other metals. Front. Aging Neurosci. **9**, article 446 (2018)
3. Emin Tagluk, M., Tekin, R.: The influence of ion concentrations on the dynamic behavior of the Hodgkin–Huxley model-based cortical network. Cogn. Neurodyn. **8**(4), 287–298 (2014). https://doi.org/10.1007/s11571-014-9281-5
4. Kager, H., Wadman, W.J., Somjen, G.G.: Simulated seizures and spreading depression in a neuron model incorporating interstitial space and ion concentrations. Am. Physiol. Soc. **84**(1), 495–512 (2000)
5. Stankevich, N.: A rare and hidden attractor with noise in a biophysical Hodgkin–Huxley-type of model. Nonlinear Sciences, Chaotic Dynamics (2017)
6. Cisternas, P., et al.: The increased potassium intake improves cognitive performance and attenuates histopathological markers in a model of Alzheimer's disease. Biochem. Biophys. Acta **1852**, 2630–2644 (2015)
7. Levi, T., Khoyratee, F., Saïghi, S., Ikeuchi, Y.: Digital implementation of Hodgkin–Huxley neuron model for neurological diseases studies. Artif. Life Robot. **23**(1), 10–14 (2017). https://doi.org/10.1007/s10015-017-0397-7
8. Vermeer, S.E., Prins, N.D., den Heijer, T., Hofman, A., Koudstaal, P.J., Breteler, M.M.: Silent brain infarcts and the risk of dementia and cognitive decline. N. Engl. J. Med. **348**(13), 1215–1222 (2003)
9. Ozer, M., Perc, M., Uzuntarla, M.: Controlling the spontaneous spiking regularity via channel blocking on Newman-Watts networks of Hodgkin–Huxley neurons. Front. Phys. **86**(4), 40008 (2009)
10. Brookmeyer, R., Johnson, E., Ziegler-Graham, K., Michael Arrighi, H.: Forecasting the global burden of Alzheimer's disease. Alzheimer's Dementia **3**, 186–191 (2007)

11. Ozer, M., Uzuntarla, M., Perc, M., Graham, L.J.: Spike latency and jitter of neuronal membrane patches with stochastic Hodgkin-Huxley channels. J. Theor. Biol. **261**(1), 83–92 (2009)
12. Bazsó, F., Zalányi, L., Csárdi, G.: Channel noise in Hodgkin–Huxley model neurons. Phys. Lett. A **311**(1), 13–20 (2003)
13. Hill, B., Schubert, E., Nokes, M., Michelson, R.: Laser interferometer measurement of changes in crayfish axon diameter concurrent with action potential. Science **196**(4288), 426–428 (1977)
14. Kalnay, E.: Atmospheric Modeling, Data Assimilation, and Predictability. Cambridge University Press, New York (2003)
15. Roper, S., Obenaus, A., Dudek, F.: Osmolality and nonsynaptic epileptiform bursts in rat CA1 and dentate gyrus. Ann. Neurol. **31**(1), 81–85 (1992)
16. Rosen, A., Andrew, R.: Osmotic effects upon excitability in rat neocortical slices. Neuroscience **38**(3), 579–590 (1990)
17. Rudolph, M., Piwkowska, Z., Badoual, M., Bal, T., Destexhe, A.: A method to estimate synaptic conductances from membrane potential fluctuations. J. Neurophysiol. **91**(6), 2884–2896 (2004)
18. Ullah, G., Schiff, S.: Assimilating seizure dynamics. PLoS Comput. Biol. **6**(5), e1000776 (2010)
19. Sun, X., Perc, M., Lu, Q., Kurths, J.: Spatial coherence resonance on diffusive and small-world networks of Hodgkin–Huxley neurons. Interdiscip. J. Nonlinear Sci. **18**(2), 023102 (2008)
20. Roberts, B.R., et al.: Rubidium and potassium levels are altered in Alzheimer's disease brain and blood but not in cerebrospinal fluid. Acta Neuropathol. Commun. **4**(1), 119 (2016)
21. Gupta, S., Singh, J.: Investigating correlation properties of Hodgkin–Huxley model with leaky integrate – and-fire model. In: Proceedings of International Conference on Advances in Computer Science, AETACS (2013)
22. Fuller, S., Steele, M., Münch, G.: Activated astroglia during chronic inflammation in Alzheimer's disease—do they neglect their neurosupportive roles? Mutat. Res. **690**, 40–49 (2010)
23. Gupta, S., Singh, J.: Spiking patterns of Hodgkin-Huxley model in Alzheimer's disease: effects caused by noise current. Int. J. Comput. Appl. (0975-8887) **94**(11), 1–6 (2014)
24. Kneller, J., Ramirez, R.J., Chartier, D., Courtemanche, M., Nattel, S.: Time dependent transients in an ionically based mathematical model of the canine atrial action potential. Am. J. Physiol. Heart Circ. Physiol. **282**, H1437–H1451 (2002)
25. Ziburkus, J., Cressman, J., Barreto, E., Schiff, S.: Interneuron and pyramidal cell interplay during in vitro seizure-like events. J. Neurophysiol. **95**(6), 3948–3954 (2006)
26. Allaman, I., et al.: Amyloid-β aggregates cause alterations of astrocytic metabolic phenotype: impact on neuronal viability. J. Neurosci. **30**(9), 3326–3338 (2010). https://doi.org/10.1523/jneurosci.5098-09.2010
27. Ullah, G., Schiff, S.J.: Personality and Alzheimer's disease: an integrative review. Pers. Disord. **10**(1), 4–12 (2019)
28. Scheffer, M., et al.: Anticipating critical transition. Science **338**, 344–348 (2012)
29. Barreto, E., Cressman, J.R.: Ion concentration dynamics as a mechanism for neuronal bursting. J. Biol. Phys. **37**, 361–373 (2011)
30. Supnet, C., Bezprozvanny, I.: The dysregulation of intracellular calcium in Alzheimer disease. Cell Calcium **47**, 183–189 (2010)

An Adaptive Framework for Human Psycho-Emotional Mapper Based on Controlled Stimulus Environment

Ayan Chakraborty[1,2]([✉]), Sajal Saha[2], and R. T. Goswami[1]

[1] Techno International New Town, Kolkata 700156, India
{ayan.chakraborty,rtgoswami}@tict.edu.in
[2] Kaziranga University, Jorhat 785006, Assam, India
sajalsaha@kazirangauniversity.in

Abstract. In the recent era, human are ruled by digital media. It can be said that for improvised Human Computer Interaction (HCI) process and security purposes, a robust authentication framework is the target of all researchers. Any CHAP or PAP based and biometric authentication techniques have been evolved in a great way to serve this purpose. Along with these widely used techniques, a new research domain Affective Computation (AC) has taken place with a different approach towards engaging human emotions into a farm computational model. In this work, a robust and adaptive framework for a Human Emotional Mapper has been introduced in details through which human emotional signature can be tracked. This emotional signature pattern can be used for authentication as well as improvised HCI.

Keywords: Human Computer Interaction (HCI) · Affective computing · Emotion · Psychophysiological responsiveness · Stimuli · Multivariate signal · Plutchick's model · Pattern · Signature pattern · Longest Common Subsequence (LCS)

1 Introduction: Affective Computation (AC)

Affect stands for emotional feelings of a human. So Affective Computation (AC) is an interdisciplinary research area spanning psychology, cognitive science, social science and computer science. It deals with the computational models which can frame human emotions and feelings in a usable way. AC has the ability to offer benefits in HCI process in a more humanly way. For instance, in an e-learning environment, an AC framework can identify when a student is frustrated and provide the best recommended learning path. In telemedicine, AC model can help doctors for quick understanding a remotely located patient's mental or emotional state. Various business application areas are recently being explored including customer relationship management (CRM), human resource management (HRM), marketing and Entertainment-On-Demand.

U. Batra et al. (Eds.): REDSET 2019, CCIS 1229, pp. 278–287, 2020.
https://doi.org/10.1007/978-981-15-5827-6_24

Most commonly used authentication processes are based on PAP/CHAP protocol. These protocols are always vulnerable to Brute Force attacks, secrecy and storage. A more advanced way of authentication is backed by biometric parameters of a human user like fingerprint, heart beat, retina pattern, face/voice recognition, DNA pattern etc. But these parameters hugely vary depending on various environmental causes. Furthermore these processes are always not fully accurate and cannot be reset once compromised. It involves costly hardware also.

From the above discussion, it is evidently observed that gradually authentication techniques are inclining on more inner parameters of a human user.

Inspired by these thoughts in present research work, a learning based adaptive framework has been proposed which is capable of integrating multivariate emotional patterns of a human being and generating a signature pattern through a robust statistical model. This paper has been organized as follows:

Section 2 discusses the Preliminaries of Human Emotional Model and Affective Computation where as in Sect. 3, Proposed Framework has been elaborated. However, Sect. 4 reports the Analysis of Algorithmic Complexity, followed by Sect. 5, which elaborates the Result Analysis. At the end, in Sect. 6 new horizon of future research and conclusion is presented.

2   Review on Human Emotional Model and Affective Computation

An emotional AI model can be framed using collective responses from facial expression, body gesture, voice modulation, speech patterns, and pupil dilation etc. against a set of stimuli. Saike He et al. in 2016 [1] depicted a futuristic framework which can featurise entrainment phenomenon and efficiently quantify its pattern and Wataru Sato et al. in 2013 [2] recorded facial electromyography (EMG) analysis from the set of corrugate supercilii and zygomatic major. The paper further derives scorings on valence scaling, experienced emotion related arousals and its polarity. Alexander Toet et al. in 2011 [3] explained the effects of various spatio-temporal dynamic texture characteristics on human emotions against the emotional experience of auditory (e.g., music) and haptic repetitive patterns. Using a unique topographical self-report method Lauri Nummenmaa et al. in 2014 [4] reveal maps of human body sensations related with varied emotions. Shikha Jain et al. in 2015 [5] reported the background study along with necessary requirements for developing emotion based computational model. This model is reported to generate artificial emotions as per external stimuli. An algorithmic approach for detection and analysis of human emotions with the help of voice and speech processing was proposed by Poorna Banerjee Dasgupta in 2017 [6]. The arousal of emotion is usually accompanied with manifestation in our external appearance, such as changes in facial expression, voice, gesture, posture, and other physiological conditions described by Amit Konar and Aruna Chakraborty in 2015 [7] whereas a survey has been done by Andrea Kleinsmith et al. in 2013 [8]. It reports a systematic review on affective body expression and perception and recognition. Stefano Piana et al. in 2014 [9] published a method where data acquired from optical motion capture system and Microsoft Kinect, has been examined on a "six emotions" recognition problem, and deploying a leave-one- subject-out cross validation strategy, achieved an overall recognition rate of 61.3% which is very near value of 61.9% obtained by human observers. The Wheel of Emotion proposed by Robert Plutchik in 2001 [10] is widely used by psychologists to map the relationships between the emotions and stimuli in human being.

3   Proposed Framework

This proposed framework for adaptive computational model to generate human emotional signature pattern is primarily based on Robert Plutchik's theory. In 2001 *Plutchik's Wheel of Emotions* [10] has been published in American Scientists. In this model human emotions are represented by eight basic emotions like joy, trust, fear, surprise, sadness, anticipation, anger, and disgust. This model illustrates the relationships between these basic emotions, their opposite emotions along with intensity (Fig. 1).

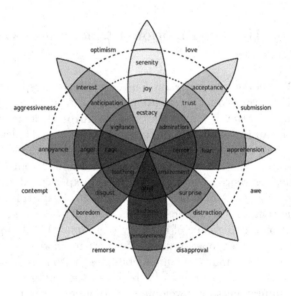

Fig. 1. Robert Plutchik Wheel of Emotions

Opposites: Every primary emotion has a reverse emotion, therefore:

- Sadness is the reverse of Joy.
- Anger is the reverse of Fear.
- Surprise is the reverse of Anticipation.
- Trust is the reverse of Disgust.

Combination: Emotions at the empty space between two petals are the combinational dyads, so that:

– Anticipation and joy leads to optimism taken together.
– Joy and trust leads to love taken together.

Intensity: Intensity of each emotion increases from periphery inwards denoted by gradual change of color from lighter shade to darker.

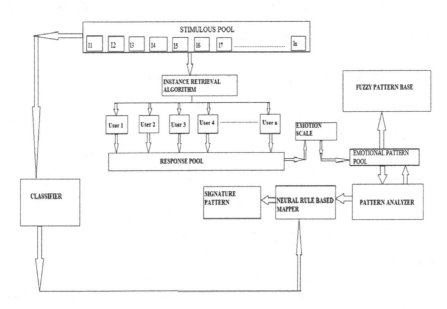

Fig. 2. Adaptive human emotional mapper

3.1   Phase 1: Creation of a Controlled Environment

Creation of a controlled environment to represent Human Psycho Emotional Behavior depending on Plutchick's Model, eight basic emotions and their primary, secondary and tertiary dyads have been formed.

- Creation of Stimulus Pool
  Multivariate stimuli has been designed using the standard dataset collected from OpenBCI and PhysioNet.
  – Psychometric questionnaire survey
  – Image Database
  – Video Database
  All of this survey has been done in Emotional Reflexive Retention time, i.e. 35 s
- Data Acquisition

- Every emotion is considered as a 2D vector with dimensions $(+)$ve/$(-)$ve and intensity
- Sample population is of size 30
- No of survey emotional have been implemented on each sample is 800
- Variance model has been created by tuning the stimuli to make one single emotion as the driving factor and others as variable according to that
- Scoring scale has been used as 0–10
- Data Analysis
  - For every variance model the Mean of the participating emotions has been calculated
  - From the Mean value, Standard Deviation has been generated.

3.2 Phase 2: Generation of Signature Emotional Pattern

In this work, a human user behavioral pattern based analyzer has been proposed by A. Chakraborty et al. in 2011. This concept is governed by the usage log pattern of an individual human user. Figure 2 shows the pattern of n symbol emotional responses and has been recorded in an Emotional_Sequence_Storage which can grow with every sessional activity of the user. Responsibility of Pattern_Analyzer Module is to read the whole Emotional_Sequence_Storage and retrieve the sequence with highest appearance in sessional log. These highly repetitive sub-sequences are considered as the Emotional_Signature_Pattern using Gen_Signature_Pattern algorithm which has been explained in later section.

Let assume that up to t^{th} sequence, t numbers of Emotional_Sequences are being generated and stored in *Set X* where $X = \{S^0, S^1 \cdots S^t\}$. After this, Pattern_Analyzer module, using Gen_Signature_Pattern algorithm derives q number of Emotional_Signature_Patterns of v length from set X. Furthermore, tuning of these patterns of length v is done adaptively within the range of two boundary values K_1 and K_2 and $q \geq 1$. So all v length newly generated Signature_Patterns form a new Set named as Y. Conclusively, by introducing the well known statistical model of Dempster Shafer rule of combination (DSRC) over the identified signature_patterns, the authentication has been considered depending on the results of Basic Belief Assignment of set Y which is basically the calculated value of *belfunc(Y)*. Here, the subset occurrence probability of Y within the superset X has been proved by the degree of belief. For a successfully authenticated user, a threshold value of *belfunc(Y)* has been set by the admin. In the light of the above discussion, the proposed framework is described here with basic three concepts: an intelligent algorithm which is capable of finding out q number of v length Emotional_Signature _patterns, to prove the authentication score, comparing with the threshold value of *belfunc (Y)* for all the possible combinations of rules, use of DSRC and analysis of the run time complexity of introduced model.

Algorithm 1: Gen_Signature_Pattern

Input: (i) *EmotionalSequence* S^t for t^{th} session, along with *EmotionalSequence*
      storage containing S^0, $S^1 \cdots S^{t-1}$ and P_s^0, $P_s^1 \cdots P_s^{t-1}$

      (ii) $K_1 = 1$ (if $t = 0$) $\parallel \acute{x}^{t-1}$ (otherwise)

      (iii) $K_2 = n$ where n = length of *EmotionalSequence*s

Output: *EmotionalSignaturePattern* P_s^t for t^{th} session sequence

0: for all x (where $K_1 \leq x \leq K_2$), do *Step 1* to *Step 2*

1: call *LCS* subroutine (Longest Common Subsequence)
      to find out repetitive sequence P and number of repetation
      r.

2: calculate $\sigma = z/x$ and if $\sigma \leq \sigma_{min}$, $\sigma_{min} \leftarrow \sigma$

3: define x for which $\sigma = \sigma_{min}$ as $\acute{x}^t$

4: $P_s^t \leftarrow P$

5: Stop.

Adaptive identification of the Signature_Patterns from the gathered knowledge of Emotional_Sequence_Storage is one of the main features of this algorithm.
Other than this, fully deterministic approach has been followed to identify the
occurrence of the mostly repetitive sequence or sub-sequences. It can be observed
in every emotional sequence that, the boundary value of K_1 is modifying and
the consecutive emotional sequence is gathering knowledge regarding any abrupt
changes through x'^{t-1} introducing the idea flow of information mechanism. The
responsibility of x'^{t-1} is to determine an dynamic way to minimize the difference between the calculated values of K_1 and K_2 which will effect the searching
process of Signature Pattern with reduced time frame.

4 Output and Level of Confidence

To analyze the confidence level to validate a user by authenticating him/her
through Emotional Signature Pattern DSRC is being introduced into the presented work. For this purpose, a non empty finite set X has been taken, which
is consisted of the current Emotional Sequence at t^{th} session, so S^t has been
directly mapped with X. Likewise the other non empty finite set Y which is
consisted of r number of Signature Pattern up to $(t-1)^{th}$ session has been taken
so that P_s^{t-1} has been straightly mapped with Y. Taking consideration $M =$
Mass Function of Belief; therefore, according to DSRC, the Belief Function of
X i.e. *belfunc(X)* is given by

$$belfunc(X) = \sum\nolimits_{Y|Y \subseteq X} M(Y) \tag{1}$$

This equation directly derives

$$M(X) = \sum\nolimits_{Y|Y \subseteq X} (-1)^{|X-Y|} belfunc(Y) \tag{2}$$

Therefore $belfunc(Y)$ can be given as

$$belfunc(Y) = \frac{i}{\sum_{Y|Y \subseteq X}(-1)^{|X-Y|}} \qquad (3)$$

where i is known as Shafer Normalization Factor and depicted as

$$i = \sum_{x_1 \cap x_2 \cdots \cap x_n = X = \phi}(M_1(x_1)M_2(x_2)\cdots M_n(x_n)) \qquad (4)$$

where $x_1, x_2 \cdots x_n$ are the scoring values of n different user activities within S^t.

The framework discussed here is run with a customized web application named as EMOFY where multiple sessions (to be precise, 200) are monitored with associated time mapped Emotional_Sequences for multiple users (some samples are shown in Fig. 3).

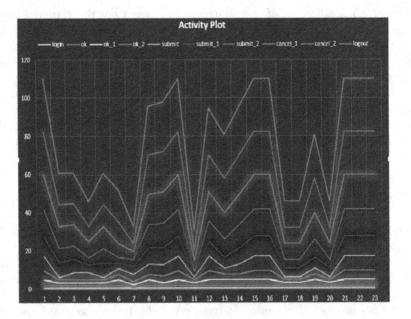

Fig. 3. EMOFY response plot

Each Emotional Sequence is treated as an authentic activity marker of a particular user for a specific session. From these information a properly formatted score list has been formed. This list has a score value which indicates the triggering of an event as identified by the admin. Here the sessional activities are plotted with time in X-axis. The Emotional Signature Patterns which have been derived out of Gen_Signature_Pattern algorithm from the specified pool of stimuli are shown in Fig. 4.

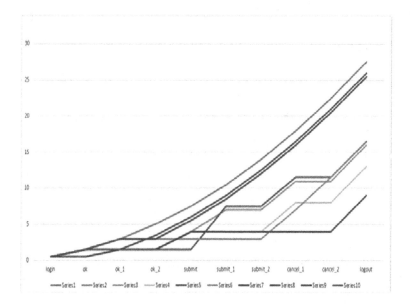

Fig. 4. Emotional signature pattern of different users

4.1   Regression Graph of BelFunc(Y)

To implement the currently proposed algorithm, users have been navigated through a controlled web environment.

To test the algorithm, 200 numbers of Emotional_ Session_Sequences are chosen at random from the pool of 8400 sequences. Hence, $t = 200$. Corresponding Emotional_ Session_Sequences $\{S^0, S^1 \cdots S^{t-1}\}$ have been processed to generate an Emotional_Signature_Pattern sequence of a specific user whose web activity navigation are trained by the system. The result shown below showings the $belfunc(Y)$ values of 200 no. of Emotional_ Session_Sequences of 25 no. of users.

Here in the following graph, horizontal and vertical axis indicates the values of $belfunc(Y)$ and the number of sessions respectively.

Figure 5 clearly explains that $belfunc(Y)$ with the value 3.0 have been attained for maximum time and this behavior is marked through red circles. The regression line, thus identified, helps to set the threshold values of K_1 and K_2.

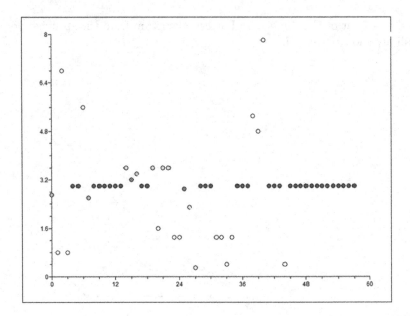

Fig. 5. Regression plot for emotional signature pattern of different users (Color figure online)

5   Analysis of Algorithmic Complexity

This searching time complexity could be more normalized by employing *LCS Algorithm* in the later part to find out the most repetitive common sub-sequence. Gen_Repetitive_Seq will consume up to $O(z(n * p)^2)$ of time to find out the longest common sub-sequence of any specific length from the Emotional Sequence storage. Therefore in the proposed algorithm, repetitive triggering of LCS algorithm will take up to $O((K_2 - K_1)r(n * p)^2)$ of time to identify desired Emotional Signature Pattern. So it can be concluded that Emotional Signature Pattern generation may be executed in polynomial time.

6   Conclusion

Current study proposes a framework for identification and analysis of session based emotional pattern within a controlled environment. Framework as explained in the current paper, features an effective and dynamic pattern management based on proven statistical computational capability. Experiment shows that this framework has a fair potential as an alternative to conventional CHAP or PAP based authentication systems. This claim can be established by the fact that here, the authentication is governed by the ever dynamic emotional responses of human brain.

References

1. He, S., Zheng, X., Zeng, D., Luo, C., Zhang, Z.: Exploring entrainment patterns of human emotion in social media. PLoS ONE **11**(3), e0150630 (2016). https://doi.org/10.1371/journal.pone.0150630
2. Wataru, S., Yasutaka, K., Motomi, T.: Enhanced subliminal emotional responses to dynamic facial expressions. Front. Psychol. **5**, 994 (2014). https://doi.org/10.3389/fpsyg.2014.00994. https://www.frontiersin.org/article/10.3389/fpsyg.2014.00994. ISSN 1664-1078
3. Toet, A., Henselmans, M., Lucassen, M., Gevers, T.: Emotional effects of dynamic textures. i-Perception **2**(9), 969–991 (2011). https://doi.org/10.1068/i0477
4. Nummenmaa, L., Glerean, E., Hari, R., Hietanen, J.K.: Bodily maps of emotions. PNAS **111**(2), 646–651 (2014). https://doi.org/10.1073/pnas.1321664111
5. Jain, S., Asawa, K.: Emotional computer: design challenges and opportunities. IGI Global **6**(2), 35–56 (2015)
6. Dasgupta, P.B.: Detection and analysis of human emotions through voice and speech pattern processing. IJCTT J. **52**(1), (2017). https://doi.org/10.14445/22312803/IJCTT-V52P101
7. Konar, A., Chakraborty, A.: Emotion Recognition: A Pattern Analysis Approach, 1st edn. Wiley, New York (2015). ISBN-13:978-1118130667. ISBN-10:1118130669
8. Kleinsmith, A., Bianchi-Berthouze, N.: Affective body expression perception and recognition: a survey. IEEE Trans. Affect. Comput. **4**(1), 15–33 (2013). https://doi.org/10.1109/T-AFFC.2012.16
9. Piana, S., Staglianó, A., Odone, F., Verri, A., Camurri, A.: Real-time automatic emotion recognition from body gestures. arXiv:1402.5047 [cs.HC] (2014)
10. Plutchik, R.: The nature of emotions. Am. Sci. **89**, 344 (2001). https://doi.org/10.1511/2001.4.344

Implementation of Common Spatial Pattern Algorithm Using EEG in BCILAB

Tanupriya Choudhury[1]([✉]), Amrendra Tripathi[1], Bhawna Arora[2],
and Archit Aggarwal[2]

[1] School of CS, University of Petroleum and Energy Studies (UPES), Dehradun, India
tanupriya1986@gmail.com, tripathiamrendra@gmail.com
[2] Amity University, Noida, Uttar Pradesh, India
bhawna2600@gmail.com, archit.aggarwal1508@gmail.com

Abstract. Massive progress has been made in the field of modeling the brain signals which are taped by the Electroencephalography (EEG), functional near-infrared spectroscopy (fNIRS) and so on. BCILAB is a toolbox in MATLAB which is composed of predefined algorithms which may expedite research for advancement of BCI methods and with that condense the time requirement for the real-time scrutinization of brain signals. Prominence is on implementation of CSP on EEG data with its steps explanation and procedure on BCI toolkit. The results obtained shows the Structure of predictive model can be visualized and the liner weights of classifier assigned to different features and the CSP model consist of six set of parameters that can be interpreted as pre channel weights and forms a map.

Keywords: Brain-Computer Interface · Interface · Electro-encephalogram · CSP algorithm · BCILAB

1 Introduction

Presently there is a huge gap between the implementation of researches obtainable and the software's that could practically be used for application. BCILAB is designed to bridge that gap. Through this paper one can stepwise learn the use of BCILAB. BCILAB is a toolbox in MATLAB which is composed of predefined algorithms which may expedite research for advancement of BCI methods and with that condense the time requirement for real-time scrutinization of brain signals. BCILAB is among the openly available toolkit available over the internet which could be easily installed by downloading and extracting in a folder along with MATLAB by setting its path to File/Set Path/Default and then using the command cd your/path/to/bcilab which would automatically open the toolkit. BCILAB is being focused here because of its easy availability, user friendly and large functionality which has both online and offline functionality. It even contains methods which have recently been published like Bayesian approaches. This paper works on EEG data which has been downloaded from the BNCI website ("bnci-horizon-2020. eu/database/data-sets"), which is already preprocessed. Analysis of EEG signal is as follow:

© Springer Nature Singapore Pte Ltd. 2020
U. Batra et al. (Eds.): REDSET 2019, CCIS 1229, pp. 288–300, 2020.
https://doi.org/10.1007/978-981-15-5827-6_25

1) Frequency generated in the range of one to four Hertz belongs to the delta category which in turn is deep sleep or unconscious state.
2) Frequency generated in the range of four to seven Hertz belongs to the theta category which includes dreaming or deep meditation.
3) Frequency in the range of seven to thirteen Hertz is known as the alpha range. This is the state in which brain activities like jogging, imagining and relaxing take place.
4) Frequency in the range of thirteen to thirty Hertz is known as the beta phase and is comprised of decision making and physical activities.

Firstly different types of BCI system have been considered in Sect. 2 and review on the technology has been given. Then steps have been shown for implementation sequentially along with screenshots in Sect. 3. Moreover the algorithm used has been deliberated in the Sect. 4 which is followed by the results in Sect. 5. Lastly the conclusion and future scope has been presented.

2 Literature Survey

The system of Brain-Computer Interface creates a new pathway for the communication that the human mind is trying to attain but is unable to due to physical restrictions which may be a consequence of real life events. Thus the interface may help in assisting people involved in any such incidence where they are deemed unable to communicate. The following are general descriptions and analysis of systems which have been implemented previously.

"Brain-Computer Interface" by Anirudh Vallabhaneni et al. [1] goes into depth while maintaining a simple proficient language. The paper has a detailed introduction. History of BCI has been given to provide better background understanding on the subject. The individual components have been explored to provide clear concepts of the system. A brief comparison of HCI and BCI is also seen in certain parts. It is depicted how BCI can be seen as a highly developing subset of BCI with potential for solving the gap between the brain and effective communication.

"High-speed spelling with a non-invasive brain–computer interface" by Xiaogang Chen et al. [2] is one of the most recent and significant developments in BCI. The paper proposes an electroencephalogram-based BCI speller which can be implemented using both invasive and non-invasive methodologies. The paper has achieved high transfer rates. Thus this paper affirms that the field of BCI can be used to improve neural communication with the outside world for those who need it the most.

"A Randomized Controlled Trial of EEG-Based Motor Imagery Brain-Computer Interface Robotic Rehabilitation for Stroke" by Kai Keng et al. [3] conducts a study to determine the ability of the BCI method combined with other technology like robotics to help subjects who have experienced a stroke and lost motor function. The conclusions drawn from the study clearly show that the use of BCI with extension of other technologies was similar, if not better than other therapeutic measures for stroke rehabilitation.

"Virtual typing by the people with tetraplegia by the use of a self-calibrating intra-cortical brain-computer interface" by Beata Jarosiewicz et al. [4] shows the difficulties associated with BCI interfaces and their prolonged need of repeated calibration. The paper attempted to combine various calibration methods in order to remove the entropy of the typing process, making it smoother and more effective. The unique approach made use of three such techniques. The results show great promise and scope for immense development. It is a step forward toward making BCI systems more compatible and practical for daily use. The system may be able to provide a degree of freedom to people with paralysis in terms of communication.

"Flight simulation using the Brain-Computer Interface: A pilot, pilot study" by Michael Kryger et al. [5] shows the successful use of their own BCI system in order to give the user control over flight using a flight simulator. The subjects were subjected to six sessions and with the careful modification of parameter over the course of these sessions, it was determined that the user was successfully able to have a full degree of control on the aircraft including advance functionality and just basic flight. This paper opens potential doors to more such activities with the help of BCI. It reassures the fact that there is no potential limit on BCI systems.

"Effects of mental workload and fatigue on the P300, alpha and theta band power during operation of an ERP (P300) brain–computer interface" by Ivo Käthner et al. [6]. The prolonged use of any system must be tested for the fatigue and stress that it may incur on the subject and thus there is a need to find indicators which may help achieve the same. The paper aimed at finding such indicators by causing variations in factors like listening tasks and the intensity of the task involved. The paper then noted variations in signals generated to determine and track fatigue. It was concluded that the groups of the signals from the time and the frequency spectrum of the electroencephalogram was successful in finding of the fatigue.

The above description of various domains of research depicts the ability of BCI systems to help a very large demographic [9, 18, 19]. These systems present us with the ability to enhance and explore the ability of the human brain beyond the constrict that is present now [7, 10, 11, 20]. The systems present potentially the most revolutionary medical advancements enabling people with disability live a regular life. The systems also present new developments in strengthening of the mind for sharper skill development. These developments present with large scope for physical, mental and economic well being. Communication will be faster and without any barriers. The general speed and efficacy of life expectations will improve vastly with mass adaptation of the systems.

The enormous potential seen with the capabilities of the system should not be allowed to overwhelm. It is necessary to maintain a degree of control on the systems while repeatedly monitoring both the positive and negative consequences the systems present [15, 16]. The prime concern with the systems that is the welfare of all mankind should be kept at priority [13, 17].

3 Implementation

3.1 Approach to Design

- Create an approximate method for particular data and implementation of it.
- Giving paper on implementation of CSP on EEG data with its steps explanation and procedure that can act as base for further research [8, 12, 14].

3.2 Simulation/Experimentation

The simulation consists of the following steps:

1) Upload the data as depicted by Fig. 1. A view of the entire data has been shown in Fig. 2. The screen in Fig. 1 shows the MATLAB view where the data set may be defined. The data is an EEG dataset. The full screen view of the entire data set with all the parameters is shown in Fig. 2.

Fig. 1. Uploading the data

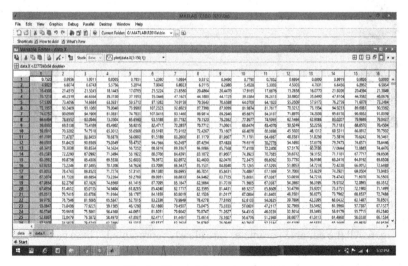

Fig. 2. View of the entire data set

2) Initiate BCILAB as shown in Fig. 3 in order to proceed for computations. The command 'bcilab' is entered in the MATLAB terminal in order to start the BCILAB toolbox. Figure 4 shows a view of the BCILAB which is the first screen after opening the toolbox bar on the screen.

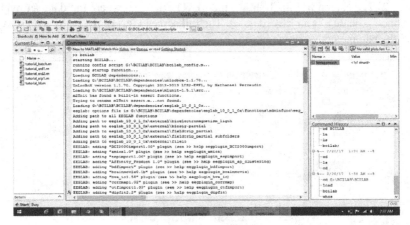

Fig. 3. Start BCILAB

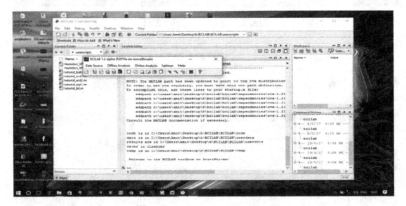

Fig. 4. View of BCILAB bar.

3) Enter the approach to be used as user requirement as shown in Fig. 5. The approach used in this particular use case is CSP. The description along with the approach is editable as per the requirements. The standard configuration for an approach is shown in Fig. 6. All the editable parameters are clearly represented. These can be modified. This is the default approach presented in MATLAB the reference to which can be found in the help documentation. The approach here is that we expect a sampling rate of one hundred units in HERTZ. The next parameter is a range of frequency we need to look for which are the upper limits of the frequency distributions used. The

epoch time is the duration in which we expect the response we are looking for to take place. The number of CSP patterns entered will be multiplied by two and generated. The last parameter is the machine learning algorithm to be used. The default has been used for the purposes of this study. The setup of the approach is now complete.

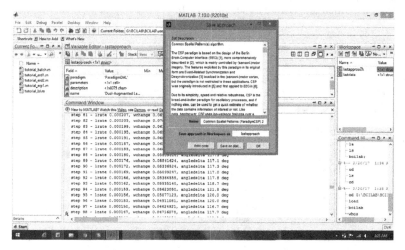

Fig. 5. Approach to be used as per requirement

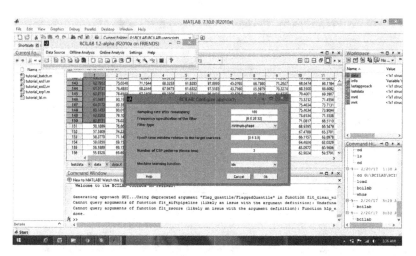

Fig. 6. Standard configuration of approach

4) Calibrate the model by setting up markers as shown in Fig. 7. The dialogue box in Fig. 7 gives us the ability to define custom markers that is classes of data which we are looking for in the data, here two default markers are specified. The parameter search asks what data we want to search for within the data set. The other options like

cross validation are optional and are based on the requirements of the experiment, here the default values have been used. A visual view of EEG markers is shown in Fig. 8. The blue and the green lines with their respective labels show the markers and the desired classes of data they generate. The visual of the commands running in the back is shown in Fig. 9. While the visualisation happens, MATLAB performs operations which are visible as seen in Fig. 9.

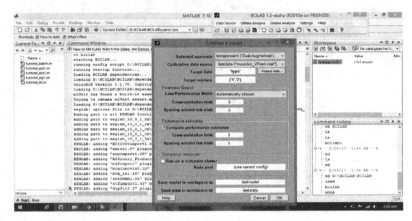

Fig. 7. Model calibration by setting up markers

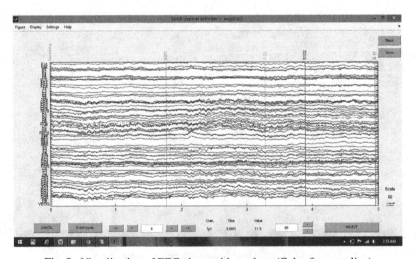

Fig. 8. Visualization of EEG along with markers (Color figure online)

5) Analyse the individual data entries as shown in Fig. 10. Each approach to analysis has various parameters. Each of these parameters is shown in this toolbox. The relevant sub parameters which are needed to be optimised are editable here. This depicts the

Fig. 9. Commands running in the background

extreme degree of control one can maintain while performing such analysis. All the default values have been used here. The screen is shown for depiction purposes only.

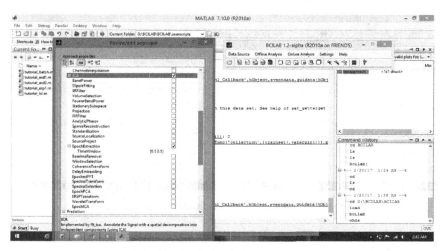

Fig. 10. Analyzing independent data

6) Select to train the model in offline analysis as per selected criteria as shown in Fig. 11. We train the model according to the approach and parameters set above. This will generate the final results.
7) In order to see the generated results in a visual format, select visualize model function of BCILAB as shown in Fig. 12. The resultant patterns are seen in Fig. 15.

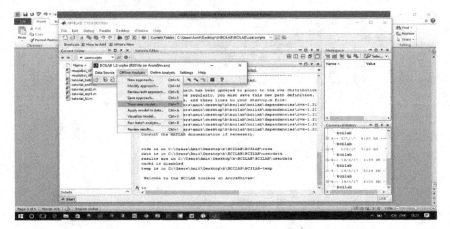

Fig. 11. Select to train the model in offline analysis as per selected criteria

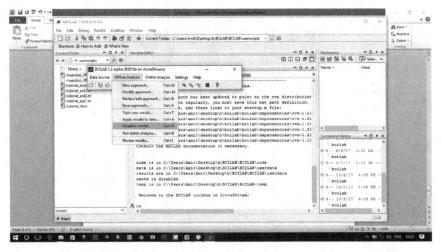

Fig. 12. Visualize the model that has been trained.

4 Process Flow

Wavelet Common Spatial pattern (WCSP) is the root for the algorithm used. A diagrammatical representation is seen in Fig. 13. The flow chart shows the steps involved clearly. The algorithm may be explained as follows:

1. Data for the purpose of study is gathered by the use of EEG experimentation and the pre-processing is done simultaneously with filtration.
2. Wavelet decomposition is used to prescribe signals to their respective sub-bands.
3. Wavelet reconstruction causes the regeneration of signals.
4. Common Spatial pattern is used to perform spatial filtration.
5. The distinctive features are determined is done from WCSP signals.

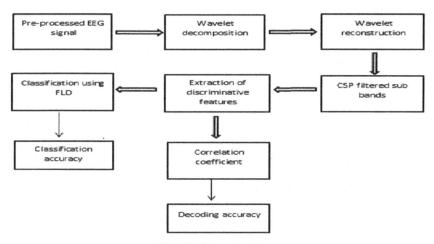

Fig. 13. Flow algorithm

6. The FLD classifier is given the training by the use of the features determined.
7. The reconstruction of the speed profile is done and the determination of decoding accuracy is found with relation to the correlation coefficient [21].

5   Results

The results obtained can be viewed in a review form as shown in Fig. 14. We see that the error result is approximately five percent which means that the model is wrong five percent of the times. The review of results in Fig. 14 shows the five set of ratings for the data set which are True positive, True negative, False positive, False negative and the error rate. The results are also available in a visual form as shown in Fig. 15 which was generated earlier. Figure 15 is a direct representation of the obtained CSP patterns based on the process flow thus concluding the experiment successfully. The optimal channels based on the EEG data after implementing the CSP model are seen in Fig. 15. The six models represent the computation of patterns on the test user data uploaded initially. This thus shows that the computation is complete and the experiment was a success. All required actions were performed successfully.

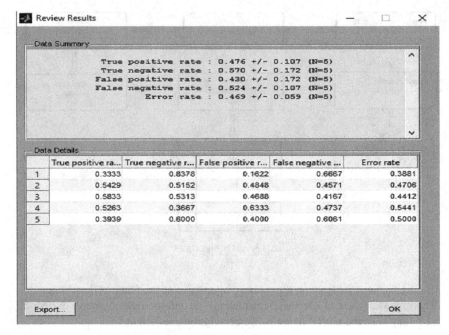

Fig. 14. Review of results

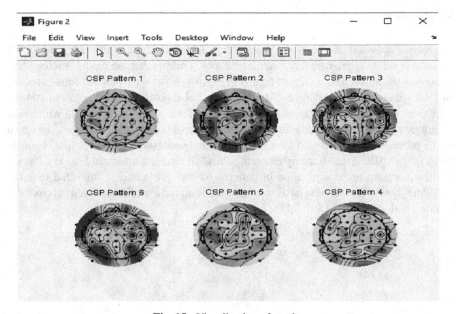

Fig. 15. Visualization of results

6   Conclusion and Future Work

The paper is based on implementation of CSP on EEG data with its steps explanation and procedure on BCI toolkit that can act as base for further research which can even be extended to hardware part by recording EEG data and analysis can be done based on it. The results obtained shows the review which has the true negative, true positive, false negative and false positive taking an average of random five inputs for every factor from the data and then calculating the error rate. Further the Structure of predictive model can be visualized and the liner weights of classifier assigned to different features and the CSP model consist of six set of parameters that can be interpreted as pre channel weights and forms a map as presented in Figs. 14 and 15. This paper can be viewed as point of beginning of the process in BCILAB.

References

1. Vallabhaneni, A., Wang, T.: Brain—computer interface. In: He, B. (ed.) Neural Engineering. Bioelectric Engineering. Springer, Boston (2005). https://doi.org/10.1007/0-306-48610-5_3
2. Chen, X., Wang, Y., Nakanishi, M., Gao, X., Jung, T.-P., Gao, S.: High-speed spelling with a noninvasive brain–computer interface. PNAS 112(44), E6058–E6067 (2015)
3. Ang, K., et al.: A randomized controlled trial of EEG-based motor imagery brain-computer interface robotic rehabilitation for stroke. Clin. EEG Neurosci. 46, 310–320 (2014)
4. Jarosiewicz, B., et al.: Virtual typing by people with tetraplegia using a self-calibrating intracortical brain-computer interface. Sci. Transl. Med. 7, 313ra179 (2015)
5. Kryger, M., et al.: Flight simulation using a brain-computer interface: a pilot, pilot study. Exp. Neurol. 287, 473–478 (2017)
6. Käthner, I., Wriessnegger, S., Müller-Putz, G., Kübler, A., Halder, S.: Effects of mental workload and fatigue on the P300, alpha and theta band power during operation of an ERP (P300) brain–computer interface. Biol. Psychol. 102, 118–129 (2014)
7. Zhang, H., et al.: A brain controlled wheelchair to navigate in familiar environments. IEEE Trans Neural Syst. Rehab. Eng. 18(6), 590–598 (2010)
8. Tangermann, M., et al.: Brain-computer interfaces: beyond medical applications. IEEE Comput. Mag. 45(4), 26–34 (2012)
9. Deore, R.S.: Human computer interface through EEG signals. In: SHOUDHGANGA, pp. 1–174 (2012)
10. Chang, C.-J., Lin, C.-T.: Brain computer interface-based smart living environmental auto-adjustment control system in UPnP home networking. IEEE SJ 8(2), 363–369 (2014)
11. Nicolae, I.-E.: An improved stimuli system for brain-computer interface applications. In: 8th ATEE (2013)
12. Henshaw, J., et al.: Problem solving using hybrid brain-computer interface methods: a review. In: 5th IEEE International Conference on CogInfo, pp. 215–219 (2014)
13. See, A.R., et al.: Hierarchical character selection for brain computer interface spelling system. In: IEEE (2013)
14. Kim, M., et al.: Toward realistic implementation of brain-computer interface for TV channel control. In: IEEE GCCE (2013)
15. Hermanto, B.R., Mengko, T.R.: Brain signal reference concept using cross correlation based for brain computer interface. In: ICICI-BME, pp. 388–390 (2013)
16. Ianez, E.: Multimodal human-machine interface based on a Brain-Computer Interface and an electrooculography interface. In: IEEE BOSTON, pp. 4572–4575 (2011)

17. Ou, C.-Z.: Brain computer interface-based smart environmental control system. In: Eighth International Conference on IIHMSP (2012)
18. Kumar, S.: Brain computer interface for interactive and intelligent image search and retrieval. In: IEEE, pp. 136–140 (2013)
19. George, K.: Design, implementation and evaluation of a brain-computer interface controlled mechanical arm for rehabilitation. In: IEEE (2013)
20. Castillo, J.: Proposal of a brain computer interface to command an autonomous car. In: IEEE, pp. 1–6 (2012)
21. Arora, B., et al.: An intelligent way to play music by brain activity using brain computer interface. In: NGCT (2016)

A Review on Enhancement of Road Safety in Vehicular Ad-hoc Networks

Chiranjit Dutta[1](✉), Ruby Singh[1], and Niraj Singhal[2]

[1] SRM IST NCR Campus, Ghaziabad, Uttar Pradesh, India
cse.chiranjit@gmail.com, rubysinghit@gmail.com
[2] Shobhit Institute of Engineering and Technology, Meerut, Uttar Pradesh, India
drnirajsinghal@gmail.com

Abstract. Vehicular Ad-hoc Network (VANET) aims at transmitting crucial information regarding road and network traffic conditions and other information pertaining to the network on timely basis. It thrives to enhance the present protection standards and efficiency of the network. The fundamental use of vehicular ad-hoc networks is in relation with traffic conditions and other applications related to road safety. This paper describes essential utility of vehicular ad-hoc networks associated with traffic conditions and road safety. Whenever the emergency messages need to be sent to the vehicles, it is of prime importance that vehicles are connected all the times. If the connectivity is not given importance, then the main objective of disseminating the important information to vehicles is not achieved.

Keywords: Information transmission · Road safety · Vehicular Ad-hoc Networks

1 Introduction

Vehicular Ad-hoc Networks (VANETs) fall under category of wireless networks which supports vast number of mobile nodes or vehicles on the road [1]. VANET aims at transmitting crucial information regarding road and network traffic conditions and other crucial information pertaining to the network on timely basis. It thrives to improve the present safety standards and performance of the network. The sorts of conversation in VANETs are automobile to roadside communication and car to vehicle communication. Below figure represents attack scenario and communication in VANET.

As shown in Fig. 1, Suppose vehicle 'X' behaves maliciously in nature and tries to misguide vehicle 'A' by transmitting a message of an accident at a location 'L' ahead somewhere in the network [2]. Henceforth, vehicle 'X' advises vehicle 'A' to take another route or exit the main road. In the same way, vehicle 'X' might not transmit emergency or priority messages sent to it by vehicle 'B' to vehicle 'A'.

VANET architecture utilizes public key signatures. For public key infrastructure, Certificate Authorities (CAs) binds amongst nodes and the majority keys [4]. Privacy and Security are two massive worries for the VANETs designer. Means, if forgotten; it could result in the vulnerable VANETs deployment. If suitable measures are taken, an expansion of attacks can be performed effortlessly, like, identification robbery, message

© Springer Nature Singapore Pte Ltd. 2020
U. Batra et al. (Eds.): REDSET 2019, CCIS 1229, pp. 301–310, 2020.
https://doi.org/10.1007/978-981-15-5827-6_26

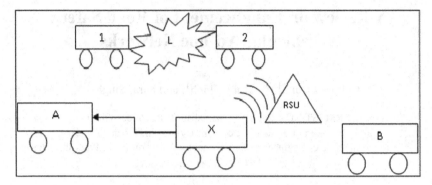

Fig. 1. VANET under attack scenario

content material amendment, fake records era, propagation and so on. Examples of some specific attacks are given below.

i)   If the integrity of message is not definite, then the malicious vehicle can modify the message content, given by other vehicles and affecting the other vehicles behaviour. Accordingly, the malicious car might also obtain several benefits at the same time as preserving its strong point indefinite. Furthermore, the car that to begin with reasons the message may also emerge as accountable for the harm precipitated.
ii) If authentication isn't always delivered, then a malicious automobile can also more-over imitate an emergency car to exceed the rate limits without being regularly going on.
iii) A malicious automobile can also file a false emergency for obtaining improved the usage of situations (like, deserted roads) and if non-repudiation isn't always promoted, it cannot be approved even supposing detected.

The general architecture of Vehicular Ad-hoc Network is depicted in Fig. 2.

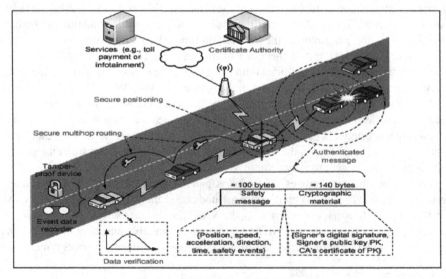

Fig. 2. General architecture of VANET

2 Techniques for Road Safety

A Road safety research strategy includes exceptional techniques ranging from quantitative to qualitative research; it's applicable in some of the sectors like health, delivery, police, welfare, insurance and others.

2.1 Supervision

It includes gathering information on character instances or assembling records from statistics and is a non-stop pastime with constructed in comments mechanisms and a motion element. Supervision produces data that assist in expertise the importance of the trouble and its characteristics, converting trends, populations at chance, stylish danger factors and the effect of interventions. A surveillance programme ought to be operational and sustainable and have to be easy, applicable, sensitive, reliable, nicely timed, and cost-powerful in nature.

2.2 Class Based Study

Class-based studies offer the most reliable data on RTIs and certainly one of kind injuries. However, those studies are costly, time consuming and requires huge property. There are only a few surveys completed in the Region at the populace degree and people researches suggest the massive burden of RTIs in contrast to information from the national reporting structures or medical institution-based research.

2.3 Risk Oriented Review

Risky factors in road safety includes not wearing seat belts, helmets, restraints from toddlers, drinking and driving, speeding, cell phone use, pedestrian behavior etc. However, this statistic isn't routinely to be had inside the countrywide facts systems with every police and the health zone. Hence, a mixture of quantitative and qualitative research wants to be employed to acquire dependable data on focused chance elements. Observational surveys, roadside interviews, focused group discussions, in-intensity interviews and precise strategies help in growing statistics on hazard factors.

3 Background

Highway protection and traffic engineers have commonplace tips that are being evolved for years and draw close now as values [10]. Throughout the time, a particular distance is travelled with the useful resource of the automobile this is inevitable.

3.1 Driver's Reaction Time

Person's response time can be described as the calculation time for responding to impulses. There are variety of factors that affects the response time, like gender, age, non-public tendencies, illness, distraction, tiredness or intoxication degree and so on [11].

3.2 Stopping Distance

The stopping distance is the distance protected with the resource of the auto within the course of the 3 tiers of automobile preventing. For the programs of avenue safety, it's far described because the predicted distance prior to which a cause pressure must find an obstacle for stopping the auto without colliding. The cruelty of accidents at diverse vehicle speeds is depicted in Fig. 3, 4 given below.

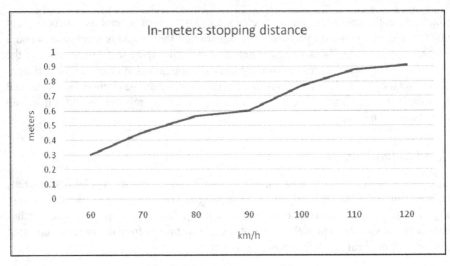

Fig. 3. Distance in wet conditions

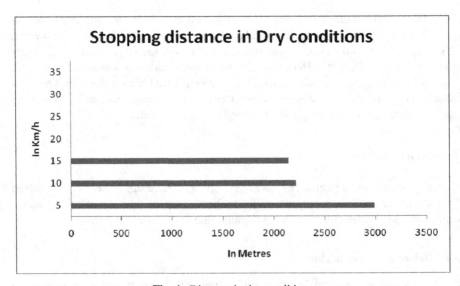

Fig. 4. Distance in dry conditions

3.3 Fatality of National Highway

The information/data has been included on the vicinity of nature of roads/accident locations, number of fatalities for the exact years and motives for commonplace injuries. The compiled records and the details are given to National toll road Indian Authority, DG (Roads) & Chief engineers of PWD of unique UTs/States and every other related for having brief and long-term corrective measures for rectifying the black spots on precedence foundation [22]. Casualties of national highway are given below in Fig. 5.

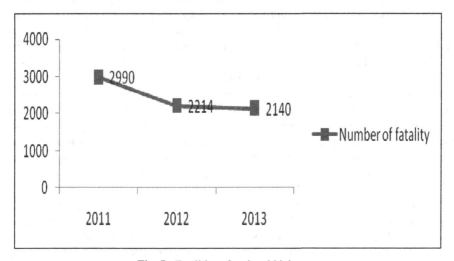

Fig. 5. Fatalities of national highways

4 Related Work

This phase describes the existing work carried out by way of diverse authors inside the area of Vehicular Ad-hoc Networks.

S. E. Carpenter and K. Harfoush [1] proposed a safety relay, a flooding-based messaging system within a geographical address forwarding area. Different sending Zone sizes as far as a few measurements alongside security mindfulness likelihood, which incorporated correspondence and portability execution, have been assessed. The mobility patterns of 250 vehicles have been captured by using simulation of urban mobility (SUMO). The vehicles moved in a two square mile urban downtown situation for more than 30 min. U. Rajput et al. [2] displayed a technique for saving security in VANET. The proposed method has incorporated the qualities of pen name conspire and the gathering mark-based plan. The proposed strategy has utilized proficient and light weight nom de plumes message verification. The parameters like end to end postpone and parcel conveyance proportion have been estimated.

V. Nguyen et al. [3] proposed a fast and efficient broadcast frame adjustment algorithm based on the three-hop neighbour information. This algorithm has improved the efficiency of the system. Authors have used MAC protocol to provide faster broadcast framework. The packet delivery ratio obtained for the proposed work is higher than the existing algorithm. D. Kim et al. [4] proposed a plan to convey Road Side Units in constrained cost. The authors have tested the viability of VANET. Three deployment strategies comprise of (i) static (ii) mobile but not controllable and (iii) fully controllable. H. Zhong et al. [5] described a method for obtaining the privacy & authentication for VANET. The proposed conspire became out to be greater comfy and effective as some distance as correspondence overhead and computational price. The proposed exhibit for the maximum element consists of three segments named as On Board Unit, Road Side Unit and Trusted Authority. K. Suriyapaiboonwattana et al. [6] proposed another versatile convention to upgrade the execution for on street safety ready application in VANET. It has enhanced the communicated storm issue utilizing versatile hold up windows and versatile likelihood to transmit. The performance parameters like number of success rate, collision and delay have been measured and compared with existing protocols.

K. Suriyapaibonwattana and C. Pomavalai [7] proposed a technique that used GPS information to enhance the performance safety and reduced the broadcast storm. Performance parameters like time and cost has been measured. C. T. Barba et al. [8] has designed a framework for information transmission about the traffic conditions that helps the driver to take decision. Intelligent Traffic Lights (ITLs) has been created which transmit data to drivers about traffic and climate conditions. X. Mama et al. [9] proposed another convention for quick conveyance of messages utilizing the control channel for Dedicated Short-Range Communication VANET. Cross-layer message need setting, dynamic collector situated bundle redundancies, most remote transfer with separate based AD timer for multihop communicate, and so on have been utilized for expanding the execution and unwavering quality of the messages. Jaap et al. [10] thought about the execution of various directing conventions like AODV, DSR, FSR and TORA in VANET recreation condition utilizing NS-3 organize test system. A model for generating Vehicular moment pattern has been developed. The comparison has shown the proactive and reactive ad-hoc routing protocol's advantages and disadvantages. C. Sommer et al. [11] examined the need for bidirectional coupling of system recreation and street movement small scale reenactment for assessing IVC protocols. For getting significant outcomes, the determination of a versatility model ought to be done in a productive way. In light of these factors, the creators have proposed a crossover reproduction structure known as Vehicles in Network Simulation.

X. Lin et al. [12] explained a model for security and authentication in VANET. The performance metrics like average message loss and average message late ratio are determined. Singhal D and Srivastava N. [21] added a WSN framework to enhance potato edit creation. By checking and understanding man or woman harvest and its conditions, ranchers can conceivably distinguish the extraordinary manures, water device and one of a kind necessity. The sensor hub, that is little in length and low in control usage, suggests big capacity in this precise condition. A water gadget administration display is displayed to evaluate agrarian parameters utilizing scientific estimations with precise case of potato trim. Utilizing WSN agrarian parameters like profundity of water, soil water pressure and framework restriction and so forth are evaluated for water machine management framework to keep up best Stationary Wavelet Transform for higher product yield and increment the software effectiveness of water machine framework with the aid of 10%. G. Han et al. [22] broke down properties of four ongoing vitality active scope systems via precisely choosing four agent related scope estimates, for example, by correspondence weighted covetous cover, advanced associated scope heuristic, covered target and associated scope; and flexible range set spreads. Through a point by point correlation as far as proportion of dead hubs, lifespan of the device, regular use of vitality and so on. Qualities of fundamental plan thoughts used to upgrade scope and system network of industrial wireless sensor networks are exemplified. Different system parameters have been mimicked in a boisterous situation to acquire the ideal system scope. The most fitting mechanical field for every calculation has likewise been depicted in view of scope properties.

Existing work done by various authors in the domain of Vehicular Ad-hoc Networks is given in Table 1.

Table 1. A glance of existing techniques

Authors	Proposed work	Parameters	Remarks
Cheng et al. [13]	Road safety services in VANET	Vehicle speed, driver's aggressiveness	The appropriateness for the QoS beneficial useful resource of diverse infotainment and avenue protection packages has been stated
Nasrallah et al. [14]	An Intelligent Road Traffic Signaling System (IRTSS) machine based totally on the VANET structure	Average waiting time and average number of vehicles, throughput and end to end delay have been measured	Road traffic has been reduced by using destination information using OBUs
Nithin K. Agarwal et al. [15]	Proposed an estimation of pedestrian protection at intersections thru Simulation and surrogate protection measures	Calculate P fee for all-manner prevent Controlled and all-way prevent managed	Focused on overcoming those barriers through developing fashions that quantify ability interactions between pedestrians and vehicle
S.P. Bhumkar et al. [16]	Proposed an accident avoidance and detection system on the highways	Calculate distances, Reaction time, Judgment and imaginative and prescient capability	Proposed a wise vehicle device for twist of destiny prevention and making the area a far higher and comfy region to stay
D. Sam et al. [17]	VANET based driver alert system	Average packet loss ratio, Average velocity of motors and simulation time	Road accident has been reduced to a great extent along with the cost

(continued)

Table 1. (*continued*)

Authors	Proposed work	Parameters	Remarks
Markowski et al. [18]	Modeling behavior in vehicular and pedestrian site visitors manual	Calculate pedestrian areas, reliability and calibration	Proposed paintings suggest the application of the models and the manner they will be used to ease and enhance format of vehicular and pedestrian regions
David Shinar et al. [19]	Proposed a protection and mobility of prone street clients: Pedestrians, bicyclists, and motorcyclists	Percent change in site visitors fatalities with appreciate to the bicyclists, motorcyclists and pedestrians	This study discusses the take a look at strategies, findings, implications, and hints for extra safety for the vulnerable road users (VRUs)
Alejandro Correa et al. [20]	Presents Automatic Car Parking method thru a Communal Vehicular Positioning Network (VPN) system based totally definitely on the tree based totally completely in tree based looking algorithms	Determine the penetration and accessibility rate.	Developed a smart parking device on pinnacle of a Vehicular Sensor Network that lets in the self maintaining and conventional vehicles to coexist within the automobile parking zone

5 Problem Statement

An essential application of vehicular ad-hoc networks is associated with traffic situations and notable packages related to avenue safety. Whenever the emergency messages need to be sent to the vehicles, it is of high importance that vehicles are related all the instances. If the connectivity isn't given importance, then the primary objective of disseminating the crucial data to vehicles isn't done. In past, many researchers have put forward strategies and algorithms to provide for the better connectivity a number of the cars. The clustering of cars is one approach, which pursuits at retaining connectivity a number of the vehicles. In this, the head of cluster is decided on the basis of centrality and speed. Initially, mean pace is computed the use of the truncated distribution model. In this, the cluster head is chosen on the basis of velocity and centrality. Initially the mean pace is computed the usage of the truncated distribution version. The automobile having the velocity closest to the advocate velocity is considered for the choice of the cluster head. Vehicles which do no longer belong to cluster head neighbor listing ought to fetch for every other cluster.

The centrality is computed using the K-method which defines three centroids consistent with transmission variety.

6 Conclusion

Vehicular Ad-hoc Network is designed for beautifying safety measures on roads & with a view to obtain the identical, numerous works and researches has been carried out. With the advancement in time, several security threats have also evolved in VANET. This paper has discussed the safety and privacy measures of vehicular ad-hoc network and the data. It also discusses the future possibilities in order to avoid security threats in VANETS.

References

1. Carpenter, S.E., et al.: Improving safety in the time constrained vehicular ad-hoc networks with geo-addressing relay. In: International Conference on Vehicular Electronics and Safety (2017)
2. Rajput, U., et al.: A hybrid approach for efficient privacy preserving authentication in VANET. IEEE Access **5**, 12014–12030 (2017)
3. Nguyen, V., et al.: An efficient and fast broadcast frame adjustment algorithm in vehicular ad-hoc networks. IEEE Commun. **21**(7), 1589–1592 (2017)
4. Kim, D., et al.: A new comprehensive RSU installation strategy for cost-efficient VANET deployment. IEEE Trans. Veh. Technol. **66**, 4200–4211 (2017)
5. Zhong, H., et al.: Efficient conditional privacy preserving & authentication scheme to secure service provision in VANET. Tsinghua Sci. Technol. **21**, 620–629 (2016)
6. Suriyapaiboonwattana, K., et al.: An adaptive alert message dissemination protocol for VANET to improve road safety. In: International Conference on Fuzzy Systems (2009)
7. Suriyapaibonwattana, K., et al.: An effective safety alert broadcast algorithm for VANET. In: International Symposium on Communication and Information Technology (2008)
8. Barba, C.T., et al.: Smart city for VANETs using warning messages, traffic statistics & intelligent traffic lights. In: IEEE Intelligent Vehicles Symposium (2012)
9. Ma, X., et al.: Design and analysis of a robust broadcast scheme for vehicular ad hoc networks safety related services. IEEE Trans. Veh. Technol. **61**(1), 46–61 (2012)
10. Jaap, S., et al.: Evaluation of routing protocols for vehicular ad hoc network in typical road traffic scenarios (2005)
11. Sommer, C., et al.: Bidirectionally coupled network & road traffic simulation for improved IVC analysis. IEEE Trans. Mob. Comput. **10**(1), 3–15 (2011)
12. Lin, X., et al.: Security in vehicular ad hoc networks. IEEE Commun. Mag. **46**(4), 88–95 (2008)
13. Cheng, et al.: Infotainment and road safety service support in vehicular networking: from a communication perspective. Mech. Syst. Signal Process. **25**(6), 2020–2038 (2011)
14. Nasrallah, Y.Y., et al.: Distributed time synchronization mechanism for large-scale vehicular networks. In: IEEE Conference on Mobile & Wireless Networking (2016)
15. Agarwal, N.: Estimation of pedestrians safety at intersections using simulation, Dissertation (2013)
16. Bhumkar, S.P., et al.: Accident avoidance & detection on highways. Int. J. Eng. Trends Technol. **3**(2), 247–252 (2012)

17. Sam, D., Raj, V.C.: A time synchronized vehicular ad hoc networks of roadside sensors & vehicles for safe driving. J. Comput. Sci. **10**, 1617 (2014)
18. Markowski, M.J.: Modeling Behavior in Vehicular & Pedestrian Traffic Flow. Ph.D. dissertation, University of Delaware (2008)
19. Shinar, D., et al.: Safety & Mobility of Vulnerable Road Users: Pedestrians, Motorcyclists and Bicyclists (2012)
20. Correa, A., et al.: Autonomous car parking system through a cooperative vehicular positioning network (2017)
21. Singhal, D., Srivastava, N.: Wireless sensor networks in agriculture for potato farming (2017)
22. Han, G., et al.: Analysis of energy-efficient connected target coverage algorithms for industrial WSNs. IEEE Trans. Ind. Inform. **13**(1), 135–143 (2017)

Intelligent Parking Using Wireless Sensor Networks: A Review

Ruby Singh[1]($\boxtimes$), Chiranjit Dutta[1], and Niraj Singhal[2]

[1] SRM IST NCR Campus, Ghaziabad, Uttar Pradesh, India
rubysinghit@gmail.com, cse.chiranjit@gmail.com
[2] Shobhit Institute of Engineering and Technology, Meerut, Uttar Pradesh, India
drnirajsinghal@gmail.com

Abstract. In current years, because of financial growth, number of cars on the roads has increased. It's not an easy task to find parking space today. Parking vehicle problem causes waste of time and fuel consumption. Intelligent Parking is the solution to this problem where the driver gets an alert about unoccupied parking which saves the drivers time and increases the efficiency of fuel for automobiles. With the enhancement in modernization, parking has also end up a completely serious difficulty. This paper describes the various Parking techniques with the usage of sensor networks. When so ever a vehicle is placed into a parking slot, its information will be shared with the parking management sensors. Applications of wi-fi sensor networks have made the arena a smooth place to live.

Keywords: Intelligent Parking · Wireless Sensor Networks

1 Introduction

I-parking is an intelligent and secure parking space management solution with latest technique designed to offer exactness and protection in vehicle access control and efficient profitability. Deficiency and lopsidedness of parking spots have turned out to be not kidding issues as of late. Drivers may pick adjacent unlawful territory for stopping when accessible parking spots are full scale of sight. To relieve issues, for example, illicit stopping, a constant parking spot checking and directing framework, numerous methods are proposed [1].

Through increasing car population, ordinary volumes of people-owned vehicles are increasing each day. But the amount of parking spaces in urban locality does not have the same number of cars to satisfy the parking area demands and to minimize illegal parking. Lack of parking spots could motive some issues, as an example, the amazingly moderate speed even as seeking parking spot, scrambling for streets with bikes, preventing by the way in risky element, or using U-flip unlawfully. These practices could now not just spoil the security and direction of transportation but in addition make commotion and dissipate property. It is anything but difficult to look at that a few cars want to seek parking spot impartial from anybody else at the same time as roadside parking spots are inadequate [2].

© Springer Nature Singapore Pte Ltd. 2020
U. Batra et al. (Eds.): REDSET 2019, CCIS 1229, pp. 311–319, 2020.
https://doi.org/10.1007/978-981-15-5827-6_27

The condition brings out self-assertive preventing, and it is likewise the number one purpose of illegal preventing. Recently, stopping issue has turned into individuals' badgering. The moderate paced city arranging has expanded the issue considerably more. The sweep for the parking vicinity is a dreary approach which impacts the budgetary sports' capability, and further the social institutions and value. Framework establishments cannot deliver revived information of the halting places of work on the net due to the fact the ceasing workplaces do now not arrange with the institutions. Certain massive automobiles aren't organized to suit into the routinely to be had parking regions. In this way there is a want for a machine; which can don't forget each single related datum, for locating the ceasing starting [3] (Fig. 1).

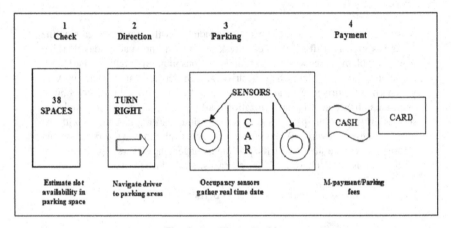

Fig. 1. Intelligent Parking

Parking guidance system comprises of four different methods named as: Traditional Blind Search, Parking Information Assistant, Reservation based Parking System and Centrally Assisted Parking system.

1.1 Traditional Blind Search (TBS)

In this method, driver searches blindly for the loose space in parking region. If he reveals the free area, then he parks the vehicle. This method was basically used in the small parking regions [6].

1.2 Parking Information Assistant (PIA)

In this technique, the records approximately parking area availability suggests on the electronic display screen like on a huge LED display screen. The drivers park their automobile primarily based on this information. But this approach results in confusion to the drivers due to the fact the message displayed at the display takes a while to replace the facts.

1.3 Reservation Based Parking System (RPS)

In this approach, users reserve the parking area with the help of net. The management supplied an ID through which the drivers need to login thru smart phone calls or message and pay via internet banking and thus reserve the distance for his or her automobiles. But this system has a drawback that after any slot has been reserved; no person can use that space although it is unoccupied.

1.4 Centrally Assisted Parking Space (CPS)

In this technique, a centralized server is used to control and takes the selection related to parking. The drivers ship a parking request to the server alongside their vacation spot.

2 Existing Parking Area Monitoring Strategies

All of present-day parking location monitored strategies are constrained to parking masses and quality supported with the resource of sensors. For example, wise parking lot makes use of Wi-Fi sensor network, Zigbee, pressure sensors. They use sensors to replace database to discover if the gap is empty. Another example is Eco-Community plan superior by manner of numerous colleges. In Eco-Community, sensors are deployed in parking regions. All adjustments in sensed facts are up to date to a database, and clients can then get the current recognition of parking areas. Practically, a few existing apps for clever telephones offer actual time repute of some specific parking lot. However, they do not offer fame of roadside parking. The foremost aim of our device is to offer actual-time repute of roadside parking via existing tool on the roads [4, 5] (Fig. 2).

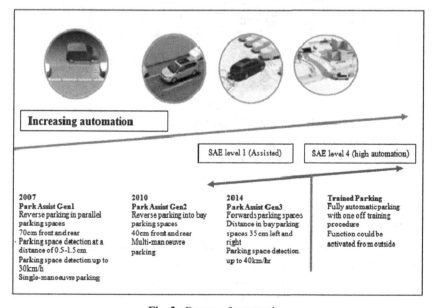

Fig. 2. Degree of automation

There are different techniques based for the degree of automation and effectiveness in intelligent parking which are as follows:

2.1 Expert Based Systems

These professional primarily based technologies can clear up the trouble associated with allotted and hard website online vacationer's environment. These expert systems or agent primarily based truly generation has useful competencies such as autonomy, social functionality, reactivity, proactively and adaptability that may be used for cracking issues that have relatively dynamic behaviours [6, 7].

2.2 Inductive Detector Lop (IDL)

It is an intrusive method, which is used for detecting single automobile. At the doorway of parking place, a coil is positioned so that it will generate a sign of frequency tiers from 10–50 Hz while the automobile passing over it. When the auto pressed the coil its inductance numerous which in flip trade the generated frequency. When the price of frequency is more than the brink frequency a signal is sent as a way to suggests that a automobile is handed. The principle of inductive detector loop is shown in parent below (Fig. 3):

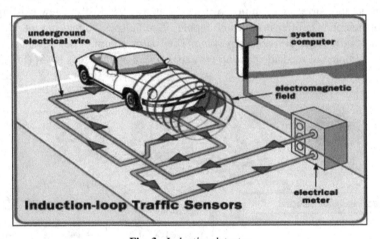

Fig. 3. Inductive detector

2.3 Microwave Radar

In microwave radar system, electromagnetic waves are used having frequency range lies between 1–30 GHz. RADAR will send the radio waves continuously, if any car occurs in its path then the signal will reflect back and thus by knowing the velocity and time of transmitting and receiving signal, we can calculate the distance of a car. It is best in case of rainy seasons because it is not affected as other systems get affected [9].

2.4 Structures Based on Sensors

A variety of low fee sensor nodes take part to shape a Wireless Sensor Network. For processing and transmission of facts, practical elements make the sensors to be installation quick and hassle free. They have vibrant destiny on the grounds that WSNs are without problems hooked up in the everyday surroundings and they offer the statistics for positioning and surveillance. There are terrible components associated with the video sensors. The first includes high price of video sensors. Second is that, sensors produce large facts at times; transmission of which thru the Wireless Network is tensed [4] (Fig. 4).

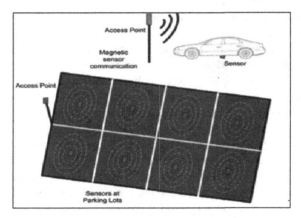

Fig. 4. Magnetic sensor based system

2.5 Global Positioning System Based Structures

Records about the location and availability of nearby parking near the holiday spot will be sent to drivers using the modern global positioning system using vehicle navigation. The data of present-day nation of the parking facility are provided. That's because they couldn't provide assurance of a parking zone whilst the purpose force gets to the capability. Cerreo had a yearlong take a look at on avenue parking, which targeted on distinct problems involved with on avenue parking mainly insurance, planning, manipulate and operations. Various techniques and awesome towns have been used for demonstrating those troubles. It also highlighted one-of-a-type challenges of on-road parking collectively with peer-to-peer alternate and garage of parking facts [19].

3 Related Work

This section describes the existing work done by number of authors in the field of Wireless Sensor Networks.

Z. Wei et al. [1] built up a multi-charging framework consolidating the commonsense battery charging highlight and plan a scholarly charging administration framework to augment the interests of both the clients and the charging administrator. Initially, for ensuring the QoS for the users, control system has been implemented. Secondly, the charging problem has been discussed. At that point, a versatile utility arranged booking calculation has been to advance the aggregate utility for the charging administrator that can firmly accomplish low assignment declining likelihood and high benefit.

S. Mama et al. [2] proposed a programmed stopping framework in light of stopping scene acknowledgment so as to tackle the stopping issues, for example, stopping scene acknowledgment strategies are less shrewd, vehicle control has a low level of mechanization and the examination extension is restricted to conventional fuel vehicles. To expand the use of parking spots and stopping accommodation, machine vision and example acknowledgment strategies have been utilized to cleverly recognize a vertical stopping circumstance, design a sensible stopping way, build up a way following control procedure to enhance the vehicle control robotization, and investigate a profoundly smart programmed stopping innovation guide. The parking accuracy has been improved by designing the automatic parking system.

Mahmud et al. [1] described various intelligent car parking services that are used for parking guidance, parking management and also become eco friendly. Different techniques like Fuzzy logic, neural network approaches, GPS Vehicular, Vision based system have been discussed for wireless sensor network system.

S. N. Shinde and S. S. Chorage [2] proposed an intelligent system for car parking. The system includes sensor nodes that gather the positioning and track the car's path. Camera based system is used to capturing the image of the car. Image processing and FPGA systems are combined to recognize the position and orientation of the vehicle. T. Sirithinaphong and K. Chamnongthai [3] proposed a system using neural network for automatic car parking system using car license plate pattern. In this system, the car license area is determined on the basis of color, shape and the area of the plate. The performance parameters like extraction rate and recognition rate have been determined. Recognition rate was 96% whereas extraction rate was 92%.

Idris et al. [9] described different smart parking system along with their technologies. Smart parking is used to solve the site visitors congestion problem that become more often than not occurs within the town regions. The main part of the smart parking technologies mostly based on sensor system. In smart parking machine cars on the street can take a look at the supply of the parking area and reserve their region inside the parking zone. By using I parking privacy of the motive force and security as well included by the usage of WSN architecture. Proposed method proved that the parking spot finding time was fast. Ranjini, R. and D. Manivannan [10] presented commonly used parking techniques and recognize the problems related to their methodologies. The methods have been studied based on scalability, complexity, cost and techniques used.

J. Owens and A. Hunter [11] presented a method to solve the problem of automatically recognize and classify the object in motion stage. Neural network has been used as a classifier. H. Ichihashi [20] proposed a camera based technology to know the availability of free space in the parking zone. A scheme known as Park Lot used as a classifier along with fuzzy C mean system. For optimization particle swarm optimization technique has been used. The results obtained by applying optimization and classification techniques have been improved. E. Cavalcanti Neto et al. [12] described a framework for distinguishing and understand automobile plates to govern automobile access utilising Brazillian format. In this framework just the enrolled clients have the consent to enter their vehicle in the stopping place. For distinguishing the number and separating the characters computerized picture preparing has been utilized.

S. Funck [13] proposed a scheme to know the unoccupied space of the car parking area based on single image camera. CCTV cameras have been used for surveillance that will automatically detect the occupancy of the car parking area. As no additional outdoor equipment required this scheme become more cost effective. For recognize car image Principle component analysis (PCA) method has been used. This method is used to compress the available data. Benenson et al. [14] presented PARKAGENT model used for parking in the city. PARKAGENT worked like a traditional parking model, in which the behaviour of each driver has been simulated in the complex condition of parking space. Thompson et al. presented a model used for knowing the search behaviour of driver. Search process was completed by using analytical procedure within the modelling framework. Parameters like size of car queue and departure rate have been calculated.

L. Yang et al. [16] proposed a multi agent scheme known as "Active Parking Guidance Information System". This scheme supports both stationary and mobile agents, automatically search for parking space, parking park and parking route guidance without the involvement of driver. Route negotiation was done by using GPS technique. K. Jiang [17] proposed a parallel parking scheme used for non-holonomic automobiles using by microprocessor alongside ultrasonic sensors. Ultrasonic sensors were used for scanning and finding the automobile. The scanned records changed into then processed to perceive the placement of the car inside the parking location.

Park et al. [18] proposed a recommendation scheme based on map that reflects driver's preference modelled by Bayesian network (BN). The proposed method gathers statistics like climate, position, time & request from customers from android smartphone and provides suitable carrier via showing the statistics on map. Vianna et al. [19] proposed a system based on telematics resources. In this system a logic architecture has been designed for processing and sending the collected information. Experiments have been performed on the data collected from the medium size Brazillian town. The results obtained proved that the traffic congestion has been lower along with air pollution.

Existing work done by various authors in the area of Vehicular Ad-hoc Networks is given in Table 1.

Table 1. Comparison of different techniques

Authors	Techniques used	Characteristics	Service provided
L. Yang et al. [16]	Agent based	Dynamic dissemination and congested activity condition	Parking guide, path agitation
T. H. S. Li et al. [15]	Fuzzy based	System is intelligent like human being	Intelligent parking strategies e.g. individual and parallel parking

(*continued*)

Table 1. (*continued*)

Authors	Techniques used	Characteristics	Service provided
Ranjini, R et al. [9]	Wireless sensor based	Implementation, maintenance is inexpensive, Consume less power	Detecting and monitoring the car parking
S. N. Shinde et al. [2]	GPS based	Constant area-based data and direction towards goal	Give records approximately the territory and accessibility of parking facility
T. Sirithinaphong et al. [3]	Vehicular conversation	Provide parking statistics about the cellular cars	Antitheft protection, regular stopping course benefit and so on
S. F. Lin et al. [8]	Vision based	Good for automobile looking in huge parking slots	Parking slot inhabitance identity, parking spot region, stopping price accumulating and so on

4 Problem Statement

Intelligent Parking is an area where the concepts of wireless sensor network can be utilized. It is assumed that every vehicle contains sensors which not only indicates the coordinates of the vehicle but also used to communicate with other vehicles or Road Side Units (RSU). When so ever a vehicle is placed into a parking slot, its information will be shared with the parking management sensors. If the parking management is made 100% manual, then there would be no use of wireless sensor network for I Parking. In such case the parking management should be automated.

5 Conclusion

The proposed research scenario addresses Intelligent Parking's various possibilities and their enhancement as well as a new view of Intelligent Parking in Wireless Sensor Network (WSN) phrases. It is also one of the maximum attentions gaining areas in this world. Looking at this in phrases of Wi-Fi sensor community not handiest makes it interesting but also enhances the possibilities of research on this vicinity.

References

1. Mahmud, S.A., et al.: A survey of intelligent car parking system. J. Appl. Res. Technol. **11**, 714–726 (2013)

2. Shinde, S.N., et al.: Intelligent car parking system. In: International Conference on Inventive Computation Technology, Coimbatore (2016)
3. Sirithinaphong, T., et al.: The recognition of car license plate for automatic parking system. In: Fifth International Symposium, vol. 1, pp. 455–457 (1999)
4. Tacconi, D., et al.: Using wireless sensor networks to support intelligent transportation systems. Ad Hoc Netw. **8**(5), 462–473 (2010)
5. Geng, Y., et al.: New smart parking system based on resource allocation & reservations. IEEE Trans. Intell. Transp. Syst. **14**(3), 1129–1139 (2013)
6. Wang, H., et al.: A reservation based smart parking system. In: Conference on Computer Communication Workshops, Shanghai, pp. 690–695 (2011)
7. Lee, S., et al.: Intelligent parking lot application using WSNs. In: International Symposium on Collaborative Technologies & Systems, Irvine, CA, pp. 48–57 (2008)
8. Lin, S.F., et al.: A vision-based parking lot management system. In: IEEE International Conference on Systems, Man and Cybernetics, Taipei (2006)
9. Idris, M.Y.I., et al.: Smart parking system using image processing techniques. J. Inf. Technol. **8**(2), 114–127 (2009)
10. Ranjini, R., et al.: A comparative review on car parking technologies. Int. J. Eng. Technol. **5**, 975–1024 (2013)
11. Owens, J., et al.: Application of the self-organising map to trajectory classification. In: International Workshop on Visual Surveillance, Dublin, pp. 77–83 (2000)
12. Cavalcanti Neto, E., et al.: Development of control parking access using techniques digital image processing and applied computational intelligence. IEEE Lat. Am. Trans. **13**(1), 272–276 (2015)
13. Funck, S., et al.: Determining car-park occupancy from single images. In: IEEE Intelligent Vehicles Symposium, pp. 325–328 (2004)
14. Benenson, I., et al.: PARKAGENT: an agent-based model of parking in the city. Comput. Environ. Urban Syst. **32**, 431–439 (2008)
15. Thompson, R.G., et al.: A parking search model. Transp. Res. Policy Pract. **32**, 159–170 (1998)
16. Yang, L., et al.: Intelligent parking negotiation based on agent technology. In: International Conference on Information Engineering, Taiyuan, Shanxi, pp. 265–268 (2009)
17. Jiang, K.: A sensor guided parallel parking system for non-holonomic vehicles. In: IEEE Intelligent Transportation Systems, Dearborn, MI (2000)
18. Park, M.-H., Hong, J.-H., Cho, S.-B.: Location-based recommendation system using Bayesian user's preference model in mobile devices. In: Indulska, J., Ma, J., Yang, L.T., Ungerer, T., Cao, J. (eds.) UIC 2007. LNCS, vol. 4611, pp. 1130–1139. Springer, Heidelberg (2007). https://doi.org/10.1007/978-3-540-73549-6_110
19. Vianna, M.M., et al.: Intelligent transportation systems and parking management: implementation potential in a Brazilian city. Cities **21**(2), 137–148 (2004)
20. Ichihashi, H., et al.: Vacant parking space detector for outdoor parking lot by using surveillance camera. In: Conference on Fuzzy Systems, Jeju Island (2009)

Review on Computational Techniques to Identify Drug Targets from Whole Proteome of Fungi and Bacteria

Reena Gupta and Chandra Shekhar Rai[✉]

University School of Information, Communication and Technology,
Guru Gobind Singh Indraprastha University, New Delhi, India
{reena,csrai}@ipu.ac.in

Abstract. Despite worldwide efforts to control bacterial and fungal diseases, there are still a large number of human fatalities due to these pathogens. Pathogens develop resistance with descend of time to the available drugs which further heightens the adversity of insufficient remedial resources. This requires exploration of novel drug targets, which will be helpful in uprooting bacterial and fungal pathogens in future. Conventional methods of designing drugs and vaccines are time taking, require intensive man power and are less in number. Moreover, development of resistance to existing drugs is a serious concern. So, there is a need for efficient and better therapeutics which are fast, reliable and accurate. Hence, improvements in complete genome sequencing combined with computational biology and cheminformatics suggest an alluring alternative technique to screen drug targets. In the present study, we have emphasized on the computational techniques to screen drug candidates from whole proteome of fungi and bacteria. Further, we have compared three target identification tools designed for identifying drug targets from proteome or genome of fungal and bacterial pathogens through subtractive or comparative channel analysis. Promisingly, this comprehensive review analyzes the tools and their protocols to identify drug targets. This will surely help biologists to decide which available tool is useful for identifying drug targets from bacteria and fungi.

Keywords: Drug targets · Target identification · DEG · BLAST · Comparative genomics analysis · TiD

1 Introduction

Revealing the enigma of life by means of computational techniques is really alluring. The paradigm transformations in biology, caused by the high throughput genomic techniques, during the past few decades have resulted in taking most of biology away from the laboratory bench and granted the amalgamation with other scientific disciplines, especially computing. This amazing blend between biology and computer science has given birth to a new discipline called bioinformatics. The outcome is the expansion of biological research in depth and breadth [1]. Biological data is a mammoth library of

© Springer Nature Singapore Pte Ltd. 2020
U. Batra et al. (Eds.): REDSET 2019, CCIS 1229, pp. 320–327, 2020.
https://doi.org/10.1007/978-981-15-5827-6_28

nucleic acid and protein sequences. Since the beginning of 1990s, many laboratories are examining the full gene sets of various species such as bacteria, yeast, fungi, mice and humans. For detecting similarities and differences between different gene sequences, thousands of nucleotides and amino acid sequences have to be analysed and examined. One of the important exercises of bioinformatics is to examine and analyse these colossal store houses or libraries of biological data set to attain crucial information for the research and expansion of the advanced product.

The primary aim of the bioinformatics is to unveil the information hidden in the bio sequences. The high throughput genome sequencing has resulted in accumulation of sequence data in the biological databases. From this raw data, biologically meaningful information has to be derived. Various computational methods like data mining, pattern recognition, machine learning algorithms, soft computing and visualization are applied on the biological data to bring out the useful information [2].

In addition to administering theoretical knowledge of background and present-day practical tools and techniques to determine and analyse nucleotides, proteins and DNA, bioinformatics helps in analysis of sequence homology and designing drugs. Traditional methods of designing drugs and vaccines are time consuming, require intensive man power and limited in number. Moreover, development of resistance to existing drugs is a serious concern. So, there is a need for efficient and better therapeutics which are fast, reliable and accurate. Therefore, improvements in complete genome sequencing combined with computational biology and cheminformatics suggest an alluring alternative technique to screen drug targets [3]. Previous studies found putative drug targets for bacteria and fungi using computational comparative genomics approach, subtractive genomic approach and online databases and tools [4]. Further, the work embodied in this article pertains to compare three different target identification tools which find putative drug targets for bacteria and fungi proteome using subtractive or genomic analysis technique in an online and offline mode.

2   Need of Computational Technique for Screening of Drug Targets

The procedure of designing and discovering drugs, including target identification, lead identification, target validation, lead optimization and launch of new drugs to the public is called drug discovery. Drug discovery as a whole is a 'hot topic' in bioinformatics. This process is very crucial as it includes analysis of the sources of diseases and discovering methods to tackle them. A flowchart of the stages used in discovery of drugs is shown in Fig. 1.

The cost of development during discovery of drug, from theoretical conceptualization into clinical trials, roughly varies from 0.8 to 1.0 billion USD [5] and it takes approximately 14 years in the whole process [6]. Such a lengthy, costly, risky and time-consuming development course has culminated in lofty attenuation rates with less success attributed to unfavourable effects on humans (10%), poor pharmacokinetics (39%), animal toxicity (11%), inadequacy (30%) and various commercial and miscellaneous aspects. Drug discovery process allowed colossal repositories of compounds to be identified and incorporated in a faster way [7, 8].

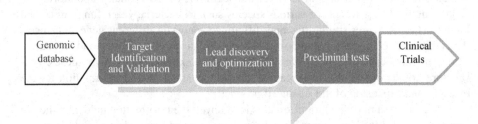

Fig. 1. Stages of in silico drug discovery methods (courtesy Myers and Baker [6])

Despite a large amount of money being invested in process of development of new drug in the previous decades, due to the low accuracy and high error rate in drug discovery process, the outcome is not commensurate to the investment [9]. Consequently, many techniques have been designed to lower the cost, shorten the cycle of research and increase the success rate for discovery of drug targets. The expense of development of drug targets could lessen by up to 50% by the usage of computational techniques [9].

Target identification is the process of identifying the direct molecular target in the active site of protein or sequence of nucleic acid. Rational drug design is a strategy of searching novel drugs based on biological target knowledge [10]. In contrast to traditional methods of drug discovery, it modulates a specific drug target that may have therapeutic properties. Designing drugs with this approach helps in lowering the frequency of disease [9]. Practically, we can simulate every feature of drug discovery process and development using *in silico* techniques. Genomics has established better and efficient methods of screening genes, which further develop new strategies for designing drugs and developing therapeutic measures to curb human diseases. Moreover, novel potential drug targets can be identified using comparative or subtractive genomics approach [11, 12].

3   Cases Studies of In-Silico Screening of Drug Targets

Shanmugham and Pan used computer based technique to screen drug targets of *M. abcessus* infections [13] by aiming at qualitative characterization of putative drug targets in three phases. In the first phase, they performed choke point evaluation, pathway evaluation, virulence factor evaluation, resistance genes analysis and protein network evaluation. The resultant gene set was filtered in second phase to identify putative drug targets through subtractive channel analysis. The outcome was the gene set necessary for the growth and survival of the pathogen, which was further non homologous to human and gut flora. This output of gene set was prioritized using cellular localization, functional annotation and druggability analysis in third phase. Hence, resultant candidates facilitated the screening of drug targets against pathogenic bacteria using novel hierarchical *in silico* approach.

Gupta *et al.* identified promising drug targets for *Leptospira* using combined approach of comparative and subtractive genomics [14]. They performed homology search using TiD, target identification tool [15]. In addition to this, they performed comparative analysis to find non-homologous genes which are necessary for broad spectrum anti-bacterial drug targets. The resultant set of genes was prioritized using protein-protein interaction network, virulence analysis, choke point analysis and genome scale metabolic network reconstruction pathway analysis. Hence, they proposed that the outcome gene set could act as possible broad-spectrum drug target against *Leptospira* using computational approach.

Rahman *et al.* found putative drug targets for *Bacillus anthracis* using *in silico* approach [16] by identifying non homology genes for human database and performing metabolic pathway analysis on necessary gene set. They predicted membrane bound proteins of the resultant gene set using PSORTb, ngLOC and CELLO for sub cellular localization analysis. Hence, they detected drug targets against *Bacillus anthracis* using *in silico* approach.

Dutta *et al.* identified putative therapeutic targets for human pathogen Helicobacter pylori using *in silico* approach [17]. Using subtractive genomics approach, they found out the gene set absent in host but necessary for the growth and survival of the pathogen. Hence, they investigated the proteins for detecting potential drug and vaccine candidates in the human pathogen using computational techniques.

Katara *et al.* searched putative target sites of drugs using *in silico* approach against *V. cholerae* [18]. They performed subtractive approach to detect possible drug targets. They mined the gene set by performing blastn with DEG (Database of Essential Genes) to homologous proteins and then, identifying non homologous proteins with human host followed by virulence factor analysis. Gene Ontology analysis was done using Blast2Go to detect the role of resultant proteins in metabolic pathways. Hence, screening of potential drug targets was achieved using *in silico* approach.

4 Comparison of T-iDT and TarFisDock with TiD

Tool for identification of drug target, T-iDT, is a tool that identifies drug targets using comparative genomics. It searches essential genes from a bacterial protein set through DEG. Further, it removes homologous proteins by screening against human protein dataset to identify putative drug targets [19].

TiD is based on the similar guidelines of T-iDT. However, TiD implements an exhaustive target mining principle as shown in Fig. 2. It surely has compelling advantage over T-iDT. The first step of TiD is to exclude paralogous proteins from the gene database using CD-HIT suite and then, the gene set was used for identification of essential genes with either DEG or CEG (Cluster of Essential Genes) dataset or both DEG and CEG based on comparative evaluation.

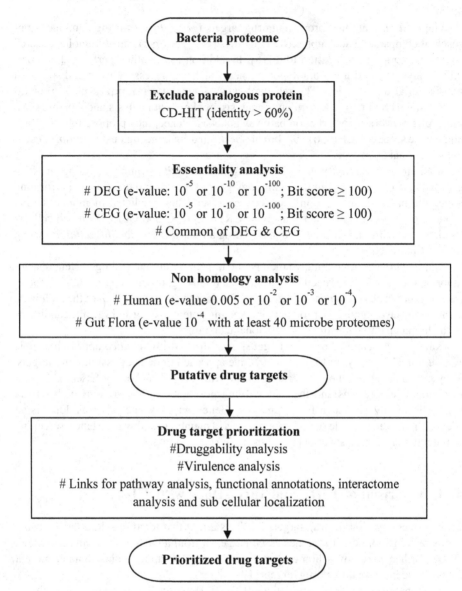

Fig. 2. Flowchart of TiD drug target mining tool (courtesy Gupta *et al.* [8])

Further, TiD incorporates protein datasets for Human, Guinea Pig, Laboratory Mice, Cow, Domestic Dog and Rhesus Macaque in Non-Homology Analysis Tab. Hence, we can analyse drug targets of pathogenic fungi and bacteria against all of these host creatures. TiD also allows the user to screen non-homology evaluation against gut flora to exclude the interference of drug targets with useful gut microbes. The resultant drug targets can be characterized as novel, virulent and existing targets with the help of TiD software. In addition to this, user can prioritize drug targets with the online links provided with TiD. A Single Click Recommended Drug Target Identification tab is also incorporated to assist a beginner in order to screen drug targets from fungal and bacterial proteome.

On the other hand, another tool, Target Fishing Docking (TarFisDock) of Potential Drug Target Database (PDTD) addresses putative drug targets for a known drug, natural product, drug candidate or new synthetic compound through a reverse docking technique [20]. TarFisDock cannot identify potential drug targets from complete proteome of a pathogenic fungi and bacteria but could aid in getting insight mechanism of reaction of a drug or synthetic compound. Therefore, TiD has compelling advantage over TarFisDock and T-iDT towards detection of possible drug targets for fungal and bacterial proteome and their computerized screening using online databases.

The comparison of three tools/softwares have demonstrated that TiD can not only detect possible drug targets, but it can also verify drug targets already suggested in literature. The approach of using CEG with DEG for detecting essential genes is implemented first time in TiD. TiD can execute target identification based on subtractive genomic analysis and prioritization on a single click. The automated Single Click Recommended Target Mining Tab in TiD is quick and authentic as it excludes possible human errors which occur due to manual examination during subtractive/comparative genomic evaluation.

TiD is potential to identify drug targets and characterized them as novel, existing and virulent without any manual error in a single platform. TiD screens minimum essential proteins in contrary to complete proteome for online downstream target prioritization applications or softwares after experimental validation. Links to online tools are incorporated in TiD for pathway evaluation, subcellular localization, interactome evaluation and functional annotations. Therefore, TiD would be an accessible tool for biologist for identifying drug targets against fungal and bacterial pathogens.

Moreover, the present-day target mining principles executed in TiD makes it an effective tool for discovering drugs from whole proteome of fungal and bacterial pathogens. Hence, we recommend that TiD is a potential tool to detect novel drug targets and to verify gene set recommended in the past as drug targets for fungi and bacteria.

5   Conclusion

In order to minimise the monetary input and time in the discovery of unique drug target molecules, all existing theoretical and experimental intelligence of the drug discovery process is being employed for designing potential leads in rational drug design. The first process of rational drug design is target identification. Moreover, computational approach will reduce time and cost for identifying drug targets from the whole proteome of fungi and bacteria. TiD employs subtractive channel analysis protocol by blending experimentally verified knowledge, essential protein and clusters of proteins of bacteria and fungi, host proteins, gut flora proteins, druggable targets, virulence factors and comparative proteomic or genomic evaluation program viz. BLAST + from NCBI and CD-HIT suite to screen possible drug targets from fungal and bacterial proteome. The compelling overlap is found in targets detected by TiD and literature which supports the applicability of the tool in excavating drug targets from fungal and bacterial proteome.

Hence, we recommend TiD for identifying drug targets for pathogens of fungi and bacteria.

References

1. Luscombe, N.M., Greenbaum, D., Gerstein, M.: What is bioinformatics? An introduction and overview. Yearb. Med. Inform. **10**, 83–99 (2001)
2. Yeh, I., Hanekamp, T., Tsoka, S., Karp, P.D., Altman, R.B.: Computational analysis of Plasmodium falciparum metabolism: organizing genomic information to facilitate drug discovery. Genome Res. **14**, 917–924 (2004). https://doi.org/10.1101/gr.2050304
3. Butt, A.M., Nasrullah, I., Tahir, S., Tong, Y.: Comparative genomics analysis of mycobacterium ulcerans for the identification of putative essential genes and therapeutic candidates. PLoS ONE **7**, e43080 (2012). https://doi.org/10.1371/journal.pone.0043080
4. Ou-Yang, S.-S., Lu, J.-Y., Kong, X.-Q., Liang, Z.-J., Luo, C., Jiang, H.: Computational drug discovery. Acta Pharmacol. Sin. **33**, 1131–1140 (2012). https://doi.org/10.1038/aps.2012.109
5. Moses, H., Dorsey, E.R., Matheson, D.H.M., Thier, S.O.: Financial anatomy of biomedical research. JAMA **294**, 1333–1342 (2005). https://doi.org/10.1001/jama.294.11.1333
6. Myers, S., Baker, A.: Drug discovery–an operating model for a new era. Nat. Biotechnol. **19**, 727–730 (2001). https://doi.org/10.1038/90765
7. Lobanov, V.: Using artificial neural networks to drive virtual screening of combinatorial libraries. Drug Discov. Today BIOSILICO **2**, 149–156 (2004). https://doi.org/10.1016/S1741-8364(04)02402-3
8. Lahana, R.: How many leads from HTS? Drug Discov. Today. **4**, 447–448 (1999). https://doi.org/10.1016/s1359-6446(99)01393-8
9. Shekhar, C.: In silico pharmacology: computer-aided methods could transform drug development. Chem. Biol. **15**, 413–414 (2008). https://doi.org/10.1016/j.chembiol.2008.05.001
10. Mavromoustakos, T., et al.: Strategies in the rational drug design. Curr. Med. Chem. **18**, 2517–2530 (2011). https://doi.org/10.2174/092986711795933731
11. Abadio, A.K.R., Kioshima, E.S., Teixeira, M.M., Martins, N.F., Maigret, B., Felipe, M.S.S.: Comparative genomics allowed the identification of drug targets against human fungal pathogens. BMC Genom. **12**, 75 (2011). https://doi.org/10.1186/1471-2164-12-75
12. Wei, W., Ning, L.-W., Ye, Y.-N., Guo, F.-B.: Geptop: a gene essentiality prediction tool for sequenced bacterial genomes based on orthology and phylogeny. PLoS ONE **8**, e72343 (2013). https://doi.org/10.1371/journal.pone.0072343
13. Shanmugham, B., Pan, A.: Identification and characterization of potential therapeutic candidates in emerging human pathogen mycobacterium abscessus: a novel hierarchical in silico approach. PLoS ONE **8**, e59126 (2013). https://doi.org/10.1371/journal.pone.0059126
14. Gupta, R., Verma, R., Pradhan, D., Jain, A.K., Umamaheswari, A., Rai, C.S.: An in silico approach towards identification of novel drug targets in pathogenic species of Leptospira. PLoS ONE **14**, e0221446 (2019). https://doi.org/10.1371/journal.pone.0221446
15. Gupta, R., Pradhan, D., Jain, A.K., Rai, C.S.: TiD: standalone software for mining putative drug targets from bacterial proteome. Genomics **109**, 51–57 (2017). https://doi.org/10.1016/j.ygeno.2016.11.005
16. Rahman, A., et al.: Identification of potential drug targets by subtractive genome analysis of Bacillus anthracis A0248: an in silico approach. Comput. Biol. Chem. **52**, 66–72 (2014). https://doi.org/10.1016/j.compbiolchem.2014.09.005
17. Dutta, A., Singh, S.K., Ghosh, P., Mukherjee, R., Mitter, S., Bandyopadhyay, D.: In silico identification of potential therapeutic targets in the human pathogen Helicobacter pylori. Silico Biol. **6**, 43–47 (2006)

18. Katara, P., Grover, A., Kuntal, H., Sharma, V.: In silico prediction of drug targets in Vibrio cholerae. Protoplasma **248**, 799–804 (2011). https://doi.org/10.1007/s00709-010-0255-0
19. Pubmeddev, S.N., et al.: T-iDT : tool for identification of drug target in bacteria and validation by Mycobacterium tuberculosis. - PubMed – NCBI. https://www.ncbi.nlm.nih.gov/pubmed/17518759. Accessed 29 Sept 2019
20. Gao, Z., et al.: PDTD: a web-accessible protein database for drug target identification. BMC Bioinform. **9**, 104 (2008). https://doi.org/10.1186/1471-2105-9-104

Innovative Smart Hoisting Assistance

Anjali Garg[✉], Vibhu Mehta, Shubham Soni, Ritika Sharma,
Himanshu Goyal, and Divyam Sachdeva

The NorthCap University, Gurgaon, India
anjaligarg@ncuindia.edu

Abstract. Mechanical Jacks that are available in the market presently are often troubling and injurious under bad weather conditions. These jacks require the user to stay in a sustained bent over or squatting position to successfully place and operate the jack. Working in such a manner for a long time can cause suffering to the user especially for elderly people or women drivers. Moreover, the safety features in today's jack are not enough for the operator to work with them in an appropriate manner. Additionally, the commercial jacks are big and bulky which raises the question for their placement and maintenance, also usually it is difficult to make out the proper position under an automobile where a jack has to be placed. This paper proposes solution to these problems. ISHA (Innovative smart hoisting assistance) is a system that will place and operate an electric car jack by utilizing power from the car battery. Using the concept of IoT and Smart Automation, the operator can just press a button from the Graphical User Interface (GUI) to change a deflated tyre without much hassle.

Keywords: Automation · Internet of Things (IoT) · Human machine interface (HMI)

1 Introduction

Transportation is a vital part of everyone's day to day life. In recent years personal transportation has become more dominant. Travelling in cars gives us privacy and is an effective way of transportation for majority of the citizens. With the development and technology advancement in present era, many features are added to cars that make our commute very easy and comfortable. However, the jacks used in the vehicle is still the same, there are two commonly used car jacks: Hydraulic car jack and Mechanical car jack [1–3] which are discussed thoroughly below.

1.1 Mechanical Jacks

These jacks use mechanical methods for lifting a car. They may use a screw for lifting and lowering of car or using a racketing system to lift a car with a notch at a time slowly. This include scissor jack in this category and the high lift jack.

© Springer Nature Singapore Pte Ltd. 2020
U. Batra et al. (Eds.): REDSET 2019, CCIS 1229, pp. 328–338, 2020.
https://doi.org/10.1007/978-981-15-5827-6_29

1.2 Hydraulic Jacks

Jacks in this category use either a horizontally or vertically mounted hydraulic cylinder to cars. Basically these hydraulic jacks takes advantages of the fact "It is really difficult to compress a fluid" [4–6]. The jack contains a reservoir full of the sometime type of oil. When the upstroke is given to the handle, oil is pulled from the reservoir. When down stroke is given, that portion of the oil flows into the central cylinder and underneath a piston. As the amount of oil increases under the piston, then pressure is also increased hence it pushes the cylinder up and lifts the car. It will stay in the same position until the oil is let out and flows back into the reservoir.

A car jack is a mechanical product that in used in lifting heavy vehicles such as cars and it allows the user to gain access to the underneath areas of the vehicle. This revolutionary device is of great advantage but in today's era when automation is taking over in each possible sector of our lives, it is quite evident that the manually operated car jacks are time-consuming and cause inconvenience for elderly & women users. These commercially available jacks is what most people are familiarized with and it's included as standard equipment for most of the new cars, Available car jacks, are typically manually operated and therefore require substantial laborious physical effort on the part of the user.

These jacks present difficulties for the elderly, women and are especially disadvantageous under adverse weather conditions. These presently available jacks further require the operator to remain in a prolonged bent over or squatting position to operate the jack. Doing work in such a way for a long period of time is not ergonomic to the human body. Moreover, the safety features in today's jack are not enough for the operator to work with them in an appropriate manner.

There are also reports on car jacks which lead to a serious number of accidents. A specified jack purposed to hold up to 1000 kg, but tests undertaken by consumer affairs have revealed that is fails to work after lifting 250 kg and may physically break when it has a weight close to its 1000 kg capacity [7–9]. Furthermore, available jacks are typically large, heavy and also difficult to store, transport, or move into the proper position under an automobile.

An automotive jack is a device used to raise all or part of a vehicle into the air in order to facilitate vehicle maintenances or breakdown repairs. Considering such inherent disadvantages of the commercially available jack, this paper proposes the revolutionary idea to encounter the above-stated problems. A Smart Hoisting Assistance System would operate an electric car jack using the concept of IoT and Smart Automation which would be easier to operate.

The paper is divided into two parts namely: Hardware and Software, that thoroughly explains the working of different modules combined to accomplish the above-stated objective.

2 Hardware Involved

The motorized screw jack [10, 11] is used to lift the small and medium automobiles. Most of the vehicles contain old screw jack that are used to lift car [3–5]. This needs very high efforts from the user and create a lot of hassle while being used. In order to avoid all the hassle caused by the screw jack, the motorized jack has been developed in a way that it can be used to lift the car with very less effort and process is also made smooth. The process is made so simple that even an old person or women can use it with ease. A D.C motor is coupled with shaft of the screw jack using a gear assembly. Now the screw jack's shaft rotation depends upon the torque of the D.C motor. Automation done is based on the concept that this is an age of automation where we are trying to replace the manual effort by mechanical power in all forms of automation [6, 7]. The process remains to be an important part of the system although with changing demands on physical effort, the degree of automation is increased. The motorized screw jack [10, 11] has been developed to cater to the needs of small and medium automobile garages. The hardware part consists of:

2.1 Chassis Design

a. The tire and the body are in-line at the edges which follows the basic Sedan style cars, to give it a proper and original look of the chassis.

Fig. 1. Setup of chassis design

b. The rack as seen in the Fig. 1 is attached with the stepper motor that is covered by its casing. The casing is firmly attached with the rack and pinion mechanism as shown in Fig. 2 that ensures the smooth movement of jack.

Fig. 2. Rack & Pinion mechanism with stepper motor

2.2 Front-Wheel Assembly

Front-wheel assembly as shown in Fig. 3 is connected using two supporting rods to the front chassis. It is designed to provide a solid layout for the tyres.

Fig. 3. Setup of the front wheel assembly

2.3 Rear-Wheel Assembly

Rear-wheel assembly as shown in Fig. 4 is connected to the rear of chassis using dead axel and supporting rods.

Fig. 4. Setup of the rear wheel assembly

2.4 Vertical Suspension Support

As seen in Fig. 5, the hollow pipe connecting the chassis and dead axel has a vertical slot, which will provide us with the desired suspension effects. When one tire of either side is lifted with the jack, the other tire which is in line with the lifted one of the same sides, doesn't get lifted too. Even if it does so, the weight of the tire will try to put it down and the downward movement will then be supported by this slot.

Fig. 5. Setup of vertical suspension support

2.5 Rack and Pinion Assembly

Rack of the Rack & pinion assembly as shown in Fig. 6 connects the front end & rear end chassis of the main frame. It is further utilized for horizontal movement of jack.

Fig. 6. Rack and Pinion

a. Support for pinion

Two plain sheets of the same length and height as that of rack is attached at the sides to provide support for the horizontal and in-line motion of the pinion. This pinion is connected to the ball bearing in the side face of the casing with the help of the motor's shaft, which further helps in the horizontal movement of the whole casing on just switching on the motor. The jack is suspended from the casing.

2.6 Ultrasonic Sensor

It is device that is used to measure distance with the help of ultrasonic waves that determines the distance where jack must be placed. It is positioned at the front & rear rack of the chassis. The trig (trigger) pin is used to trigger the sound pulses of ultrasonic sensor. The sensor along with its respective pins are shown in Fig. 7.

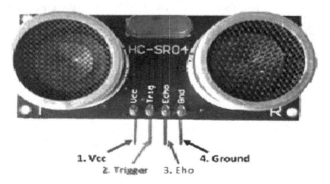

Fig. 7. Ultrasonic sensor

3 Hall Effect Sensor

A Hall effect sensor as shown in Fig. 8 is used to see the effect of magnetic circuit. These sensors are utilized for closeness/proximity sensing as well as speed detection, and positioning applications. They are placed on both the racks to monitor the positioning of the jacks. The sensor contains four pins but only three are used in the project namely: Ground, Positive and A0 (Analog Pin).

Fig. 8. Hall effect sensor

3.1 Raspberry Pi

The Raspberry Pi as shown in Fig. 9 is a low cost, controller that can be used with a laptop/computer device. It provides options to program in languages like Scratch and Python. It functions on Linux operating system and is available in different type of models that serves many purposes. Pi consist of 40 pins in which there are twenty-four General-purpose Input/Output Pins (GPIO) along with four power supply pins each of 3 V and 5 V. There are 8 available ground pins which are connected with jumper wires.

The commonly used models are: Raspberry Pi 1 model B +, Raspberry Pi 1model A, Raspberry Pi Zero, Raspberry Pi 2, Raspberry Pi 3 mode. Raspberry pi is brain of our prototype [8, 9].

Fig. 9. Raspberry Pi 3B+

3.2 Stepper Motor

The stepper motor shown in Fig. 10 is primarily being used to move the jack horizontally. It consists of four pins which are attached to its driver board.

Fig. 10. Stepper motor

3.3 Tyre Pressure Monitoring System

Tyre pressure monitoring system (TPMS) as shown in Fig. 11 is used to monitor the pressure of each tyre and to further display this to the user so that appropriate action could be taken.

Fig. 11. TPMS with display

4 Software Involved

Using Raspberry Pi 3B, we can control the movement of jacks used to lift the car. It will take the input and will lift the side of the car accordingly.

Depending upon the values given by the TPMS as described in the flow chart of Fig. 12, it is decided to know the tire which needs replacement and the location of jack.

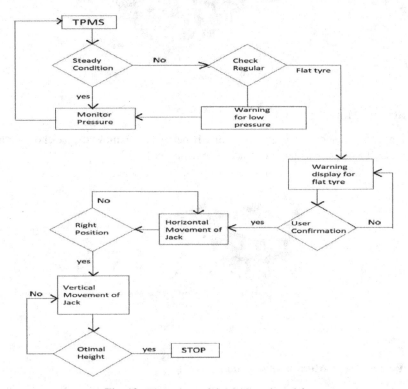

Fig. 12. Flow chart of the proposed model

It will decide the horizontal movement, vertical movement and height of the jack to lift the car.

It will also tell the pressure of the tyres and provide warning accordingly to the user.

Once the tyre is replaced, it will help to reduce the height of the jack to bring the jack and hence the car to its original position.

The detailed working is as follow:

- Tyre Pressure Monitoring System (TPMS) would run continuous checks on the tyre's pressure in the vehicle. The tire pressure monitoring system (TPMS) aims to provide constant monitoring of the tires and warn you when any one of the tyre is considerably inflated or developing an unsafe driving condition. It is classified into two types: direct TPMS (dTPMS) and indirect (iTPMS)

- It will check the pressure in all the tyres and provide real-time information about the tyre's condition. If the tyre condition stays steady i.e. normal tyre pressure change it would continue monitoring its health, carefully observing its data.
- The controller will check for low pressure or a flat tyre. In the case of low pressure, a constant low-pressure message will be displayed to the user on the visual board/display board till the pressure becomes normal in the tyres.
- In case of a fatal occurrence like a deflated tyre, the system would display a warning message and would wait for further instruction from the user. Till the momentarily period when the user stops the vehicle and clicks on the "*Start Button*" on the Web iOPI, the process of upliftment of car activates.
- The jack reaches the faulty tire using a stepper motor which is supported by a rack and pinion system. The confirmation that the jack has reached the specified position is done by the Hall Effect sensor placed near the tire system.
- Then the jack starts to open using a DC motor until a specific height has been reached and so it is safe to remove the tire off the car.
- Further, the system waits so that the replacement of tyre can be completed by the user. When the user presses the "*Complete Button* "on the Web iOPI. The folds the jack and places it back to its original position.
- Finally, the system rechecks all the parameters and confirms that the jack has been placed back properly and the car is good to go again.

5   Features

Following are the features of the proposed system which makes it unique and innovative for all the car users:

- Supports Smart Innovation & IoT
- User-friendly Graphical user interface
- Reduces the number of accidents due to a deflated tyre
- Confirms cooperative replacement of flat tyres
- Improves women and elderly people safety
- Provides Real-time tyre pressure data
- Saves manpower and time

6   Conclusion

Accounting all the commercially available car jacks, this paper provides a way to improve the characteristics of the jacks by only adding a few alterations on the features and design. The paper presents an automatic car jack system that will be easy to operate, able to lift and lower the car without much physical effort and chiefly provide safety to the user.

The scope of the paper is to design a car jack that provides safety, reliability and is easy to operate, the paper describes the development of a car jack that is powered by car battery and automated with graphical user interface (GUI). The designed system would provide many benefits such as user-friendly interface, confirms cooperative replacement of flat tyres, saves manpower and time and at the same time providing real-time tyre pressure data. The proposed system is low cost, easily operated, user-friendly and safe, provide proper ground clearance, low weight and it is beneficial to all categories of people, be it women, old age people or anyone else.

References

1. Balkeswar singh, Chatpalliwar, A.S., Bhoyar, A.A.: Optimizing efficiency of square threaded mechanical screw jack by varying Helix angle. Int. J. Mod. Eng. Res. (IJMER) **2**(1), 504–508 (2012)
2. Patel, N.R., Dalwadi, S., Thakor, V., Bamaniya, M.: Design of toggle jack considering material selection of screw- nut combination. Int. J. Innov. Res. Sci. Eng. Technol. **2**(5), 1748–1756 (2013)
3. Haribaskar, G., Dhenesh Kumar, N., Arun Kumar, C., Hari Haran, P., Boobalan, M., Sadha Sivam, C.: Research article remote controlled scissor jack to lift the vehicle. Int. J. Adv. Res. **3**(3), 1279–1282 (2015)
4. Sharavanan, R.: Design of built-in hydraulic jack for light motor vehicles. Int. J. Mech. Eng. Technol. (IJMET) **8**(8), 1649–1655 (2017)
5. Noor, M.M., Kadirgama, K., Rahman, M.M., Sani, M.S.M., Rejab, M.R.M.: Development of auto car jack using internal car power. In: Malaysian Science and Technology Congress, MSTC 2008, 16–17 December 2018. KLCC, Malaysia (2008)
6. Jadhav, S.S., Patil, P.K., Khara, A.R.: The automatic hydraulic Jack. IJEDR **5**(2), 323–325 (2017)
7. Patil, M., Gaurav, U., Rajesh, P., Nilesh: Automated car jack. Int. J. Curr. Eng. Technol. **4**(4), 323–325 (2014)
8. Madhusudhan, B.P.M., Prabhushankar, M.R.: Development of electro mechanical jack for auto leveling of vehicles. Int. J. Innov. Res. Sci. Eng. Technol. **3**(5) (2014)
9. Thomas, J.P.: Vehicle lift system. United States Patent Issued on 6 January 2009, Patent Number: US 7472889 B1
10. Farhad, R.: Apparatus and method for an electric jack. United States Patent Issued on 8 November 2007, Patent Number: US 2007/0256526 A1
11. Masiwal, A., et al.: Design and fabrication of Hydraulic Jack system for four wheelers. Int. Res. J. Eng. Technol. (IRJET) **05**(04) (2018)

Computational Hybrid Approaches for Routing and Security Optimization in Networks

Nida Iftekhar, Sherin Zafar, Samia Khan, and Siddhartha Sankar Biswas[(✉)]

Jamia Hamdard, New Delhi, India
nida.iftekhar@jamiahamdard.ac.in, zafarsherin@gmail.com,
samia.khan20@gmail.com, ssbiswas1984@gmail.com

Abstract. Portable Ad-hoc Network also referred as Mobile ad-hoc Networks (MANET) is a no established, foundation less system worked for different military, law, salvage activities and these days most prevalent are Online Social networks (OSN). Since the applications where MANET is used for, requires explicit and upgraded security and steering strategies, breaks should be stayed away from for execution improvement in OSN. MANET's are crucial against different assaults and posture steering and security challenges just as circumstances so the proposed computational Route Amassed (RA) and Adroit Iris Testament (AIT) directing and security approach connects the tradeoff in MANET and beats different impediments winning in customary procedures of MANET. Because of fame and acknowledgment of biometrics against different security ruptures, iris is a standout amongst the most solid and remarkable biometric quality that is used in this chapter for security upgrades in MANET. The proposed Route Amassed approach attaches a focal controller eluded as focal lead, into the MANET task which generally pursues a dispersed methodology. The expansion of a focal lead which is chosen with the assistance of an irregular capacity, renders the quicker location of courses and subsequently, quicker conveyance of parcels, which is further aide with the procedure of course accumulation which enables the courses to be amassed at the focal lead and just the location of the focal lead is publicized in the system and hence it abbreviates the steering tables of different hubs. So the examination approach talked about, broke down and actualized in this chapter initially investigates verified methodology and produces grave biometric signature for beating different security worries through MATLAB test system and afterward further through NS2 test system upgrades QOS parameters like however put (throughput), start to finish deferral (packet delivery ratio) and bundle conveyance proportion (end-to-end delay) through Route Amassed Approach subsequently giving a verified just as course improved methodology for MANET.

Keywords: MANET · Route Amassed (RA) · Adroit Iris Testament (AIT) · Biometric · Cryptography · QOS

1 Introduction

The development of specially appointed systems [1] has supported in upsetting the system activities crosswise over various fields. A portion of the fields incorporate the

© Springer Nature Singapore Pte Ltd. 2020
U. Batra et al. (Eds.): REDSET 2019, CCIS 1229, pp. 339–354, 2020.
https://doi.org/10.1007/978-981-15-5827-6_30

unfriendly landscapes in military applications, crisis tasks, for example, inquiry and salvage under debacle conditions, community oriented figuring for example gatherings and so forth and most prevalent these days are Online Social Networks (OSN) where framework arrangement was not practical. Impromptu system is a type of system set up for a specific session. The main impetus behind the task of a specially appointed system is shared correspondence. The taking part gadgets work without any focal facilitator. The system is fit for distinguishing new joining hubs definitely and enlisting them faultlessly. The correspondence between the gadgets inside one another's remote range happens legitimately utilizing radio waves, for gadgets not in the scope of one another, the middle of the road hubs work as switches and information is hence exchanged through various bounces. Be that as it may, the plan and advancement of such a system additionally represents various issues and difficulties [2]. This chapter contemplates the foremost issues influencing the advancement and execution of specially appointed systems and proposes answer for improving the steering and upgrading the security of MANET used for OSN.

1.1 MANET's Issues

The Practically all the impromptu system applications use the Industrial, Scientific and Medical (ISM) band which don't include any permitting. In this way, specially appointed systems have restricted channel data transfer capacity available to them alongside the inalienable mistake inclined remote channel. The different issues experienced while conveying specially appointed system are examined underneath and furthermore delineated in Fig. 1:

a. *Medium gets or the Medium Access Control (MAC) layer to conspire*

The essential capacity of the MAC layer [3] incorporates to play out the methodology important while exchanging the information among at least two gadgets inside the system. Macintosh layer is likewise in charge of redress of irregularities showing up from the physical layer. Macintosh layer straightforwardly controls the dependability and proficiency of information to be transmitted between the hubs along the course in the system, Quality of Service (QoS) [4] of the system likewise relies upon the MAC layer convention. The prime duty of MAC convention is to give conveyed arbitration to shared channel to exchange the parcels. The plan of MAC convention in this manner ought to include least overhead, least impacts, greatest usage of channel, and least postponement, moderate the aftermaths of concealed terminals and the controlling of uncovered terminals.

b. *Routing*

To consolidate the remarkable highlights of self-designing portable specially appointed system or the MANET, steering of information withstands an excessive number of issues. This likewise triggers a requirement for uncommon directing conventions [5] to be intended for MANETs absorbing the necessities. The MANET directing conventions are responsible for finding a plausible course between the source and the goal, choosing the course for transmission and keeping up the course alongside sparing the rare assets. The principle deterrents over the span of directing convention configuration are:

i.   Versatility: The essential normal for specially appointed systems is profoundly portable hubs, bringing about the successive area changes thus, repeating way breaks, impacts of parcels, presence of stale course data turns into a noteworthy issue for the directing convention to manage.

ii. Data transmission Limitation: The normal channel represents the constrained transfer speed for each hub.

iii. Restricted Resources: Ad hoc system associated gadgets have constrained capacity limit, registering power and thorough battery control.

iv. Blunder inclined remote channel: Channel is inclined to blurring and different mistakes.

c.   *Energy Constraint:*

The lifetime of the system relies upon the battery control accessible with the hubs, to continue the system activities. Under the nonappearance of any huge improvement in the battery inquire about; the vitality the executive's task winds up urgent for the specially appointed systems which incorporates finding ways with insignificant vitality utilization, lessening the dispersal of processor intensity of the figuring gadgets.

d.   *Scalability*

Impromptu system ensures a practical, foundation free correspondence and in this way is drawing in intrigue quickly. The expansion in the quantity of hubs in the system offers ascend to versatility issues. The directing convention configuration must have highlights to build the versatility of the system with the end goal that the presentation of the system isn't influenced by the additional number of gadgets into the system.

e.   *Security*

Retribution the applications, specially appointed systems are utilized for, essentially military, security of information transmitted is exceptionally critical. Since, impromptu systems work without any focal facilitator and all the taking an interest hubs share a typical remote channel, likelihood of it getting assaulted increments. The investigation of broad security dangers [6] consequently winds up essential to develop an answer (Table 1).

Table 1. Challenges and attacks to each layer.

Layer	Attacks	Security issues	Challenges
Physical layer	Eavesdropping interceptions jamming, denial of service attacks	To prevent jamming of signals, and attacks related to denial of service	Bandwidth, power consumption
Data link layer	Traffic analysis, malicious behavior of nodes	To protect the MAC protocol and securing the link layer	Bandwidth, power consumption, wireless media
Network layer	Black Hole, sink hole, gray hole, worm hole, byzantine attack	To protect the forwarding protocols and ad hoc protocols	Scalability, infrastructural, wireless media, cooperativeness, power consumption
Transport layer	Session hijacking, SYN flooding	To authenticate and secure end to end communication with the help of encryption	Bandwidth, wireless media, power consumption
Application layer	Repudiation, data corruption	To detect and prevent the virus, worms and other malicious codes	Software and application, infrastructural, power consumption

2 Related Work

The creators have foregrounded the issues engaged with framework less working MANET with very portable hubs, the essential difficulties attempted in this paper are enhancement, QOS parameters and security leaps as far as MANET [7]. The propounded calculation depends on biometrics based extraction of iris picture. The calculation additionally includes hereditary calculation. The ease, adaptable and profoundly usable, proficient methodology is bolstered by very amazing outcomes. Cyber Secure CIB; authors have filtered the differing assaults and other security issues looked by MANETs. The paper endeavors to advance security in digital world by joining discrete recognizable proof components. Security ruptures are substantiated to be forestalled by Crypt-Iris based (CIB) procedure. The outcomes are illustrative of the productivity of the system [8]. Secure Routing in MANET; authors have attempted the investigation of biometrics approach focused to improve security. The paper assesses the pantomime issues and assesses the changes with information. The outcomes finish up the upgraded presentation of the proposed methodology [9]. Novel Crypt Approach; authors have used cryptography to additionally upgrade the security limits of MANET. The outcomes are characteristic towards the improvement in QOS parameters of MANET [10]. The creators have understood the methodology of information total and have executed conglomeration to indisputably prune the information to be transported out. The collection procedure is hence demonstrated to lessen clog in the system just as a decrease in the vitality utilization. The paper exhibits a capricious collection approach which is pleasing to changing traffic situations and is successful in diminishing system clog and vitality devoured while transmission of information [11].

3   Key Challenges of MANET

3.1   Security

The quirk of impromptu system can be depicted by its capacity to associate exceptionally portable, remote hubs with no requirement for a fixed foundation. The radio associated hubs accomplish bounce by-jump transmission of data by going about as switches for one another, yet this helpless open system and other unconventional highlights present constraining difficulties on specially appointed systems. MANET represents no limitations on the hubs portability (hubs can openly leave or join the system) and along these lines, verifying the system limits is a test. The creators in this chapter [12] give a point by point knowledge into the security challenges looked by MANET. The exploration in the paper shows the basic security parameters dependent on security needs remembering the peculiarity of MANET. The section likewise assesses and examinations different sorts of assaults in MANET.

3.2   Routing

The one of a kind highlights of MANET force a basic constraint for the directing of information parcels in MANET. The steering conventions utilized for wired systems can't along these lines, be utilized for MANET and It winds up significant to build up a directing convention for MANET fusing all the interesting highlights and relating issues and limitations, into the plan. There are a few conventions structured and proposed in MANET. The first of its classification is Proactive Protocols [13] which dedicatedly propagate the contemporary data of the courses to every one of the hubs of the system yet this methodology adds to the additional utilization of transfer speed while refreshing the courses. The second classification of MANET directing Protocols are known as the Reactive conventions [14] which trigger the course disclosure system simply after the course is mentioned. This helps sparing the data transfer capacity however adds to the inactivity inside the system. The third classification is the amalgamation of the initial two methodologies into the activity, called the cross breed steering conventions [15]. MANET directing conventions need enhancement.

3.3   QOS Parameters

Security and steering are the two most significant issues for QOS (Quality of Service) [18] improvement in MANET. The consolidated Conspicuous RA and AIT approaches proposed in this examination ponder decrease the tradeoff and give an instrument of verified and steering advancement approach whose depiction is given in Fig. 1.

Fig. 1. Key challenges of MANET

4   Proposed Conspicuous RA (Route Amassed) and AIT (Adroit Iris Testament) Approaches for Routing and Security Optimization in MANET for OSN

Security and steering are the two most significant issues for QOS (Quality of Service) improvement in MANET. The proposed consolidated Conspicuous RA and AIT approaches proposed in this exploration ponder decrease the exchange off and give a component of verified steering streamlining approach whose total flowchart portrayal is given in Fig. 2. The proposed Adroit Iris Testament approach is one of the advancement procedure received in this exploration consider for verifying and upgrading protection and confirmation of MANET. AIT uses solid biometric highlight iris alongside cryptographic highlights to build up an exceptionally trust situated mark that abuses bi-symmetrical based sluggish wavelets to cover biometric signature based information. Mix of biometric and cryptographic highlights makes the proposed methodology twofold verified against different security ruptures. Belo are examined two novel AIT and RA approaches which are used in this examination investigation.

4.1   Adroit Iris Testament Approach

AIT based approach generates domains of cryptography and private key. It selects individual iris image and first perform iris disjuncture for detecting the circular iris and pupil boundaries through linear Hough transform approach. Iris disjuncture extracts the area of interest of iris image and removes the unwanted parts from it and generates accurate input for upcoming normalization phase which is performed by histogram equalization technique.

This process of histogram equalization enhances iris image contrast through transformation of intensity image and thus improves global contrast of the selected iris image. Followed by normalization is template encoding phase done through 3.5 bi-orthogonal wavelets that breaks the 2D normalized pattern into 1-D signal. Novel lifting scheme is explored for construction of bi-orthogonal filters. This process results in faster implementation of wavelet based transformation. Two criterions i.e. Hamming Distance and Normalized Correlation Coefficient are explored for matching process. Hamming distance incorporates noise masking and normalized correlation coefficient accounts local variations in image intensity, achieving best and accurate matching results. Cryptographic based Hashing technique is then utilized to generate the domain and private key and authentication is then performed further. Following MATLAB function is utilized for authentication preservation in MANET.

```
function                      [authentication_sucess,ip_iris_pal]              =
fun_user_authentication(total_classes,images_per_class,
base_class,ip_iris_image_path,re_train,matching_tech,show_figure)
if re_train == 1
    % Iris Database Training for Authentication Process
```

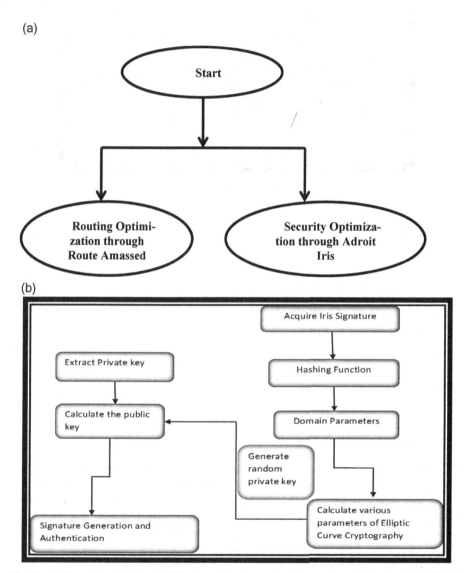

(a)

(b)

Fig. 2. (a) Conspicuous RA and AIT approaches for routing & security optimization in MANET (b) flowchart of adroit iris testament approach for securing MANET (c) Flowchart of route amassed approach for routing optimization in MANET

(c)

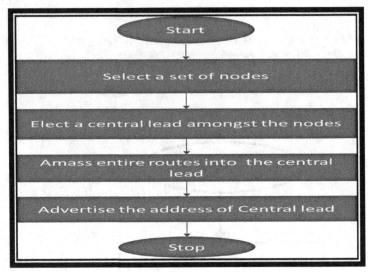

Fig. 2. (*continued*)

```
      fun_train(total_classes,images_per_class);
         % End
end
% Iris I/P Matching for Authentication Process
img_path = ip_iris_image_path;
[~,~,ip_iris_pal] = fun_create_pal(img_path,show_figure);
[matched_class]                                                    =
fun_search(total_classes,images_per_class,ip_iris_pal,matching_tech);
if (matched_class == base_class)
      authentication_sucess = 1;
else
      authentication_sucess = 0;
end
% End
end
```

4.2 Route Amassed Approach

The proposed approach annexes a central controller referred as central lead, into the MANET operation which otherwise follows a distributed approach. The addition of a central lead which is selected with the help of a random function, renders the faster detection of routes and hence, faster delivery of packets, which is further adjunct with the process of route amassment which allows the routes to be amassed at the central lead and only the address of the central lead is advertised in the network and thus it helps shorten the routing tables of the other nodes. In case of any failure, such as the central lead quitting the network or changing its position in the network, the proposed framework also incorporates the updating of the central lead. The route amassed approach thus puts a check on the bandwidth, reduces the computational loads on the processors, prunes the memory requisites and also helps in diminishing the latency problems and therefore, renders in the achievement of optimization in routing.

5   Results and Discussion

The conspicuous RA and AT approaches for routing and security optimization in MANET first starts with an effective authentication mechanism exploring strong biometric trait; iris as well as cryptographic features through well-developed MATLAB simulator. Figure 3 shows the encryption parameters of sender A and receiver B generated through corresponding iris templates.

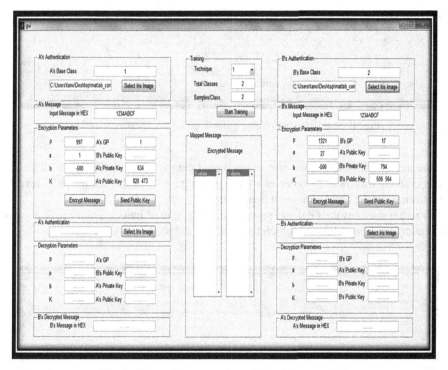

Fig. 3. Encryption parameters of A and B generated.

Figure 4 depicts scatter plot of elliptic group E p (a, b) = E997 (1,-500), where X-axis and Y-axis represents different values of x and y which are calculated with the help of equation $y^2 = x^3 + ax + b \bmod p$. All the points generated by elliptic curve are utilized for mapping purpose. Plain text point's p_m will be encrypted as cipher text points with the help of the points given in the scatter plot.

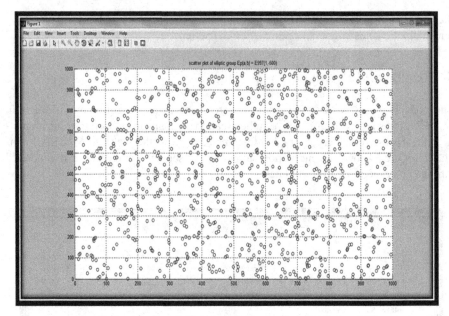

Fig. 4. Scatter plot of elliptic group E p (a, b) = E997 (1, −500)

Figure 5 represents scatter plot of encrypted data E 997(1,-500) where all points are encrypted with help of receiver's (A's) public key. Thus the scatter plots reveals effectiveness of AIT authentication approach.

Figure 6 signifies the GUI and process of encryption of message and Fig. 7 depicts authentication being achieved which thus validate the proposed AIT approach.

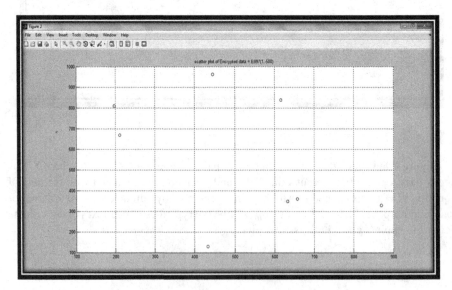

Fig. 5. Scatter plot of encrypted data E 997(1, −500)

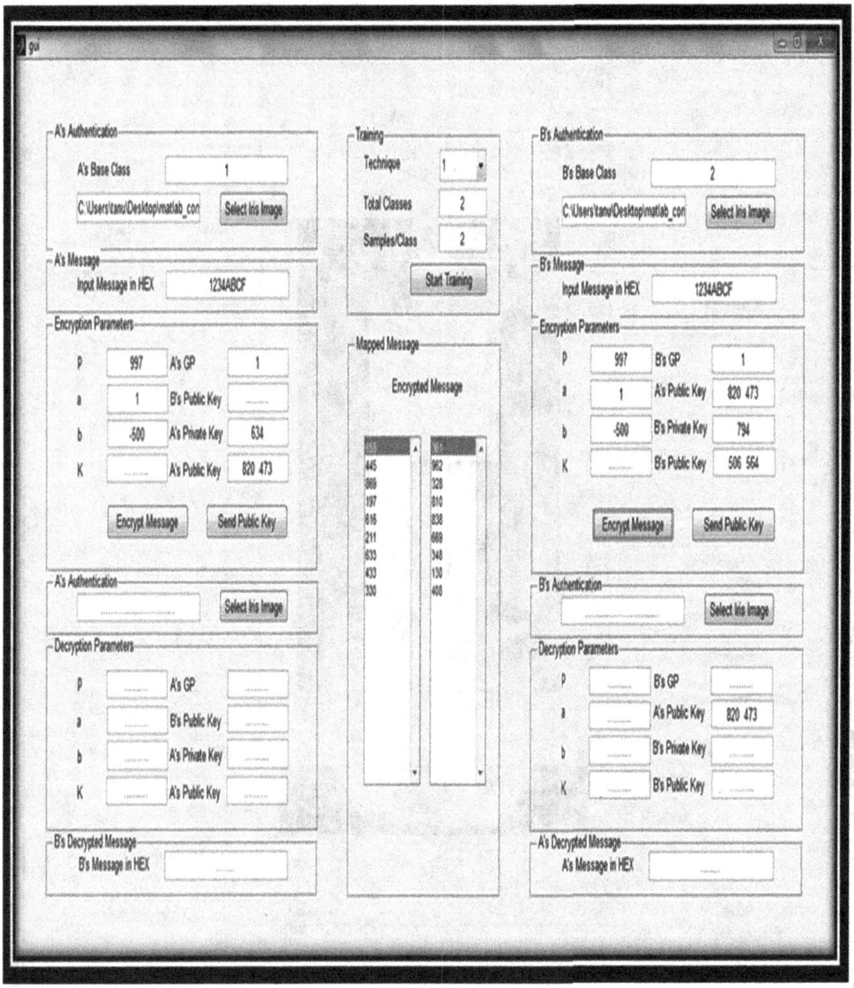

Fig. 6. Message being encrypted

After instilling security features in MANET through proposed AIT approach next is optimization through RA approach by various effective QOS results like throughput, packet delivery ratio and end-to-end delay. NS2 simulator results are depicted through Fig. 8, 9 and 10 which validates the proposed approach.

Figure 8 provides a comparison analysis of traditional shortest path routing approach and RA approach and red line in the graph shows how with increase in number of nodes the proposed approach optimizes throughput and provides effective results. Similarly, Fig. 9 provides a comparison analysis of traditional shortest path routing approach and RA approach and red line in the graph shows how with increase in number of nodes the proposed approach optimizes packet delivery ratio and provides effective results.

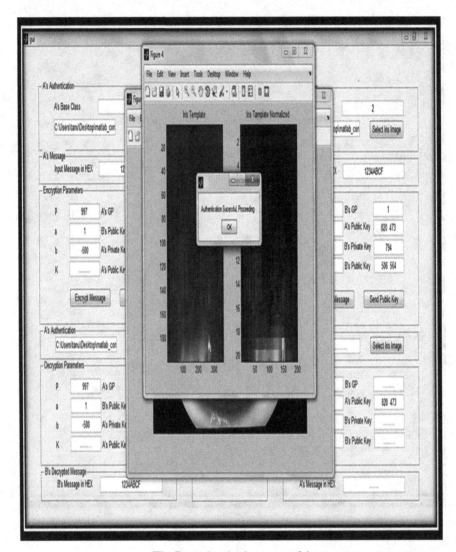

Fig. 7. Authentication successful

Similarly, Fig. 10 provides a comparison analysis of traditional shortest path routing approach and RA approach and red line in the graph shows how with increase in number of nodes the proposed approach optimizes end-to end delay and provides effective results.

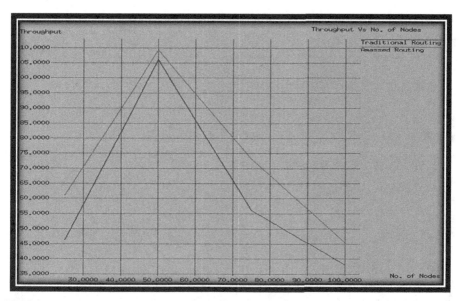

Fig. 8. Comparison analysis of Route Amassed approach and Traditional Approach with throughput as a QOS parameter.

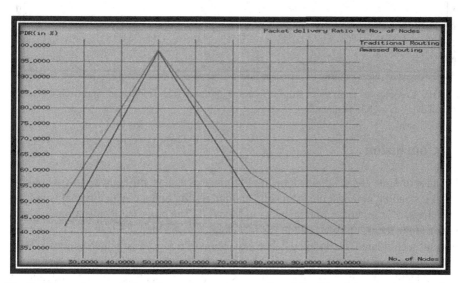

Fig. 9. Comparison analysis of Route Amassed approach and Traditional Approach with packet delivery ratio as a QOS parameter.

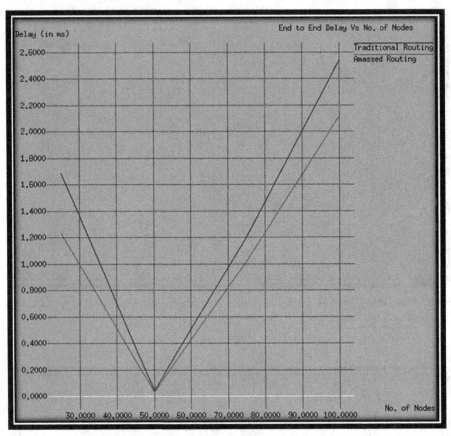

Fig. 10. Comparison analysis of Route Amassed approach and Traditional Approach with end-to-end delay as a QOS parameter

6 Conclusion

Because of fame and acknowledgment of biometrics against different security ruptures, iris is a standout amongst the most solid and interesting biometric quality that is used in this chapter for security improvements in MANET. The proposed Route Amassed approach adds a focal controller alluded as focal lead, into the MANET task which generally pursues a circulated methodology. The expansion of a focal lead which is chosen with the assistance of an arbitrary capacity, renders the quicker recognition of courses and subsequently, quicker conveyance of parcels, which is further aide with the procedure of course gathering which enables the courses to be amassed at the focal lead and just the location of the focal lead is promoted in the system and hence it abbreviates the directing tables of different hubs. So the examination approach talked about, broke down and actualized in this chapter initially investigates verified methodology and produces sepulcher biometric signature for defeating different security misgivings through MATLAB test system and after that further through NS2 test system enhances QOS parameters like however put, start to finish deferral and bundle conveyance proportion through Route Amassed Approach consequently giving a verified just as course upgraded methodology for MANET. Execution of enhanced RA and AIT approaches is broke down and portrayed in above areas. Two client verification framework is created through AIT procedure that accomplishes confirmation through fulfillment of least Hamming Distance = 0 and greatest Correlation Coefficient = 1, in this way permitting just coordinating hubs transmission and correspondence in the system. Classification is guaranteed by getting to touchy data just to expected sender and beneficiary. Uprightness is safeguarded by permitting just those hubs to enter the system that accomplish least hamming separation and most extreme connection coefficient. Non-renouncement is accomplished by validating mark of both senders just as collector. Accomplishing security objectives like confirmation, secrecy, respectability and non-revocation restrains the event of different dynamic assaults in MANET. Further by NS2 test system Route Amassed approach is reenacted consolidating sepulcher iris mark to accomplish productive QOS parameter aftereffects of throughput, start to finish delay, parcel conveyance proportion, when contrasted and conventional steering and verified methodologies of MANET.

References

1. Adibi, S., Mobasher, A., Tofighbakhsh, M.: Fourth-Generation Wireless Networks: Applications and Innovations. IGI Global (2010)
2. Alslaim, M.N., Alaqel, H.A., Zaghloul, S.S.: A comparative study of MANET routing protocols. In: The Third International Conference on e-Technologies and Networks for Development (ICeND2014), pp. 178–182 (2014)
3. Arrobo, G.E., Gitlin, R.D.: Improving the reliability of wireless body area networks. In: 2011 Annual International Conference of the IEEE Engineering in Medicine and Biology Society, EMBC, 30 August–3 September, pp. 2192–2195 (2011)
4. Barakah, D.M., Ammad-Uddin, M.: A survey of challenges and applications of Wireless Body Area Network (WBAN) and role of a virtual doctor server in existing architecture. In: 2012 Third International Conference on Intelligent Systems, Modelling and Simulation (ISMS), 8–10 February 2012, pp. 214–219 (2012)
5. Corson, S., Macker, J.: Mobile Ad hoc Networking (MANET): Routing Protocol Performance Issues and Evaluation Considerations. Network Working Group, RFC2501 (1999)
6. El-Masri, S., Saddik, B.: An emergency system to improve ambulance dispatching, ambulance diversion and clinical handover communicationâ-a proposed model. J. Med. Syst. **36**, 3917–3923 (2012)
7. Hanzo, L., Tafazolli, R.: A survey of QoS routing solutions for mobile ad hoc networks. IEEE Commun. Surv. Tutor. **9**(2), 50–70 (2007)
8. Istepanaian, R.S.H., Zhang, Y.T.: Guest editorial introduction to the special section: 4G health, the long-term evolution of m-health. IEEE Trans. Inf Technol. Biomed. **16**, 1–5 (2012)
9. Jovanov, E., Milenkovic, A.: Body area networks for ubiquitous healthcare applications: opportunities and challenges. J. Med. Syst. **35**, 1245–1254 (2011)
10. Perahia, E., Gong, M.X.: Gigabit wireless LANs: an overview of IEEE 802.11 ac and 802.11 ad. ACM SIGMOBILE Mob. Comput. Commun. Rev. **15**, 23–33 (2011)
11. Keikhosrokiani, P., Zakaria, N., Mustaffa, N., Wan, T.-C., Sarwar, M.I., Azimi, K.: Wireless networks in mobile healthcare. In: Adibi, S. (ed.) Mobile Health. SSB, vol. 5, pp. 687–726. Springer, Cham (2015). https://doi.org/10.1007/978-3-319-12817-7_30

12. Redieteab, G., Cariou, L., Christin, P., Helard, J.F.: PHY+MAC channel sounding interval analysis for IEEE 802.11ac MU-MIMO. In: 2012 International Symposium on Wireless Communication Systems (ISWCS), 28–31 August 2012, pp. 1054–1058 (2012)

13. Tian, H.: Hermes: a scalable sensor network architecture for robustness & time energy awareness. A Dissertation Proposal Department of Computer Science University of Virginia (2003)

14. Xiaoyi, Z., Doufexi, A., Kocak, T.: Throughput and coverage performance for IEEE 802.11ad Millimeter-Wave WPANs. In: 2011 IEEE 73rd Vehicular Technology Conference (VTC Spring), 15–18 May, pp. 1–5 (2011)

15. Zain, A.S.M., Yahya, A., Malek, M.F.A., Omar, N.: 3GPP long term evolution and its application for healthcare services. In: 2012 International Conference on Computer and Communication Engineering (ICCCE), 3–5 July, pp. 239–243 (2012)

16. Zafar, S., Soni, MK., Beg, MMS.: An optimized genetic stowed approach to potent QOS in MANET. Procedia Comput. Sci. **62**, 410–418 (2015)

17. Zafar, S.: Cyber secure corroboration through CIB approach. Int. J. Inf. Technol. **9**(2), 167–175 (2017). https://doi.org/10.1007/s41870-017-0018-7

18. Zafar, S., Soni, MK.: Secure routing in MANET through crypt-biometric technique. In: Proceedings of the 3rd International Conference on Frontiers of Intelligent Computing: Theory and Applications (FICTA), pp. 713–720 (2014)

An Empirical Analysis of Supply Chain Risk and Uncertainty in Manufacturing Sector to Achieve Robustness

Surya Prakash[1(✉)], Gianesahwar Aggarwal[1], Archit Gupta[1], and Gunjan Soni[2]

[1] BML Munjal University, Gururgam, Haryana, India
suryayadav8383@gmail.com
[2] Malaviya National Institute of Technology, Jaipur, Rajasthan, India

Abstract. The primary purpose of supply chain risk management (SCRM) is to check the vulnerability of the supply chain and link the risks with strategies to manage them to improve the supply chain performance. The risks involved can be from the supplier side, production, transportation or even from the customer experience. The major part of the risk is due to the uncertainty in demand and risks caused by supplier issues. The robust supply chain needs to be conceived to manage the risks. The present study aims to investigate the correlation between uncertainty, risk, and robustness in the complex supply chain network. The research starts with data collection from 53 manufacturing firms about various supply chain risks. Structural equation modeling method for empirical data analysis is deployed to study the correlation among the three proposed SCRM tactics and hypothesis testing is carried out. The result shows that managing risk and uncertainty leads to achieving robustness in the supply chain. There is a positive correlation between risk and uncertainties. The empirical research outcomes can be further used to improve the risk management in supply chain network design.

Keywords: Supply Chain Risk Management (SCRM) · Uncertainty · Risks · Robustness

1 Introduction

A supply chain consists of a set of suppliers, plants, distributors, and customers. The aim of a typical supply chain is to provide the product from supplier to customer with efficiency and responsive manner. In a supply chain network design, there is always some uncertainty from the customer as well as from the supplier side (Aras and Bilge 2018). Due to this, there is always some level of risk present. The supply chain risk management practices is being used to achieve some robustness against the impact of risks (Wieland and Wallenburg 2012). A study conducted by McKinsey revealed that risk would continue to grow over the future years (Gyorey 2010).

In this paper, we have investigated the possible complicated relationship among risk and uncertainty coming from the supplier side. There is need for studying the methods/approaches to achieve the robustness for the manufacturing sector. There are

© Springer Nature Singapore Pte Ltd. 2020
U. Batra et al. (Eds.): REDSET 2019, CCIS 1229, pp. 355–364, 2020.
https://doi.org/10.1007/978-981-15-5827-6_31

numerous example of disruptions in the supply chain caused by risks from supplier, customer and logistics domain (Tang and Christopher 2006). More the number of inter-connections within the supply chain, there will be escalation in disruptions and risks events, which can result in bankruptcy, breakdowns, unsatisfied customer, etc. In other classification, risk can be internal or external i.e. they can be sourced within the supply chain network or with the service providers. The risks may arise due to multi-product multi-period mechanism of the modern supply chain (Mital *et al.* 2018).

Uncertainty and internal risks cause more disruption and affect the performance of the supply chain further (Manuj and Mentzer 2008). Thus, every organization must try to take managerial decisions for mitigating the uncertainty which results in business integration. In many articles, the quantitative models are extensively used for the above purpose to quantify the uncertainty. The major causes of uncertainty lie in the efforts of improvement in delivery time, quality of the product, product reliability, and product life cycle.

In order to resolve the uncertainty, the internal capabilities and technical resources need to be configured (Prakash *et al.* 2017). The level of uncertainty is determined by its causes to get substantial impacts (Ganbold and Matsui 2017). Resources and capabilities of the firm are noted methods to provide the solution for uncertainty management. The robustness is directly linked with uncertainty and risk management evaluation and mitigation (Prakash *et al.* 2019). The robustness is the outcome of implementing supply chain risk management (SCRM) strategy in organizations. It increases transparency and provides the flow of information to manage the situations (Hartmann *et al.* 2019). The present study aims to investigate the correlation between uncertainty, risk, and robustness in the complex supply chain network. The data collected through a survey from the experts in the existing industry and hypothesis testing and structural equation modeling approach was used. The research starts with data collection from 53 manufacturing firms about various risks. In methodology, data analysis, modeling and hypothesis testing are used.

2   Methodology

There is a number of risks involved in the supply chain network. These risks and uncer-tainty involved results in chaotic situations in the supply chain. Some examples of risk can be due to delivery time, demand uncertainty, transportation or supply of raw mate-rial. Figure 1 shows the flow diagram of the research methodology adopted. Initially, a survey was designed to collect data from practitioners and industry experts in order to identify possible relationship elements.

After initial proof reading and experimental pilot study to refine the survey and validated. Then the survey was sent to the 200 manufacturing industries from India to get responses. This exercise yielded 65 filled responses. After applying data cleaning in received survey samples, 53 relevant and complete responses were used for data analysis. The SPSS Amos tools were used to model the path diagram and analysis carried out.

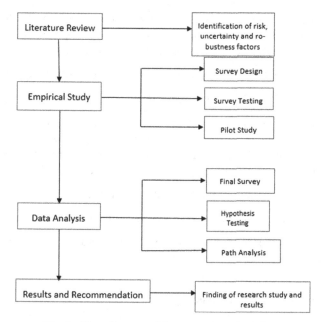

Fig. 1. Flow diagram of the research methodology

2.1 Hypothesis

As we know that in the statistical analysis, hypothesis testing has a fundamental role (Kumar 2015). In the first step, the initial research hypothesis are framed in the form of null and alternative hypotheses. However, to start the process, various fundamental terms were used which needs initial understanding in the given context. The key terms are defined as follows.

Uncertainty: For uncertainty, we have considered the variation in the demand of the customer and how it is dependent upon the supplier variations and uncertainty can occur due to any environmental or climatic or politic instability in a region.

Risk: The risk involves an unwanted set of events that affects the performance of the supply chain negatively. It covers all the delivery time issues, logistics service provider or miscommunication with supply chain partners.

Robustness: It is the capability of the supply chain and its partners to handle risk and/or uncertainty. This empirical study is made to check the relationship among risks, uncertainty with robustness. The uncertainty entirely affects the production limit, supply limit, logistics infrastructure, and other internal capabilities.

Following hypothesis were framed to analyses the situations.

H1A: Addressing uncertainty related to customer demand results in a robust supply chain.

H0A: Uncertainty management does not have much impact on achieving robustness.

Nowadays due to many internal risks, there is turbulence in the supply chain. The volatility of demand in the market is the primary cause of the disturbance. The product life cycle also plays a crucial role in it. Every industry needs to be technology efficient for handling the vulnerability of the supply chain. A robust supply chain can be a better solution to deal with such risks. This results in the succeeding hypothesis.

H1B: Addressing risk related to logistics and supplier will lead to achieving robustness.

H0B: The logistics and supplier issues are not much important for achieving robustness.

SCRM strategies aim to encapsulate the decisions taken in the organization. SCRM manages the risk resulting in the reduction of supply chain risks associated with drivers. A descriptive and systematic approach can provide significant results. Looking into it following hypothesis is also considered.

H1C: Managing the uncertainties yields significant risk reduction.

H0C: Managing the uncertainties does not yield significant risk reduction.

The above all hypotheses are tested by considering data analysis, path analysis using the survey data..

3   Data Analysis and Discussions

The path diagram was made considering all the parameters and the hypothesis is given above are tested. There were two variables taken, observed and unobserved. All the dependency to support the unobserved variables in the form of questions were assigned to each unobserved variable accordingly as observed variables. A unique variable was added in the form of error to the existing variables to support the observed variables and to take care of all the unwanted and unexpected errors that may occur while proving the hypothesis. Figure 2 shows the path diagram of the proposed model.

The number of different variables used by us to calculate the model results and prove our hypothesis is 34 out of which observed variables are 15 and unobserved variables is 19. After running the model, it was observed that the degree of freedom is 86. Hence the model is over identified, and we do our estimates. The Chi-squared value observed is 124.298 which is justifying the model fit. Our model can achieve the ideal fit as probability value (p-value) of our model is 0.05. Table 1 present the regression weight estimates.

P-value is the significant value of the calculated probability to find the results of the hypothesis. There is one pre-chosen probability level known as a significant level. If the p-value is lesser than the significant level, then we need to reject the null hypothesis, i.e. H0 in this case. The null hypothesis is the negation of the alternate hypothesis. In this research, we have taken 5% of the significance value. It means all the null hypotheses are rejected if p-value is less than 5% ($p < 0.05$). As seen from the tables we are getting p-value < 0.05 for every hypothesis testing which means all the null hypothesis is rejected and are study is giving expected results.

We have also used the Cronbach alpha test to check the reliability of the data. We were getting consistent data with alpha value close to 1 which signifies the reliability of data. This shows the accuracy of the results. Table 1 shows estimates of the regression weights of the correlated factors. The standardized error is the distance between the regression

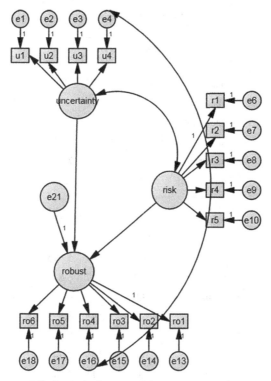

Fig. 2. Path diagram of the proposed model

line and the observed value when plotted for the prediction model, is also calculated and listed in it. Further, it contains critical ratio value which tells the significance between all loadings. It is the ratio of estimate and standard error. The accepted value of which should be greater than modulus of 1.96.

Table 2 shows the standardized regression weights and their estimates. These are the results of estimates that have been standardized to make variance 1 of exogenous and endogenous variables. Table 3 shows the covariance estimates along with standard error value, critical ratio value and calculated p-value between uncertainty and risk. Further, Table 4 shows the correlation estimates between uncertainty and risk.

To check the reliability and correlation among the independent variable to support the hypothesis, we use variances which are being calculated in Table 5 along with the standard error, critical ratio, and p-value. The table provides the paths of supply chain risk management to uncertainty and risk showing the variance of 77% and 47.2%, respectively and further shows the variances estimated of each error on the dependent and independent variables. The total execution time for running the model came out to be 0.596 out of which minimization is done is 0.047 and miscellaneous is done is 0.549.

Table 1. Regression weight estimates

Element		Regression weight	Estimate	S.E.	C.R.	P	Label
robust	<—	risk	−.638	.187	-3.420	***	
robust	<—	uncertainty	−.460	.141	-3.266	.001	
u1	<—	uncertainty	1.000				
u2	<—	uncertainty	1.014	.133	7.620	***	
u3	<—	uncertainty	1.020	.136	7.486	***	
u4	<—	uncertainty	.964	.128	7.524	***	
r1	<—	risk	1.000				
r2	<—	risk	1.172	.190	6.177	***	
r3	<—	risk	1.042	.164	6.337	***	
r4	<—	risk	1.018	.189	5.395	***	
r5	<—	risk	1.374	.207	6.626	***	
ro1	<—	robust	1.000				
ro2	<—	robust	1.247	.149	8.391	***	
ro3	<—	robust	1.029	.122	8.456	***	
ro4	<—	robust	1.163	.150	7.746	***	
ro5	<—	robust	.913	.115	7.918	***	
ro6	<—	robust	.819	.112	7.332	***	

Note- The "***" value indicates that the p-value is less than 0.01.

3.1 Model Fit

There is three model fit which is used to check the accuracy and evaluate results based on which hypothesis is tested and is passed or nullified. This fit test is used to find the discrepancy between observed values and the values expected under the model. The first one is the absolute model fit which works based on statistical formulas and uses data for model generation. The observed parameters in absolute model fit is the chi-squared value, root mean squared error of approximation (RMSEA) and goodness fit index.

Model chi-square ($\chi 2$)
The chi-squared test is used to test how much-observed distribution is due to chance. It is used to "evaluate model fit the correlation between the sample and fitted covariance's matrices" (Hu and Bentler 1999). A good model fit would have chi-square value should not be very high as compared to degrees of freedom, but it cannot only decide the fitness of model as there are many more parameters used to decide it. In our model, the chi-squared value comes out to be 124.98 which is decent as compared to degrees of freedom.

Table 2. Standardized regression weights

Element		Standardized regression weights	Estimate
robust	<—	risk	−.508
robust	<—	uncertainty	−.467
u1	<—	uncertainty	.832
u2	<—	uncertainty	.819
u3	<—	uncertainty	.810
u4	<—	uncertainty	.813
r1	<—	risk	.746
r2	<—	risk	.785
r3	<—	risk	.803
r4	<—	risk	.696
r5	<—	risk	.834
ro1	<—	robust	.877
ro2	<—	robust	.843
ro3	<—	robust	.847
ro4	<—	robust	.808
ro5	<—	robust	.818
ro6	<—	robust	.784

Table 3. Covariances estimates

	Covariance		Estimate	S.E.	C.R.	P	Label
uncertainty	<–>	risk	.646	.157	4.127	***	

Root mean square error of approximation (RMSEA)
As per Byrne, "The RMSEA tells us how well the model, with unknown but optimally chosen parameter estimates would fit the populations covariance matrix" (Byrne 1998). It is very much sensitive towards estimated results of the model and helps to get the best fitness index for the model to prove our hypothesis. For a model to have a better fit, the value of RMSEA should be less than 0.1 and in our model, the value of RMSEA comes out to be 0.091 which is justifying our model.

Goodness-of-fit statistic (GFI)
It is one of the major procedures to calculate the estimated which further helps us in accepting and rejecting our hypothesis. According to (Diamantopoulos *et al.* 2000), GFI tells us "By looking at the variances and covariances accounted for by the model, how closely the model comes to replicating the observed covariance matrix". In our model, the value of GFI is calculated as 0.784 which very much better than the accepted value of

Table 4. Correlations estimates

	Correlations			Estimate
uncertainty	<->		risk	1.072

Table 5. Variances estimates of the model

Variance	Estimate	S.E.	C.R.	P
uncertainty	.770	.207	3.717	***
risk	.472	.148	3.185	.001
e21	.010	.021	.504	.614
e1	.343	.066	5.220	***
e2	.388	.074	5.238	***
e3	.420	.080	5.248	***
e4	.367	.070	5.260	***
e6	.377	.072	5.236	***
e7	.404	.077	5.228	***
e8	.283	.054	5.216	***
e9	.521	.100	5.229	***
e10	.389	.075	5.172	***
e13	.223	.050	4.412	***
e14	.470	.102	4.601	***
e15	.311	.068	4.586	***
e16	.536	.113	4.719	***
e17	.306	.065	4.692	***
e18	.313	.066	4.781	***

0.90. The next model fit calculated for the hypothesis to prove is Incremental fit indices. It consists of three terms as mentioned. The accepted value of each procedure is near to 0.9 (Hooper *et al.* 2008).

Adjusted goodness-of-fit statistic (AGFI)
It is very much related to goodness fit index and helps in adjustment by reducing fit, by saturating model based upon degrees of freedom. In our model, the AGFI value comes out to be 0.703 which is little bit less but due to more dependency on other factors, the value will not have much impact on the model results.

Normed-fit index (NFI)
This statistical procedure evaluated the model by comparing the $\chi2$ value of the model to the $\chi2$ of the null model. (Bentler *et al.* 1980). In our model, the value evaluated is

be 0.850 which is very much near to the accepted range and hence will not impact the accuracy of our hypothesis.

Comparative fit index (CFI)
The CFI works on the sizes of samples. It performs even when the data collected in the sample size is very small. It assumes that the variables that are not directly observed are uncorrelated and compares the covariance with this null model Byrne 1998. In our model, the calculated CFI is 0.949 which is within the accepted range.

Parsimony fit indices
(Mulaik *et al.* 1989) recommended using PFI in tandem along with other measurement tools in statistics to prove the hypothesis. In our model, the value of 0.829 which is within the accepted range.

4 Conclusion

This research aimed to find the correlation between the risk, uncertainty, and robustness in the supply chain. In order to increase the efficiency and responsiveness of the supply chain, we come across some risks and uncertainties, both external and internal. This bridges the gap of supply chain networks with real-life scenarios. An empirical study with the deductive approach shows the results depicting the dependency. SCRM strategy is used to determine the internal and external risks, uncertainties and how it affects the supply chain. Some hypotheses made in our study talks about the dependency of risk, uncertainty, and robustness with each other. The study of the relationship is essential to increase the overall performance of the supply chain. As such, risks impact the supply chain from the customer and supplier side causing supply chain disruptions. The hypothesis testing with a significance level of 0.05 gives the result as a rejection of the null hypothesis. This means all the alternative hypotheses are accepted.

The implementation of SCRM in this study results in an active correlation between risk, uncertainty, and robustness, which can be compared to real-world situations. All the supplier side problems lad to demand risk and variation in the customer demand results in demand uncertainty. This all will affect customer experience and its responsiveness. High variation in the supply of raw materials and the demand leads to disturbance in the internal capabilities of the firm. Also, it impacts the logistic services. It becomes necessary to create a robust supply chain network in order to deal with such risks and uncertainties. Robustness deals with some variations of risk alerting the administrative level of a firm to manage the internal and external capabilities. After all, every firm wants to increase the performance of the supply chain.

References

Wieland, A., Wallenburg, C.M.: Dealing with supply chain risks. Int. J. Phys. Distrib. Logist. Manag. **42**, 887–905 (2012)

Bentler, P.M., Bonett, D.G.: Significance tests and goodness of fit in the analysis of covariance structures. Psychol. Bull. **88**, 588–606 (1980)

Byrne, B.M.: Structural Equation Modeling with LISREL, PRELIS and SIMPLIS: Basic Concepts. Applications and Programming. Lawrence Erlbaum Associates, Mahwah (1998). https://doi.org/10.4324/9780203774762

Hooper, D., Coughlan, J., Mullen, M.R.: Structural equation modelling: guidelines for determining model fit. Electron. J. Busi. Res. Methods **6**, 53–60 (2008)

Diamantopoulos, A., Siguaw, J.A.: Introducing LISREL, pp. 150–192. Sage Publications, London (2000)

Hartmann, H.S.: Defusing the supply chain: how the application of IoT changes SCRM. Acad. Manag. Proc. **2019**, 15–17 (2019)

Hu, L.T., Bentler, P.M.: Cutoff criteria for fit indexes in covariance structure analysis: conventional criteria versus new alternatives. Struct. Eqn. Model.: Multi. J. **6**(1), 1–55 (1999). https://doi.org/10.1080/10705519909540118

Manuj, I., Mentzer, J.T.: Global supply chain risk management strategies. Int. J. Phys. Distrib. Logist. Manag. **38**(3), 192–223 (2008)

Kumar, A.: Hypothesis testing in medical research: a key statistical application. J. Univ. Coll. Med. Sci. **3**, 53–56 (2015)

Gyorey, T., Jochim, M., Norton, S.: The challenges ahead for supply chains. McKinsey Q. (2010)

Mital, M., Del Giudice, M., Papa, A.: Comparing supply chain risks for multiple product categories with cognitive mapping and analytic hierarchy process. Technol. Forecast. Soc. Change **131**, 32 (2018)

Mulaik, S.A., James, L.R., Van Alstine, J., Bennett, N., Lind, S., Dean Stilwell, C.: Evaluation of goodness-of-fit indices for structural equation models. Psychol. Bull. **105**, 430–445 (1989)

Aras, N., Bilge, Ü.: Robust supply chain network design with multi-products for a company in the food sector. Appl. Math. Model. **60**, 526–539 (2018)

Ganbold, O., Matsui, Y.: Impact of environmental uncertainty on supply chain integration. J. Jpn. Oper. Manag. Strategy **7**(1), 37–56 (2017)

Prakash, S., Soni, G., Rathore, A.P.S., Singh, S.: Risk analysis and mitigation for perishable food supply chain: a case of dairy industry. Benchmarking: Int. J. **24**(1), 2–23 (2017)

Prakash, S., Kumar, S., Soni, G., Jain, V., Rathore, A.P.S.: Closed-loop supply chain network design and modelling under risks and demand uncertainty: an integrated robust optimization approach. Ann. Oper. Res. (2019). https://doi.org/10.1007/s10479-018-2902-3

Tang, C.S.: Perspectives in supply chain risk management. Int. J. Prod. Econ. **103**, 451–488 (2006)

Preliminary Evaluation of Navigation and Timing Capability of IRNSS/NavIC at The Northcap University

Kartikay Saini, Pankaj, C. D. Raisy, Preeti, Sharda Vashisth[(✉)], and Amitava Sen Gupta

Department of Electrical, Electronics and Communications Engineering, The Northcap University, Gurugram, Haryana, India
kartikay.saini98@gmail.com, pankajrajniwal81@gmail.com, chungathraisy@gmail.com, preeti.khokhar19@gmail.com, {shardavashisth,amitavasengupta}@ncuindia.edu

Abstract. Global Navigation Satellite System (GNSS) is a system which uses the satellites to provide geo-spatial positioning. It allows the receivers to determine their location (i.e. latitude, longitude and altitude) and time up to very high precision. The most common GNSS is the Global Positioning System(GPS) which is developed by USA. Russia's GLONASS is also a fully functional GNSS. Other GNSS include BeiDou Navigation System of China and Galileo of the European Union. India (ISRO) has recently developed and launched the Indian Regional Navigational Satellite System(IRNSS). This paper analyses the basic performance indicators such as data quality, data usability, uncertainty in position and the uncertainty in time of the data provided by the IRNSS receivers.

Keywords: GNSS · IRNSS/NavIC · DOP · Real-time data · IRNSS receivers · L5 band · Data quality

1 Introduction

India named its regional navigation satellite system as Indian regional navigation satellite system (IRNSS) (Thoelert et al. 2014). IRNSS is an autonomous satellite system that provides accurate real-time navigation and timing services by transmitting L5-band and S-band signals. IRNSS constellation comprises of 3 Geostationary satellites (GEO) and 4 Geosynchronous satellites (GSO) (Majithiya et al. 2011 and Ganeshan 2012). The locations and other vital details of these satellites have been mentioned in Table 1. After achieving fully operational constellation, IRNSS's name was changed to a new operational name, Navigation with Indian Constellation (NavIC) (Zaminpardaz et al. 2017a, b, c). The area covered by the NavIC system is from Latitude 30° S to 50° N and Longitude 30° E to 130° E (Zaminpardaz et al. 2016). Primary service area includes the India mainland and Indian Ocean while secondary service area includes areas around Southeast Asia, Eastern Europe, Eastern Africa, Western China and Western Australia (Harde et al. 2015). The accuracy is better than 20 m over the Indian Ocean region

© Springer Nature Singapore Pte Ltd. 2020
U. Batra et al. (Eds.): REDSET 2019, CCIS 1229, pp. 365–374, 2020.
https://doi.org/10.1007/978-981-15-5827-6_32

and 10 m accuracy over mainland India. Currently, NavIC is fully operational and is undergoing evaluations all over India.

The three onboard atomic clocks of IRNSS-1A malfunctioned in 2016 which lead to the loss of this satellite. In 2017, ISRO launched NavIC's eighth satellite IRNSS-1H to reconstitute the constellation in place of the failed satellite, but as the heat shield could not be detached, the launch resulted in failure (Cozzens 2017). A total of 24 MHz bandwidth of spectrum is allocated in the L5-band (1176.450 MHz) and in the S-band (2492.028 MHz) for IRNSS (ISRO 2014).

2 Experimental Setup

At The Northcap University (NCU), two accord IRNSS user receivers have been received from Space Application Centre (SAC), ISRO, Ahmedabad under the MoU signed between SAC and NCU. These two receivers have been used to collect the data for the analysis of basic performance indicators. Data is received in a raw satellite navigation format known as Receiver Independent Exchange Format (RINEX) which is then converted into a readable format by the software and received in excel sheets for further analysis. However, a few arbitrary spikes observed in the data might be due to some complication in the receiver as the data received is highly sensitive. The IRNSS receivers in dual mode (L5 and S band signal) are used to collect the information for data analysis. Also, it can be seen from Table 1, that there is no Pseudo-Random Noise (PRN) assigned to IRNSS-1I GSO satellite, but in the data received by the receivers, PRN I09 comes with the data received from this satellite. Therefore, I09 has been used to mention the data received from IRNSS-1I in the assessment.

Table 1. Information of satellites in NavIC system

Satellite	PRN	Type	Orbit	Launch Date	Current Status
IRNSS-1A	I01	GSO	55° E, 29° E inclined orbit	01/07/2013	Failed in orbit
IRNSS-1B	I02	GSO	55° E, 29° E inclined orbit	04/04/2014	Operational
IRNSS-1C	I03	GEO	83° E, 5° E inclined orbit	15/10/2014	Operational
IRNSS-1D	I04	GSO	111.75° E, 31° E inclined orbit	28/03/2015	Operational
IRNSS-1E	I05	GSO	111.75° E, 29° E inclined orbit	20/01/2016	Operational
IRNSS-1F	I06	GEO	32.5° E, 5° E inclined orbit	10/03/2016	Operational
IRNSS-1G	I07	GEO	129.5° E, 5.1° E inclined orbit	28/04/2016	Operational
IRNSS-1H	–	–		31/08/2017	Launch failed
IRNSS-1I	–	GSO	55° E, 29° E inclined orbit	12/04/2018	Operational

3 Data Analysis

3.1 Uncertainty in Position

The IRNSS receiver in dual mode (L5 and S band signal) is used to collect the information to observe the basic performance indicators. Difference between the mean of position received (reference coordinates) and the Single point position in each direction is used to analyse the uncertainty in the position. The position is received as latitude (North), longitude (East) and altitude (Height). The latitude, longitude and altitude of the receiver at The Northcap University are taken into account and the jitter over it is measured. Latitude and longitude are in degrees which are then converted into radians and then to meters for the assessment. The values have been normalized such that the center data has mean 0, to observe the jitter which would indicate the performance. Figure 1 shows the jitter of the North, East and Height data received by the IRNSS receiver of one day. Table 2, shows the average jitter found in North, East and Height data over a period of a week received by the indicators.

Figure 2 shows the deviation of latitude against the deviation of longitude in NavIC system. Latitude varies more than the Longitude in NavIC.

3.2 Uncertainty in Time

Timing information given by the IRNSS receiver is one of the most important information as it holds its significance in many real-time applications. This timing information is highly accurate since it purely depends on the onboard atomic clock of the satellites, but due to some noise present in the atmosphere and other factors, there is some jitter in the time. This jitter becomes less significant when taken over a longer period of time. Figure 3 shows the jitter in the time received by the IRNSS receiver at The Northcap University. The jitter is found to be approximately 19.8 ns.

3.3 Data Quality

Data quality is assessed by observing the C/N_0 of the signal received by the IRNSS receiver. It gives the signal strength as it is the ratio of the Carrier Power to the Noise. The higher this ratio is the better is the strength of the signal. As shown in Fig. 4, C/N_0 can be observed for the 7 satellites over the duration of 24 h. The variation in the C/N_0 of the three GEOs is found to be less and is seen to be more stable than the GSO satellites. This is because the GEO satellites are relatively stationary with respect to the receiver and hence less variation of C/N_0 is observed.

The range of C/N_0 over the duration of 24 h for all the seven satellites is found to be between 35 Hz-dB to 52 Hz-dB.

Table 2. Jitter found in the basic performance indicators of NavIC System

	North	East	Height
Jitter	2.75 m	0.58 m	4.8 m

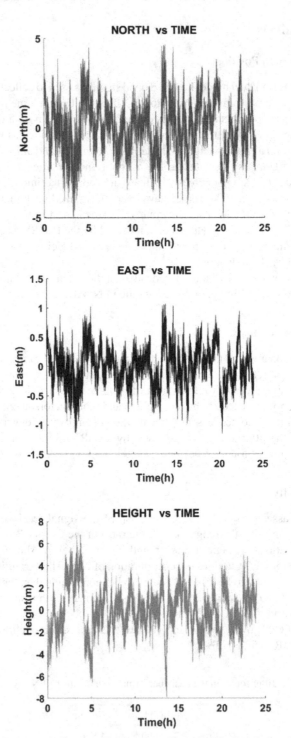

Fig. 1. Basic Performance indicators, North (m) vs Time (hour); East (m) vs Time (hour); Up (m) vs Time (hour)

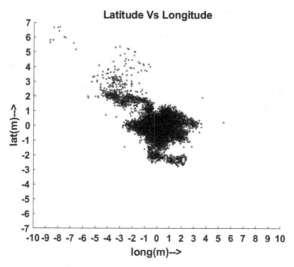

Fig. 2. Latitude vs Longitude of NavIC

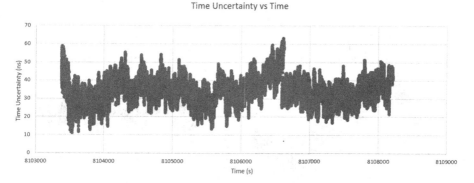

Fig. 3. Jitter in the time received by the IRNSS receiver

Figure 5, shows the graph of C/N_0 plotted against the elevation angle of the satellite. It is seen that the variation of C/N_0 against the elevation is less for I03, I06 and I07, it is more stable. This might be due to the fact that the relative position of these receivers remains almost the same for different elevation angles. While for other satellites the C/N_0 increases with the increase in elevation angle and is maximum when the elevation angle is at its peak. Geosynchronous satellites are continuously moving and when the elevation angle is maximum it is directly pointing towards the receivers giving the maximum C/N_0.

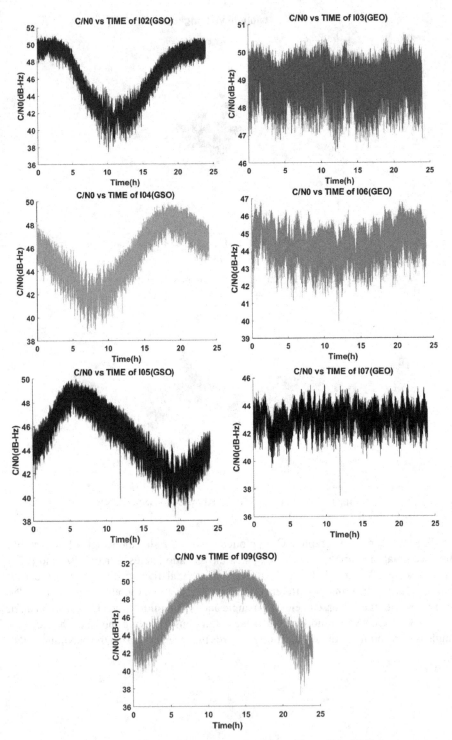

Fig. 4. C/N$_0$ (dB - Hz) vs Time (hour) of the 7 satellites of NavIC System

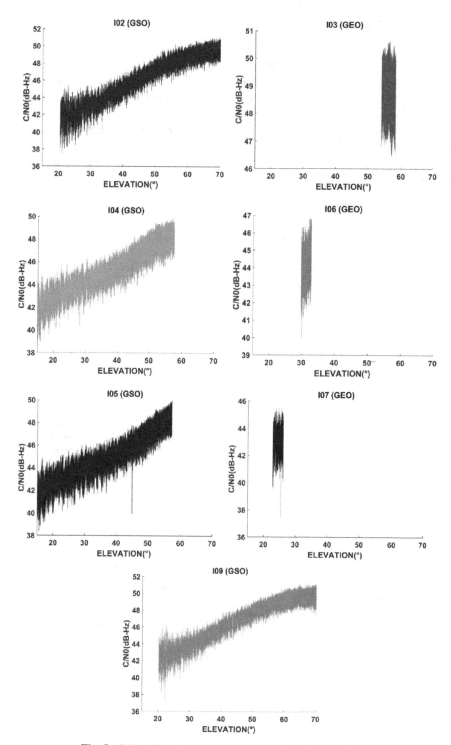

Fig. 5. C/N$_0$ (dB - Hz) vs elevation angle (°) of the satellites

3.4 Data Usability

Usability of the data is assessed by observing the DOP (Dilution of Precision) values received by the IRNSS receiver. DOP indicates the error caused by the relative position of the satellites. In this contribution GDOP (Geometrical Dilution of Precision), VDOP (Vertical Dilution of Precision), PDOP (Position Dilution of Precision) and HDOP (Horizontal Dilution of Precision) have been assessed over the duration of 24 h. The ideal value of DOP is 1, which indicates that the data received is highly accurate and precise. When the satellites are spread apart from the receiver's point of view, a good GDOP is received but when the satellites are close, poor GDOP is received. Table 3 shows the average values of different DOP calculated over a period of a week. Figure 6, shows the variation of the values of GDOP, PDOP, HDOP and VDOP over the duration of 24 h.

Table 3. Average values of DOP

	GDOP	PDOP	HDOP	VDOP
Average value	3.81	3.17	2.04	2.42

These values are considered to be good for positioning and navigation services.

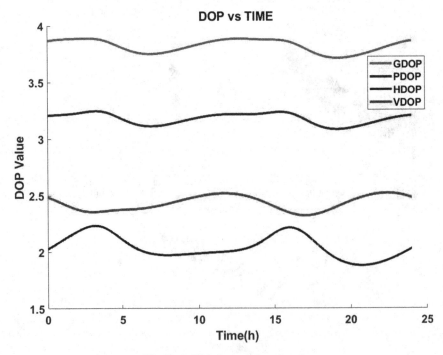

Fig. 6. DOP values vs time (hour)

Figure 7, shows the plot of the position uncertainty against the corresponding GDOP value. When poor GDOP is received it undermines the precision of the data received and hence the position uncertainty for the poor GDOP will be more. It can be seen from the increasing slope of the plot, as the GDOP increases the position uncertainty also increases.

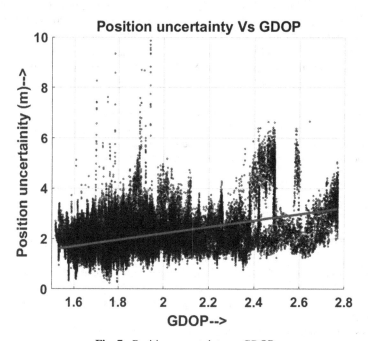

Fig. 7. Position uncertainty vs GDOP

4 Conclusion

In this paper, the analysis of basic performance indicators such as the uncertainty of position, uncertainty of time, data quality and data usability of the NavIC System have been done using data collected from the IRNSS receivers at The NorthCap University donated by the SAC, Ahmedabad.

Basic performance indicators have been taken into account for analyzing the uncertainty in position. GPS with more than 24 operating satellites in its constellation and having better coverage over the earth has less jitter in the basic performance indicators than the jitter in the basic performance indicators of NavIC.

The NavIC consists of 7 operational satellites 4 IGSOs and 3 GEOs. Therefore, the NavIC receivers perceive these satellites in their South direction. Hence, the position uncertainty in the North direction of NavIC is higher than that of in the East direction. In the case of GPS, the satellites are available in all directions as it has more satellites in its constellation thus yielding better results.

As satellites in NavIC has less spread and appear to be in one direction when viewed from the receiver the deviation increases. The latitude has more deviation as the satellites appear to be in the South direction thus relatively decreasing the spread in North direction when compared to the spread in East direction (longitude).

IRNSS/NavIC gives good results over the mainland of India. Strength of the signal received is also good and even the GDOP received is considered good for the navigation services. The jitter in time received is of 20 ns which is small and becomes insignificant when considered over a longer period of time. In the future due to some circumstances, if India is denied the use of GPS satellites, the IRNSS/NavIC can be used instead.

To further prove the effective use of NavIC system the next step of the study will include the applications of the data received for the navigation and time services.

Acknowledgments. The data from the IRNSS receivers has been collected and shared by Mr. Nikhilesh Kumar, lab assistant of NavIC lab at The NorthCap University. We are thankful to Space Application Centre (SAC), ISRO, Ahmedabad and the management of the university for providing the infrastructure to carry out the research. Their support is gratefully acknowledged.

References

Cozzens, T.: IRNSS-1H navigation satellite launch unsuccessful. GPS World, 31 August 2017 (2017)

Ganeshan, A.S.: Overview of GNSS and Indian navigation program, GNSS User Meet, 23 February, ISRO Satellite Center, Bangalore (2012)

Harde, H., Shahde, M.R., Badnore, D.: Indian regional navigation satellite system. Int. J. Res. Sci. Eng. 1(SPI), 36–42 (2015)

ISRO: IRNSS SIS ICD for standard positioning service version 1.0 configuration. ISRO, Bengaluru (2014)

Majithiya, P., Khatri, K., Hota, J.K.: Indian regional navigation satellite system: correction parameters for timing group delays. Inside GNSS 6, 40–46 (2011)

Thoelert, S., Montenbruck, O., Muerer, M.: IRNSS-1A: signal and clock characterization of the Indian regional navigation system. GPS Slout. 18(1), 147–152 (2014)

Zaminpardaz, S., Teunissen, P.J., Nadarajah, N.: IRNSS stand-alone positioning: first results in Australia. J. Spat. Sci. 61(1), 5–27 (2016)

Zaminpardaz, S., Teunissen, P.J., Nadarajah, N.: Single- frequency L5 altitude determination from IRNSS/NavIC and GPS: a single and dual-system analysis. J. Geodesy 91(12), 1415–1433 (2017a)

Zaminpardaz, S., Teunissen, P.J., Nadarajah, N.: IRNSS/NavIC L5 attitude determination. Sensors 17(2), 274 (2017b)

Zaminpardaz, S., Teunissen, P.J., Nadarajah, N.: IRNSS/NavIC single-point positioning: a service area precision analysis. Mar. Geodesy 40(4), 259–274 (2017c)

Artificial Intelligence Supervised Swarm UAVs for Reconnaissance

Saatvik Awasthi[1]([✉]), Balamurugan Balusamy[1], and V. Porkodi[2]

[1] School of Computer Science and Engineering, Galgotias University, Greater Noida, India
saatvikawasthi1998@gmail.com, kadavulai@gmail.com
[2] Department of Information Technology, Lebanese French University, Kurdistan Region, Erbil, Iraq
porkodi.sivaram@ifu.edu.krd

Abstract. The unmanned aerial vehicles (UAV) have great potential to support search tasks in unstructured environments. These are agile, small and lightweight which can incorporate many sensors that are suitable for detecting an object of interest across various terrains. These UAVs or Drones are perfectly suited for reconnaissance and perimeter sweeps. However, these have their limits and are vulnerable when operated alone. The solution to the problem is using a number of these drones to form a swarm. The swarm of drones can cover a larger area in a short period. The drones will be resembling the flocking nature of birds and the hive nature of bees which means there would never be a single drone operating alone. These drones are connected and the main controller i.e. the hive. The Hive is a narrow AI which is a goal-based system. The goals can be sweeping an area or periodic border patrols. The hive monitors the drones, organizes them. The drones communicate in the swarm wirelessly creating a Flying Adhoc Network. For navigation, this network utilizes GPS technology. This project aims to develop an AI-based system that controls these drones and achieve the goal that is assigned to it.

Keywords: Swarm drones · FANETS · UAVs · Artificial intelligence

1 Introduction

THE Unmanned Aerial Vehicle (UAV) [3] is an aircraft which does not require an onboard pilot. The aircraft can be remotely controlled by a controller at the ground station or by an onboard microcontroller. This gives the freedom to make these vehicles to small, agile, lightweight, fast. It is also easier to conceal these vehicles. These are less expensive than traditional aircrafts. These aerial vehicles can be used to various kind of jobs. These are currently being adopted by the military and civilians. These are helpful in performing various tasks like surveillance, disaster management, hazardous environment operations. These drones can also be mechanized to perform targeted operations like striking targets in a vicinity and surgical strike.

The UAVs are a very good vehicle but their features are the disadvantage for them. These being small in size cannot fly for very long time due to battery and energy limitations. Being the smaller in size also makes them vulnerable. A single UAV can cover a smaller area and cannot be used for very larger areas.

To overcome this, we can use multiple UAVs working together. These UAVs can be combined virtually forming a swarm. The swarm is a group of vehicles working together, communicating each other to achieve a common goal. The swarm nature extends the capabilities of the UAVs while overcoming the limitations. The whole swarm functions as a large UAV giving the larger ground and distances. The swarm can go on forever as the UAVs can be swapped as required.

The swarm can be self-autonomous following the command of the leader UAV. They will still require a supervision as the microcontroller onboard is not sufficient to supervise all the drones. Here the drone swarm requires a hive. The hive is an artificial intelligence system i.e. goal driven. This agent serves as ground control to all the drones. It supervises over all the swarm activities. The Hive acts as the interface between the human and the swarm. The Hive acts as delimitation to the autonomous swarm. The allocates the missions, control the behavior of the swarm. It is responsible to switching out drones as and when required.

2   Related Work

The Particle Swarm Optimization (PSO) [10] algorithm has been used for plotting the waypoint and optimizing the swam. PSO is a heuristic algorithm used for optimizing problems. These algorithms are not predictable and have high time complexity. The solution to this was using Distributed Particle Swarm Optimization algorithm was given by Hereford et al. [10]. This algorithm was to perform search tasks. Wang, Bai, Liang, Wang, Zhang and Fu [13] proposed three optimized algorithms for reconnaissance missions accomplished by utilizing UAV swarms. These three algorithms are Maximum Density convergence DPSO (MDC-DSPO), fast cross-over DPSO algorithm (FCO-DPSO) and accurate coverage exploration DPSO algorithm (ACE-DPSO).

The vision is the most promising sensory modal that an autonomous system can achieve. Utilizing computer vision backed by deep learning algorithms can provide much information as compared to other sensory modals. Schilling, Lecoeur, Schiano, and Floreano [4, 8] proposed a vision-based flight for drone swarms. They proposed a data-efficient imitation learning approach to coordinate the drone swarm. Inspired from this our system utilizes it for coordinating the flight pattern for target tracking and object identification.

3   Proposed System

The system proposed here is a UVA swarm that is supervised by an Artificial Intelligence System as shown in Fig. 1. The system is divided into 2 sub-systems that are combined to work as one. One system is an autonomous drone swarm. The other being an Artificial Intelligence enabled Ground Control system called the Hive. These two systems work together to achieve a common goal.

The swarm is one part of the complete system. The swarm carries out the activities instructed by the Hive. The swarm takes its own decisions using the onboard controller and algorithms like keeping collision free as shown in Fig. 2. These decisions involve keeping on flight path, keeping the UAV paths collision free, following the target, calculating path to the rendezvous point. The swarm executes the commands given by the Hive. The commands that are received from the hive are when to break the swarm, when to return back, when to reform, sending data back to the Hive. The swarm utilize flocking and path planning algorithms to manage the swarm. It utilizes vision flight algorithm for target tracking and object identification.

The second part of the system is the Hive. It is a goal based Artificial Intelligence system that supervises the swarm using the decision-making algorithms. The swarm is autonomous but receives it goals by the Hive. The Hive is responsible for the formation of the swarm in the beginning and decommissioning it when the mission is completed. The Hive firstly calculates the mission requirements and the number of UAVs required to complete the task. Then the swarm is assembled and the mission is assigned. The also responses to the requests of the swarm like UAV replacement or breaking formation.

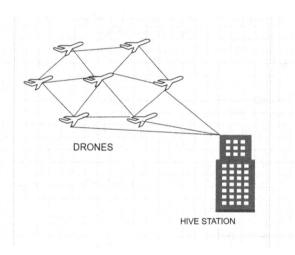

DRONES

HIVE STATION

Fig. 1. The swarm structure and supervision to the AI ground station

3.1 Limitation in Previous Systems

The previous swarm systems that have been proposed all deliver refined flight controls and flocking mechanisms but lack decision making capabilities. They cannot make the decisions and fulfill the mission requirements independently. The limitations that the proposed algorithm aims to solve are listed below.

- The limitation in the current swarm methodologies is that they are decentralized and are not backed up with Artificial Intelligence capabilities. This makes them very narrow working machines.

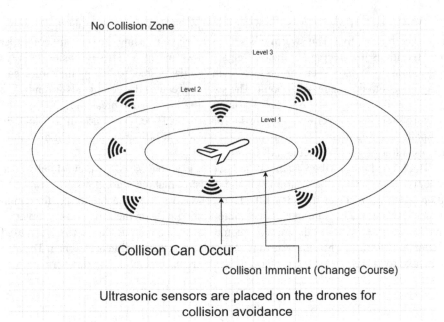

No Collision Zone

Fig. 2. The collision avoidance by a drone using ultrasonic sensor

- The current systems are decentralized, hence lack powerful processing capabilities as utilizing on-board processing.
- The current swarms cannot process and find predictive paths for target tracking as the current swarm methodologies rely only on on-board controllers.
- These swarms are autonomous but require a lot of human intervention and cannot complete a mission on their own without supervision.

3.2 Proposed Improvements

The proposed improvements are utilization of multiple algorithms for flight control, coupling the swarm with artificial intelligence, utilizing the ground control to provide improved swarm management and better data procession. The addition of artificial intelligence and machine learning in the system makes decision making more accurate and chances of completing a successful mission are increased drastically.

4 Features and Applications

4.1 Flocking Nature of Swarm

The swarm nature of the drones allows them to work together. The is resembled from the nature of bees. The swarm forms a pattern or formation as required. This is derived from the flocking nature of birds. The flocking algorithm we are utilizing is autonomous flocking swarm control algorithm [7, 12]. This allows multi-layer flocking. This is a low energy consuming algorithm and helps the other UAVs or drones in the network to maintain the formation autonomously. The ground control has to only send the signals to the main UAVs. The secondary UAVs will follow the main of root UAV. They utilize the hierarchical structure. The message is transferred to the main UAV and it transmit it to the secondary UAVs. Our algorithm follows a different approach to this.

All the UAVs are treated as equal. The commands are broadcasted to all the UAVs then the UAVs follow the individual command. It is not necessary to broadcast the command to each and every UAV. [6] Our algorithm utilizes mesh network topology of the drones. Each node is connected to at least on nearby drone creating an Adhoc network. Even if one UAV receives the command it is send to nearby connected drone. Its like a handshake that I have something new do you have it? Like this it is all communicated to all the UAVs in the network.

4.2 Reconnaissance

The UAV swarm is capable to perform the reconnaissance over the area allocated. The swarm is assumed to be equipped with wide angle lens cameras. The swarm capture the images together from each node which is sent to the ground control Hive. The AI at Hive utilizes the image stiching algorithm to generate a wide area view of the area. The reconnaissance algorithm finds the targets as the commands from the ground control system. The DSPO algorithm is used for swarm UAV reconnaissance [2]. The algorithm works individually on each UAV. When the target is achieved then the swarm is informed and reconnaissance is complete.

4.3 Rendezvous Planning

The swarm has times to break into smaller sub swarms as per the mission requirements. When the swarm breaks a rendezvous, point is decided. The path formulation algorithm formulates the path for each and every drone to meet at rendezvous point to form a formation. Distributed Cooperative particle swarm optimization (DCPSO) can be used to update the velocity and positions of the UAVs. The paths generated are collision free as they are non-cooperative. This helps to keep the swarm connected after dispersing. The swarm can get into formation effectively and in shortest path followed without collision using this algorithm.

4.4 Endless Swarm

The swam can go on performing its mission or task endlessly. This is possible due to the expendable feature of the swarm. Being in a swarm the drones work function as a one large system rather than an individual. The UAVs are replaced as when they require change. If one UAV faces a problem it is replaced with another. In case of a problem the UAV communicates the Hive and returns itself to the Hive. The Hive replaces the UAV by sending another one. This helps the swarm to let the mission on going as long its required.

The drones are periodically changed as per their battery capacities. For a task a UAVs half-life is calculated. Half Life is the time by which the drone consumes half of its energy in battery. When it reaches half its capacity it is either swapped with a new battery or replaced by another UAV.

4.5 Vision Flight

The UAVs utilize a secondary algorithm for vision-based flight. It works alongside flocking algorithm [6]. The vision algorithm utilizes neural engine to follow the points plotted by the flocking and path plotting algorithm. It helps to guide the drone swarms to be aware of their surroundings and also help to avoid obstacles. The vision flight implementation allows the UAV to utilize object identification path following in case of absence of GPS navigation. The GPS based navigation highly depends on connectivity but in case of absence of connectivity with the GPS or Hive The swarm can use visual navigation to travel to rendezvous or the targeted location. This visual flight allows the swarm to be capable for terrestrial navigation techniques.

The vision-based technique helps in the target tracking more effective. The UAVs can follow or track a target without needing any external target identification and tracking parameters. The target can be tagged and identified using vision tracking. The trajectory is plotted of the target and followed as its patterns. The Hive can utilize the path plotting of the UAV and suggest predictive patterns to follow the target or relocate the target.

4.6 Energy Efficiency

The swarm highly relies on connectivity. It also in continuous communication with the Hive. This results in too much energy consumption over data transfer. This can minimize using effective data routing algorithms. The algorithm uses a multi-hop routing technique for a faster data transfer and shorter delay.

At a point of time all the UAVs need not to utilize all of it sensors. The drones at the center and middle of the swarm won't need to keep all their sensors turned on as they are at the center. The drones at the center will rely on the flocking and path plotting algorithm and turn off the sensors for visual flight, surrounding awareness, etc. The drones at the edge of the swarm can be replaced by the drones in the center of the swarm.

4.7 The Hive

The UAVs swarm is a semi-autonomous system that is supervised by the goal-based Artificial Intelligence System that utilizes decision making algorithms to make decisions for the swarm and plan out a formation as per mission requirements. The Hive is responsible for the formation of the swarm in the beginning and decommissioning it when the mission is completed. It calculates the effort or the number of drones required for the swarm to form, number of replacement drones needed and as and when the drones are needed, etc. It also responses to the requests of the swarm like UAV replacement or breaking formation.

5 Motivation

5.1 Security

The major motivation behind the idea was security. India share a vast border with its neighbors Pakistan and China. As relations between the countries are bitter the borders are heavily manned throughout the year. This requires a lot of man power. Added to this the constant rising of tensions the terrorist activity to invade the borders are constantly increasing. To this lot of reconnaissance is required and the border needed to be constantly watched by perimeter sweeps. Here the Swarm drones come into play that can autonomously work together and cover a large area for perimeter sweeps, keep a close eye on border activities.

5.2 Elasticity

The UAVs in the swarm are of expendable nature. This gives the swarm elasticity of being of any size from being in tens to thousands. This elastic and expendable nature motivates the nature that the swarm can grow and shrink as per the requirement as the mission. This also keeps the swarm to go on endlessly and recover no matter how great the damage is done. Even if most of the drones are destroyed, they can quickly replace by new ones and the presence of a Hive supervision provides data security and redundancy. The new drone taking place of the previous one has the data for the previous one and can continue the task as it has to be proceeded with.

6 Use Cases

There are numerous use cases for the swarm to be implemented. The use cases vary from area of deployment and the severity of the situation. The system is fully capable of achieving its goal by precision planning and decision-making techniques.

6.1 Perimeter Sweep

The UAVs swarm can be used for a perimeter sweep. The perimeter sweep involves looking for a particular area for hostile presence. This can be achieved by utilizing the swarm of drones which are separated as individual and each drone is given a non-collision path that are unique. These paths are such that each and every corner of the perimeter is searched for the hostile. This gives a multiple view of a corner by using overlapping paths. Each and every path is unique and speed of the UAVs are coordinated to avoid collision.

6.2 Area Reconnaissance

The UAVs swarm can be used for area reconnaissance. The area reconnaissance involves the performing patrols on the borders or an area. These drones can be used in place of soldiers to patrol a large area. Multiple drone swarms are used to patrols where they allocated a particular area to sweep. These drones continuously scan for any unidentified hostile object in the vicinity. The drones are replaced and swapped out providing endless coverage without blind spots.

6.3 Target Tracking

The UAVs can be utilized for target tracking. The swarm can break its formation into smaller groups. It will utilize vision flight algorithm to track moving objects and plot path to track the target. In case of desynchronization with the target the ground station Hive can use path predictive algorithms to re locate the target organize the swarm to track it.

6.4 Remote Area Surveillance

The UAVs is very helpful in remote area surveillance. The UAVs are smaller in size hence can fit into tight positions and can be utilize to surveillance at remote locations even under unfavorable weather conditions. This is one of the major use cases of the swarm UAVs. Being in a swarm they can cover a larger area as well as the data is also secured due to data redundancy. Being in a swarm it is security increases than being a single drone.

6.5 Hazardous Area Monitoring

The UAVs is very helpful in remote area surveillance. The UAVs are smaller in size hence can fit into tight positions and can be utilize to surveillance at remote locations even under unfavorable weather conditions. This is one of the major use cases of the swarm UAVs. Being in a swarm they can cover a larger area as well as the data is also secured due to data redundancy. Being in a swarm it is security increases than being a single drone.

6.6 Disaster Management and Damage Control

The UAV swarm is of much help in case of disaster management and control. In occurrence of a disaster the drone swarm can be deployed in the area of impact to scan for survivors and analyze the damage done. The drones can locate the pinned survivor's location precisely and the help can be provided quickly and effectively.

7 Comparison

The comparison of drone swarms with single drones and how effective can the drone swarms be when coupled with an AI.

7.1 Time

Let consider the area A of length D and breath B. The time taken to calculate the flight path is taken as a constant C. The speed taken is constant of S. The time taken T will be

$$t = \frac{D}{S} + C$$

Let the sweep width of the UAV is X then, it will require B/X passes to cover the area A. Then the total time

$$T = \frac{B}{X}t$$

When considering a swarm of N drones, time taken to make a single pass is same t. The load is parallelly done by N drone hence the total time taken is t.

Considering a reconnaissance scenario, the area A is divided into a matrix. Of rows and columns. The drone has to travel all the possible paths from point P_1 to P_2. The number of possible paths is $M_1...M_n$. Distance travelled by each UAV is $D_1 ... D_n$.

Then the time taken by single drone is:

$$T = \frac{D_1 + D_2 + ... + D_n}{S} + C$$

The time taken in the case of a drone swarm is way less as all the paths are followed by individual drones.

$$T = \max\left(\frac{D_1}{S} + \frac{D_2}{S} + ... + \frac{D_n}{S}\right) + C$$

The maximum time is the time taken to sweep the longest path which is way less than the time in case of a single drone.

Assumptions:

- All drones are considered identical.
- The drones don't require replacement for recharge.
- Each and every drone speed is constant.

Table 1. Comparison of single drone vs a swarm of drones

Parameter	Single	Swarm
Time	Maximum	Minimum
Energy Efficiency	Minimum	More than Single drone
Range	Half-life of UAVs battery	Unlimited (Theoretically)
Communication	Limited to onboard antennae	Can be extended by placing UAVs linear fashion and hoping the signal

Table 1 shows the comparison on various parameters how drone swarm is better than single drone.

8 System Architecture

The system comprises of 2 main components:

- The Swarm of UAVs
- The Ground Station (Hive) (Fig. 3).

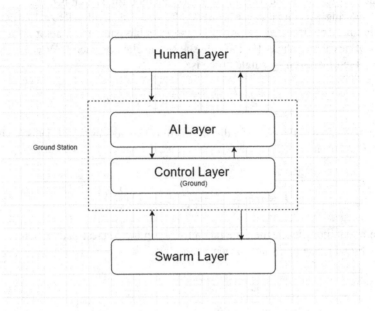

Fig. 3. The various layers of the system

8.1 Proposed Algorithm

The Fig. 4 shows the complete flow control and decision made at various layers to achieve the mission objective. The above mission terminates in two conditions weather its completed or the mission validation fails. The initial layer computes all parameters before starting the mission. If there is a mission failure possibility the mission is not executed.

8.2 Human Layer

The Human Layer is the interface through which the human interacts. Its responsibility is to collected the accurate mission objectives and required parameters, validate those before feeding it to the AI layer. The human layer keeps the track for the progress of the mission and continuously getting updates from the AI Layer.

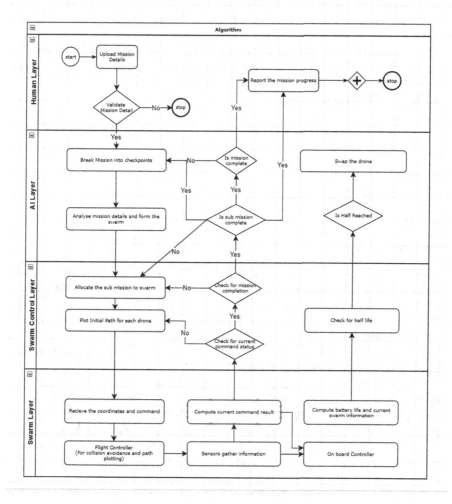

Fig. 4. The flow of data through various layers

8.3 Ground Station (Hive)

The Hive is separated into 2 sub parts one being the controller and communicator for the swarm other being the Artificial Intelligence program that controls the controller.

The AI sub layer comprises of decision making and predictive algorithms. It also comprises of greedy and path finding algorithms for path plotting and swam formation. It utilizes these algorithms to govern and supervise the swarm. The mission data is fed to the AI system. The AI calculates the number of drones required to complete the mission. It estimates the initial swarm number and the number of replacement drones required to swapping. The swarm is assembled. The mission is divided into smaller tasks that needed to be performed. These smaller tasks are checkpoints to the mission progress.

As the mission progresses the AI allocates new tasks or objective to the swarm. The AI decides when the swarm needs to be formed, when it needed to be dispersed or the drones needed to be replaced. The AI is responsible for all the data crunching and utilizes the ground station protocols and algorithm to control the swarm.

The ground station provides complete monitoring and interaction with the swarm. It comprises of protocols for communication and algorithms for replacement of the drones, formation of the swarm, flocking algorithm, data communication.

Algorithm for drone replacement:

```
If(current_level == half_life)
    Request_change()
Else
    E = Estimate_time()
    Schedule_change_time(E)
```

8.4 Swarm of UAVs

The swarm is initiated by the Hive (Ground Station). The initial flight paths are computed by Hive. The swarm then follows that path and in case of any change utilize the onboard controllers to take the necessary decision. The is decentralized [1] in nature and all drones are treated equally. There are various algorithms that are being utilized to form the swarm, keep it in position, for rendezvous planning and vision-based flights. FANETS [5, 14] are used to provide continuous communication among the swarm and also providing data efficiency with effective data routing.

The flocking nature of the swarm is maintained by multiple algorithms. These follow a DSPO[] based scheme. FEI DAI [7] have proposed 3 DSPO based intelligent flocking control algorithms that are utilized in various kind of scenarios. Flocking and topology control is critical for the robust running and maintenance of multi- Unmanned Aerial Vehicle (UAV) system. This paper proposes a swarm intelligence inspired autonomous flocking control scheme for UAV Networks (UAVNs) [14] to help them maintain their topology during the flying process, while ensuring the Quality of Service (QoS) of them with low energy consumption. The Situation Perception Consensus (SPC) algorithm [11, 12] provides the UAV swam with better stability to perform mission in hostile and complex environments. In this, the UAV swarm cooperative SPC is analyzed, the consensus evaluation indices are established and evaluation method based on three-parameter interval number and HM operators is designed. The evaluation indices are established from six aspects based on IQ evaluation theory and the characteristics of swarm cooperative engagement.

The swarming algorithm for target recognition is a swarming algorithm [15] for distributed ATR using software agents embedded on UAVs. This algorithm has shown that distributed ATR using a swarmed model improves the scalability of the system, both in the number of UAVs deployed and the number of targets in the AOI, as compared with a centralized model for ATR. This makes the system less dependent on the central location by confirming targets using cooperative local computations on UAVs and improves the susceptibility of the system to malicious attacks on the central location.

Vision Based flight algorithms are used to provide better coordination in the swam as well as target tracking is enabled by using them. The utilization of vision-based flight provides and added advantage of navigation if the Hive is offline. Fabian Schilling [4, 9] has suggested two methods one for target tacking and one for cohesive swarm collision avoidance. These provide the vison flight capability to the swarm hence making it autonomous.

References

1. Cooley, R., Wolf, S., Borowczak, M.: Secure and decentralized swarm behavior with autonomous agents for smart cities. In: 2018 IEEE International Smart Cities Conference (ISC2) (2018). https://doi.org/10.1109/isc2.2018.8656939
2. Zeng, Z., Sammut, K., Lian, L., Lammas, A., He, F., Tang, Y.: Rendezvous path planning for multiple autonomous marine vehicles, 0364-9059 © 2017 IEEE (2017)
3. Hildmann, H., Kovacs, E., Saffre, F., Isakovic, A.F.: Nature-inspired drone swarming for real-time aerial data-collection under dynamic operational constraints, 4 September 2019. Received: 31 July 2019; Accepted: 28 August 2019
4. Schilling, F., Lecoeur, J., Schiano, F., Floreano, D.: Learning vision-based flight in drone swarms by imitation. IEEE robot. Autom. Lett. **4**, 4523–4530 (2019)
5. Khan, M.A., Khan, I.U., Safi, A., Quershi, I.M.: Dynamic routing in flying ad-hoc networks using topology-based routing protocols, 14 August 2018. Received: 18 June 2018; Accepted: 9 August 2018
6. Dai, F., Chen, M., Wei, X., Wang, H.: Swarm intelligence-inspired autonomous flocking control in uav networks, 9 May 2019. Date of current version 23 May 2019, Received 4 April 2019, accepted 27 April 2019
7. Vikranth, D.R.: UAV swarm co-ordination and control using grossberg neural network. Int. J. Comput. Sci. Trends Technol. (IJCST) **5**(4), 1–7 (2017)
8. Schilling, F., Lecoeur, J., Schiano, F., Floreano, D.: Learning vision-based cohesive flight in drone swarms. arXiv:1809.00543v1 [cs.RO], 3 September 2018
9. Zhu, X., Liu, Z., Yang, J.: Model of collaborative UAV swarm toward coordination and control mechanisms study, In: ICCS 2015 International Conference on Computational Science, vol. 51, pp. 493–502 (2015)
10. Hereford, J.M.: A distributed particle swarm optimization algorithm for swarm robotic applications. In: IEEE International Conference on Evolutionary Computation (2006). https://doi.org/10.1109/cec.2006.1688510
11. Gao, Y., Li, D.: UAV swarm cooperative situation perception consensus evaluation method based on three-parameter interval number and heronian mean operator. IEEE 20 November 2018. Electronic ISSN 2169-3536
12. Majd, A., Ashraf, A., Troubitsyna, E., Daneshtalab, M.: Using optimization, learning, and drone reflexes to maximize safety of swarms of drones. In: 2018 IEEE Congress on Evolutionary Computation (CEC) (2018). https://doi.org/10.1109/cec.2018.8477920
13. Wang, Y., Bai, P., Liang, X., Wang, W., Zhang, J., Fu, Q.: Reconnaissance mission conducted by UAV swarms based on distributed PSO path planning algorithms, vol. 7, pp. 105086–105099. IEEE Access 30 July 2019. Electronic ISSN 2169-3536. https://doi.org/10.1109/access.2019.2932008

14. Liu, D., Wang, J., Xu, Y., Xu, Y., Yang, Y., Wu, Q.: Opportunistic mobility utilization in flying ad-hoc networks: a dynamic matching approach. IEEE Commun. Lett. 1 (2019). https://doi.org/10.1109/lcomm.2019.2899602

15. Dasgupta, P.: A multiagent swarming system for distributed automatic target recognition using unmanned aerial vehicles. IEEE Trans. Syst. Man Cybern. - Part A: Syst. Hum. **38**(3), 549–563 (2008). https://doi.org/10.1109/tsmca.2008.918619

Using Virtual Reality as a Cost-Effective Substitute for Engineering Labs in Underdeveloped Countries

Alalade Adesoji[1], Sanjay Misra[1(✉)], and Ravin Ahuja[2]

[1] Covenant University, Ota, Ogun, Nigeria
Alalade.Adesoji@stu.cu.edu.ng,
SanJay.misra@covenantuniversity.edu.ng
[2] Shri Vishwakarma Skill University, Gurgaon, India
ravinahujadce@gmail.com

Abstract. Engineering education in underdeveloped countries is lacking on multiple fronts, majorly, the insufficiency of practical and technical know-how of engineering graduates. This problem stems deeply from a lack of experimental laboratories and at best inadequate training equipment for students to carry out practical knowledge. This paper is centered on the introduction of virtual laboratories as a less expensive and more dynamic means of carrying out engineering practices in graduate and undergraduate programs to make up for the lack of actual laboratories in these underdeveloped nations. This paper proposes the introduction of Virtual Reality into engineering education to bridge this gap between underdeveloped nations and developed nations as an educational aid in engineering. Also conducted is a comprehensive literature survey on already in-practice VR technology in institutions world-wide, the benefits this tech has provided these institutions and the benefits it will afford underdeveloped nations.

Keywords: Virtual reality · Virtual environments · Engineering education · Engineering laboratories · Underdeveloped nations

1 Introduction

In the 21st century, the most powerful nations in the world have attained such a revered position because of economic stability, scientific edge and technological advancements which can be traced back to the quality of the educational institutions in those nations. Countries like these such as The U.S.A, Japan, Russia, Germany, France, China, and etcetera have attained superpower status because of the influx of investments of these countries in education [1]. Engineering single-handedly has even transformed the economies of these superpower nations most notably Germany and Japan. This powerfulness is a direct reflection of the strength of the academic institutions in these nations [1] with emphasis on the engineering aspect. Engineering as a course is very practical and technical and to be fully productive as a graduate of an engineering program, people must have these practical hands-on solutions. In regards to globalization of any economy and speeding up the development of new technology, the importance of engineers,

© Springer Nature Singapore Pte Ltd. 2020
U. Batra et al. (Eds.): REDSET 2019, CCIS 1229, pp. 389–401, 2020.
https://doi.org/10.1007/978-981-15-5827-6_34

which includes but not limited to designing, operation and maintenance of complex technical devices and systems, production of new materials and technologies cannot be overstated [2]. Engineers from institutions of more developed countries are at their peak because of the training and standards inculcated in them by means of theoretical, practical and hands-on educational aids in the form of laboratory engagements, field trips to established worldwide recognized bodies, and also the use of the numerous technological accomplishments made in recent times. All of these mentioned put these developed countries significantly ahead of underdeveloped nations in all things engineering related. Thus, this paper seeks to provide a bridge for the gap between developed and underdeveloped economies as relates to engineering by introducing the VR technology in higher institutions as an effective substitute for standard laboratories in higher institutions.

Virtual Reality (popularly called VR) refers to computer-simulated environments that implicate or give a real sense of physical presence in a place in the real world, and also in fictional worlds [3]. In another definition, VR can be defined as a simulation utilizing computer graphics to conceive a realistic looking world [4]. This virtual world is very dynamic and can be interacted with via inputs from an operator(s). Such inputs consist of gestures and verbal commands and they are achieved via specialized equipment [5]. We look at the capacity and capabilities of Virtual Environments (VE) utilizing VR for education and tutoring activities. These VEs are already being utilized in several engineering realms from automobile manufacturing and some more complicated systems design regarding to space [6]. VEs have a small branch tagged Virtual Learning Environments (VLEs) which are developed and designed solely for pedagogical purposes and are applied for tutoring uses in higher institutions [6].

Virtual Environments offer the consumers the opportunity to carry out the activity of interest they want to, from operating or piloting an aero plane, installing technical devices, analyzing complex systems, and etcetera without actually having to engage in the real-life process itself. This removes the threats of hazards, wastage of resources, and at worst, loss of life. Every economy requires the innovation and unique dynamism of engineers skill set to play the crucial role of creation and development of new technology, new materials and operation of technical machineries [7, 29].

1.1 Defining the Problem

The problem this paper intends to tackle stems from a gross lack of training equipment and state-of-the-art laboratories to effectively inculcate solid practices in engineering students in underdeveloped countries. What we have represented so far led us to think about the importance of capable engineers in an economy. Taking Nigeria as a case study, compared to the amount of graduates that emerge from universities per year from engineering programs, the amounts of students with actual hands-on experience is very low when faced with real-time real world engineering problems due to lack of appropriate practical knowledge and this creates a lag in the economy because of lack of know-how to apply the bulk of acquired knowledge [8]. Knowledge retention amongst students in engineering is not satisfactory and must be rectified to remain competitive in a growing and more demanding local and global economy. The learning pyramid presented by the National Training Laboratories shows that learning by doing is 75% more sufficient for learners as compared to just visual inputs (20% sufficient) or audio materials (10% sufficient) [4, 30]. This physical act of "doing" should traditionally be achieved with the use of a state-of-the-art laboratory in a professional academic setting. Seriously to note though is that, fully functional laboratories with state of the art equipment are very costly to implement and pose a major challenge for higher institutions in underdeveloped nations who work with very limited budgets, and from the primitive days of engineering education, functional and practical laboratories have played a crucial role in graduate and undergraduate programs. In point of fact, before engineering science became emphasized, most engineering instruction was conducted in the lab or workshop [9, 31].

Ensuing below are the research question and its sub-questions, which is a guiding motive behind the study of this issue.

The research question emerges: Is Virtual Reality Engineering an innovative enough and sufficient substitute for Engineering Laboratories and Workshops in underdeveloped nations?

The sub-question follows; if it is, how can it be efficiently implemented in an institution where budget is very minimal and must be maximized?

This paper is divided into five sections. After the introduction, the second chapter is related works showing a detailed study of similar literature. Third section is methodology, fourth is discussions of the role of this technology and lastly the conclusion.

2 Related Works

The term Virtual Reality is very aptly defined by one of the earlier papers on Virtual Reality in Engineering Education as a highly realistic, highly interactive, highly immersive computer-simulated environment which may be graphics or text based. This article [10] being one of the pioneers of literature on VR Labs categorized it into three budget levels; low; USD10,000–12,000, medium; USD10,000–50,000 and high; greater than USD50,000. Thanks to advances in technology, VR which has been around over 40 years, in present day can be acquired relatively cheaply by the privileged everyday user and researcher, this gap is covered by Stuchlikova et al. [4] and Zavalani [11]. Zavalani [11] also points out that on the world-wide web (WWW) are free VR demo modules that can be easily downloaded for use in educational institutions where budget restrictions make acquisition a challenge. In [11] also, a more recent article on Virtual Reality, VR was more accurately described VR as a surfacing computer interface branded by outstanding levels of immersion, believability, and interaction, with an expected intention of causing the operator to be completely convinced, that he/she is in the simulated environment, contrary to being on the outside looking in. Virtual reality executions traditionally utilize superior speed, superior quality 3-D graphics, 3-D audio and particular VR gear such as head mounted displays (HMDs), wired clothing, etcetera to produce high degrees of reality and believability [12].

Cecil et al. [6] adequately described three levels of immersion in VR tech; none, semi and full immersion where he described non-immersive environments as similar to a typical 2D computer screen; being the most basic of VLEs. Semi-immersive environments as dynamic 3-D sound systems enabled representations of target environments where operators can interact with the VE using sensors, 3-D goggles and trackers. A computer monitor or a much larger wall sized screen, can be used as the means of display on which the consumers are able to intercommunicate with the 3-D environment if need be, but mainly observe. Fully immersive environments are VEs in which all relations to the user's environment are completely phased out (the immersion is 360°). The HMDs being worn on the head houses lenses on which VE is projected thereby immersing the user completely in the virtual environment [6].

Numerous literatures exist on Virtual Reality in Engineering Education in which different models were proposed, some effective, some not making much of an impact but essentially the systems are too complex and bogus with cost of implementation being on the high-side. Abulrub [13] discussed a highly effective but quite complex and costly to implement VR model designed in the University of Warwick that can be used to simulate both 2-D (non-immersive) and 3-D (fully immersive) environments. This model combines hardware devices such as integrated camera-based infrared real-time tracking systems, projectors, x-ray CT scanning systems, VR gear alongside Autodesk software packages such as Autodesk Showcase and Autodesk Inventor to simulate the start to finish processes of manufacturing of cars. Valdez et al. [14] and [15] proposed non-immersive VR models for electrical engineering students to acquaint them to various types of electronic components that could be challenging to obtain and circuit designs that would be otherwise unfeasible to execute for a variety of reasons. [15]. Valdez in [15] proposed a VEMA (Virtual Electric Manual) environment comprising software such as Wirefusion to view models, and 3ds Max, Vizup and Java to design models. This VEMA environment was targeted at replacing a measurements and instrumentations laboratory in its entirety, although easy to implement and completely cost-effective, model is non-immersive and therefore very limited as a virtual environment platform.

Sampaio [16] and Dinis [17] proposed fully immersive VR models for undergraduate civil engineering students. The model in [16] allows visualization of the physical progression of construction processes from details of the form of each element used in achieving the work, roof design to type and method of operation of the equipment utilized in the construction. 3D geometric models are created and viewed via a platform called Eon Reality Systems [1]. In [17], it was proposed that the adoption of game-based Virtual Environments for Architectural, Engineering and Construction (AEC) courses which have been widely accepted in academia [18–20] designed via 4D CAD and Autodesk Revit software be utilized by potential civil engineers to explore 3D models of various infrastructure and simultaneously discover various disciplines of civil engineering. Jing [21] elaborated a collaborative simulation technology for complex integrated mechanical and electro-hydraulic system, using ADAMS control system module which easily interfaces with MATLAB. These systems although highly effective and bringing very complex real-life engineering systems to a virtual environment, they are quite costly and time consuming to implement.

Other articles focused not only on VR in engineering pedagogy generally only but streamlined it to a very specific purpose under a very specific program, some of such scenarios include [22] where the authors focused on semi-immersive VR technology singularly on replicating chemical laboratories and plants because of the risk of exposure of amateurish students to extreme levels of radioactive toxicity and curbing those

---

[1] https://www.eonreality.com/systems/.

risks. For this, virtual laboratory accidents are simulated in these plants and students and experience repercussions so as to be properly educated on chemical danger. Also Wolfartsberger [23] elaborated on a VR based environment for review of 3D engineering designs using native CAD, 3D editable mesh and Unity3D software packages to create the VR design environment and HTC Vive hardware to access it. This system is highly effective as surmised from the users as it visualizes complex engineering data and provides a set of multimodal tools to inspect a 3D model on various levels. Di Giorgio [24] streamlined his study in VR to Satellite Engineers to replicate experiments that cannot possibly be done in space due to sheer expense of technology that it will require, along with manpower and time investment. Virtual reality provided a technological option to actual real life implementations of different engineering programs as can be seen in all the articles in this paper. VR allows for the creation of 3D models of already existing engineering components, devices and facilities that can be interacted with using dedicated software and hardware, also to model various pre-conceived ideas before production and implementation [2, 25].

This study revolves around a fully immersive 3-D VR model that is simplistic to implement with very minimal cost incurred and improves on previous related works with its simplicity to create and implement various 3-D VR models using the Unity3D [2]. VR software design platform and an Oculus Rift HMD.

3 Methodology

Even with the simplest of designs, the process of creating a 3D model for a VR exercise requires some investment, with respect to finances, time and effort. The whole process has to begin with gathering of information and analysis of this information. The research methodology is divided into two parts; Firstly is proper collection of data through interviews and questionnaires about the familiarity and interest of young engineers in the technology, thorough analysis and assessment of this data and secondly, utilizing the analysis to carefully guide the creation and implementation of VR 3D models.

3.1 Questionnaire Guiding VR Design

For the purpose of this paper, the following are analytic questions (questionnaire) to which answers were sought out by oral interviews I conducted with students of the department of Engineering, Covenant University.

1. Are you familiar with Virtual Reality technology and its concepts?
2. Have you used this technology before?
3. Will you be interested in using VR technology in conjunction with your program?
4. What kind of experiment can you suggest to be conducted using VR technology?
5. Overall, do you encourage the implementation of new technology in Nigerian education?
6. Would you say this technology posed any threat to Nigerian education? If yes, what are those threats?

---

[2] https://unity3d.com/.

3.2 SWOT Analysis of Responses Given to Questionnaire

A cumulative amount of 50 students were orally interviewed from various five programs of the College of Engineering. These programs are Electrical Engineering, Telecommunications Engineering, Computer Engineering, Mechanical Engineering and Civil Engineering. The response and feedback from the students of the university showed a high level of enthusiasm of students in the technology and a high expectation for this technology to be a perfect substitute for traditional and conventional teaching aids. After the first and second question, a lot of responses indicated that majority of engineering students were familiar with this technology but had never been hands-on save for a few who have utilized the technology but majorly for gaming and entertainment purposes. After explanation of the technology and its potential benefits, interests from the students surged and multiple inputs and suggestions were offered (Table 1).

Table 1. SWOT analysis of the cumulated data acquired in response to the questionnaire; This analysis is a guide that governs the steps that follow showing the implementation of VR into the university as an adequate substitute means to the lack of standard facilities.

Strengths	Weaknesses
-Large interest of the students in the concepts and introduction of VR technologies -More zeal from student to engage in actual practical and not only conventional theoretical practices -Flexibility of experiments that can be conducted with VR -VR serves as a gateway for students to research and apply more technology in advancement of education	-High price of VR equipment and also more advanced and intricate designs will require higher cost -Too many suggestion for experiment which will require a lot of time to develop those intricate designs -High computational power needed, security issue also prevails
Opportunities	Threats
-Involvement of students in construction and design of VR systems -Creation of applications that use 3D interfaces -Simplification of the technology so students can take bolder steps	-Insufficient funds for procuring, maintaining and servicing equipment -Disregard for traditional and conventional modes of teaching

3.3 Tabular and Graphical Representation of Responses

Tables 2 and 3 below represent the responses of students to the questionnaire, by experiment of interest of each student against their familiarity, experience and interest in VR tech (Graphs 1 and 2).

Table 2. Cross-tabulation of experiment of interest vs. familiarity with VR technology

Experiment of interest	Familiarity with tech		Total
	No	Yes	
Nil	3	0	3
Electrical eng.	4	9	13
Telecomms eng.	0	4	4
Computer eng.	1	2	3
Civil eng.	1	6	7
Mechanical eng.	4	16	20
Total	13	37	50

Table 3. Cross tabulation of experiment of interest vs. interest in implementation of VR technology

Experiment of interest	Interest in tech		Total
	No	Yes	
Electrical eng.	0	13	3
Telecomms eng.	0	4	13
Computer eng.	1	3	4
Civil eng.	1	7	3
Mechanical eng.	1	20	7
Total	3	47	50

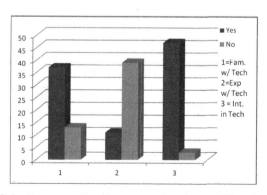

Graph 1. Representation of response of students to VR technology

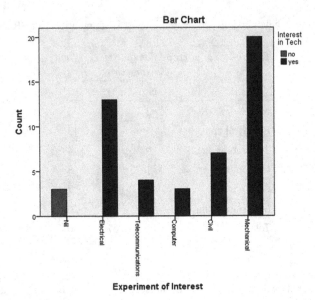

Graph 2. Representation of cumulative choice experiment of interest per program

3.4 Proposed Model

The hardware system comprises a VR headset or head mounted device (HMD), in this case, Oculus Rift, a gesture sensor such as Leap Motion, and a 360° camera, Ricoh Theta S, integrated together with Unity3D software which is pre-installed and operational on a PC [26]. Figure 1 below shows an interconnection between these components.

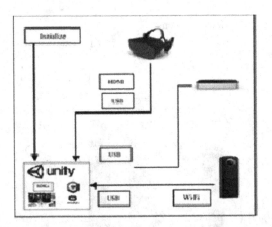

Fig. 1. Hardware and software components of a VR system [26]

As can be seen above, this system is a mock up of the proposed hardware to implement VR on in an institution initiating this technology. VEs can be designed by contracted

VE designers or any qualified personnel. After design, the VE is simulated via the HMD either by means of a portable device that can be inserted in the HMD or in the case of a more robust HMD such as HTC Vive or Oculus Rift which is more advisable, it can be connected via dedicated connectors to the computer and the VE run directly from the computer but simulated on the HMD.

This model is very simplistic, yet directly creates a solution for an enormous problem. At initial stages, three of the model should be satisfactory enough to go through a maximum of 15 students to conveniently and appropriately disburse knowledge. If the ratio of students to set-up should at any point exceed 5 to 1, it will pose a threat to the complete engagement of the students to the exercise and the aim, thus defeated. With increase of population, addition of more models is definitely recommended.

3.5 Implementation of VR in Engineering Education in Nigeria

A 10-step methodology to implement VR in Engineering Education in institutions without adequate provision laboratory/workshop;

Step 1: The specific course objectives (i.e. the topics to be conducted in a VE) are established.
Step 2: The objectives requiring simulation, either computer-generated simulation, or virtual reality (i.e. 3D simulation) as a measure or means for completion are chosen. Rationale for the utilization and benefits of utilizing simulations and VR are examined when composing the selections.
Step 3: The composed list will be refined by selecting those that are capable of utilizing 3D simulations, using VR, as a measure or means for completion of the targets of the course.
Step 4: For each target in the list, the sub steps below are performed;
  Sub-step 4a; Standard of realism needed is determined, on a scale of very figurative to very real.
  Sub-step 4b; Level of immersion and presence necessary is determined, from a range of zero immersion required (e.g. Desktop VR) to complete immersion (by use of VR gear such as HMD, joysticks, etc) or from level of physical presence needed to none.
  Sub-step 4c; Nature of intercommunication with tactile input and output to and from, the VE needed, (e.g. haptic-tactile, 3D sound, text-based, audio, visual, and/or gesture) is determined.
Step 5: Depending on choices made in Step 4 above, VR software, hardware and/or delivery system (e.g. the Net, WWW pages) are selected.
Step 6: The VE is devised and created with VR software in this case Unity3d. In conjunction with the targets intended to be met, the VE may be created;
  • By the tutor or professional VE designers can be contracted
  • By the students
  • Or direct acquisition prebuilt and refitted to course objectives
Step 7: After the VE is generated, it is appraised via means of a pilot group of students.
Step 8: Appraisal outcome is used to revise the VE. Steps 7 and 8 are reiterated until the VE appropriately achieves all the targets intended for the course.
Step 9: The VE is then appraised by testing on the target population.

Step 10: Appraisal outcomes are used to revise the VE. Steps 9 and 10 are reiterated as necessary to ensure the VE remains consistent with the course objectives at any given time. Appraisal and revision has to continue and be maintained pending the period the VE will be used with the target population (Fig. 2).

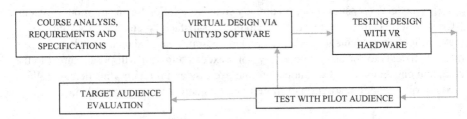

Fig. 2. Major steps in implementing VR

4   Role of VR in Teaching and Developing Future Engineers

Virtual Reality initiates a ground-breaking instructional tool for engineering that empowers engineering undergraduates and graduates to evaluate the value of provision of solutions requiring application of relevant knowledge and insight to various real-life complex challenges. The interactive Virtual Environment contributes a well-suited instrument to reduce complicated problems into very basic and simple ones and create homogeneity between them to produce an unparalleled, authentic and practical solution [13].

Producing the 3D VR models should be done with precise designations and motives which will determine how detailed the final model will be. These details must be completely fitting for the target goals the designer seeks to accomplish with the model. This technology makes provision of real-life experiments without having to use real-life experiments possible via the virtual experiment training system. This simulates different types of actual existent engineering problems that will not normally be easily created in a conventional classroom, lab or workshop for various reasons such as cost, health and safety [27]. This technology contributes a lot of importance in developing educational organizations in ways such as:

- It decreases cost of assets overtime as it solves the problem of purchasing and installing training machinery/instruments, while navigating restraints brought on by time and costs.
- Diminishing the risks of damaging materials and practices in teaching and training environments.
- It enhances the possibility to survey normally remote and hazardous regions such as highly radioactive environments.
- It reduces the effect on climate by minimizing wasteful materials produced and also eliminates damaging mistakes from amateurs and learners.
- It enables engineering students with disabilities to experience an environment where normally it would have been hardly possible.

- It makes student learning experience extraordinary which helps in developing the students and giving them a special appreciation for the subject matter.
- It also creates a scholarly reputation for any institute that incorporates the technology and makes them a desired choice for engineering students.

An effectual engineering teacher and in essence, leader, should definitely possess future awareness alongside tenacious technical and technological knowledge to be able to think creatively and rigorously to designate different feasible solutions to engineering problems. This Virtual Reality technology can also produce positive effects on engineering leaders and learners individually in helping them develop invaluable virtues such as intellectual motivation, effective communication and intercommunication, individual confidence and collective team collaboration [28]. Ways that Virtual Reality can institute these attributes on leaders/learners include;

- It enhances young engineers drive and mindset to acquire knowledge as it actively engages the students.
- It permits empirical learning by aiding in comprehension of real-life elements being simulated.
- It provides an avenue for young aspiring engineers and also professionals to research and probe technology in a hands-on manner.
- It encourages engaged attentiveness, participation and amplifies student interaction.

5 Conclusion

In conjunction with the dire state of underdeveloped countries, the industries and SMEs face a quite challenging business environment. Hence, properly cultivating future engineers demands a concise and adequate understanding of the industry requirements in the present and also, the challenges faced by the industries because there is a requirement for engineers to possess enlightened practical problem solving skills and correct theoretical application to real-life challenges. Therefore, engineering programs must be incorporated in such a way as to meet the needs of the industry.

3D VR technology will facilitate engineers to leave school with an in-depth understanding into the utilization of innovative technology to create products that have great value, save costs on this production and quickly move these products to meet the needs of consumers. The economy of these underdeveloped nations sorely require graduates of engineering who possess peculiar knowledge and skillet, and can achieve innovative solutions with minimal costs and zero wastages, increase profit recoupment, create unique and outstanding brands, provide genuine quality assurance and in general much better products.

With Virtual Reality the goal of this paper has clarified a way to actively achieve all of these qualities in a growing economy by integrating the powerful technology into the educational sector and training of upcoming engineers to create value in the products of engineering institutions in underdeveloped nations and to fulfill the industry needs thereby strengthening economic structure.

Acknowledgment. The authors wish to appreciate the Center for Research, Innovation, and Discovery (CU-CRID) of Covenant University, Ota, Nigeria, for partly funding of this research.

References

1. Glenda, K., et al.: Higher education and economic development: the importance of building technological capabilities. Int. J. Educ. Dev. **23**, 22–31 (2015)
2. Makarova, I., et al.: The application of virtual reality technologies in engineering education for the automotive industry. In: International Conference on Interactive Collaborative Learning (ICL), Florence (2015)
3. Nesamalar, E.K., Ganesan, G.: An introduction to virtual reality techniques and its applications. Int. J. Comput. Algorithm **01**(02), 28–30 (2012)
4. Stuchlíková, L. et al.: Virtual reality vs. reality in engineering education. In: 15th International Conference on Emerging e-Learning Technologies and Applications (ICETA), Bratislava (2017)
5. Martín-Gutiérrez, J., et al.: Virtual technologies trends in education. Eurasia J. Math. Sci. Technol. Educ. **13**(2), 469–486 (2017)
6. Cecil, J., et al.: Virtual learning environments in engineering and STEM education. In: 2013 IEEE Frontiers in Education Conference (FIE), Oklahoma (2013)
7. Kamp, A.: Engineering Education in a Rapidly Changing World, 2nd Revised Edition edn., p. 92. 4TU. Centre for Engineering Education, Delft (2016)
8. Afonja, A.A., et al.: Engineering Education for Industrial Development: Case Studies of Nigeria, Ghana and Zimbabwe. African Technology Policy Studies Network (ATPS), Nairobi (2005)
9. Potkonjak, V., et al.: Virtual laboratories for education in science, technology, and engineering. Comput. Educ. **15**(C), 309–327 (2016)
10. Pantelidis, V.S.: Virtual reality and engineering education. Comput. Appl. Eng. Educ. **5**(1), 5–12 (1997)
11. Zavalani, O., Spahiu, A.: Use curiousity for virtual reality as a hook in engineering education. In: 15th International Conference on Interactive Collaborative Learning (ICL), Villach, Austria (2012)
12. Bell, J., Fogler, H.: The investigation and application of virtual reality as an educational tool. In: Proceedings of the American Society for Engineering Education, Anaheim (1995)
13. Abulrub, A.G., et al.: Virtual reality in engineering education. In: IEEE Global Engineering Education Conference (EDUCON), Amman, Jordan (2011)
14. Travassos Valdez, M., et al.: Virtual labs in electrical engineering education - the VEMA environment. In: Information Technology Based Higher Education and Training (ITHET) Conference, York, UK (2014)
15. Travassos Valdez, M., et al.: 3D virtual reality experiments to promote electrical engineering education. In: Information Technology Based Higher Education and Training (ITHET) Conference, Lisbon, Portugal (2015)
16. Sampaio, A.Z., et al.: Interactive models used in Civil Engineering education based on Virtual Reality technology. In: Human System Interactions (HSI 2009), Catania, Italy (2009)
17. Dinis, F.M., et al.: An immersive virtual reality interface for civil engineering dissemination. In: Experiment@International Conference (exp.at 2017), Faro, Portugal (2017)
18. Heydarian, A., et al.: Immersive virtual environments versus physical built environments: a benchmarking study for building design and user-built environment explorations. Autom. Construct. **54**, 116–126 (2015)

19. Deshpande, A.A., Huang, S.H.: Simulation games in engineering education: a state-of-the-art review. Comput. Appl. Eng. Educ. **19**(3), 399–410 (2011)
20. Messner, J.I., et al.: Using virtual reality to improve construction engineering education. In: American Society for Engineering Education Annual Conference & Exposition, Washington DC (2003)
21. Jing, L.: Integrated mechanical and electro-hydraulic system modeling and virtual reality simulation technology of a virtual robotic excavator. In: 2009 IEEE 10th International Conference on Computer-Aided Industrial Design & Conceptual Design, Wenzhou, China (2009)
22. Bell, J.T., Fogler, S.H.: The application of virtual reality to chemical engineering education. In: IEEE Virtual Reality (VR 2004), Chicago, IL, USA (2004)
23. Wolfartsberger, J., et al.: A virtual reality supported 3D environment for engineering design review. In: Virtual System & Multimedia (VSMM), Dublin, Ireland (2017)
24. Di Giorgio, F., et al.: Virtual reality in satellite integration and testing. In: Systems Engineering (ISSE), Edinburgh, UK (2016)
25. Manseur, R.: Virtual reality in science and engineering education. In: Frontiers in Education, 2005. FIE 2005, Indianopolis, IN, USA (2005)
26. AlAwadhi, S., et al.: Virtual reality application for interactive and informative learning. In: 2017 2nd International Conference on Bio-engineering for Smart Technologies (BioSMART), Paris, France (2017)
27. Pantelidis, V.S.: Reasons to use virtual reality in education and training courses and a model to determine when to use virtual reality. Themes Sci. Technol. Educ. **2**(1–2), 59–70 (2010)
28. Zuljan, M.V., Vogrinc, J.: Facilitating Effective Student Learning through Teacher Research and Innovation, Ljubljana, Slovenia: Faculty of Education, University of Ljubljana, Slovenia (2010)
29. Egoeze, F., MIsra, S., Maskeliunas, R., Damasevicius, R.: Impact of ICT on universities administrative services and management of students' records: ICT in university administration. Int. J. Hum. Capital Inf. Technol. Prof. **9**(2), 1–15 (2018)
30. Oyebiyi, O., Misra, S., Maskeliunas, R., Damasevicius, R.: Application of ICT by small and medium enterprises in Ogun State, Nigeria. Commun. Comput. Inf. Sci. **799**, 459–471 (2018)
31. Sowunmi, O.Y., Misra, S., Omoregbe, N., Damasevicius, R., Maskeliunas, R.: A semantic web-based framework for information retrieval in E-learning systems. Commun. Comput. Inf. Sci. **799**, 96–106 (2018)

Distinctive Type of Fall Detection Methods Using Wearable Device Safety and Security of Elderly Person

R. K. Aggrawal and Mamta Gahlan[✉]

Department of Computer Engineering, NIT Kurukshetra, Kurukshetra, Haryana, India
mamtagahlan@gmail.com

Abstract. Falls is a main risk for the elderly man living without assistance. Rapid and fall detection events can reduce the rate of Humanity and raise the chances to survive and independent living of old person. In the last few decades, several technological and medical treatment solutions for detection of falls were published, but most of them suffer from vital limitations. We will discuss the various challenges and concept related to fall detection system for elderly person, A lot of research being conducted is being aimed at finding solutions for helping the elderly and their caretakers in case of incidences of falls; fall detection mechanism and notification alarms in case of falls have been developed in order to reduce fall consequences. Recently, the medical and behavioral history of elderly patients has also been taken into account for predicting the possibility of falls and devising better fall likelihood prediction systems.

Keywords: Fall detection · Elderly monitoring · Physical damages · Fall prevention and machine learning

1 Introduction

Some of the researcher has developed the home network applications detection of fall in healthcare. Fall is a very serious issue at the old age group person. According to survey of the china by 2050 more than 30% person will be aged at the age of above 40 years. more than 70% of person is hip fracture at the age of 70 years. It is the main reason of the circumstance like Psychological, Medical, Environmental and Biological behavior of person depend upon the history of the different person. A serious fall is one of the most life threatening risks to an elderly person It severely injures, and sometimes even kills the victim, especially old person. Therefore there is need for fall find out will help these people when they do fall and are not able to call for help. But one of the problems of these detection systems is that they are contact based i.e. they can sense the fall only when someone in physical contact with systems. Hence a system based on sensors is more desirable for those who are unable to call for help after a fall. In this paper we can describe the methods of fall detection, Fall prevention Technique and flow chart. It describe the challenges face in fall detection and future work.

2 Literature Review

Kinsella and Phillips [1, 2] discuss the population above 65 and over aged person issue of the health and coming next 10 to 15 year this ratio is decrease. It can be easily control and improve the life of human being better way to control using electronic device.

Popescu [3] one third of adult population above the age of 65 year according to the survey of united state. If a person lives alone in house, fall can cause head injuries.

Zhang and Ren [4] it can describe the, all over world the cost of health finance are increase day by day. Below poverty line people can not provide a better facility and awareness according to WHO survey, in this paper better technique to detect a person in homely environment. Overall discussion about the sensor technology, audio and video new system developed and how to overcome the false alarm.

Bai et al. [7] the overall paper discuss the track a person through GPS technology, WHO can describe the second main issue regarding health profile. Psychological effect better way to improve over health issue and daily activity.

Yu et al. [8] main purpose of this paper is when a person sitting or lying in the chair it can make difficult angle provide better resolution. Possibility of false alarm 70% may be reduce.

Igual et al. [12] it is very complex process, not provide a better solution, health consequence are decrease day by day. Analysis of different studies in order to determine the nature with time.

Gravina et al. [16] this paper work on hidden markav model and machine learning approach and describe the decision tree which is used to detect various factor such as muscle weakness and many more for the improvement.

3 Types of Fall Detection

Many of the researchers use some of the medical and sensor networks to tracks the activity of human being. There are basically three type of fall detection system

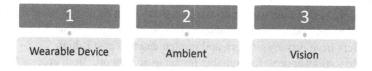

1. Portable device based
2. Ambient based
3. Vision type

Wearable Device Based Methods: It can be used like a watch and sensor can be detect and process Sensor device can be wear in clothes so the movement of person easily detect. Wearable device based on sensor networks (SN) are increasing day by day in medical system. The main objective of this SN to observes the physiological, medical and other activity. Most significant sign of this ECG, Heart rate, blood pressure and position of the body. Sensor network put on any part of patient body, such as hands waist.

Zhang et al. [4] this can be detect by using accelerometer, picture and better solution to using email and other resource.

Abbate et al. [5] we can use fall activity and detected by mobile phone and machine learning or deep learning approach to better solution to provide us to aged person.

Bagalà et al. [6] this researcher provide a algorithms and true and false alarm can't trigger. Direction of the person set according to accelerometer and better solution provide us.

Bai et al. [7] it can be implemented using smart phone with GPS location better function to the user battery backup is more important than foreground and background.

Yu et al. [8] this paper improve the result of fall detection and it can be extract by using post processing and false alarm possibility can be neglect.

Rougher et al. [9] this paper can be analyzed track of person when fall and different technique find out the better result.

Ambient Based Methods: Based on home network and daily activity of a person can be observed some of the drawback of this system person cannot track with in camera range [9, 10]. Sensor can be detect when a person walking and false alarm rate can be high. It can not discuss the testing methodologies, validation and verification

Some of the research gaps in ambient system

- Lack of knowledge of prediction system
- Low risk of death rate to prevent the technique of fall
- To prevent falls, user friendly interface of system and feedback from patients should be considered.

Yan et al. [11] when we wear a device or sensor it can be detect our home network location. Video method is more suitable and relevant then the ambient methods. This method suffers from privacy concern and implementation cost is high.

Wearable sensors approach is suitable for acoustic network. Both approach it can be used to detect daily activities.

Vision Based Methods: Vision based method are related space and time feature, change of position of body moment. It can be work on segmentation, feature extraction and data acquisition.

4   Fall Prevention Technique

This Fig. 1 shows the different number of detection prescribe, behavior of different personality reflect when ever Fall risk detect different, psychological behavioral Geographical and other factor define fall condition Risk factor depend upon categories area (Fig. 2).

Fig. 1. Model of acoustic sensor approach

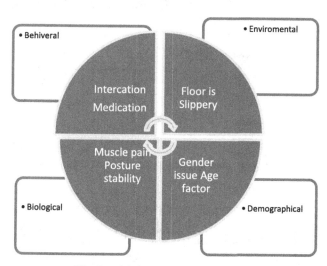

Fig. 2. Risk factor when a person fall

This flow chart describe the signal obtained from sensor data that is connected to the Wi-Fi -network. Accelerometer rotate in x, y, z axis and sensor send the data to the mobile phone and this data is stored in the cloud. Person can observed our data using mobile application send the fall message to the detect the location of the person and take care in situation (Fig. 3).

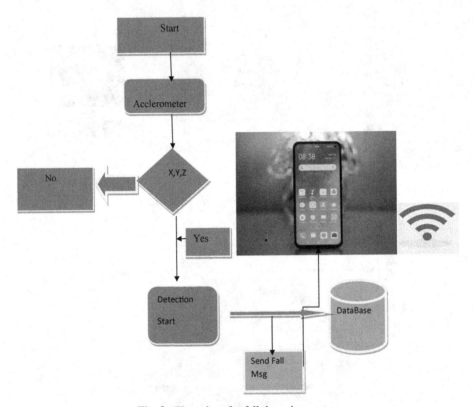

Fig. 3. Flow chart for fall detection system

The figure shown that sample of the different age group person it can be reflect in this graph variation can be arise, when 21%, 30%, 42% respectively when we use different participant, different age group person would some changes in the daily activity. Some sample in this bar graph clearly shown the age factor and behavior of the different environment effect the person health (Fig. 4).

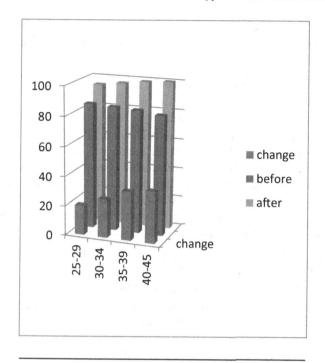

Fig. 4. Age factor changing ratio

5   Challenges

A wide range of challenges are faced by the mentioned fall prediction, Often times these systems achieve high accuracy when tested in experimental settings, but they are applied to all world situations, [12] they do not yield such impressive results. A major reason for this is that these fall prediction and prevention systems use data from young adults; all experiment that are conducted do not incorporate data from older people. Fall prediction and prevention systems often have a constraint on the energy budget allocated for these systems, this is a major challenge faced by such systems. To address this energy optimization issue all future work done must focus on energy optimization [13]. Smart phone based systems need to address the storage issue as well. Cloud computing is often used to combat this issue.

Another challenge faced by fall prediction systems is that there is little focus on user feedback in IOT-enabled monitoring systems for fall detection. The existing systems detect user data by pervasive monitoring and then simply transmit this data to a device like a smart phone; there is no role of users in this process. Since user feedback is not taken into account these fall detection systems are not very popular among older adults.

Another big concern associated with such systems is maintenance of privacy and ensuring confidentiality of the personal data that has been collected about the user's health. [14]. In case of the IOT- enables fall prediction systems, the data collected and stored in smart phones is prone to attacks as it is transmitted over wireless networks.

Hence, ensuring user privacy is a huge challenge [15]. Many recent systems are mobile cloud based; such systems provide numerous benefits for data privacy and security.

6 Suggestion and Work in Future

1. Information about machine Learning

Falls are predicated through patients various behavior patterns like uneasiness, we can say that it can observe with the help of network. Survey was conducted by Gravina et al. [16] which showed distinguishable properties which result should concentrate on the use of knowledge from one content to another. Deviation in behavior can be done with algorithm such as HMM (Hidden Markov Model), which is used to check decision trees to detect various factor such as muscle weakness and many more for the improvement.

2. Uncertainly is caused because of multiple heterogeneous

Sensors and predication systems. Future work play a major role for the uncertainty concept. Bayesian graphical method is one such method.

3. Feedback provide to patients through interface

With the advanced technology of Smartphone, user friendly application can help to registered to receive medical treatment and to engage in the observe the process. Future work ensures that application is easily used at the receivers end.

4. Cell phone based fall observation and forcast

Accuracy of the detection algorithm is one of the main matters that is focused. Digital phone being employed for the purpose should have better battery [17] capacity as the other application consume the battery.

5. Enviromental Fall risk Factor

Fall risk factor such as poor lighting, wet floors etc. should be looked upon. As a prevention, interactive 3Dgaming application come into role play [18].

6. Comparison of IOT –Enabled system with clinical system comparison of IOT fall risk assessment and clinical assessment should be a major concern for future work. Various researches should be done for the comparison [19, 20].

7. Biomedical signal

Diseases such as (PD) Parkinson's disease [21] and (FOG) are common cause of falls which are predicated through electronic signal like ECG and EMG.

8. Accuracy of fall predication

New technique should be implemented along with various assessments and algorithm BBS, TUG, FGA, still demonstrate not required data. Duncan et al. [22] analyzed the fact that five -month review shows precise result than a twelve month effect. Future wok should based on more requirements for older people as they are prone to disease.

7 Conclusion

In this paper we conclude fall perception on the Wi-Fi and sensory device it will detect the accidental of person fall. Serious fall is one of the most life threatening risks to an elderly person. We can use the information from electronic device this can prevent the activity of daily life. It severely injures, and sometime seven kills the victim especially old people Therefore, there is a need for fall detection systems, that will helps these people when they do fall and not able call for help. But one of these problem of these detection system is that they can sense the fall only when someone is in physical contact with the system. Hence, a system that is based on sensors is more desirable for those who are unable to call for help after a fall. We can conclude it's a tough task. Frequent falls amongst the elderly and injuries caused as a effect the same have highly degraded their quality of life; and hence, it is needed to provide aged people with convenient means of detecting and preventing falls. Despite considerable research, fall detection and prevention systems face several challenges which have been previously discussed.

References

1. Kinsella, K., Phillips, D.R.: Global aging: the challenge of success. Popul. Bull. **60**, 3 (2005)
2. Tabulation on the 2010 population census of the people's republic of China, China Statistics, May 2013. On-line
3. Popescu, M., Li, Y., Skubic, M., Rantz, M.: An acoustic fall detector system that uses sound height information to reduce the false alarm rate. In: Proceedings of 30th International IEEE Engineering in Medicine and Biology Society Conference, pp. 4628–4631, August 2008
4. Zhang, Q., Ren, L., Shi, W.: HONEY a multimodality fall detection and telecare system. Telemed. e-Health **19**(5), 415–429 (2013)
5. Abbate, S., Avvenuti, M., Bonatesta, F., Cola, G., Corsini, P., Vecchio, A.: A smartphone-based fall detection system. Pervasive Mob. Comput. **8**(6), 883–899 (2012)
6. Bagalà, F., Becker, C., Cappello, A., Chiari, L., Aminian, K.: Evaluation of accelerometer-based fall detection algorithm in real-world falls. PLoS ONE **7**(5), 1–8 (2012)
7. Bai, Y.W., Wu, S.C., Tsai, C.L.: Design and implementation of a fall monitor system by using a 3-axis accelerometer in a smart phone. IEEE Trans. Consum. Electron. **58**(4), 1269–1275 (2012)
8. Yu, M., Rhuma, A., Naqvi, S., Wang, L., Chambers, J.: A posture recognition-based fall detection system for monitoring an elderly person in a smart home environment. IEEE Trans. Inf. Technol. Biomed. **16**(6), 1274–1286 (2012)
9. Rougier, C., Meunier, J., Arnaud, A.S., Rousseau, J.: Robust video surveillance for fall detection based on human shape deformation. IEEE Trans. Circ. Syst. Video Technol. **21**(5), 611–622 (2011)
10. Ozcan, K., Mahabalagiri, A., Velipasalar, S.: Automatic fall detection and activity classification by a wearable camera. In: Bobda, C., Velipasalar, S. (eds.) Distributed Embedded Smart Cameras, pp. 151–172. Springer, New York (2014). https://doi.org/10.1007/978-1-4614-7705-1_7
11. Yan, H.R., Huo, H.W., Xu, Y.Z., Gidlund, M.: Wireless sensor network based E-health system: implementation and experimental results. IEEE Trans. Consum. Electron. **56**(4), 2288–2295 (2010)
12. Igual, R., Medrano, C., Plaza, I.: Challenges, issues and trends in fall detection systems. Biomed. Eng. Online **12**(1), 66 (2013)

13. Rajagopalan, R.: Smart and pervasive health systems—challenges, trends, and future directions. In: Arai, K., Bhatia, R. (eds.) FICC 2019. LNNS, vol. 69, pp. 408–419. Springer, Cham (2020). https://doi.org/10.1007/978-3-030-12388-8_29

14. Ding, W., Jing, X., Yan, Z., Yang, L.T.: A survey on data fusion in internet of things: towards secure and privacy-preserving fusion. Inf. Fusion **51**, 129–144 (2019)

15. Stone, E.E., Skubic, M., Rantz, M., Popescu, M.: U.S. Patent Application No. 16/108,432 (2019)

16. Gravina, R., Alinia, P., Ghasemzadeh, H., Fortino, G.: Multi-sensor fusion in body sensor networks: state-of-the-art and research challenges. Inf. Fusion **35**, 68–80 (2017)

17. Habib, M.A., Mohktar, M.S., Kamaruzzaman, S.B., Lim, K.S., Pin, T.M., Ibrahim, F.: Smartphone-based solutions for fall detection and prevention: challenges and open issues. Sensors **14**, 7181–7208 (2014)

18. Webster, D., Celik, O.: Systematic review of Kinect applications in elderly care and stroke rehabilitation. J. Neuroeng. Rehabil. **11**, 108 (2014)

19. O'Sullivan, M., Blake, C., Cunningham, C., Boyle, G., Finucane, C.: Correlation of accelerometry with clinical balance tests in older fallers and non-fallers. Age Ageing **38**, 308–313 (2009)

20. Greene, B.R., O'Donovan, A., Romero-Ortuno, R., Cogan, L., Scanaill, C.N., Kenny, R.A.: Quantitative falls risk assessment using the timed up and go test. IEEE Trans. Biomed. Eng. **57**, 2918–2926 (2010)

21. Allen, N.E., Schwarzel, A.K., Canning, C.G.: Recurrent falls in Parkinson's disease: a systematic review. Parkinson's Dis. **2013**, 906274 (2013)

22. Berg, K., Wood-Dauphine, S., Williams, J.I., Gayton, D.: Measuring balance in the elderly: preliminary development of an instrument. Physiother. Can. **41**, 304–311 (1989)

Role of Fuzzy Set Theory and Kappa Coefficient in Urological Disease Diagnosis

Sunil Singh[1]($\boxtimes$), Navin Ram Daruka[2], Megha Shukla[3], and Ashok Deshpande[4]

[1] Department of Computer Science & Engineering, CSVTU Bhilai, Bhilai, India
sunilkumarbit32@yahoo.com
[2] Aaroygom Urocare Center, Bhilai, India
drnavinurology@gmail.com
[3] Department of Computer Science & Engineering, SSTC Bhilai, Bhilai, India
megha16shukla@gmail.com
[4] Berkeley Initiative Soft Computing (BISC) Special Interest Group (SIG) Environment Management System (EMS), COEP Pune, Pune, India
ashok_deshpande@hotmail.com

Abstract. Invariably, no two physicians think alike in diagnosing a disease and therefore, medical science is imprecise/ fuzzy. Probability theory has witnessed successes in several areas of science and technology however, it may not be possible to apply two valued based probability in medical disease diagnosis as medical documentation is always in words and never in numeric terms. Realizing ground reality, we believe that fuzzy set theory- human centric modeling could be an effective armamentarium in medical disease diagnosis in general, and urological disease diagnosis in particular. The limited study carried out by the authors in the past infers that expert urologists can achieve around 90% accuracy in urological disease provisional diagnosis for above 40 years male patients using fuzzy theoretic operations. In this papers, apart from urological disease diagnosis, the authors tried to take a deeper look into concentration operators used in fuzzy set theory and also application of kappa coefficient in urological diseases diagnosis by expert and upcoming urologists via sonography images. Comparison of one of the existing software designed for disease diagnosis with the one developed by the authors is an integral part of the study.

Keywords: Urological disease diagnosis for male · Fuzzy set theory · Perceptions of urologist · Cohen's Kappa coefficient

1 Introduction

Patients while describing symptoms to a physician uses linguistic terms such as *very hot body temperature, there is severe pain in my stomach* and alike. In other words Patient-Physician dialogue is never probabilistic. We therefore, believe that computing with Words via fuzzy sets and fuzzy logic could be a promising technique that can easily capture the required medical knowledge and come up with sound diagnostic decisions [1]. Practically, an expert physician tends usually to specify his/ her experience in rather

© Springer Nature Singapore Pte Ltd. 2020
U. Batra et al. (Eds.): REDSET 2019, CCIS 1229, pp. 411–419, 2020.
https://doi.org/10.1007/978-981-15-5827-6_36

fuzzy terms, which is more natural to him than trying to cast his knowledge in rigid rules having abrupt premises.

The paper is organized as follows Sect. 2 refers to brief description on sonography as this test is frequently used in urological disease diagnosis while Sect. 3 refers to author's contribution on Fuzzy logic in Urological Disease Diagnosis. Section 4 presents the need and relevance of the study, delineating three important issues. Methods/ techniques used are covered in Sect. 5. Section 6 is a brief outline of methodology covered while Case Study in details including results and discussion is presented in Sect. 7. Conclusion and Further scope for research are the contents of Sect. 8.

2   A Word on Urology

2.1   Sonography

Sonography is a diagnostic medical test that uses high-frequency sound waves also called ultra-sound waves to bounce off structures in the body and create an image. Test is often referred to simply as an ultra-sound or as a sonogram and is a non-invasive imaging test and has no known complications.

It is useful for evaluating the size, shape, and density of tissues to help diagnose certain medical conditions. Traditionally, ultra-sound imaging is great for looking into the abdomen without having to cut it open. Abdominal ultra-sound in particular, is often used to diagnose gallbladder disease or gallstones, kidney stones or kidney disease, liver disease, appendicitis, ovarian cysts, ectopic pregnancies, uterine growths or fibroid and other conditions [3, 4].

2.2   Why Study Images?

Invariably sonography a part of imaging, is suggested for Kidney-Ureter-Bladder(KUB) for Urological disease diagnosis as this area of physician is well known to Urologist/Uro-surgeon [5]. The possible reasons for the sonography in urology are as under

1. Urologist initially recommends X-ray to find size of cyst and stone
2. The expert suggests sonography when they have to operate the patients because he is not sure size and exact position of stone. Expert Urologists advice patients that without recommendation don't do sonography as it is harmful for tissues for Kidney-Ureter-Bladder (KUB) as it is soft organ of body [6].

3   Authors Contribution on Fuzzy Logic in Urological Disease Diagnosis

Attempts were made by the authors in medical disease diagnosis using fuzzy relational calculus and arrived at the conclusion that 13/ 81 urological patients are diagnosed for Urethra Stricture disease. Expert Uro surgeon has confirmed that 11/ 81 patients are correctly diagnosed for single disease with concentration operator as 2 proposed by Professor Zadeh was used in fuzzy model explained in brief [11].

A patient says "I have high body temperature and fuzzy logic expert assigns membership grade based on his/ her perception for the linguistic description " high" in average fuzzy set (type1 fuzzy set) drawn on the advice of 15–20 seniors domain experts, in this case expert urologists. But the patient describes his/ her symptom as "very High Body Temperature". The expert opined that he/she is not in a position to assign membership to very high body temperature. This is a real issue in computing with words via fuzzy sets and fuzzy logic [2]. Professor LotfiZadeh, based on intuition proposed membership grade as 2 for Very High Body Temperature.

The other issue relates to examine sonography images correctly by urologist.

4   Need and Relevance of the Study

There has been phenomenal increase in patients with urological diseases in several countries. Ever increasing cost of investigating tests and surgery are unaffordable to the poorest of the poor. We have addressed these issues in our paper [11].

The three issues for research stand out in urological disease diagnosis:

Issue 1: Concentration Operator in Fuzzy Set Theory
Professor Zadeh proposed to use concentration operator as 2 for the adjective "Very" which is, needs to be confirmed. We used various concentration operators (1.85 to 2.5) in the model based on seven urologists perceptions was evaluated.

Issue 2: Imaging as a method of Urological Disease Diagnosis
Sonography has been one of the effective test in urological disease diagnosis. It is important to statistically test performance of senior and junior urologists who diagnose a disease based on these images.

Issue 3
We do know that concerted efforts are being made efforts in development of software using machine learning or deep learning algorithms for medical disease diagnosis. The paper also tries to compare performance of one of the available model and the formalism developed by the authors.

The paper is modest attempt to address the above three issue.

5   Mathematical Preliminaries

The two important fuzzy set theoretic approaches are used in this study. These are:

5.1 Fuzzy Relational Calculus (FRC)

A Fuzzy Relation R is a mapping from the Cartesian space $X \times Y$ to the closed interval [0, 1], where the strength of the mapping is expressed by the membership function of the relation for ordered pairs from the two universes, or $\mu_R(x, y)$. Relations can be used to represent *similarity between the two elements*. Suppose R is a fuzzy relation on the Cartesian space $X \times Y$, S is a fuzzy relation on $Y \times Z$, and T is a fuzzy relation on $X \times Z$, then fuzzy max–min composition (also termed as compositional rule of inference) is defined in terms of the function-theoretic notation in the following manner [8]:

$$\mu_T(x, z) = \vee_{y \in Y}(\mu_R(x, y) \wedge \mu_S(y, z)) \tag{1}$$

It is important to transform fuzzy tolerance relation to fuzzy equivalence as the analyst would need crisp output with a defined alpha cut or possibility level [8]. A fuzzy tolerance relation can be transformed into fuzzy equivalence relation by almost $(n - 1)$ compositions.

$$R_1^{n-1} = R_1 \circ R_1 \circ R_1 \circ R_1 \ldots \ldots \ldots \ldots \circ R_1 = R \tag{2}$$

5.2 Cohen's Kappa Coefficient in Brief

Cohen's kappa coefficient (κ) is a statistic that is used to measure inter-rater reliability (and also Intra-rater reliability) for qualitative (categorical) items [1]. It is generally thought to be a more robust measure than simple percent agreement calculation, as κ takes into account the possibility of the agreement occurring by chance [10]. There is controversy surrounding Cohen's kappa due to the difficulty in interpreting indices of agreement. Some researchers have suggested that it is conceptually simpler to evaluate disagreement between items.

6 The Method

Medical diagnosis usually involves careful examination of a patient to check the presence and strength of some features relevant to a suspected disease in order to take a decision whether the patient suffers from that disease or not.

Let us assume fuzzy set A of the symptoms observed in patient Rs = (pxs) and the fuzzy relation R representing the medical knowledge that relates the symptoms in set S to the diseases in D. These could be expressed in two forms: 1. fuzzy occurrence relation Ro = (sxd) and 2. Conformability relations Rc = (sx d). Then the fuzzy set B of the possible diseases of the patient can be erred by means of the compositional rule of inference [8] A – Always, VO- Very Often, O – Often, NS- Not Specific, S – Seldom, N- Never.

$$B = A \circ R \tag{3}$$

Or B (d) = max [min (A(s), R (S, d)] $s \in S$, for each d $\in$ D.   (4)

The procedure was adopted in the computation of max- min fuzzy resemblance/ composition procedure. Java based computer code was developed as it is an iterative process. These indication relations are:

Fuzzy occurrence indication relation

$$R_1 = Rs \ o \ Ro \tag{5}$$

Fuzzy conformability indication relation

$$R_2 = Rs \ o \ Rc \tag{6}$$

From Eq. 5, the relation between patient -symptom (p and s) and symptom-disease (s and d) is worked out using compositional rule of inference. From Eq. (6), it could be inferred that in initial screening process, the patient is confirmed for a single disease with membership value of 1.

7 The Study

Before start of urological disease diagnosis, it is important to state that there is world knowledge based on expert's perception - termed as implicit knowledge available with expert urologist. In urological diseases, it can be stated that invariably diseases other than Benign Prostatic Hyper hyperplasia (BPH) can occur below age of 40 for male patients [7]. In the study, the diagnostic label attached to the by the model (without considering age of the patient) is urethra stricture (US). The limited study refers to a few important facets of urological disease diagnosis.

Final outcome of three issues outlined in Sect. 3 are detailed in this section.

7.1 Results and Discussion

In this subsection, we present the results and discussion of the three issues considered for the study:

Issue 1: Concentration Operator

In urological diseases, it can be stated that invariably diseases other than Benign Prostatic Hyper hyperplasia (BPH) can occur below age of 40 for male patients. In the study, the diagnostic label attached to the by the model (without considering age of the patient) is urethra stricture (US). Though fuzzy occurrence and conformability indication relation (R_C) as we are interested in a single disease diagnosis. Among the five operators and five experts, the highest disease computed and then confirmed by the experts are with 1.95 and then among the diseases maximum common single disease patients are 1. Urethera Structure (US) 35 and 2. Urinary Tract infection (UTI) 9. Patients and the perception of five expert urologists was obtained for a single disease diagnosis. In the computation, we have considered o conformability Table 1 presents the output of the model based on fuzzy relational calculus for five (1.85 1.90, 1.95, 2.0 and 2.10) concentration operators for 240.

Table 1. Five concentration operator value for experts

Expert urologists	Oper 1.85			Oper 1.90		Oper 1.95		Oper 2.00		Oper 2.10	
1	US	IC		US	IC	US	IC	US	IC	US	IC
	49	6		48	7	53	6	50	7	47	4
2	UTI	US	Epidi	UTI	US	UTI	US	UTI	US	UTI	US
	44	23	2	45	22	48	23	48	22	41	19
3	KC	US		KC	US	KC	US	KC	US	KC	US
	1	9		3	8	4	11	5	9	6	7
4	PC	P		PC	P	PC	P	PC	P	PC	P
	8	2		6	2	11	3	9	3	7	2
5	KC	UTI		KC	UTI	KC	UTI	KC	UTI	KC	UTI
	9	10		9	13	11	14	11	13	7	9

Table 2. Senior Uro-expert kappa coefficient

Experts	E1	E2	E3	E4
E1	1	.59	.63	.69
E2	.64	1	.71	.67
E3	.65	.70	1	.63
E4	.68	.75	.73	1

Issue 2: Imaging as a method of Urological Disease Diagnosis

Medical test report of 50 patients whose sonography images were examined by 4 senior Urologists and their Kappa Coefficient values are worked out as per the defined procedure;

Step 1:- Compute (P_o) observed agreement

$$Po = (a + d)/n = 26 + 15/50 = 41/50 = 0.82$$

Step 2:- Compute (P_e) Expected disagreement by chance

$$Pe = [(32/50) * (29/50)] + [(18/50) * (21/50)] = .48$$

$$\text{Kappa Coefficient } k = (P_o - P_e)/(1 - P_e) = (.82 - .48)/(1 - .48) = 0.69$$

We tried to evaluate the performance of Group senior urologists and junior urologists in examining sonography images for diagnosing urological diseases. Cohen Kappa Coeff K was worked and it was inferred that the value of K is 0.69, 0.57 and 0.53 for senior urologists and it was 0. 11 and 0.44 for the two groups of junior urologists whose experience ranges between 5–10 years.

Table 3. Junior Uro-expert kappa coefficient

Experts	E1	E2	E3	E4
E1	1	.21	.33	.19
E2	.24	1	.31	.27
E3	.35	.30	1	.23
E4	.18	.25	.27	1

Issue 3: Comparison Between Available Software and Fuzzy Logic Based Software Developed by Our Team

We tried to investigate performance of our model for 30 patients for urological disease diagnosis by senior experts (over 20 years of experience) and tried to compare with one of the software freely available on Google Search. In our view, the best computational approach is to use Kappa Coefficient (k) for this comparison (Table 4).

Table 4. Kappa for issue 3 based on available software

Comparison	Kappa value
1. Uroexpert & Model	.26
2. Uroexpert & available s/w	0
3. Model & avalaible s/w	0

To our surprised Kappa Coefficient, K, ranges between 0 and 0, 26 for the freely available software while it was 0.69 for fuzzy model developed by the authors of this paper.

Discussion

In depth study of evaluating the most suitable concentration operators for the symptoms of 240 patients based on perception of the expert urologists reveals the following:

The computations made for single disease diagnosis, based on the perception of all the five senior urologists, concentration operator 1.95 ranks first, at lease in urological; disease diagnosis; amongst them- maximum common single disease patients were diagnosed with two diseases 1. Urethra Structure (US) 35 and 2. Urinary Tract Infection (UTI) 9. These diseases are also confirmed by uro physician. Therefore we argue that especially for urological disease diagnosis using fuzzy relational calculus the analyst may use 1.95 as the concentration operator though Professor Lotfi Zadeh has proposed it as 2.0 [2]. The analyst may not go very wrong if he/ she uses 1.95 as the linguistic hedge very [9].

We can infer from the Table 2, 3 that imaging as detailed in the paper for urological disease diagnose should be seen by senior urologist (say over 20 years' experience as their Cohen's Kappa coefficient is ranges between 0.53 to 0.67 which is much higher than upcoming urologist. In sum, senior urologists could be more reliable in examining the images.

"Experience cannot be substituted by any other thing but only by experience" – Says Dr. K.L Rao a very senior Indian Engineer and former Union Minister, Government of India.

Should we use not rigorously tested software for disease diagnosis, even if these are based on mathematical analysis [2] wherein the domain experts experience in the form of their perception is not given that much importance as it should be?

The limited study infers that it should not be used by any one, at least for urological disease diagnosis. We do realize that much more experiments should be conducted.

8   Concluding Remarks and Further Scope for Research

The study results detailed in this sequel are the testimony of the fact that fuzzy sets and logic via computing with words has played and will continue to play an important role in medical disease diagnosis including urology. The authors can state in no uncertain terms that collecting only patient-symptom data from the hospitals with no concern to knowledgebase of the domain experts will never be able to come up acceptable disease diagnosis. What is needed is not just machine intelligence but Human Level Machine Intelligence (HLMI).

There are several important issues to be studied such as Disease diagnosis-prognosis-diagnosis, construction of a faulty for diseases with causes, medical imaging. And many more.

The biggest room in this world is the room for improvement. So we must improve.

Acknowledgement. The authors express their gratitude to Dr(s). P K Rai, Varun Sharma, Rishi, Samir, Ashish, Yogesh Lotus, R P Singh and many mores. We are confident that they will continue to assist the team in future.

References

1. Zadeh, L.: Fuzzy sets. Inf. Control **8**, 338–353 (1965)
2. Zadeh, L.: Outline of a new approach to the analysis of complex systems and decision processes. IEEE Trans. Syst. Man, Cybern. **SMC-3**, 28–44 (1973)
3. Garraway, W.M., Collins, G.N., Lee, R.J.: High prevalence of benign prostatic hyperplasia in the community. Lancet **338**, 469–471 (1991)
4. Litwin, M.S., Hays, R.D., Fink, A., et al.: Quality-of-life outcomes in men for localized prostate cancer. JAMA **273**, 129–130 (1995)
5. Berry, S.J., Coffey, D.S., Walsh, P.C., et al.: The development of human benign prostatic hyperplasia with age. J. Urol. **132**, 474–479 (1984)
6. Gormley, G.J., Stoner, E., Bruskewitz, R.C., et al.: The effect of finasteride in men with benign prostatic hyperplasia. N. Engl. J. Med. **327**, 1185–1191 (1992)
7. Barry, M.J., Fowler, F.J., Oleary, M.P., et al.: The American Urological Association symptom index for benign prostatic hyperplasia. J. Urol. **148**, 1549–1557 (1992)
8. Ross, T.: Fuzzy Logic with Engineering Applications. Wiley, Hoboken (2003)

9. Cohen, J.: Weighted kappa: nominal scale agreement with provision forscaled disagreement or partial credit. Psychol. Bull. **70**, 213–220 (1968)
10. Anthony, J., Viera, A.J., Garrett, J.M.: Understanding interobserver agreements kappa statistic research series. Fam. Med. **37**(5), 360–363 (2005)
11. Singh, S., Ram Daruka, N., Deshpande, A.: International World Fuzzy Conference ISIS-IWCS (2018)

Analyzing Balancing of Heterogeneous Load on Cluster-Based Web Server

Praveen Kumar[1]([✉]), Garvit Singhal[2]([✉]), and Seema Rawat[2]

[1] Amity University, Tashkent, Uzbekistan
pkumar3@amity.edu
[2] Amity University, Noida, Uttar Pradesh, India
garvit114singhal@gmail.com, srawat1@amity.edu

Abstract. With increasing workload experienced by many websites, distributed web-server cluster has become a popular choice for site managers to expand the capacity of the webserver system. A web-server cluster consists of multiple web servers with a load distribution scheme to spread client requests among servers. This report focuses on dispatcher-based architecture. We study the performances of different scheduling algorithms by means of trace-driven simulation and then propose a more time-efficient approach for heterogeneous loads.

Keywords: Cloud computing · Cluster · Distributed systems · Service

1 Introduction

A distributed web-server system consists of multiple server hosts with a load distribution scheme to spread client requests among server resources [1]. Several cluster-based web-server architectures are proposed and implemented [2]. Currently most distributed web-server architectures implement simple job (client HTTP requests) scheduling schemes such as Round-Robin job scheduling algorithm and scheduling based on server-workload information that is determined by the number of active network connections. The main design consideration is the simplicity and thus is easy to implement with low overhead. This minor project will focus on dispatcher-based architecture. We will give a theoretical model for balancing a heterogeneous load in this project and later we will try proving our model by experimental analysis.

1.1 Project Goals and Objectives

The project objective is to propose a more time-efficient way to distribute different types of load on various web servers. A thorough study of various papers, articles will be conducted. It is the continuation of the paper "Comparison of Load Balancing Strategies on Cluster-based webserver" by Teo Yong Meng in which the server and load were homogeneous. The experimental analysis will be performed in the future.

© Springer Nature Singapore Pte Ltd. 2020
U. Batra et al. (Eds.): REDSET 2019, CCIS 1229, pp. 420–432, 2020.
https://doi.org/10.1007/978-981-15-5827-6_37

1.2   Related Work

Figure 1 shows the most important steps of client-server interaction on the Web. A client request is processed in two major steps:

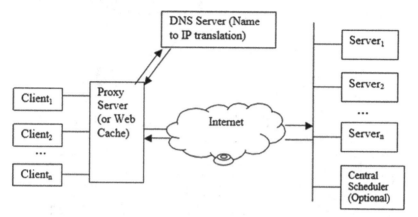

Fig. 1. An overview of client-server transaction on the web

a.   URL address name to IP address mapping. The address format used by routers and servers on the net is IP address (e.g. 137.132.88.88). However, human beings are much more comfortable with the name address (e.g. www.comp.nus.edu.sg). To bridge the gap between IP and name address, DNS (Domain Name Server) are setup on the Internet to translate name addresses to IP addresses [7, 8].
b.   Retrieval of files from the web servers. After a client obtains the IP address of the destination server, it sends a HTTP request to the server [9].

1.3   Distribution at the Dispatcher

As one of the famous way of cluster of multiple servers, based on dispatcher architecture which features an entity which is at the centre called as dispatcher which is further responsible for distributing the incoming client request to the server which is backend. The architecture is shown below in Fig. 2.

Recently there are many academic prototypes and industrial products that are based on the dispatcher-based approach.

• Four switching Layer with two forwarding packet (L4/3)
• Four switching Layer with three forwarding packet (L4/2)
• Seven switching Layer with either two/three packet forwarding (L7)

The underlying idea of this classification scheme is that client request packets must go through the network protocol stack of the dispatcher at least twice (once up and once down) before being directed to the back-end servers (Fig. 3).

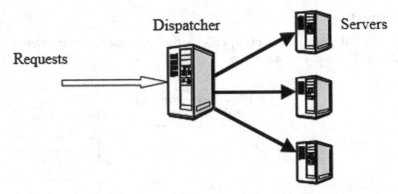

Fig. 2. A high-level view of a dispatcher-based server cluster

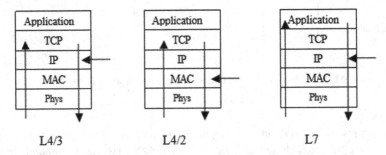

Note: The horizontal "◄—" denotes address re-mapping at the pointed layer

Fig. 3. Classification of dispatcher based web server architectures

1.3.1 Distribution at the Servers

In this approach, the overhead due to inter-communication among peer servers may be intensive. In addition, changes to the network protocol kernel of all servers are required. This makes it hard for implementation and maintenance.

2 Project Constraints

There are various constraints that we will be taking under consideration for this project. They are as under:

1. The overhead of scheduling is negligible (The time that is needed by the processor to assign a new task is negligible),
2. The overhead of communication is negligible (The time needed for a server to receive a message from dispatcher is negligible).
3. The bandwidth is sufficient to handle the traffic outgoing,

   Since we have done this similar work earlier, and the experiments performed previously revealed that the capacity of the outgoing link will be bottlenecked when the number of servers exceeds 8. Hence we assumed the unlimited capacity of the outgoing link.

3   System Modeling

3.1   A Dispatcher-Based Web-Server Cluster

The simulation model which we have used is similar to the testbed in our lab. The testbed is made up of 16 homogeneous PCs interconnected by a 100 Mbps Ethernet. 15 Pc's act as a dispatcher while one of them acts as a dispatcher. Specification of each of the PC is Pentium-II 400 MHz processor and 256 Mb of memory. All of them are running on Linux.

We will be focusing on two important models. One is dispatcher and the other one is the backend-web server. The dispatcher model as a queuing system is shown in Fig. 4.

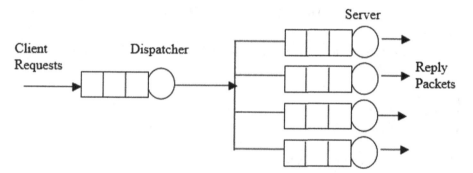

Fig. 4. Model of a web-server cluster

3.1.1   Model of Dispatcher Service Time

By taking measurement on PCs in our cluster we determine the dispatcher service time function:

$$\text{Dispatcher Service Time } (S1) = L/K1 + C1$$

Where L is the size of the request in bytes, K1 is the linear factor and C1 is the constant factor with values:

$K1 = 1.4 * 10^8$ bytes/second;
$C1 = 120 * 10^{-6}$ s

In our model of cluster dispatcher, we assume that the dispatcher takes no time to select the server.

3.1.2 Model of Web Server Service Time

Compared with the model of the dispatcher, web server model is more complicated because it involves nearly all components of a computer system. A general architecture of a web server in the form of queuing model is shown in Fig. 10 [3] (Fig. 5).

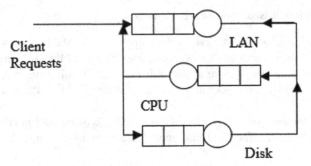

Fig. 5. A general webserver model

In general, there are three delay sources that affect the request for service time. They are given as under-:

1. CPU Time
2. Disk Access Time
3. Network Delay Time

Therefore we simplify our model-

1. All the files on the server are in cached memory. Hence, disk access delay is out of consideration.
2. The LAN Transmission delay is out of consideration.

So we consider only processing time of CPU + Memory access time for servicing a request.

3.2 Scheduling Algorithms

In the design of job scheduling algorithms, one crucial task is to measure the system workload. Good measurements are those that faithfully reflect the state of servers and easy to measure as well. The following can be used to estimate the server load:

a. The sum of service time of pending jobs on server
b. The total number of open (live) TCP connections
c. The current CPU utilization, the memory usage of the machine.

Distinguished by whether the server workload information is required in the scheduling and the definition of workload, we introduce three scheduling algorithms-:

a. Baseline Algorithm (Baseline)

In this scheme, the dispatcher distributes a coming client request to the server that has the lowest workload (sum of the service time of all requests pending on the server). The purpose of this algorithm is to establish a performance upper bound because this algorithm minimizes the waiting time of each new incoming request. The baseline algorithm takes into account the dynamic changing of server workload and avoids saturating any server by routing new requests to servers with a lower workload. The baseline algorithm is hard to implement in reality because it requires the dispatcher to sample all servers intensively (at the arrival of each new request) for workload information and the servers have to check out the size of all outstanding requests in the queue.

b. Round-Robin Algorithm (RR)

The dispatcher distributes client requests to different servers in turn without considering the state information of the servers. Compared with the baseline algorithm, round-robin scheduling is at the other end of the spectrum. It does not consider any state information of back-end servers.

The round-robin algorithm is easy to implement at the dispatcher as it just needs to keep a modulo counter to direct requests to the servers.

c. Least Connection Algorithm (LC)

The dispatcher directs requests to the server with the least number of live network connection(s).

The least connection algorithm is in between the above two algorithms. The workload information it collects is the number of network connections (i.e. number of requests) the servers have. However, it does not take into account the size of each request. Although this workload information is not as accurate as of the baseline algorithm, it is much easier to obtain.

What the dispatcher needs to do is to establish a connection table containing the number of connections for each back-end server and update the table entries constantly.

4   Simulator Implementation

4.1 Trace-Driven Simulator Using Java

To compare the performance of three algorithms that we discussed in Chapter 5, a trace-driven Java simulator is developed. The structure of the simulator is shown in Fig. 6:

The design of the simulator follows the object-oriented programming paradigm. Each entity in the physical cluster is abstracted to a class in the program. As shown in Fig. 4, there are the following main classes in the program:

- Dispatcher: This is a driver-class in the program. It reads from the trace file and sends the request (in the form of a string) to trace parser. After getting the formatted request back from the trace parser, the dispatcher directs it to one of the servers to process the request based on whichever scheduling algorithm it is using. Moreover, the dispatcher

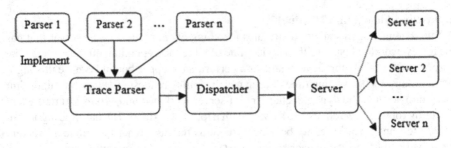

Fig. 6. Higher-level structure of the simulator

also implements the three scheduling schemes and a dispatcher queue to hold pending requests.

- Trace Parser: This is an interface class that can handle multiple input trace formats. Trace Parser class is implemented by multiple subclasses, each of which is used to parse and analyze a specific trace format.
- Server: A number of server objects will be instantiated according to the total number of servers in the cluster. Each of the processes the arrived requests sent by the dispatcher.

The main loop of the program is shown in Fig. 7.

```
void main(){
    while ( there is more request in the trace) {
        parse (request);
        Dispatcher_Queue (request);
        SelectServer (Algorithms);
        Server.process (request);
    }
}
```

Fig. 7. Pseudo-code of the simulator main loop

4.2 Performance Measurement

For the performance comparison of different algorithms, we have identified the metrics of performance which are given below:

i.   Average waiting time for each request (W): The interval of time between the request arrival and service start.

ii. Average response time for each requests (R): The interval of time between the request arrival and service end.

iii. Server Utilization (Ui) and Average server utilization (U)

Ui = Total amount of time server i is busy/total elapsed time; and

$$U = \Sigma Ui/n, \text{ where n is the number of servers}$$

A highly skewed utilization among servers may cause under-utilization of some servers while others may be over-exploited. A good scheduling algorithm should avoid the problem.

A sample output of the simulator together is shown in Appendix B.

4.3 Simulator Validation

To show the correctness of the simulator implementation, we compare the analytical results of an M/M/1 and an M/M/c queuing models with the outputs from our simulator, results of ñ' and w'. We see that our program functions correctly with a single server configuration.

4.3.1 Multiple-Server Cluster vs. M/M/c

Multiple-server cluster is coupled with scheduling algorithm(s) [4, 5]. The Round Robin scheduling just partitions the work into k equal parts and then assigns it to one server to process. Therefore it can be checked with the M/M/1 model we used above. For the other two scheduling algorithms, it seems much more complicated. Fortunately, if we ignore the dispatcher overhead, we have an analytical model [6] that is equivalent to a multi-server cluster with the baseline schedule.

The queuing model of this M/M/c model is illustrated in Fig. 8:

Compared to the web Cluster model of Fig. 10, we see that this model does not allow queuing on the server-side and put all the pending requests in a common buffer. The request in the head of the common buffer will be sent out to the first available server and the dispatching overhead is 0. It is interesting to note that in our baseline algorithm, the server with the lightest workload (that is the server to be selected) will be the first one to be available as well. The only difference lies in the fact that in the Baseline the request may have to wait in the server queue instead of a common buffer. However, since the dispatching overhead is assumed to be 0 in this M/M/c model, the time period that the request has to wait is the sum of the service time of the outstanding requests that have been assigned to the same server. This is the same as our Web-server cluster model. We can see this point more clearly from the comparison.

Theoretical results for average waiting time W in M/M/C model. It can be seen that our simulator performs correctly under a multi-server configuration. The multi-server validation provides a level of confidence for the results of the simulations. For a different input distribution model, the simulator will still function correctly because the three algorithms do NOT consider what kind of inter-arrival time and service time distributions model are used in the input trace.

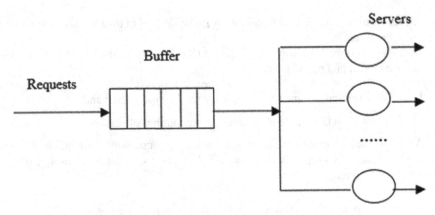

Fig. 8. An M/M/c queuing model

5 Experiment Design and Analysis

5.1 Experiment Design

To do a comprehensive study of the performance of three scheduling algorithms, we organize the performance analysis as follows:

Experiment 1: Server Capacity
The experiment's aim is to find a single server capacity. The threshold is important because it helps us to find the appropriate workload for a multi-server cluster. To facilitate further experiments, we define server capacity in terms of arrival rate (requests/second).

Experiment 2: Comparison of scheduling algorithms
Under different workloads using a four-server cluster configuration, we study the performance of algorithms under different workloads, i.e. request arrival rates.

Experiment 3: Scalability Analysis
We study the scalability of algorithms by analyzing the relative performance of three algorithms with an increasing number of web servers. This is carried out as follows:

Experiment 3.1
In this experiment, we keep the power of the servers unchanged and the no. of servers increases. Meanwhile, we increase the cluster's workload proportionally. i.e., if we have n servers, we increase the workload (request arrival rate) to n * X (the single server limit).

Experiment 3.2
The aim of this experiment is to study the effect of replacing a single server by a cluster with n less powerful servers. We keep the total power of the cluster constant. i.e., if we have n servers, the power of each server is reduced by a factor of n.

To able to compare these three algorithms, we have used the following Normalized measurements:

1. $Normalized\ Waiting\ Time = \dfrac{Average\ Waiting\ Time}{Average\ Waiting\ Time\ of\ Baseline\ Algorithm}$

2. $Normalized\ Response\ Time = \dfrac{Average\ Response\ Time}{Average\ Response\ Time\ of\ the\ baseline\ Algorithm}$

The baseline algorithm acts as an upper bound, a normalized value $= 1$ means a better performance otherwise poor performance. We apply the same set of experiments to both traces. Note that time units in all the following experiments are millisecond (10^{-3} s) unless otherwise specified.

5.2 SURGE Trace Performance Analysis

Experiment 1: Capacity of a Single Server
In Fig. 9, we observe that the average waiting time increases from about 0.8 s to 3.5 s when workload increases from 225 requests/second to 250 requests/second. In the utilization curve, we can observe that it is close to 90% which suggests that the capacity of the single server (X) is about 250 requests/second.

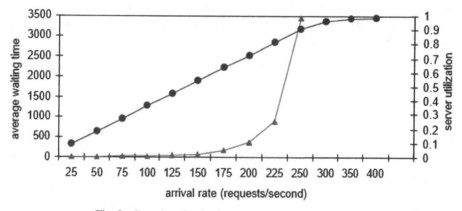

Fig. 9. Capacity of a single server system (SURGE trace)

Experiment 2: Comparison of scheduling algorithms under different workloads (4 servers)

We observer that a cluster of 4 servers can serve 1,000 requests/second with a lower average waiting time (only about 1 s compared with the previous 3.5 s in a single server case Fig. 8) even with the worst algorithm (Round Robin).

The Waiting time (Normalized) in Fig. 10 depicts that with low utilization the gap between the performance of these three algorithms are wide with Round Robin fifty times worse than and Least Connection about five times worse than the baseline algorithm at the utilization of 22.5%. However, as the arrival rate i.e. workload increases the waiting time (normalized) of these two given algorithms converges to 1. It is clear that the Least Connection Algorithm is much better than the Round Robin for it comes much closer to the performance of the baseline (with normalized waiting time close to 1).

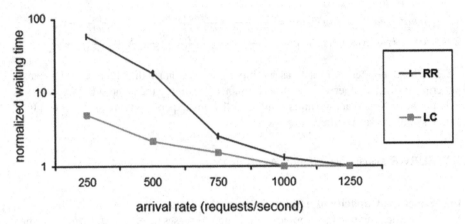

Fig. 10. Normalized waiting time vs. arrival rates (4-server cluster)

Experiment 3: Scalability Analysis

Experiment 3.1: Servers with the same power (X) and workloads increase proportionally. From Fig. 11, we observe that with the growth in the number of servers, the average waiting time keeps declining.

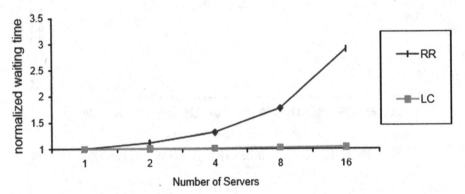

Fig. 11. Normalized waiting time vs. number of servers (power X)

From Fig. 11, we see that the relative performance of the Round Robin algorithm is going worse with the number of serves growing whereas the Least Connection algorithm comes very close to the baseline algorithm (at most 5% worse with 16 servers).

6 Summary of Analysis

The following summarizes our observations:

a. With the increase in workload, the performances of the three algorithms converge; and the Least Connection approaches the baseline algorithm in a much faster pace than Round Robin (Experiment 2) This suggests at high utilization there is a lesser need for load balancing and the Least Connection are better than Round Robin under various workloads.

b. The scalability analysis shows that the performance gaps between three algorithms grow with the number of servers in the cluster increasing. Compared with the baseline algorithm, the performance of the Round Robin algorithm deteriorates much faster than Least Connection. Round Robin scheduling does not consider the state of the server. Consequently, we can see that it does very poor in load balancing, especially with a large number of servers. The server utilization variation is always higher than the other two algorithms. In contrast, the simple counting function in the least Connection algorithm performs nearly as well as the Baseline scheme.

c. A cluster with n server with power X will outperform a single server system with power n* X in terms of average waiting time (W). We show this fact in experiment 3 using both traces. This exhibits the advantage of the clustering technique in web service.

Combining the above observations together, we conclude that the Round Robin job scheduling leaves much room for improvement especially under the condition of low to medium workload (<80%) with a large number of servers. The least Connection algorithm delivers a performance very close to the baseline algorithm under various scenarios.

7 Conclusions

Previously, Starting from a queuing model for the dispatcher-based webserver cluster and three job-scheduling (or load balancing) algorithms, I design and implement a simulator to measure the performance of the three load balancing algorithms. Both synthetic and real server trace is used in our simulation to ensure the validity of the analysis. The main finding of this project is to see how important it is to do a good choice in scheduling algorithms irrespective of the type of load. My work is by no means completed and future projects may be built upon it. Currently, my focus is on heterogeneous load on a heterogeneous web server clusters. A more general scenario is to consider the extension of the project towards other clustering techniques. For example, we may use the data partition strategy to replace the replication of files among servers. The comparison of these two schemes will be a very interesting topic to explore.

In the past four months, I have gained much knowledge and experience in system design and modeling, queuing theory, simulation techniques and experiment analysis. In completing this project, I do hope this project will in some way contribute to the understanding and the improvement of web-server clustering techniques.

References

1. Rani, D., Ranjan, R.K.: A comparative study of SaaS, PaaS, and IaaS in cloud computing. Int. J. Adv. Res. Comput. Sci. Softw. Eng. 4(6), 158–161 (2014)

2. Kepes, B.: Understanding the cloud computing stack: SaaS, PaaS, IaaS. From support.rackspace.com (2011)
3. Vaughan-Nichols, S.J.: The best infrastructure-as-a-service solutions of 2016, 1 February 2016
4. Kumar, S., Goudar, R.H.: Cloud computing – research issues, challenges, architecture, platforms and applications: a survey. Int. J. Future Comput. Commun. 1(4), 356 (2012)
5. Case Study of Rackspace. http://broadcast.rackspace.com/hosting_knowledge/whitepapers/CaseStudy_LiveSmartSolutions.pdf
6. Buyya, R.K., Yio, C.S., Venugopal, S.K.: Cloud computing and emerging IT platforms: vision, hype, and reality for delivering computing as the 5th utility. Future Gener. Comput. Syst. 25, 599–616 (2009)
7. Calheiros, R.N., Ranjan, R., Beloglazov, A.: Cloud sim: a tool kit for the model in and simulation of cloud computing environments and evaluation of resource provisioning algorithms. In: Software: Practice and Experience, vol. 41, pp. 23–50. Wiley Online Library (2011)
8. Zhang, S., Chen, X.: Cloud computing research and development trend. In: 2010 Second International Conference on Future Networks (2010)
9. Winans, T.B., Brown, J.S.: Cloud computing a collection of working papers. In: Deloitte (2009)

Author Index